SEEING RED

SEEING RED

*A History of Natives
in Canadian Newspapers*

MARK CRONLUND ANDERSON AND CARMEN L. ROBERTSON

UNIVERSITY OF MANITOBA PRESS

Seeing Red: A History of Natives in Canadian Newspapers
© Mark Cronlund Anderson and Carmen L. Robertson 2011

21   20   19   18   17   5   6   7   8   9

University of Manitoba Press
Winnipeg, Manitoba, Canada
Treaty 1 Territory
uofmpress.ca

Cataloguing data available from Library and Archives Canada
ISBN 978-0-88755-727-9 (PAPER)
ISBN 978-0-88755-406-3 (PDF)

Cover design by David Drummond
Interior Design by Jess Koroscil
Cover image: Deligalugaseitsa and Sepistopota, Sarcee, near Calgary, AB,
about 1885, McCord Museum, MP-1973.49.195
Interior images: Victoria *Times Colonist*, 14 March 1922; Toronto *Globe*,
12 April 1922; Toronto *Globe*, 18 April 1922; Regina *Leader*, 8 March 1913;
Toronto *Globe*, 18 October 1924.

Printed in Canada

The University of Manitoba Press acknowledges the financial support
for its publication program provided by the Government of Canada
through the Canada Book Fund, the Canada Council for the Arts, the
Manitoba Department of Sport, Culture, and Heritage,
the Manitoba Arts Council, and the Manitoba
Book Publishing Tax Credit.

Funded by the Government of Canada | Canadä

MIX
Paper from
responsible sources
FSC
www.fsc.org   FSC® C004071

CONTENTS

ACKNOWLEDGEMENTS

We want to express our thanks to the excellent research assistants who played a vital role in this project. These include Bridget Keating, Andrew Osbourne, Samra Sahlu, Haley Sichell, and Allison Szeles. We are also grateful for a research grant we received from the Social Science and Humanities Research Council of Canada (SSHRC), without which the research would likely never have concluded.

We also thank Dagmar and Madelaine for endless inspiration. Finally, a thanks to David Carr at the University of Manitoba Press for his early and ongoing support of this project.

SEEING RED

INTRODUCTION

Eskimo families which live in clean, modern homes and in which
the father is a steady, skilled worker have fewer children that die in
infancy than Eskimo families with more traditional life styles.
—*GLOBE AND MAIL*, 12 JULY 1974

Canada is home to more than 600 Indigenous nations as well as roughly one-
half million Aboriginals living off-reserve. Prior to the centuries-long European invasion, these groups spoke dozens of different languages, exhibited wide
variety in architecture, child rearing, clothing, diet, gender relations, material
culture, religion, rituals—in short, they varied in all the ways one might expect
of an enormous region occupied by a wide range of cultural groups.[1] All told,
in excess of 1.3 million Canadians claim some Aboriginal heritage, according
to the 2001 census. This includes First Nations, Inuit, and Métis.[2] Yet the country's most ubiquitous agent of popular education, the newspaper, has tended to
conflate all of these peoples into one heavily stereotyped monolith, patterned
on a colonial ideology that flourishes to this day.

This may come as a surprise if you think that colonialism is dead, a best-
forgotten relic of days gone by in Canada. It may also surprise you if you think
that the press is strictly objective and non-partisan. Indeed, if this is the case,
you will be surprised to discover that the evidence shows something strikingly
different. An examination of press content in Canada since the sale of Rupert's
Land in 1869 through to 2009 illustrates that, with respect to Aboriginal peoples, the colonial imaginary has thrived, even dominated, and continues to do
so in mainstream English-language newspapers.[3] Further, the press has never
been non-partisan or strictly objective in Canada. A wealth of studies, and
observations from daily life, readily demonstrate this.

Colonialism has always thrived in Canada's press. This is not a shock given
Canada's imperial birth and its enduring colonial behaviour with respect to
Aboriginals since the country's nominal founding at Confederation in 1867.[4]

It is what David Spurr refers to when he writes that "the colonizer speaks as inheritor."[5] Paul Nesbitt-Larking notes that "the medium of print is strongly associated with the politics of imperialism and colonialism."[6] In this way, Canadian nationalism becomes imperialism because it shares of the same dream.[7] Further, these colonial actions become double-edged because the mainstream positions itself as rightful owner of Aboriginal lands as well as inheritor of an English pattern of positioning itself with respect to Aboriginal peoples. Two examples exemplify the point.

The first is the treaty system that, to begin with, effectively stripped Aboriginals of the vast majority of their lands at the end of a gun barrel or with the implied threat of violence. This amounted to naked military conquest, though it is rarely portrayed as such in Canada. Instead, the nation insists that violence was the American way, a projective tale that serves the high and mighty purposes of elevating Canadiana over Americana at the same time as promoting the disingenuous and misleading idea that Indigenous peoples sought the protection of the Canadian government in their desire for treaties. Again and again in the 1870s the press made it clear that Canada chose not to engage in all-out war because it was simply too expensive and not because it was somehow unwarranted.

While it is true that the United States engaged in a centuries-long assault to conquer Aboriginal lands with few holds barred, it would be a serious mistake to conclude that Canada's emergence as a nation-state ultimately reflects a substantively kinder, gentler process. In the absence of, at the very least, the threat of overwhelming force, why would Aboriginals have willingly given up 95 percent of the territory they had possessed since time immemorial? Of course, there were other issues, including the sustainability of traditional ways of life in the face of dwindling buffalo herds. But the treaties all derived, ultimately, from the fact of white invasion, which was inherently aggressive. The idea that Aboriginals desired to cede their lands, imperialism notwithstanding, clearly makes no sense at all unless one embraces a colonial ideology that endorses imperial land theft. Why would anyone freely give up huge regions of traditional territory in return for a degraded status on small areas of marginal land? Aboriginals were compelled by force or the threat of the use of force. And that is precisely how the press portrayed it in the latter nineteenth century. Today, at least since 1997, even the Supreme Court of Canada recognizes the unsubtle and deliberate colonial intentions the federal government displayed in treaty relations. Yet Canadiana, crucially aided and abetted by newspapers, and even scholars who should know better, has for decades denied it, persisting instead in believing the dreamed colonial version of history. In this way, Canada, like all nations, is an "imagined community."[8]

The residential school system that between 1879 and 1996 sought to disappear Aboriginal culture by vigorously educating it out of existence serves as the second example of how the mainstream positions itself as owner of Aboriginal lands. Detractors accurately call it a systematic attempt at cultural genocide. Even its few lingering supporters accept that it was morally flawed and disastrously run; and Canadian Prime Minister Stephen Harper offered a formal apology for the system on 11 June 2008.[9] As with the treaties, the historical record of residential schools is unequivocal: this was a system predicated on aggressive violence. Aboriginal children were forced to school, yanked from their families, banned from speaking their languages, and often not returned for a decade or more. Sometimes years would pass and parents were not allowed even to see, let alone hug or just spend time with their children. Many children were physically, sexually, and/or emotionally abused by their teachers. Many died at the hands of vicious pedagogical authorities, including clergy. These horrific tales have been recorded in documentary film, government reports, and several excellent books.[10] John Milloy notes that "in their attack on language and spirituality, the schools had been a particularly virulent strain of that imperial epidemic sapping the children's bodies and beings."[11] J.R. Miller has termed them "merely one important cog in a machine of cultural oppression and coercive change."[12]

Both national projects, that is, the treaty system and residential schools, exemplified belligerent colonial policy at work, what one might refer to as hegemonic assimilation, an idea borrowed from Antonio Gramsci,[13] in which an imperial power attempts to impose its cultural world views upon the Other.[14] Both efforts were specifically and proudly colonialist in intention, premised first upon notions of alleged white superiority and corresponding Aboriginal inferiority, broadly conceived. Additionally, colonial ideology, draped in virulent, angry, and self-righteous Christianity, lent the works a triumphal air. White Canadians could bask self-righteously in the idea of "killing the Indian to save the white man," a concept resting at the heart of the colonial enterprise in Canada.[15] It had God's own stamp of approval. After all, the residential schools were run by clergy and keyed on religious instruction in the widest sense.

We stress these two colonial enterprises to underscore that press coverage did not and cannot occur in a vacuum.[16] If colonialism has permeated Canadian society—in a sense *is* Canadian society at its deepest level—as treaties and residential schools attest, then one might reasonably expect attendant ideological saturation to surface in the printed press. In short, as the scholars Augie Fleras and Jean Lock Kunz have observed, "mainstream media have proven complicit in fortifying the cultural hierarchy and moral authority at the heart of an existing social order."[17] Has the mainstream press expressed ideas and representations congruent to and supportive of the thinking that underwrote and gave rise to treaties and residential schools? The short answer is, yes; the long answer, with voluminous evidence, is detailed in this book.

RULE OF THREE

The establishment of treaties and residential schools was not accidental. They were created deliberately and for specific reasons. The language that aided and abetted and in turn reflected these colonial endeavours and thinking oozes from the pores of Canadian mainstream culture. In other words, the reasoning that engendered the creation of the treaty system and residential schools was, for their duration, also the *lingua franca* of mainstream newspapers. In general it avers that Aboriginals, when compared to white Canadians, exemplify three essentialized sets of characteristics—depravity, innate inferiority, and a stubborn resistance to progress. These representations cross-pollinate and contain within them a wide variety of elements. Collectively, on the one hand, this imagery has served to informally yet persuasively teach countless Canadians about imagined Native inferiority (that is, the Other in its many guises); and, on the other hand, the portrayals have served to reinforce prevalent mainstream notions about Aboriginal peoples, all of which degrade, denigrate, and marginalize. In this way, the press has both reflected naturally and regurgitated spontaneously and necessarily the culture from which it emerged at the same time as reinforcing and teaching prevailing social norms to youth and newcomers. "Along with notions of common history and traditions and shared systems of cultural representations," Bhodan Szuchewycz writes, "a significant element in the discursive construction of nations and national identities involves the articulation of difference and contrast with respect to other nations and national identities."[18]

The idea that Canadians of Aboriginal ancestry epitomize moral depravity is as old as the press in Canada. The notion finds expression in a variety of ways, including identified sneakiness, poor parenting, thievery, whorishness, dishonesty, laziness, ungodliness, and a tendency for debased afflictions associated with the body (such as sexual debauchery, alcoholism, and capricious violence).

The second perception also dates in the press to at least as early as Confederation. It asserts that Aboriginals exhibit inherent racial inferiority, though newspapers mostly remained mum on how they understood the flexible term of "race." Early on, the press critically embraced then-common social Darwinist concepts. Such presumed inadequacy leads, for example, to alleged stupidity, poor decision making (with links to depravity), and childish, irresponsible, frequently irrational behaviour. It is often conflated with and used to explain espied archetypal savagery, the alleged Aboriginal proclivities for wanton violence, violent crime, viciousness, and a general tendency toward mayhem.

Third, the press throughout Canadian history has cast Aboriginals as mired in an unprogressive and non-evolving past, as if they exist outside of linear time. Behaviour associated with this theme includes excessive stubbornness, childishness, and maladaptive cultural characteristics that make it difficult for Aboriginal culture to progress in the ways understood and appreciated by the mainstream. Additionally, this theme reinforces cultural depravity and racial inferiority in ways that buttress all three colonial essentialisms. For example, note that childishness may be lumped in with alleged innate inferiority because adults (whites) are smarter and more advanced than children (Aboriginals). By the same token, childishness may be associated with racial inferiority insofar as the superior (white adults) stands above the inferior (childish Aboriginals). The point is simply that identifying three prominent varieties of treatment is useful for the purposes of analysis and discussion, yet the three tropes themselves behave as is their wont, following their own internal colonial logic, and frequently overlap.

Variations on the three perceptions include popular archetypal packaging such as the moribund Native, the savage, the Indian princess, the stoic or noble Native, the childish Native, the intemperate Native (a.k.a., the drunkard), and so on. The list frequently decussates itself. What the archetypes share in common is that each is constructed by the characteristic three aforementioned essentialisms. For example, the Indian savage archetype typically exhibits depravity, is often identified as racially inferior, and epitomizes

Native atavism—all imaginary, that is, empirically mistaken yet nonetheless persistent in Canadian culture.

Thus Aboriginals fit in the Canadian colonial project as Others, designated outsiders in their own homeland. The rub is that the constructed Other, as noted, bears little resemblance to reality, as is clearly the case with stereotyped Aboriginals. Yet the Other has a key role to play for in Canada the imaginary Aboriginal serves to remind the mainstream about the value of its own self-perceptions while using Aboriginals' espied behaviour, portrayed through colonial lenses, as a means to gauge itself in positive ways. Of course, colonialism likewise remains active and discernible across a wide range of cultural markers—in movies, television, advertising, politics, song, and so on.[19]

EMPIRE OF "COMMON SENSE"

Insofar as the content of newspaper imagery derives from the larger culture in which its readers participate, one might reasonably expect a consonance between press content and pre-existing reader bias.[20] The result is that the news constitutes a kind of national curriculum, which emerges organically, as if nothing were more natural. In short, as curriculum news images do not present new material so much as they simply reinforce the status quo.

Exemplifying the ways in which Western colonial ideology operates, the archetypes and their various behaviours have been essentialized such that for the Canadian mainstream they operate altogether naturally, what the anthropologist Elizabeth Furniss in her careful study of colonialism in Williams Lake, British Columbia, calls Canadian "common sense."[21] In this way, for example, images of drunken Aboriginals or reports of violence against Aboriginal women may elicit nothing more than tsk-tsks and knowing nods of the head. That is mainstream common sense. In a related development, the press itself, in form and function in recent decades a product and progenitor of the ideology of liberal pluralism, adopts and strikes a non-partisan pose, championing the assertion that it remains uncontaminated by ideology (an ironic twist from the late nineteenth century when newspapers were energetically and unapologetically partisan).[22]

Instead, what we witness is a sort of generic hegemony at work, where the imperial agent embodies the dominant normative, naturalizes it, and assumes the right to define and then to impugn and punish the Other.[23] The point is that mainstream Canada gazes at the world in a certain way and acts on these beliefs. That is just how any culture works. It is neither new nor uniquely

Canadian. In the beginning English Canada adopted it and adapted it from the British who had established what would in time become the country. In the absence of this sort of culture-binding glue—as the great African novelist Chinua Achebe notes—*things fall apart.*[24] Such positive self-perceptions are the adhesive that binds culture together. Collectively, they constitute Canada's national mythological order, imagined Canadiana. Empirical reality is quite beside the point. Yet because the country adopts one set of ways of looking at the world it also necessarily rejects other possible ways, and sometimes this includes rejection of the people who practise and think in other ways.

Culture tends, in this way, as the scholar Peter Kulchyski holds, to "totalize" its existence.[25] It becomes everything. And it remains so, even if one tempers Kulchyski with Spurr's observation that colonizing discourse may be understood as a series "marked by internal repetitions."[26] As a consequence, virtually any presumed Aboriginal behaviour may become a colonial synecdoche, where the part stands in for the whole. This includes, for example, visual signifiers such as feathers, bows and arrows, and buckskins, as well as prosaic signifiers such as drunkenness, licentiousness, and laziness. Because the possibilities are delimited only by the colonial imagination, you find colonial culture, by definition, everywhere—in and among relationships, gender, politics, race, film, song, dress, diet, holidays, and religion. To put it another way, if our assertion is that Canada has been and remains a colonial entity, then evidence of it should abound in the press. After all, the newspaper remains the mother of all mass media since the birth of the Dominion and continues to be a significant player in popular culture today. According to a 2008 Canadian Newspaper Association study, 48 percent of Canadians over the age of eighteen read a newspaper daily and 73 percent read such a paper at least once per week. Further, 19 percent read a daily on-line newspaper at least once a week and 77 percent read either a printed or an on-line daily newspaper each week.[27]

Colonial representations as common sense, naturalized and totalized, comprise the guts of what reflects Canada's past and present colonial imaginary in the printed press. They adhere faithfully to global patterns of colonial representation of the racialized Other, and dovetail neatly with and within a larger cultural colonial project. Yet remarkably, these pop cultural monuments have received scant close critical reading in Canada. Here we are thinking about an obscure 1971 title, *The Canadian Indian as a subject and a concept in a sampling of the popular national magazines read in Canada, 1900–1970*, by Ronald Haycock; the kitchen-table historian Daniel Francis and his engaging and highly original, if overreaching book, *The Imaginary Indian, The Image of the Indian in Canadian Culture*; anthropologist Sandra Lambertus's study, *Wartime Images and Peacetime Wounds, The Media and the Gustafsen Lake Standoff*; R. Scott Sheffield's *The Red Man on the Warpath, The Image of the 'Indian' and the Second World War*; some work on the 1990 Oka crisis in which the media figured prominently; and Furniss's *The Burden of History, Colonialism and the Frontier Myth in a Rural Canadian Community*.[28]

Haycock's idea, well expressed by its title, is exemplary and deserves more and better study than the author affords it. The volume exhibits virtually no theoretical grounding and the methods employed are mostly random. In fact, the book employs some of the very stereotypes it deplores. Further, it overstates and likely misrepresents the influence of the Civil Rights movement in the 1960s. It holds that Canadian magazines unfairly and inaccurately portrayed Aboriginals in negative ways but that improvement was on the horizon by 1970.

Francis's book is written for the non-scholar, an advantage in that it is penned in an approachable style and not clogged with jargon or notation. Its value stems from originality and breadth, not depth; and its significant weakness is its underdeveloped theoretical framework (which some readers, we admit, might identify as a strength). The book examines the various ways in which Canadian popular culture historically has portrayed Natives. The results are "imaginary," as the title implies, because, Francis finds, the deeply demeaning and heavily racialized depictions say a great deal about mainstream Canada's imagination but basically nothing about empirical reality. The book is widely cited because it stands alone as the most ambitious and comprehensive study of its kind. In fact, it is the only study of its kind. Francis has also written *National Dreams: Myth, Memory, and Canadian History*, which provides a useful companion to *Imaginary Indian*, in particular a chapter about the myth of the Mountie—also an "imaginary" construction—in Canadian history.[29]

Lambertus's work, by contrast, is written for an audience of scholars. While the book is marred slightly by an underdeveloped methodology, we agree with its richly researched observation that "the media act as both the recipient and the transmitter of pressures to conform to the dominant ideology."[30] Lambertus finds that the results led, in the case of the 1995 standoff at Gustafsen Lake in British Columbia, to knee-jerk racist media depictions. She argues convincingly that journalists presented, more or less automatically, a media frame redolent with war-time imagery.

Sheffield's carefully argued study finds malleability and continuity in the ways in which the press depicted Indigenous peoples in the 1930s and through World War II. The former emerges from the very nature of stereotypes[31] as well as "reacting to the strains produced by the war."[32] The latter reflects the deeper structure of Canadian society and its own cultural durability. The author argues that the war produced net minor improvement for the imagined Native, though he stresses that the pejorative framings clearly outlived the conflict.

The scholarship engendered by the 1990 Oka crisis, which we discuss at greater detail in chapter 11, finds that the press quickly and naturally presented the Mohawks and Natives more generally as garden-variety savages, classic Indigenous Others who revelled in violence and mayhem. But the amount of work done on the topic remains somewhat thin (though it actually offers the bulk of what exists on the topic of Native representation in the press in Canada) and tends to be poorly informed by theory.

Elsewhere, Robert Harding has compared and contrasted news reports of Natives from the 1860s and the 1990s in British Columbia and finds enduring racism a common element in the temporally disparate portrayals. This is an important finding because it suggests Canadian society has progressed less than we may imagine. In a limited way—limited by the scope of the research, neither by the evidence nor the line of argumentation—it confirms Sheffield's point about durability and refutes Haycock's exaggerated and simplistic optimism. That said, Harding finds a positive development in that, in the 1990s, "the voices of aboriginals people…have been selectively incorporated into discourse."[33] In its attempt to establish a historical context and frame of reference, Harding's study is unique.[34]

Two books by Frances Henry and Carol Tator have plumbed contemporary Canadian English-language newspapers and found widespread evidence of what they refer to as a recurring "racist ideology" that "organizes, preserves, and perpetuates a society's power structures. It creates and preserves a system of dominance."[35] Though neither book focuses exclusively, or even heavily, on media treatment of Native peoples, the conclusions, especially of the latter book, remain prescient. The authors unearth wide evidence of racial profiling in Canada's English-language press in the 1990s, though their sampling of news content is somewhat random and limited. Still, "racial profiling exists in Canada," they meticulously conclude, "yet it does not keep its citizens safer from violence, because it is an act of violence—an act that challenges the ideals and core values of a democratic liberal society."[36]

Two books have examined how the press has imagined Aboriginal peoples in the United States. John M. Coward's *The Newspaper Indian, Native American Identity in the Press, 1820-90*[37] explores news representations from the latter part of the nineteenth century in the lands west of the Mississippi River. Coward shows how an expansionist ideology, Manifest Destiny (that is, American continental imperialism[38]), provided a way to depict and diminish Aboriginals in nearly every respect. Negative stereotypes, he writes, "proved incredibly useful and durable in the business of building a nation and creating a distinct national identity. Through the ignoble savage, Americans could imagine nation-building as a great triumph over savagery."[39] Mary Ann Weston's *Native Americans in the News, Images of Indians in the Twentieth Century* temporally picks up where Coward left off, though with less theoretical nuance. Still, she usefully reveals how news content reflected mainstream "common sense,"[40] again with imagery identified that mirrors the three tropes—depravity, innate inferiority, and a stubborn resistance to progress. Likewise, two studies have identified similar colonial projects at work in the representation of Aboriginal peoples in Australia.[41]

A variety of essays has been published that consider the press and Aboriginals in the United States, for example, on the topics of Natives in the colonial American press[42] and as gendered constructions.[43] Canada offers no counterpart. This gap becomes more pronounced when comparing study of the history of journalism or newspapers in the two countries. For instance, virtually every major American newspaper has been studied in depth; in many cases this has occurred on a variety of occasions. Journalism as a profession has received close and extensive examination in the United States, but not in Canada. Any university library contains dozens of such studies, but only a handful for Canada. In the latter case this short list includes Mary Vipond's brief and pithy *The Mass Media in Canada*,[44] Wilfrid Kesterton's *History of Journalism in Canada*,[45] Douglas Fetherling's *The Rise of the Canadian Newspaper*,[46] Minko Sotiron's *From Politics to Profit*,[47] and Paul Rutherford's excellent study of Canada's late nineteenth-century press, *A Victorian Authority*,[48] a study that foregrounds much of the other work.

Likewise, biographies and autobiographies abound about American editors, writers, and publishers.[49] This puts Canadian researchers at a distinct disadvantage. For example, to study coverage from, say, the Los Angeles *Times*, several in-depth studies exist to contextualize the work, depending on temporal interest.[50] This is important because ownership and editorial decision making may have clear repercussions for content. William Randolph Hearst, for example, was a vocal nationalist and jingoist who influenced heavily the ways in which his newspapers reported on the Mexican Revolution.[51] For Canada no comparable body of literature exists.

The same observation can be made for the work of journalists in the field. Study has shown, for example, that during coverage of the Indian Wars in the United States, especially the period after George Armstrong Custer's famous death in 1876 and the murderous assault at Wounded Knee in 1890, reporters regularly fabricated events in stories and stories themselves, all of which served to promote racial hatred. Because of the paucity of research done in Canada, it is not known whether something similar happened—but there are good reasons to think that it did. First, both countries had for centuries been engaged in conquests of Aboriginal populations, though the American version tended to be more violent. Yet the press rhetoric in the two countries bore close rhetorical resemblance. Greed, white indifference, and a colonial mentality drove the American fabrications. These needs also existed in the Canadian west where newspapers desperately sought to improve circulation and where whites clearly loathed Natives. To turn an old phrase, the absence of evidence is not the same as the evidence of absence.

The paucity of Canadian scholarly study is shocking for two basic reasons. First, consider the topic of media influence. The press exerts formidable suasion that effectively serves to instruct audiences and teach readers, and this "agenda-setting" function has been well established by scholars.[52] Paul Kellstedt terms it "social learning" and stresses its particular influence "in the case of race."[53] Agenda-setting theory illustrates how the press has the power to instruct an audience *what to think about*.[54] Miller and Ross explain the process as integral to news production. It begins when "news producers transform discrete bits of news information into socially meaningful and powerful narratives that contribute to the social construction of race and identity."[55] More than that, the press additionally has the power to tell an audience *what to think*. This remarkable conclusion was pioneered by the work of social scientists Maxwell McCombs and Donald Shaw in the 1970s.[56] Edward Said, the great literary scholar, has argued, in an analysis of the ways in which Western press imagines Islam in richly colonized garb, that the typical American receives 90 percent of his/her information regarding Islam from the media.[57] In this way, he concludes, we live in "second-hand worlds."[58]

And we do not just read newspapers, we look at them, too. Headlines, composition, layout, editorial cartoons, photographs, and advertising all impact on how we negotiate meaning when we pick up a paper. For example, a front-page story with a prominent headline and a provocative photograph signifies something different from a small report with no photograph buried near the end of the publication. Newspapers have increasingly been permeated by visual images serving a variety of purposes, with many intended effects. Often photographs serve as documentary evidence of objective circumstances just as they connote culturally and contextually specific meanings.

This format and framing has the power to suggest meaning. Reading and interpreting images is one way that we have assessed the papers in this study. However, because of the poor quality of reproduction of images and microfilm we have chosen to focus our analysis on textual news accounts. Still, over the course of this text, from scrutinizing the jammed four-page papers published in the 1870s filled with both stories and advertising to the more recent slick offerings by newspapers to include colour photographs, maps, diagrams, and website links to in-depth applications and blogs, the act of looking has influenced our conclusions.

IMAGINE CANADA

This book considers the ways in which Aboriginals have been portrayed in English-language newspapers in Canada since 1869. Viewed as a whole and in the absence of an expert ability to disentangle historical fact from fiction, the reportage collectively tells us little, certainly nothing accurate, about Aboriginal people *per se*, but it tells us a great deal about Canadiana, that is, the Canadian mainstream imagination, about Canada as an "imagined community," as well as how Canada's newspapers operate ideologically. Conjuring Marshall McLuhan and Harold Innis,[59] Andrew Perrin and Stephen Vaisey put it this way: "The modern polity is itself the historical product of communications technologies that enabled citizens to imagine a unified public in the face of practical limits on physical interaction: a collectivity of citizens removed from one another."[60] The picture revealed is not flattering. Warren Skea notes that "hegemony enables ideology sustaining the political and economic status quo to be latently published in newspapers without any skepticism by the reading public."[61] While the term may be tweaked in various ways, Jeannette Mageo and Bruce Knauft capture it effectively by referring to hegemony as "an ideology that presents itself not as a philosophy with which one might or might not agree, nor as a moral system that describes how things should be, but rather as the way the world *is*."[62] That such imagery persists to this day suggests strongly that the country lives in denial—even self-loathing, as John Raulston Saul has it—as well as summarily failing to live up to its ballyhooed boosterism of the cultural mosaic.[63]

Consider the following commentary from a speech given in 1873 by the outgoing president of the Canadian Press Association, John Cameron of the London, Ontario, *Advertiser*:

> Much has been said, at one time and another, of the influence of the
> Press. That influence augments year by year. The number of readers
> is multiplied. No class of society is entirely exempt from the direct or
> indirect influence of the Press, while large sections of the community
> are dependent entirely for opinions as well as for news on the daily
> or weekly journal. This influence may be for good or for evil. It is a
> terrible thing to vest power in the hands of men without any sense of
> responsibility; but a conscientious journalist will never forget his moral
> obligations…. further, it may be laid down as a sound business axiom
> that the Press cannot afford to make a statement it cannot prove.[64]

Cameron here, as reported in the staunchly Liberal Toronto *Globe*, baldly asserted the core agenda-setting premise: the press influences and even shapes its audiences. It leads yet is led by what its paying public desires to read, yet in some sense already believes, or is likely to accept. Newspapers in the late nineteenth century made no apologies for the political partisanship that defined them.[65] In other words, the denial is as old as Canada.

The proposition that newspapers tell us what to think brings us full circle back to a consideration of colonialism. Press coverage is important because it serves as a mirror, albeit imperfect, of public sentiment.[66] No clear consensus exists among scholars about the precise contours of this relationship. For example, Noam Chomsky has argued famously that press content necessarily promotes the interests of its corporate owners.[67] Poststructural critics such as Stuart Hall and Edward Said proffer a different reading, arguing that press content, because the press is necessarily grounded in and reflective of the culture in which it operates, invariably promotes core cultural attributes (which in themselves tend to ape elite values, in many postmodern conceptions).[68] It is, as Szuchewycz summarizes the literature, "the historical and continuing prevalence of systemic racism has been documented in a wide range of Canadian social institutions, including the legal and criminal justice systems, immigration, education, and employment.... A broad-based popular ignorance of Canada's history of discrimination and civil rights against visible and cultural minorities remains prevalent."[69] And so it goes for the fourth estate.[70] In the Canadian case, if Chomsky and Hall and Said are correct, one might expect newspaper content to promote and defend Canadian colonialism because it provides the fabric upon which Canadian culture has been embroidered and because the economic system upon which Canadian colonialism was and remains predicated benefited an elite that itself effectively directed editorial policy in the national press. In this way the press operates as a sort of colonial genre. As American literary historian Richard Slotkin has written, "the historical development of [a] culture's repertoire of genres is driven not only by social and cultural change but by the specialized discourse of artists and producers who work in that form and by the institutions that control the production and distribution of their artifacts."[71] In a similar vein, historian Lyle Dick has concluded, "since Confederation the national media based in central Canada have been oriented to historical representations aligned to expansionist imperatives."[72] In short, colonialism provides a discursive means for understanding the representation of Aboriginal peoples in Canadian newspapers.

FROM RUPERT'S LAND TO THE TWENTY-FIRST CENTURY

What changes have occurred since 1869 in the ways in which Canada's press has imagined Aboriginals? A common sense view holds that everything has changed, and further, that colonialism was and is something practised by other countries. Not Canada. Perhaps never Canada. Treaties and residential schools can be explained away, in this view, as remnants of what people used to call the "olden days," a time in which people perhaps meant well but did not know any better.

But what we discovered through a discourse analysis of Canadian newspapers is that little has changed. As best we were able, we have sought to allow the papers to speak for themselves. Sometimes this makes for cluttered pages, what with the many quotations and citations, but it also presents the reader with a more organic sense of the news as news.

The book is ordered chronologically, beginning in chapter 1 with the sale of Rupert's Land in 1869. Were Natives sold along with it? How was the purchase justified insofar as the lands were occupied, even owned, by Métis and Aboriginals? Chapter 2 considers Treaty 3, which gobbled up a huge swath of northwestern Ontario. How was the treaty presented? What of the Natives on those lands?

Chapter 3 examines the ways in which a truly national press, suddenly reaching the breadth of the country as it exists today, depicted Louis Riel and the 1885 war in the west. The reporting reached near-frenzied proportions, pitting Liberals and Conservatives into a vicious debate. Yet these opposing sides, as they had in 1869 and 1873, tended to agree on the wholesale inferiority of Natives.

Chapter 4 considers the Yukon press, 1898–1905, in and around the Klondike gold rush. This frontier land bore some close resemblance, in press reports, to the mythical American frontier. Chapter 5 explores the 1913 death reportage of the Canadian Native poet Pauline Johnson. In death the press mourned Johnson by claiming ownership of her as an Indian princess. Then in chapter 6 we turn to Grey Owl, nee the alcoholic self-promoting and beloved Archie Belaney, the enormously popular pretended Aboriginal. We examine how the press dealt with the news, which became public only after his death in 1938, that he was not in fact Native but was only faking it.

Chapter 7 investigates the depictions of 1948. Many Aboriginals had fought and died fighting for Canada in Europe. Did such sacrifice affect news portrayals? In 1969 Canada released the infamous White Paper, which in part advocated the elimination of reservations. It failed but in the meantime elicited substantive debate in the press about the nature of Aboriginal peoples and their perceived roles in Canada, which we explore in chapter 8.

In 1974 a group of Aboriginals occupied a local park in a small Ontario town, Kenora, claiming the land as their own. Chapter 9 explores the ways in which the local press presented the story as the town appeared ready to explode with racialized violence, according to the local newspaper.

Chapter 10 queries the lack of reportage associated with the passage of Bill C-31 and its attempt to erase sexual inequities inherent in the Indian Act. Press imagery of the Indian princess and the Indian "squaw" abound in coverage of issues related to Aboriginal women and inform the reading of 1985 events.

Letters to the editors published in Prince George, British Columbia, and Moncton, New Brunswick, dailies provide a frame for analysis of a discrete form of press coverage during the Oka crisis in 1990, in chapter 11. Savagery and terrorism emerge as common constructions in the letters, themes that resonated in hard news stories from the period.

In chapter 12 we investigate three news threads that dominated the four major newspapers in Saskatchewan and Alberta in 2005 during the celebration of the two provinces' centennial. Looking back 100 years earlier, we consider 1905 news reports from both Saskatchewan and Alberta dailies directly to compare changes in press imagery that occurred over a century.

Seeping through each of the chapters, then, are cross-pollinating attributes of the three noted perceptions that consistently situate Aboriginals as Other within the Canadian colonial project. By scrutinizing a wide and diverse sampling of diachronically organized printed news sources such as local, regional, and national dailies, and types of stories from so-called hard news to editorials, letters to the editor, obituaries, and human interest pieces, we seek to demonstrate how conjunctions of news sources and a normative imagined Canadian identity constitute the basis for an unambiguous narrative of a thriving colonial imaginary in the Canadian press.

CHAPTER ONE

THIS LAND IS MINE
The Rupert's Land Purchase, 1869

As for the future of this country, it is as
inevitable as tomorrow's sunrise.
—TORONTO *GLOBE*, 4 JANUARY 1869

Canada owes its existence to the purchase of Rupert's Land in 1869. This vast territory, which included most of the west and much of the north (with the exceptions of British Columbia and the high Arctic) multiplied the size of the country several times over.[1] It was sold to Canada by the Hudson's Bay Company. In a sense, the persons living there were sold along with it, having no say in the matter. Mostly these were Aboriginals or Métis (usually people of Indigenous-French or, to a lesser extent, Indigenous-Scotch or Indigenous-English heritage). Subsequent immigration to the west then engendered the country as it is today.

Purchase of the land was not an end in itself. The federal government sought the territory as part of an effort to build a nation-state that would grow and prosper in its own right (and, yes, the east, especially Ontario, would benefit immensely from this arrangement) as well as provide a bulwark against the threat of Yankee expansionism. That the land had been (and was presently) occupied for many thousands of years by Aboriginal peoples in no way diminished the craving for it. Just the opposite, in fact, as Canada argued from across its political spectrum that the usurpation of Indigenous lands was necessary on moral, not just economic or strategic, grounds. God himself, according to the press, wanted white Canada to take that land.

Newspaper reportage in Toronto and Montreal in 1869 was attentive to the purchase of Rupert's Land. The story dominated the front pages during that year. This chapter explores the attendant imagery, in particular the ways in which the press served to naturalize the massive imperial land aggrandizement by casting the land as free for the taking and Aboriginals as essentially unfit in several ways.

This process of naturalization, a kind of acculturated hegemonic ordering in the sense employed by Gramsci and others,[2] incorporated a variety of inter-related elements. For example, the press noted that the peoples of the Prairies had in effect been sold.[3] The press likewise espied the threat of American expansionism for Canada's west,[4] which became more immediate in the fall of that year when some in the Red River Settlement near what would become Winnipeg, led by Louis Riel, briefly established a parallel government.[5] Similarly, the press largely denied that the purchase and settling of Rupert's Land was in fact an imperial project, while at times depicting it as precisely that. For example, the Toronto *Globe* recorded in March 1869: "The interests which point so forcibly in this direction are chiefly imperial... and it is because of our love for the Empire and for the extension and consolidation of British authority, that the authorities of the Colonial Office have been pressed so urgently to make that region an integral part of the Canadian Dominion."[6]

In all cases, whether reporting Métis gripes about the land sale, the continental geopolitics of the purchase, or the infrequent and incurious admission that growth amounted to unabashed colonialism, portrayed favourably, the larger and more compelling news frame situated the "growth" of Canada as the inevitable maturation and blossoming of a plant in a well-tended garden. "The inevitable grandeur of [the] country's future," the *Globe* phrased it,[7] and the Montreal *Gazette* agreed.[8] Such reports were typical. For example, the *Globe* on another day recorded: "No sooner will the immigrant, who has tended his way four hundred miles westward from Lake Superior, emerge from the wilderness of weeks than he will feast his eyes upon one of the richest prairies tracts in America. One is almost afraid to speak what is merely the sober and now familiar truth, lest it should be imparted to imagination."[9] That garden, of course, was Rupert's Land. And Canada was not an imperial power, despite overwhelming evidence to the contrary. In North America that epithet was reserved for the United States. In a related theme, the press without much nuance sought to champion Canada by denigrating its southern neighbour. In comparison to the United States, Daniel Francis observes, "Canadians have always seen themselves as distinct, morally superior."[10] In the press, from this colonial launching pad gushed a barrage of relentless colonial imagery that sought to portray Aboriginals for Canadian audiences.

It is also important to remember that Canada's press remained deeply partisan in the decades after Confederation. Political parties in the years after 1867 employed press organs to promote their platforms with a vigour that would startle today's readers.[11] More than a few prominent politicians earned their stripes in the newspaper trenches. For example, George Brown, one of the fathers of Confederation, established the Toronto *Globe* (forerunner to today's *Globe and Mail*[12]) in 1844 and then for decades ran it.[13] That Brown was a devoted partisan Liberal and that the paper championed his party was balanced, in a sense, by the Conservative leaning of other prominent dailies such as the Montreal *Gazette*.[14] Typically, moreover, a given paper might benefit handsomely if its own party won office in Ottawa. In some cases, a paper might earn valuable government printing contracts or other perks.[15] Yet the *Globe* and *Gazette* were also considered to be "quality newspapers" that "remained aloof from sensationalism," according to one scholar.[16]

Not surprisingly, then, the political stakes were high. Papers fought tooth and nail for audience share perhaps as much as they did to secure their party's victory during elections. Yet though the papers bickered, sometimes with considerable vitriol, in at least one basic way they shared a common aspiration: the idea of Canada. They shared certain ideological assumptions about the inherent value of a nation-building exercise peculiar to the later nineteenth century, a project built on emerging neo-liberal capitalism and a burgeoning democracy erected on colonial architecture inherited proudly from imperial Britain. Rutherford notes that "the dogma was built on three apparent certitudes, the ideas of progress, nationality, and democracy."[17] So where the *Globe* and the *Gazette* might differ on matters such as tariff reform, for example, they agreed heartily that Canada ought to develop itself in ways commensurate with its colonial heritage. The procurement of Rupert's Land and the fashioning of Treaty 3 (1873) and Treaty 4 (1874) serve as cases in point; these events also provide an initial Canadian opening for exploring what Daniel Francis has pithily referred to as the "imaginary Indian,"[18] a construct unstuck from empirical reality but one lodged firmly in the mainstream Canadian imagination. In fact, the modern nation-state, Canada included, is itself an imaginary construct, as Benedict Anderson has shown. "It is *imagined* because even the members of the smallest nation will never know most of their fellow-members, meet them, or even hear of them, yet in the minds of each lives the image of their communion," he observes.[19] And newspapers played a key role in 1869 in helping to forge that sense of community, especially as the country itself experienced phenomenal growth with the purchase of Rupert's Land.

Historian Patricia Seed has detailed and assessed the various ways in which competing European colonial powers justified land seizures in the Americas from Columbus through the mid-seventeenth century. In order to claim legal ownership of Aboriginal lands the Spanish, for example, erected crosses and had priests read the "requirement," a sort of bellicose preemptive legal statement that offered Aboriginals an unpalatable choice—embrace Spanish imperialism or be warred upon.[20] The French, by contrast, engaged in parades and other public celebrations that, providing the French could discern a level of Aboriginal participation, according to French custom and law, conferred ownership. In both cases the respective ceremonies devolved from centuries-old cultural contexts.[21]

The English saw ownership emerge from particular usage of the land. This reflected a unique way of reading the Christian invocation that humankind should follow God's will to tame and thereby improve the land. "Englishmen found a scriptural authority," writes Seed, "for their occupation of the land in Genesis: 'Go forth and multiply.'"[22] The English understood the invocation to refer to agriculture more than to human fertility. The second facet of the English ceremony of possession, understood immediately today by any Canadian homeowner or anyone familiar with the government of Canada's approach to Aboriginal land claims, was built on the proposition that "ownership of the land could be secured by using it, engaging in agricultural or pastoral activities."[23] This, for the English, included building bridges and roads, erecting fences and cultivating gardens, and establishing permanent structures.[24] In this respect Canada's intentions were clear in the west in 1869, the *Globe* reported. Beyond encouraging and rewarding settlement and agriculture the government would "build telegraphs, railroads, open roads, develop the resources of and improve the country."[25] In one extraordinary admission, the *Globe* referred to it as Canadian "manifest destiny," underlining its earlier statement that "unoccupied land is free to any person to take up."[26] In this way, by virtue of the fact that they were not English and therefore did not (and could not) behave culturally as Britons, Natives did not and could not own the land upon which they had lived for millennia. And any assertion that the Natives inhabiting western Canada might lay legal claim to it was as absurd, according to the *Globe*, as if the inhabitants of Patagonia had claimed it.[27] One result is that Aboriginals were not fully seen as owners of the land, merely as its heathen occupants.

Yet the *Globe* and *Gazette* also recognized the existence of "Indian title." Publishing the same report, the papers acknowledged undisclosed Aboriginal "rights." But the recognition extended only so far as the federal government allowed as it negotiated treaties. In this way, the papers opined, "there will never be any difficulty...The Indian is perfectly open to fair treatment and will always stand by it."[28] Another time the *Globe* recorded that "the claims of the Indian tribes to compensation for lands required for purposes of settlement will be considered and settled in conformity with the equitable principles which have uniformly governed the British Crown in its dealings with the aborigines."[29] Further, it warned: "There will never be any difficulty in treating them for their rights, and if all treaty stipulations are properly carried out upon the part of the Government, there will never be any trouble with them. Of course they must not be humbugged with unscrupulous agents. Such rascality was the cause of all of the difficulty which the Americans have to contend with."[30] While the apparent benevolence of the phrasing was undermined consistently and repeatedly by nearly every issue of the paper in 1869, the passage points to how both papers sought to portray Canada's imperial endgame as necessary, inevitable, and just. The result? "We have only to calculate on giving them as an equal exchange [that is, for the lands ceded in the subsequent treaties], the scanty food and the scanty clothing to which he has become accustomed," the *Globe* decreed.[31] Not exactly free then, but inexpensive.

Centuries later these ideas have remained alive in Canada's press, especially in the decades after Confederation in 1867. More than that, the press framed the sale of Rupert's Land in precisely the same way and with nuance equal to the explication provided by Seed's deeply researched study. The press, as a result, presented conquest as simply a given; it really needed no particular explicit justification because it emerged ineluctably and organically from English-Canadian culture. Further, it was not considered "conquest" as one might understand the term today, with its negative and demeaning connotations. Instead, this was God's work, not simply necessary but desirable, according to the press. News reports, as we shall demonstrate, strongly illustrate this point. Likewise, press coverage enveloping the treaties cast Aboriginals as vastly inferior to white Canadians in virtually every meaningful way. The results elicited the conclusion that Aboriginals so needed to be conquered that it would have been, in a way, impolite not to have purchased the land and forced them on to reservations via treaties.

"THE GARDEN OF THE WORLD"

The sale of Rupert's Land elicited strong and ongoing comment from Canada's two leading English-language daily newspapers in 1869, the Toronto *Globe* and the Montreal *Gazette*. The former commented upon it almost every day. For example, long reports from the Northwest Territory and Red River Settlement at Winnipeg, garrulous coverage presented over several years in the form of standing columns, provided key refrains central to framing the sale of Rupert's Land. The coverage included the ongoing and teasing reminder of the land's ripe plenty.

Without equivocation the *Globe* referred to the lands as "the path of empire and the garden of the world."[32] It issued an invitation: "We have land for millions of settlers,"[33] expressing hope that "thousands of thrifty emigrants from Great Britain and Canada would rush in."[34] It explicitly endorsed the inevitability of English-style imperial practice taking root in the newly formed Canada, serving as a kind of primer for Canadian colonization of Rupert's Land. This amounted to "the opening up of a new territory for colonization,"[35] one focus of which was the creation of a white "homogenous whole."[36] Applying a biblical symbol of Eden the paper recorded, "For the hundredth time we are told of its extraordinary fertility and great resources of the country...[it is] a perfect garden."[37] On another occasion it offered, "Like Moses, the Dominion of Canada...has sight of the promised land."[38] Not surprisingly, the *Globe* linked civilization with progress and progress with Christianity.[39] Thus the Christian had a duty to evangelize.[40] And the mutual attraction of Canadians to agriculture became obvious: it was the "most fertile land in the world,"[41] "exceedingly rich and fertile,"[42] "the fertile belt,"[43] "superior,"[44] "incredibly fruitful,"[45] "inconceivably rich,"[46] a "virgin."[47] Such "wild lands" begged to be tamed[48] by Canada's "able and energetic capitalists."[49] Lest the point about possession-taking not be obvious, the *Globe* reinforced it by noting that the mixed-blood "half-breed" in the west would "do anything but farm." Further, "the country is *great*—inexhaustible...Farming here is a pleasure—there is no toil in it and all who *do* farm are comfortable and some wealthy.... The half-breeds are the only people here who are starving. Five thousand of them have to be fed this winter, and it is their own fault they won't farm. They will hunt buffaloes, drive ox-carts 500 miles up and 500 miles back...at the rate of twenty miles a day.... As for the farmers, Scotch, English, and French, not one of them requires relief."[50]

The *Gazette* countered with a closely similar account on the same day: "The starvation here threatens 5,000 of the half-breeds, but only those. The farming classes are effected very little, if anything at all by it. The half-breeds are a strange class. They will do anything but farm...This is great country, and is destined, before ten years, to contain a larger population than the Canadas. The climate is delightful."[51] Crucially, the *Globe* remonstrated: "The morality and prosperity of nations advance according to their knowledge and practice of the specific duties and virtues of the Christian religion as we find it in the New Testament."[52]

The stakes thus were high. "Ours is a contest between civilization and barbarism," the *Gazette* warned.[53] Teleologically, the *Globe* pined for a day in the west "when a higher state of civilization shall be established, and barbarism and semi-barbarism shall disappear."[54] In fact, the process had been underway for centuries, said the *Gazette,* as if to reassure readers.[55] In August it provided a clear example under the headline, "Lo the poor Indian...gradual extinction of the tribe." The article detailed the alleged disappearance of the Mi'kmaqs "who once were strong, now they are weak—the white man comes with his rum and the Indian drinks and dies."[56]

The conclusion that the *Globe* took from such sketches was simple and direct: "The all-important thing is to get the territory as soon as possible."[57] So, while the Liberal paper predictably and often sanctimoniously derided Canada's Conservative government under the direction of John A. MacDonald and his government's efforts in the negotiation and purchase of the territory,[58] it left no doubt about its support for the colonial expansion of the Dominion: as soon as possible. Even as recently as 2007 MacDonald's most recent biographer called the land "bald, empty prairie."[59]

The *Gazette* offered significantly less coverage of the sale, and less news generally, and it tended to cast the purchase in an entirely favourable light where the *Globe* took issue with everything from the asking price to the style of government that would follow the purchase. In short, while the two papers agreed on the inestimable need and desirability of the land, they squabbled over the details. Once the land was secured, the tone and nature of the partisan bickering would grow more vitriolic in the early 1870s. Still, in 1869 the *Gazette* concurred with the *Globe*'s assessment of the appeal of the territory, terming it "the greatest place for game, ever,"[60] a "colony,"[61] "great—inexhaustible— inconceivably rich,"[62] "rich and productive,"[63] a "fertile belt,"[64] and "a scene so lovely."[65] The *Gazette* put it more plainly on another occasion: "let us bless God that he has brought a vine into this wilderness; that he has cast out the heathen."[66] Such was the allure of the west's "natural fertility."[67] It followed then that "as soon as this country becomes a portion of the Dominion of Canada…it will fill up very rapidly…emigrants from Great Britain and Canada would rush in. Why not?"[68] In short, "Here is a country," the paper wrote, echoing Seed, "possessing all of the properties of greatness if once developed."[69]

Yet the west was viewed very much too in the press as the "wilds,"[70] which was not incongruous because it framed the land then to be in dire need of taming. Relatedly, the land's occupants were also seen as simultaneously wild, barbaric, and correspondingly in need of control, tutelage, taming—the uncivilized "red skin."[71] Further, the fact that Natives were nomadic, "roving bands,"[72] "wandering listlessly,"[73] contributed to the view that Natives did not in fact own the land they so pointlessly roamed.[74] As the *Globe* opined, "Their nomadic life negates almost every attempt to Christianize or civilize them."[75] The notion that Aboriginals were childlike lent weight to this conclusion.[76] For example, the Sioux in Manitoba, according to the *Gazette,* were "cleanly enough, but there is a lack of that homeliness which weds a Canadian to his hotel with sure affection."[77]

This western territory, according to press reports—was coveted too for geopolitical reasons, that is, to foreclose the potential of American annexation. As the *Globe,* before the sale of Rupert's Land was effected, put it: "It is much to be regretted, indeed, that the Imperial authorities cannot be induced to hand over the Northwest Territory to the Dominion. That would strengthen our position wonderfully. Even the prestige of possessing that great territory would give us faith in our future, which would be a better defence against annexation than a great army."[78] "Self preservation," the *Globe* articulated the sentiment brilliantly as it endorsed American meddling in Cuba, "it seems, is the great law of nations."[79] Viewed in this way, the purchase of Rupert's "virgin" Land was not just desirable but tactically prudent, even necessary—*realpolitik* in action.

"HOPELESS STAGNATION"

Before commencing a discussion about how the press framed Canada's Natives, it is worth noting that such condemnation was not reserved only for Canada's indigenes. Instead, the *Globe* and *Gazette* damned all non-white peoples without compunction, in a sense providing a context for Aboriginal stereotyping.

Mexico, a country that like Canada and the United States also sought to subdue its Indigenous populations in a period of late-nineteenth century neo-liberalism,[80] was depicted by the *Globe* as a land of degraded "half-breeds," "Mongrel races,"[81] and as a result suffered from "a chronic state of confusion and bloodshed."[82] The *Gazette* agreed, disparaging Mexico's moribund Indigenous population at the same time as depicting Mexico's dominant Roman Catholicism as essentially corrupt.[83] Meanwhile, Natives in Guyana, fuelled by alcohol, the *Gazette* told, perpetuated "atrocious murder."[84]

Among Asians, "Chinamen" figured prominently, in part because of Chinese immigration to the United States. The resulting sketches were consistently unflattering in ways that denigrated the Chinese and smeared the United States with racial intolerance in comparison to Canada.[85] For example, the state of California was set to violate the core principles of democracy, according to the *Globe*, by refusing to extend suffrage to Chinese-Americans.[86] The *Globe* sought to have it both ways, too, simultaneously deploring American racial intolerance, not so subtly asserting greater Canadian tolerance, while consistently demeaning the Chinese. For example, one read that "a Chinese couple have been arrested in San Francisco for killing a female child; an act, which according to their culture, is not a crime."[87] On other occasions a reader might learn about how a Chinese labourer "murdered a whole family of seven persons in Peru"[88] or how the Chinese, displaying lack of moral fibre, had an appetite for opium, prostitution, and other assorted vices.[89] While the *Gazette* on one occasion appeared to praise the "Chinaman" (the singular standing in for all) for his industry in the laundry business, the paper snidely expressed hope then "that they might learn to wash themselves."[90]

Other Asians also fared poorly. Siamese twins on display in London, England, constituted a sort of freakish character. "The twins are old men, and their wrinkles and worn features make them the spectacle some degrees more repulsive than before," the *Globe* commented in March 1869.[91] Oddities abounded. One story cited a scientific expedition in Borneo that was searching for "tailed men and women" who went about stark naked and spoke in "gibberish." One might scoff at this but the *Globe* "had no difficulty in believing" such reports because "science, in one sense, almost requires it."[92] The Japanese compared favourably to all other Asians. While the tone of the *Globe* commentary condescended to them it also identified qualities the paper strongly endorsed, such as cleanliness, good housekeeping, politeness, courage, dignity, and formal education.[93] Egyptians, on the other hand, had historically bathed themselves in wanton violence, causing the *Globe* to query, "Can society learn no moral from this…bloodshed?"[94]

As noted, reported American racial intolerance served to champion Canada over the United States, which in turn served to lay a plank in emerging Canadian nationalist boosterism. Nowhere was this more pronounced than in the ways in which the *Globe* and *Gazette* portrayed the treatment of American blacks and "Indians." The portrayals incorporated a subtheme that characterized the United States as a dangerous place, a land rife with violence, much of which was racialized, that stood in stark contrast to more sober and peaceful English-Canadian ways, according to press depictions. The *Globe* deplored the American "miserable bigots" who, it said, maintained "the popular prejudice against the coloured." It "crops out at every turn [as] unreasonable, malignant, and disgraceful as ever."[95]

Thus a reader encountered many sensational passages in 1869. For example, with neither attribution nor motivation explained, in early January the *Globe* presented a story about how members of the Ku Klux Klan "attacked the house of a colored man." Subsequently, the Klan members "literally shot the man to pieces, and then with knives disemboweled him."[96] Likewise, the *Gazette* reported on how the Klan was burning Chinese schoolhouses in California.[97] Certainly readers would have been justifiably appalled by such gruesome and deplorable behaviour. The Klan deserved condemnation, without question. However, the larger *Globe* frame also employed such reports to serve a nationalist project of elevating Canada over the United States. Tales of comparably senseless racial violence filled pages of print in Toronto in 1869.[98] The Klan was to blame on some occasions but more typically blacks were at fault. In January readers would have learned how "a negro woman" killed a "little girl in Kentucky from the effects of boiling soup poured down her throat."[99] While the alleged murderer was identified by race ("negro"), in a classic example of how whiteness is naturalized as normative, a reader would have understood the girl to be white because she was not identified as such. In June the *Globe* reported that some "negroes" in Georgia unsuccessfully attempted to raze a community and "massacre" its inhabitants; yet the local sheriff ably turned the tables on them and "shot and killed" those who resisted arrest.[100] In November the *Gazette* narrated a fable-like tale in which "coloureds" beset officers attempting to break up a disturbance at a church: "Some held the officers while others beat them with clubs and stones…others with knives and razors."[101] Not all reported black crime—and nearly all of the news stories in which blacks figured included some sort of legal transgression—was violent. Blacks also specialized, the *Globe* reports laid clear, in theft.[102]

So what was a reader to conclude? Clearly, a key message for readers was to be afraid. Moreover, the *Globe,* despite its own coverage, sought to portray Canada as racially tolerant on an otherwise racially intolerant continent. Yet such a conclusion would not have been warranted, as the following excerpt taken from a *Globe* story on 7 August 1869 well illustrates. This is a reported exchange between a black man and a policeman at the police station in Philadelphia:

> "What is your name?"
> "Gracchus Johnson, sah."
> "Crackers Johnson, did you say?"
> "No, sah. My fader was not a baker, sah; my mudder, sah, called me
> her 'jewel,' sah. De-reason dat my fader called me Gracchus, sah, was,
> 'cause Mrs Gracchus called her children her jewels (with dignity).'"

The passage continues in this vein, attempting to elicit humour by casting Gracchus as comically stupid. But was it funny? The prevalence of such material in both papers under consideration suggests that a reader may well have found it so. Here is the *Gazette* typing an African American: "yellow eyes, blubber lips, and tufts of coarse wool in place of hair."[103] Small wonder, perhaps, that the *Gazette* endorsed an idea widely held by whites about non-white peoples at that time. "The negro race is doomed," a headline proclaimed. Incredibly, the paper argued, in the absence of slavery, only recently outlawed in the United States, blacks would simply disappear.[104] And they were not alone.

Australia's "now disappearing" Natives mired in "hopeless stagnation," said the *Globe,*[105] while the *Gazette* reported how New Zealand Maoris had been "massacring" English families.[106] And like Canada's Native population, as was widely held in the nineteenth century, these "miserable aborigines...are now disappearing."[107] Greenland's Native population amounted to "slatterns."[108]

Given the consistency and tenacity of the tone and content of the ways in which the *Globe* and *Gazette* portrayed non-Canadian people of colour, it will come as little surprise that Canada's Aboriginal population fared no better. This can be identified in two basic steps: first, a consideration of the papers' portrayals of American Natives, which again speaks to the matter of Canadian boosterism; second, a consideration of the portrayals of Canada's Natives.

"HE SURPRISED AND DESTROYED TWO VILLAGES"

Both papers portrayed the United States as a violent land beset with racial tensions and intolerance. Depictions of American Indians contributed importantly to this chauvinism. Curiously, one result tended to portray Indigenous peoples as considerably more violent in the United States when many such groups were culturally indistinguishable from their Canadian brethren. That is, the Blackfoot, Ojibwe, Mohawk, Cree, Sioux, and so on, had traditionally occupied both sides of the Canada-United States border.

War was a constant. For example, the *Globe* and *Gazette* reported identically in early spring:

> The Indian tribes of the [American] plains are very different
> from their docile brethren in Canada—they are constantly on the
> war path and, though they have always been friendly with those they
> call King George's men, yet they look with a jealous eye on the pale
> face intruders...those best acquainted with the Indian character
> anticipate rough times. For the honour of country I hope some
> satisfactory arrangement can be made with those tribes—they are
> loyal to our flag, but, as they say, they don't like to give their lands
> for nothing. Our American neighbours place a very light value
> on the life of an Indian.[109]

The passage gives rise at several points to the question, why? For example, why might Canada's western Aboriginals feel any loyalty to the crown? Why might they be loyal to the flag? At any rate, the papers declared but did not explain.

While American society was, according to the press, more violent, the war it waged against Indians mostly resulted from Native predilections. For example, a typical *Globe* report from January: "A few minutes later a scene was witnessed to call forth the rebuke of every benevolent and enlightened mind...lay sixteen human bodies all that remained of Elliot and his party...There was not a single one that did not exhibit evidence of fearful mutilation...the throats of a number were cut, and several beheaded."[110] The rub of such reports lay in the smug conclusion that the American violence derived from an absence of Canadian-like restraint; that Canadian restraint, itself a tempered imperialism, juxtaposed with a more democratic colonialism in the United States, press reports averred. This took many forms, though the oft-employed term "savage" covers it well enough. In essence the *Globe* and *Gazette* cast savagery as the absence of its opposite, civilization. In this way, reportage drew upon a wide range of binaries to lend emotional weight to the signifiers at work. For example, where Natives loved war whites preferred peace, where Natives maintained little self-control whites exhibited much, where Indians inclined to alcoholism whites did not, where whites were honest Indians were sneaky, thieving, and so on across a range of attributes. What then was wrong with America's Indigenous populations, according to the *Globe* and *Gazette*?

What was wrong, in part, was also wrong with the United States: too much violence. But while the Canadian press championed Canada over the United States on this issue, it in no way sided with the Natives upon whom war was waged. Instead, it was American Indians who waged aggressive war against the United States, the papers related. An innate love of violence characterized the Indians; whereas the United States returned the fight in order to protect, preserve, and project civilization. Such reports abounded in the *Globe* and *Gazette,* often detailing the exploits of the American military as it sought to crush any and all Aboriginal resistance to westward expansion.[111] A typical and matter-of-fact report in January recorded: "Col. Rice has organized an expedition against savages. He surprised and destroyed two villages, and killed eleven and captured 20 Indians."[112] Nowhere do such reports explain that soldiers routinely murdered innocents, including pregnant women, children, Elders, and the infirm, as the historical record amply demonstrates.[113]

American Indians, according to press reports, loved killing: "the body of a white man was found, perfectly naked and covered with arrows and bullet holes. The head presented the appearance of having been beaten with a war club. The top of the skull was broken into a number of pieces and the brain was laying partly in the skull and partly on the ground."[114]

The *Gazette* reported in late February a veritable nightmare, set in Minnesota seven years earlier:

> Some of the barbarities practiced upon the captives were perfectly
> terrible. In one instance the savages took possession of a school-house
> full of children. They first ravished the teacher, and murdered her,
> and then nailed the children, alive in rows, along the walls. One
> they thrust into the stove, where its remains were found charred to
> a cinder, with the exception of the feet which had been dropped off
> upon the floor; and others were impaled upon rough wooden sticks
> longitudinally through the body. They roamed indeed over the

country like so many demons, wreaking a blind and terrible
revenge upon young and old.[115]

Such stories offered a variety of common stereotypes, and they occupied much space in the newspapers. Clearly, the violence was considered to be unwarranted, the mutilation both unjustified yet fully expected. Payback—even preemptive payback—was deserved. On many occasions the papers reported almost gleefully that Americans in turn responded with unmeasured violence, as in the *Globe:* "We will scalp the damned Injun on the river, old or young."[116] One way to "compel the Indians to settle down" would be to decimate the number of buffalo available on the plains, the *Globe* explained, "until they became too scarce to support the red-skins."[117]

Additionally, the *Globe* and *Gazette* reported that American Indians were "treacherous,"[118] polygamists, purchased wives (so long as they could catch them),[119] thieving,[120] and cannibalistic "wretches."[121] In late July the *Globe* presented a captivity narrative in which a white woman had been rescued after two years.[122] Her family had been "butchered." She bore witness during the kidnapping as a "savage sunk his tomahawk into one of the women." Leaving little to the imagination, the paper reported how the woman had become the forced mistress, first, to "Buffalo Man," then to "Tall Tree," after the latter paid the former a "couple of ponies."[123]

Seldom did either paper attempt to provide any explicit explanation of the discerned "savage" behaviour. That said, partially refuting its stand on the future of the African-American, the *Globe* opined in late July: "A pure American Indian is always a subject of interest—destined as he seems to be to disappear from the face of the earth, in order to make room for the negro, the Aryan, and the Mongol, the three races who at present show no sign of decadence...he has had his fair innings."[124]

In sum, then, American Indians were characterized as red devils, moribund yet nonetheless dangerous savages, well beyond the pale of Canadian-style civilization. Press portrayals of Canada's Aboriginals were framed as no less demeaning or empirically inaccurate. However, a key difference lay in the portrayal of American Indians locked in a ferocious battle that pitted America's more violent settler civilization against naturalized Aboriginal savagery. The necessarily martial context served two basic purposes for these newspapers. Such portrayals, first, confirmed the larger and broader presentations of Americans as unduly violent. The second portrayal debased Natives by casting them as one-dimensional savages and kill-crazy heathens. Thus, the second purpose becomes enmeshed with the first—stereotyping Natives *and* Americans (though obviously Aboriginals fare disastrously in the comparison) in order to champion and, indeed, justify Canada's very existence. So while the *Globe* would criticize the United States for its espied interest in annexing Cuba—"we want Cuba and we mean to have it"[125]—it would not recognize that Canada's position on Rupert's Land might be characterized much the same way.

"BEYOND ALL PRAISE"

The socio-religious imperative to subdue and absorb Canada's west in 1869—hegemonic assimilation—emerged clearly in the *Globe* and *Gazette:* get the land (which did not belong to Natives), minimize the threat posed by Aboriginals by dividing and conquering them via treaties and reservations, convert the heathens, tutor the children, root out wickedness and sin, and farm and otherwise exploit the resources in a way that God might endorse. The application of such notions necessarily had to bend to empirical reality (even if the ideas themselves did not precisely stem from it). For example, Red River had suffered a blight of grasshoppers so severe by 1869, reported the *Globe*, that Canada's Christian conscience might only be assuaged by providing relief. Such rhetoric and, indeed, commensurate actions were framed as the work that a mature and attentive parent might engage in to aid a growing child, a Christian lending a hand to a pagan, God putting an exclamation point on the need for conquest. In this way, "this deplorable state of suffering and starvation" might be alleviated by "the benevolent public,"[126] the *Globe* preached on one of several occasions.[127] Red River was synonymous in both papers with Roman Catholic "half-breeds," a people who could not even properly feed or clothe themselves, according to the *Globe*. They were "dependent on the charity of the world for their daily bread," though how this was so was not explained. Further, their food preparation was "simple and inferior," again without elaboration as to how this was so.[128] Whitefish, a staple, "is beyond all praise." Work itself, and here the expectation is that farming would prevail, fared poorly because the "half-breed system of farming is careless and unscientific."[129] One outcome, admonished the *Gazette*, was "starvation" in the colony, the result of an admixture of laziness and lack of intelligence captured in the exasperated words of the paper: "They won't farm…[they will do] anything but farm."[130] At least part of the problem, especially the material poverty and the inability to advance economically, stemmed from nominal adherence to Roman Catholicism, though how it differed in theological substance from Protestantism the paper did not explain.[131] The "half-breeds" were in fact responsible for fashioning a "horror" in the settlement.[132] Lest there be any mistake, the paper was usually careful to note that they were half Indian, and all Aboriginals tended to be indistinguishable except on rare occasions. The only positive characteristics evinced by this half-caste group was its "hospitality" and the fact that its women tended toward the "shapely" before lives of toil rendered them less attractive, the latter conjuring up the female as sexual object. Fortunately, the paper stressed, they were tractable, "easily dealt with and easily controlled."[133] In short, a correspondent for the *Globe* summarized, "A more squalid looking set of beings I never saw, inferior, I should judge, in all the elements of civilization."[134]

One "problem" then was what to do with, to, and about Natives. On this issue the papers spoke with one colonial voice,[135] and social Darwinism was the norm.[136] While the *Globe* and *Gazette* endorsed the view that American Indians were savage, portrayals of Canada's domestic Indigenous population, while nodding to savagery,[137] tended be more fully dimensioned, if no less stereotyped. In this way, the ensuing portrayals were far richer but also significantly more comprehensive in their damnation of all things Native. In general, two overlapping allegations filled many hundreds of instances the papers provided. These include assertions that Natives were debauched and backward. Such imagery served to justify the purchase of Rupert's Land and the subsequent treaties that cemented indefinite white hegemony.

Depictions of Canada's "savages," as a result, remained prominent, as in reports of a "massacre" committed by Indian "murderers,"[138] yet were complemented with closer examinations of Indigenous culture. In the former case, for example, in late May of 1869 the *Globe* reminded readers, "they [Aboriginals in Canada's west] are very different from the timid and cringing creatures who are now the sole representatives of the Indian race in the back settlements of [eastern] Canada."[139] Notice the common conflation of all Indians as a single monolithic construction. The Natives to the near east of Rupert's Land, that is, the Lake of the Woods region, were also "numerous and warlike,"[140] whereas in the west the Blackfoot were "the really wild Indians."[141] The *Gazette* agreed almost verbatim, noting that the western Natives were "constantly on the war path."[142]

"AS DEGRADED A SET OF SAVAGES AS CAN BE IMAGINED"

Beyond the well-worn "savage" tag, who then were these Native people of Rupert's Land? What, if anything, differentiated the various groups of Indians from one another and from the "half-breeds"? Were all "half-breeds" the same? These were not idle questions, and the two papers in question endeavoured at great length to explain them, if inconsistently. In this respect, the arrogance of the colonial framing was presented as what the writer Arundhati Roy has termed "everydayness"[143] in, for example, simple questions put to the *Globe:* "Could half-breeds be hired as stock-keepers...are they trustworthy?" (The short answer was, no).

"Half-breed" and *pure* Natives sometimes differed in press coverage. While the two publications tended to conflate them, on occasion the papers articulated discrete qualities espied in each group. For example, the *Globe* in August reported, "The half-breeds are generally better looking than the full-blooded Indians; but are delicate and short lived. The girls of the mission school are narrow chested and weak lunged creatures, and generally die of consumption."[144] Yet on another occasion the paper identified "half-breeds" as physically more robust, citing the ease with which "full-bloods" were stricken with consumption.[145] French "half-breeds," partly because they were identified with Roman Catholicism and partly because they were held to be most at fault for Louis Riel's short-lived government, were ranked beneath English and Scottish "half-breeds."[146] The *Globe* confidently labelled the French Métis "foolish and misguided," which "affords a striking illustration of their character."[147] "The Scotch and English half-breeds are disgusted with the course of the French half-breeds" in supporting Riel, with some satisfaction the *Gazette* and *Globe* noted identically.[148] English "half-breeds" were more "staid" than the French while the Scottish "half-breeds" were "close-fisted, canny [and] thrifty."[149] At the same time, both "Indians" and "half-breeds" displayed an animal-like hardiness: "They can subsist upon what a white man would die upon. They can go for days without food. They are inured to hardships of every kind."[150]

The papers also occasionally characterized specific Aboriginal nations. For example, the Sioux were renowned for having in 1862 "drenched Minnesota with blood." A *Globe* report from Winnipeg said "the Sioux Indian should be driven from the territory back to the United States, there to receive punishment for their atrocities on American soil in 1862. Only small bands remain in the territory but these are doubly dyed villains; and notwithstanding the destitution of the settlement, are constantly robbing the farmers of horses and cattle."[151]

They were also reported to have designs to "devastate" Portage la Prairie, Manitoba, in a raid that never occurred.[152] The *Gazette* too identified them with the "horrible outrages in Minnesota."[153] The Blackfoot further west, meanwhile, had "murdered several Christian Indians."[154] This latter group, though "handsome"[155] were "wild Indians...their posts have been abandoned, their agents murdered,"[156] noted the *Globe*. Almost verbatim the *Gazette* concurred, throwing the Plains Cree into the mix, calling them "the real Indians, wild and eloquent," yet at the same time diminishing them as childlike in their need to supplicate to the "Father" represented by the incumbent federal representative from Ottawa.[157] The "Ojibways," east toward the Lake of the Woods, specialized in "theft and debauchery...drunkenness [and] gambling."[158] The "Swamp Indians" (Cree) presented "as degraded a set of savages as can be imagined."[159] The Mohawk, who inhabited southern Quebec, were cast as "smugglers" by the *Gazette*, living in a "howling wilderness," closely associated with debased nature, "stalwart...brandishing both his knife and tomahawk."[160]

The *Globe* explained the origins of the Métis as "the half-breed, a race which has sprung into existence in the last 70 or 80 years...a hardy looking people." The white fraction of the mixture rendered them braver and more fierce than Indians and so the latter made peace with them, the paper continued.[161]

That said, perhaps the most common Canadian stereotype with respect to Natives alleged an innate predilection for alcoholism and related behaviour that speaks to a basic absence of self-control. For example, "For whiskey almost anything can be purchased from an Indian," proclaimed the *Globe*.[162] In short, the term "Indian," sometimes substituted as "aboriginal," "native," "indigene," "red man," red skin," or "savage," signified drunkard or drunkenness, among other things; and drunkard signified moral weakness, a lack of self-control. These portrayals did not attribute themselves to any sort of verifiable authority, a hallmark of contemporary journalism. Instead, the papers presented what amounted to hearsay as fact, confusing opinion with conclusions drawn from actual evidence. This speaks to the operation of hegemonic naturalization, as if such assertions lay beyond the realm of the necessity of evidence and proof.[163]

Thus drunkenness and a love of drink featured prominently in the coverage, from commonplace observations such as, "drinking fire-water"[164] to allegations including, "You all know [the Native] drinks too much," in the

Gazette.[165] Lassitude dovetailed neatly with the claim that Indians were intemperate in their thirst for alcoholic beverages. Both the *Globe* and *Gazette* noted Indigenous laziness as evidenced by an unwillingness to farm. In fact, "half-breeds" were so opposed to engaging in the principal economic activity of the colonial settlement that they would choose starvation before taking up the plow.[166] This led to a situation in which they were "all dependent on the charity of the world for their daily bread," according to the *Globe*.[167]

Another feature of alleged Native backwardness lay in their inability to rise above the intemperate demands of the flesh, as already suggested by love of drink, laziness, and also the devotion to atavistic (and occasionally amusing)[168] outbursts such as the war dance.[169] This might lead directly to "demoniacal orgies through the influences of the fire water upon the savage nature of the Indian," reported the *Globe*.[170] In another example, an article narrated the practice of "squaw kissing" when oversexed "Indian and half-breed women go about kissing every one of the opposite sex whom they meet…Hiding from the keen scented squaws is impossible, and the readiest way of getting through the ceremony is to take it manfully."[171]

It might have been unsurprising then for *Globe* readers to learn that "polygamy is practiced in the tribes…A man may have as many wives as he can keep, but he must buy them. The universal price of a wife is a pony…A squaw once purchased becomes the immediate property of the purchaser, but he must catch her."[172] On the other hand, why not? "Many of their women are remarkably shapely," the *Globe* insinuated.[173]

"THEY ARE CONSUMMATE BEGGARS"

Curiously, despite their espied savage nature, the press also noted that Aboriginals "are easily dealt with and easily controlled."[174] "No Canadian farmer should hesitate for an instant on their account," the *Globe* boasted.[175] In other words, westward imperial expansion into Rupert's Land would not be undermined by a little savagery. Despite a proclivity for warring, another article explained, "qualified [Indian] agents could easily settle" them down.[176] Thus, the savage also earned status as a lowly and slightly pathetic creature, as the *Globe* had it, "the poor Indians."[177] More hopefully, citing comments made in Parliament, the *Globe* even suggested that under select conditions some Natives might become modestly "civilized."[178] Other reports claimed that "there is no fear of violent molestations from the Indians…[because] They are consummate beggars."[179] Less charitably, and citing a litany of stereotyped gripes, the *Globe* opined: "The Indian…is almost useless. He is inert and uncleanly. He is only driven to the chase by the direct extremity of hunger. He walks about in stately indolence, and is full of a not ungraceful pride, none of which is lost or forgotten when seeking alms. When he begs he begs with the bearing of a man about to confer a favour."[180]

Ultimately, these sorts of characterizations contributed to the infantilization of Natives, "who are to be taken care of as little children."[181] On one of the few occasions that either paper commented favourably on Roman Catholics, the *Globe* reassured readers that "Jesuits control the Indians like children."[182] French "half-breeds," after news of the Riel insurgency came to dominate the front pages, also were called "childish."[183] Additionally, the *Globe* offered: "Of all savages those that live by fishing…are the most degraded. I was surprised at the thoroughly Mongolian type, with broad, flat faces and oblique eyes, or pure breeds. The older women were horribly withered, bleared and smoke dried, extremely suggestive of the witches in Macbeth."[184]

Both papers concluded forcefully that Aboriginals required domination and subjugation. White Canadian society through its democratic government must "act as guardians to their interests, and to promote their Christianization and civilization." The paper did not identify a potential conflict in these goals—that is, how might Christianity benefit Natives? Such was the "heathen" lot of the "poor Indian."[185]

It would be an error to automatically assume consonance between press and public opinion—though this often occurs; the story here is more complex. Instead, as noted, the work of agenda-setting theorists shows how the press not merely frames issues for readers but primes readers, providing them with ready-made consumable opinions. In 1873, the Montreal *Gazette* boldly championed the agenda-setting power of the press. In an article endorsing a view printed first in the New York *Tribune*, it recorded:

> Newspapers are getting to be much more than mere transcripts of the news and gossip of the day. They are pioneers in learned explorations; they are foremost in geographical and historical discovery; they are the teachers of social science…The reporter of today is the adventurer who penetrates the desert and the jungle, the scholar who researches for relics of the forgotten past, the courier who bears the news of

victory…across a wilderness and through hostile armies…we can hardly doubt that it is destined in a very short time to be the foremost of all the secular professions—the most powerful in its operations, the most brilliant in its rewards, and the most useful to mankind.[186]

Yes, in those days they were all heroic self-made men.[187] And, after all, "journalistic language is a kind of palimpsest," David Spurr writes.[188] Ongoing colonialism completes the picture, rendering the sorts of portrayals presented in the chapter not simply as accurate but even as desirable, natural, and inevitable. Put simply, colonialized images promote and support what Peter Kulchyski has identified as "totalizing" colonial practice.[189] In this way, the press served as a primary teacher about important public issues such as the construction of race and identity.

American reporters frequently exaggerated or simply fabricated news about Aboriginals in the late nineteenth century. Sharon Murphy has termed it "outright lying," and attributed it to greed on the part of writers who were paid by the column inch. Thus, "they faked 'reliable sources' and 'eyewitness accounts' and wrote propaganda disguised as news."[190] John Coward argues that such behaviour was largely predictable. As the news business professionalized and competition grew fiercer in North America after the American Civil War and Canadian Confederation, journalists were pressured increasingly by tighter deadlines, which contributed to sloppier attention to detail and accuracy. But, the key point Coward makes for the United States, and one that fits equally well for Canada, is that the press itself shared the same world views as its audience. For example, in the United States, reporters "happily fired at Indians whenever they had the chance."[191] Thus colonial cultural visions prevailed in press depiction because they constituted "the racial ideology of the age as well as the particular historical circumstances that brought Indians into popular consciousness."[192]

CHAPTER TWO

FIFTY-SIX WORDS
Treaty 3, 1873

We cannot but think that the treatment of the Indian to the east of the Rocky Mountains is a very serious matter, and that a material force of disciplined men will be necessary to enforce law and order. It is quite possible that as cultivation makes its way the grasshoppers will disappear, and the mosquitoes will follow them, but the whole history of the continent tells us that the savage is an incubus not so easily removed. We say incubus, because he is untameable and must be provided for. Bred as he has been to consider the country his own, he can never be made to understand that he should be dispossessed of it.
—MONTREAL *GAZETTE*, 4 JUNE 1873

When the Gomery Commission, the body charged with investigating the sponsorship scandal in Quebec, summoned sitting Canadian Prime Minister Paul Martin to testify in early 2005, the press drew attention to the fact that the last sitting prime minister called upon to testify at such proceedings was also Canada's first, Sir John A. MacDonald. The Pacific Railway Scandal, which seemed to consume federal politics and the national press in 1873, summoned MacDonald and thereby established a precedent upon which Justice John Gomery acted when he beckoned Martin. Such framing by the press lent weight to the seriousness of the commission's work.

Such a framing also lends support to the convention among Canadian historians that the Pacific Railway Scandal loomed as the biggest political story and certainly the key news story of 1873.[1] After all, legality and politics aside, the core of the issue hinged on the common goal of settling the Canadian west. Liberals and Conservatives differed in their respective approaches to this issue but shared a basic goal: white Christian immigrants should fill the lands west of the Great Lakes. In a sense, the railroads played a minor, if salacious, role in this larger Canadian metanarrative.

It should come as no surprise then that the pre-existing condition upon which western settlement was predicated in 1873—that is, Indigenous occupancy of western Canada—would also have been of some interest to the press. Treaty 3, third of the eleven numbered treaties, was signed in 1873 and effectively turned over an area that today includes twenty-eight First Nations—reaching in the south from the Northwest Angle at the Lake of the Woods northward through Red Lake, eastward to beyond Upsala, and westward into Manitoba, 14,245,000 hectares in all—to the Crown, which then turned aggressively to promote white settlement.[2] The importance of the treaties can hardly be overstated. Without them there would be no Canada as it is known today. Yet in the country's two most widely read and influential English-language newspapers, the Montreal *Gazette* and the Toronto *Globe*, Treaty 3 earned just one short paragraph of coverage in total in the *Globe* and none at all in the *Gazette*.

While the signing of Treaty 3 received little direct attention, on other occasions the idea and practice of treaty making were discussed in detail by the papers. Canada's Natives west of the Great Lakes purposefully sought treaties, the *Globe* explained. They did so, the argument ran, in order to invite the protection of the white Protestant community at the same time as the gesture demonstrated an acknowledged inability to govern their own affairs. In short, at some level sensible Aboriginals endorsed colonialism—and treaties—as good for themselves.[3] These portrayals tended to project, invert, and package the idea of treaties in such a way as to reverse cause and effect. Following this line of reasoning, whites did Aboriginals a favour by seizing the vast majority of their lands. Much of the subsequent Othering evinced in news reports importantly serves to rationalize the land usurpation inherent in the treaty-making process. Treaties had, in fact, the *Globe* reported, been advantageous for American Natives.[4]

Typically, Aboriginals were portrayed as desiring treaties, explicitly for their own good. Moreover, such assertions were presented as givens, declarations of simple common sense—never quoting or, for that matter, attributing such statements to any specific person or persons—and couched with a caution that for any such treaties to be successfully negotiated the Canadian government must make a strong show of "force," because Aboriginals tended to be mercurial and potentially dangerous, the *Globe* asserted.[5]

As noted in the previous chapter, this "prairie land" was highly desirable; but it had lamentably been turned into little more than a "desert" through Aboriginal misuse, according to the *Gazette*.[6]

"A MAN CANNOT BE BOTH A HUNTER AND A FARMER"

In 1873, these two papers—one Liberal and one Conservative—identified the other as the "opposition"; after all, Canada underwent a change in government as Macdonald was ushered out of office and Alexander Mackenzie came in. Predictably, then, the papers battled mightily on such issues as the Pacific Railway Scandal and the Reciprocity Treaty with the United States—issues of significant electoral import.

Yet on an issue arguably of greater weight—the "Indian Problem," as it was frequently known—the papers spoke as if from one partisan colonial voice, as they had in 1869. The attendant tropes deeply and consistently stereotyped Indigenous people in the most pejorative of ways—colonially racist, to put it simply—and certainly belied the notion that the press could marshall evidence to "teach" Canadians with any degree of accuracy about Indigenous peoples, as claimed by the *Gazette*.[7] Such imagery was simultaneously blistering in its condemnation of Native peoples yet awkwardly heartfelt. In short, the two fierce ideological rivals presented a unified colonial indictment of Canada's Native populations. This continuity, mirroring that of 1869, is then important because it suggests that little changed in the few years after the purchase of Rupert's Land.

The Canadian west was only just opening up to settlement in 1873 and the federal government was determined to push a railway through to the Pacific Ocean. The west was portrayed vividly in the press as the "wilds"—and inhabited, correspondingly, by the uncivilized "red man"[8] ("man" in this case standing in for everybody of any identifiable Aboriginal ancestry while "red," colour of passion, served as a ubiquitous signifier of essential Nativeness). According to press reports, this territory was an untapped garden. The *Gazette* wrote: "It is deserving of the most energetic efforts on the part of the government that no pains should be spared to assist immigration to the Northwest. Every man that can handle a spade or axe, every homestead that rises on the boundless prairies that lie awaiting the hand of the husbandman, every acre of land brought into cultivation, will be an additional assistance to the great national enterprise which is ultimately to span the continent."[9] Indeed, the land was coveted for geopolitical reasons but also as a source of wealth—a principal source of which was expected to be rich agricultural lands.[10]

The pith of the argument continued to derive from inherited English cultural assumptions about how specific forms of land usage bestowed and signified land ownership. God wanted the land settled by white Protestant Christians. Yet divine sanction was not sufficient in itself. Gaining legal title to Rupert's Land was one thing and effectively securing it was another. Large-scale white settlement was thus key; but before that could happen the Aboriginal population had to be dealt with. The most basic solution was to establish treaties. In this way, by compelling Natives to take treaties and relocate themselves to restrictive reservation lands and the regulatory apparatus through which the federal government would manage them, the country could take shape. This occurred in the west over a number of years after 1869 (although the north was all but ignored in this respect till the late twentieth century). For example, Treaty 1 and Treaty 2, covering most of southern Manitoba, were struck in 1871 and 1872 respectively. Treaty 3, which usurped some 14 million hectares in central Canada in and around the Northwest Angle, reached eastward from Treaty 1, was struck in 1873. Treaty 4, which covers most of southern Saskatchewan west from Treaty 2, was signed in 1874. Treaty 5 in 1875 spanned the northern reaches of the four earlier treaties.[11] And so on, through Treaty 11 in 1921.

A simple question foregrounded much of the news rhetoric: how could peoples for whom senseless wandering personified a way of life possibly make good use of the land?[12] Natives exhibited an atavistic and reductive "migratory"[13] impulse derived from hunting, which conflicted with the press's notions of the desirability of progress. Hence, when the *Globe* stated, "a man cannot be both a hunter and a farmer," the implied comparison naturally favoured the latter occupation.[14] This logic had served as a primary justification for usurping it in the first instance.[15] Protestant Christianity, which infused Canadian politics in the 1870s, also demanded that Natives be settled, pacified, and taught, as best one might—and both newspapers endorsed the use of force, if necessary.

Canadian colonialism, then, as presented in the press, lay grounded in one key assertion: Aboriginals did not own the land upon which they had lived, loved, and died for thousands of years. As historian Patricia Seed has documented, the basic premise upon which English conquest in the Americas lay, emerged from the observation that Indigenous peoples failed to exploit the land in ways commensurate with English custom and law.[16] By neglecting to build fences, construct bridges, and erect permanent structures, and tame the land as Britons might—the essence of which, when duly practised, conferred ownership—Natives lost any claim to full ownership.[17] In other words, by failing to act like Britons *cum* Canadians, Natives effectively invited the Canadian government to take it away—hence the treaty system.[18] The *Gazette* reported in January 1873 that "it is questionable that these Indians have been upon the lands for so long a period as to raise a presumption of right."[19]

"FIRST, THE INDIANS MUST HAVE PRESENTS"

In a sense Treaty 3 was barely a news story at all: the *Globe* passed off its signing in fifty-six words—among them that "the terms are very liberal towards the Indians,"[20] whereas the *Gazette* simply declined to notice it. In late September the *Globe* made passing mention of the likelihood that its signing would be postponed by ten days because of the intransigence of an Ojibwe leader[21] who led a group of "obstinate," "polemical" and "crafty" Natives,[22] and then in late October the *Globe* printed excerpts of the treaty, advising readers that the shiftless Aboriginals might now be effectively "quieted" by white Canada.[23] After that, the *Globe* remained silent on the treaty.

Natives, however, did not escape substantive notice in either paper. In fact both publications had much to say about them—ultimately leading to the conclusion that the lack of interest in the treaty as news reflected a "thick" sense[24] that the treaties were minor incidents in the larger narrative of triumphal Anglo conquest. Still, on one occasion in July, the *Globe* reported that Natives on the Prairies, with the exception of the Blackfoot, were "anxious" to strike treaties, though it gave no indication why.[25] In order to effect treaties, the paper counselled, the government must be prepared to bribe the childlike Natives with baubles and cheap trinkets such as beads.[26] "First, the Indians must have presents," the *Gazette* explained.[27]

In no case did the *Globe* or *Gazette* promote physical genocide. This was unnecessary because in the publications asserted that homogeneous Native culture along with its practitioners, would shortly fade away and die out. In the late nineteenth and early twentieth centuries, Aboriginals as a whole on the North American continent were believed to be in a state of demographic disappearance, "dying out before the white man,"[28] as the *Globe* put it on one of several occasions, even on occasion dying of starvation in the extraordinarily rich lands of Saskatchewan.[29]

Both broadsheets expressed much interest in political news, in particular Canadian and English. On balance, the *Globe* displayed greater attention to Ontario politics where the *Gazette* favoured political reportage tilted eastward toward Quebec and the Maritimes. Both featured a lot of advertising, including typically as much as 50 percent of the front pages alone—for items such as cigars, railways, book binding, sugar and syrups, grocers, liquors, furnaces, mechanics wanted, medical and dental services, the legal profession, board and lodging, and such. Both also, in the style of the day, ran serialized literature. Meanwhile, mesmerism was taken seriously in 1873, as was phrenology. Religious news, especially in the *Globe*, figured prominently. The *Gazette* pitched itself as the "best commercial newspaper in Canada."[30] Sports, meanwhile, gained scant attention. On the other hand, news from the United States earned a standing front-page column in both publications, including ongoing snippets which tended to focus on violence, crime, and disease.[31] A close reading of such reports reveals a framing that positions Canada as not so subtly woven of more durable moral cloth than the United States.[32] Citing the English positivist Herbert Spencer, the *Globe* agreed that "there is no instance on record in criminal statistics of a man who rose up against the laws of society who was not deficient [when] considered as an intellectual being."[33]

"LET US BLESS GOD THAT HE HAS BROUGHT A VINE INTO THIS WILDERNESS"

One of the principal all-purpose wrongs attributed to Natives by these press organs stemmed from the contention that they were essentially uncivilized. This entailed, first, that Indigenous peoples were not properly Christian— in particular, because the papers also expressed a pronounced disdain for Roman Catholicism, this meant Protestant Christianity—which, the *Gazette* assured readers, Natives preferred.[34] Without a trace of irony the *Gazette* denounced Catholics for engaging in "religious persecution."[35] In fact, the Catholic Church behaved in altogether unchristian ways in its dealings with thieving and needy Aboriginals, the paper warned. Various Christian churches, among whom the Catholic constituted a single if prominent entity, that aided and abetted the disenfranchisement of Natives from their lands and culture the papers lauded because it was "to their advantage."[36] Reporting the results of an interview, the *Globe* offered: "Asked if he could name any positive improvement in morality that had resulted from the missionaries' labours, 'Yes, Christianized Crees would not steal your horses—at least not openly—when you were passing through their country'...[and] they had all been polygamists to as great an extent as they could afford and they used to exchange wives to suit each others' convenience."[37]

As the *Gazette* put it on another occasion, "let us bless God that he has brought a vine into this wilderness; that he has cast out the heathen."[38] Further, the *Globe* charged, even when converted to any variety of "nominal" Christianity, Natives were probably just faking it, either because they were not trustworthy, could not understand basic Christian dogma, or, most charitably, yet implying unintelligence, needed more time to gain an understanding of the new religion.[39]

The papers denied the existence of Indigenous religious traditions.[40] According to the *Globe* and the *Gazette*, it was a mistake to identify Indigenous belief systems as religions because their first premises included the promotion of aggressive violence, patricide, polygamy, and infanticide.[41] Moreover, "missionaries have made no impression on them," the *Globe* expressed its exasperation.[42] Meanwhile, sweat lodges, which remain central to Plains culture to this day, allegedly served no religious function but instead provided a means by which the "miserable, starved-looking," superstitious, "idlers" could and did plot mischief and criminal activities in "great Indian natural luxury," the equivalent of Russian baths taken to an extreme, a long article in the *Globe* related.[43] In particular, according to the *Globe*, the attendant medicine man used gatherings in the "sweating booths" to plot vengeance upon personal enemies, employing other hapless Natives as so many transfixed pawns to aid and abet criminal activity.[44] Yet on other occasions Native religion was merely derided as silly, childish, and not only pointless but counterproductive.[45] The Métis, by contrast, the *Globe* portrayed as simply too "passionate" for the abstemiousness required of a good Christian.[46]

The allegation that Natives lacked intelligence framed many news stories, going so far in the lack of control of their faculties as to be "insane," opined the *Gazette*.[47] For the French Métis, likewise, "the yoke of celibacy is too heavy; and fiddling, dancing, and hunting and a wild roving life have too many charms" to resist, including cavalier inebriation.[48] Then there existed just plain idiocy; how else might one explain their love of trinkets, and the fact that Aboriginals were easily duped, the *Globe* advised readers.[49]

First peoples were often depicted as being simultaneously barbaric— "bloodthirsty" and "dangerous"—and yet cowardly, quick to retreat from a fair fight.[50] This fated them, in the *Gazette*'s estimate, as suggested by a headline, "The Trouble With Indians"—to be sneaky, light-fingered, treacherous, and apt to turn tail at the first sign of resistance to their nefarious behaviours.[51] What more might one expect of a people bred on horse-theft as a way of life, helpless yet excitable to an unnatural degree?[52]

Natives additionally emerged in press reports as needy and not self-reliant, "the unsophisticated children of the plains."[53] Resisting honest farm work in favour of hunting was simply lazy "child's play."[54] Indeed, treaties, claimed the *Globe*, would "train them in the habits of self-reliance" and maturity. "They cannot always be kept," the paper puffed with impatience, "in a state of pupilage."[55] Yet the bribery served an identified purpose: Aboriginals needed to be controlled, for while on the reservation the Native was invariably a "pauper" whereas away from the reserve he became an "outlaw."[56]

The Indigenous predilection for inactivity, meanwhile, was only exacerbated, the *Gazette* warned, when combined with a love of drink.[57] Alcohol was a peril for all, it proclaimed on a variety of occasions.[58] In fact, the *Gazette* championed temperance as the best option for all Canada, white and non-white.[59] That said, Natives not only had a weakness for inebriation, but, in turn, such a characteristic reinforced the sense that temperate whites therefore needed to teach Aboriginals the proper way to behave, to the extent that they could be taught, chimed the *Globe*.[60]

In sum, the smear of being uncivilized, from allegations of cultural backwardness, paganism, love of violence, dishonesty, profligacy, and so on, expressed itself in many ways, which in themselves frequently cross-pollinated. These stereotypes denied Aboriginal humanity and agency in ways that, following their own internal logic, rendered documents like Treaty 3 just and reasonable settlements, desirable for all inhabitants of Canada, Aboriginal and settler. Natives were not the only group cast as Other in the *Globe* and *Gazette*, yet they fell in with the alleged weakest of three groupings, loosely identifiable by skin pigmentation and geographical location.[61] In the first and best case, white Europeans such as the French and Scottish stood above all others. A second category included Turks, Chinese,

Japanese, and Persians. They occupied an area of mid-level damnation. And then, third, non-white Aboriginal peoples from anywhere on the planet constituted the sorriest and most deplorable bunch.

Stereotypes of Canada's Natives, while universally uncomplimentary, were not entirely consistent. They were simultaneously depicted as both partially tractable and yet entirely intractable. Canadian Indigenous artisanship, for example, compared favourably with more "primitive" Japanese and Chinese work, the *Globe* judged.[62] Still, the *Globe* made it clear that in Canada an ordered hierarchy, however poorly articulated, existed among the "races." In Canada whites came first, followed by Natives, the "pure Indian," in turn followed by overtly sexual, drunken, violent, and criminally inclined "half-breeds" (French-Native sometimes being preferable to Scotch-Indian), children, and then dogs.[63] The "half-breeds" were lazy and continued to favour virtually all activities to productive farm work, the *Globe* opined.[64] The Scottish and the French admixture another time differed. The Scottish, it seems, improved the line by contributing shrewdness, steadiness, and industriousness, according to the *Globe*:

> There is a great difference between the Scotch and French half-breeds. The French, who intermarried with the Indians in some respects became as the Indian. Just as the Spaniards in Mexico and South America who later intermarried with the natives sunk to their level. The children have all the Indian characteristics. They excel the Indian in strength of body and endurance. They best him in his own field of hunting, running, riding, power of eating, or when necessary, of abstinence; with these are united much of French vivacity, love of amusement, hospitality, patience, courtesy or manner, and warmth of affection. When a Scotchman married a squaw, her position, on the contrary, was frequently not much higher than a servant's. He was 'the superior person of the house.' He continued Christian after his fashion, she continued pagan...The children of such a couple take more after the father than the mother. As a rule they are shrewd, steady and industrious. A Scotch half-breed has generally a field of wheat before or behind his house, stacks, barn and provision for a year ahead in his granary. The Metis has a patch of potatoes or a little barley, and a year of scarcity draws his belt tighter or starves.[65]

Likewise, the papers took delight in casting Louis Riel, "great chief" of the insurgent Métis movement of "Banditti" in Red River, as a racialized murderer.[66]

The stereotyping of other Europeans emerges as rather tame by comparison. Jews were money-grubbers.[67] Norwegians, Danes, Dutch, and Germans were "economical."[68] Juxtaposed with portrayals of Natives, these attributes, while unflattering, seem nearly harmless. Italians, however, the *Globe* cautioned, were associated with slavery.[69]

Both papers expressed strong aversions for the Chinese. Well-known pejoratively as "Chinamen," the *Gazette* labelled them as physically diminutive, imitative, comical, and crafty.[70] In this way, nothing had changed from the 1869 press coverage. The *Globe* agreed, opining that they were "celestials," "little," "small," "pig-tailed," "resist" civilization's "influences," "heathen," yet potentially make good servants.[71] Still, the *Gazette* held, the Chinese, Japanese, Turks, and Persians appeared to be coming out of their collective "oriental darkness" and "are letting in the light of western civilization."[72] And the *Globe* concurred, proclaiming that Canada must play its part, "to be a light to the dark places of the earth."[73] The *Globe* had particular hope for Japan. "Western light," it claimed, "having once entered...will be impossible to exclude."[74] Mexicans, though, understood as "half-breeds," were dangerously criminal.[75] And Spaniards had without warning "sunk" to the level of Natives.[76]

As an enterprise, colonialism, therefore, was just and necessary "not only for children, but for humanity in general," the *Gazette* explained in an editorial titled, "THE HEART OF AFRICA,"[77] a continent and its inhabitants that exhibited alleged retarded social evolution.[78] Africa acted as the "White Man's Grave," a *Globe* headline cautioned. The accompanying news story related how Africans dressed like lunatics, revelling in exotica and attracted as if by magic to trifles. Further, they were unintelligent, as evidenced by their poor command of the English language.[79] The Ashantee still engaged in slavery.[80] On the other hand, more promisingly, Persia had begun "to let in the light of western civilization," the *Gazette* chirped. The result "will have a wholesome effect," the paper predicted.[81]

American blacks, serving the chauvinistic purpose of championing Canadian civil society over that of the United States, earned nearly total condemnation. Typically, reports noted white lynchings of preternaturally vicious black men who had "ravished" white women, in one representative case, "after knocking her on the head with an axe."[82] Blacks predictably exhibited "obnoxious characteristics," were "smelly...fat niggers," suffered from an "absence of self-will," and were no more intelligent than dogs, the *Gazette* charged.[83] The *Globe* summed it up in a headline: "Two Blacks Won't Make One White."[84] The United States as a whole, too, was portrayed as existing in nearer chaos: "The epidemic of murders and suicides is raging to an alarming extent on the other side of the line," the *Globe* warned.[85]

Among Indigenous Others, Hawaiians earned probably the most favourable portrayals. They were merely ugly and dressed strangely.[86] Likewise, the Maori, in a single article in the *Globe*, gave "hope that at least one aboriginal race will not die out before civilization, but become absorbed by it."[87] The need for Mexico to defeat its marauding northern Indigenous tribes was stressed by the *Globe*.[88]

Fijians stood out as among the worst of the Others identified by the *Globe* and *Gazette* in 1873. At some length, these island people were tarred as unmitigated beasts in an article detailing a "shocking massacre." A certain Mr. Burns, it seems, had been "clubbed and tomahawked; his brains were beaten out." His wife had been raped and murdered and their child likewise barbarously dispatched. All this resulted, the *Gazette* insinuated, from an inability to control crazed Native libidinal impulses.[89] The *Globe* agreed, reporting on the same story, but embellished it with the charge of cannibalism. The report continued, "The savages had taken [a little girl] by her legs and dashed her brain out against the post of the bedroom door."[90] American Natives, as in 1869, earned blistering condemnation. The Modoc war, set in Oregon, for example, gained ongoing coverage. On the plus side the Modoc fought well, almost akin to "civilized people." Yet they ultimately were cowards, retreating when confronted directly, the *Globe* reassured.[91] The American response, which echoes 1869 coverage wherein the United States was cast as an unnecessarily violent land, a prime signifier of the better sense of imagined Canadian sobriety and calm, conjured up savagery itself.

The "war-like"[92] Sioux were still remembered for the "Minnesota Massacre" of 1862. As a result, the mere presence of the Sioux in Manitoba in 1873 was used as a pretext for near panic. Similar to the cautionary moral structure of a fairy tale, the *Globe* story on 16 June 1873 began with an attempt to frighten readers by invoking the monster and then proceeded to reassure its audience that, if the proper rules were followed (that is, by acting civilized), punishment (that is, the rage of the monster) might be averted. It continued:

> There has been in this country a sense of insecurity in the minds of the settlers. The general feeling is, that the Government is weak, incompetent, and time-serving. Then there is the strife of races, the jealousy of religious sects, and the Sioux Indian war-scare, all bringing forth their damaging fruits. As far, however, as we can learn, there is very little danger of an Indian war at present. The Sioux Indians know full well that their only friends are on this side of the lines...They know that there is still in the minds of the Americans the bitter remembrance of the great 'Minnesota Massacre.'[93]

Indigenous peoples were held to be human—but at a vaguely substandard level, as the discussion of racial hierarchy implied. As the *Gazette* put it, "all the American Indians are supposed, on good grounds, to belong to one variety or family of the human species."[94] They compared well, the *Gazette* said, to mosquitoes and grasshoppers (the latter of which in reality plagued Manitoba's crops again in 1873).[95] And savages were sometimes "picturesque"—for example, "properly tinted and tasseled, plumed with war-eagle plumes and manteau"—the *Gazette* explained in a lengthy and glowing obituary of the imperialist American Romantic artist George Catlin,[96] but in a primitive way, the *Globe* reminded.[97] Yet they remained dangerous and violent, the *Globe* intoned consistently, as an article in late January 1873 reported. In this case, even "squaws took part in the battle and one soldier was killed by the squaws." The United States prevailed, as usual, the story reassured readers, because civilization was destined to conquer savagery and, in this case, because the army employed a howitzer.[98]

Possibly because they were found the furthest from Ontario, British Columbia's Natives stood out as the most deplorable of a bad lot. The *Gazette* explained that they were "thievish and licentious" murderers, engaged in slavery, and practised cannibalism as a religious ritual. Yet with some relief the paper reported that these habits might be overcome through forceful education. Interestingly, the paper argued that some of the difficulties with Aboriginals had been caused by an untoward association with poor whites, conflating a racist slur with classism.[99] Natives in the far west were "excitable," helpless, imploring, automatically cast as in need of direction. They were not trustworthy. They inclined naturally to violence, the

Globe reported.[100] Another time they were identified as "semi-civilized" who "fight greatly amongst themselves" and lacked the "slightest degree" of the benefits of Christianity. They practised abortion and polygamy and infanticide, continued the *Globe*. They trafficked in alcohol and sold their women as whores to certain white men. In short, "very little progress has been made.... Evidently a great deal needs to be done before the condition of British Columbian Natives is in any way creditable either to themselves or to their white neighbors."[101] Additionally, they were identified as "dangerous," "primitive," and "bloodthirsty."[102] The Blackfoot exemplified this, too, for the *Globe*, in a somewhat rare story that detailed Native violence against other Natives. The narrative pitted Cree against Blackfoot and featured scalping and a bluff that won victory for the Cree.[103] According to the paper, poor communication might have been the culprit engendering violence between the groups. The Chinook Natives of British Columbia spoke a "barbarous lingo" that consisted of "one or two hundred words, first introduced by the Hudson's Bay agents."[104]

But on the issue of Indigenous peoples and education the two broadsheets wanted to have it both ways. The Sioux were terrifyingly wicked yet fundamentally harmless.[105] The Native was tamable insofar as he was educable, penned the *Gazette*.[106] On the other hand, because he is nothing short of an "incubus," the *Gazette* reported, "he is untamable and must be provided for"—again, like a needy and stubborn child.[107] The *Globe*, however, still maintained that enforced education tendered the best solution, because it promised the only real chance that Aboriginals might "progress" and master "self-reliance," however imperfectly.[108] The challenge was to overcome Aboriginal "proclivities" for "obstinacy" and "craftiness," the *Globe* asserted.[109] Plus, Natives were closely associated with nature and with animals more plainly, both traits which required taming in order to be made productive.[110] The *Gazette* reported on a public lecture by a Mr. C. Robb: "The lecturer concluded by saying: 'The nature of the Indian, in the reproachful sense of the word, seems to be incapable of eradication, and, to use their own phrase, 'ducks will be ducks for old hen, he hatch 'em.' But the watchword for humanity is still onward and upward, and the march of civilization is ever in the same direction. Meanwhile, let us bless God that he has brought a vine into this wilderness.'"[111]

What are we to make of such imagery? Given that Canada inherited an imperial tradition from its English forebears and that it plied its own colonial path
with respect to Indigenous peoples after 1867, behaviour steeped in ambigu-
ous yet nonetheless strident hegemonic colonial racism, the press treatment in
1873 presented and discussed here seems largely predictable.

That said, some change had occurred since 1869 in the ways that these
two newspapers imagined Aboriginal peoples. First, now that the purchase
of Rupert's Land was itself history, the country turned its energies to settling the west. This had become the dominant national news story by 1873.
The result led to significantly increased news coverage of the west as well,
correspondingly, to a greater depth of interest in all things Aboriginal.
Press content, as presented in this chapter, belies the popular notion that
stereotypes run skin deep. The 1873 imagery cut to the bone, fleshing out,
to follow the metaphor, supposed Indigenous inferiority virtually everywhere imaginable.

John Cameron, publisher of the London *Advertiser* and president of the
Canadian Press Association, waxed on in the *Globe* about the greatness of
Canada's media and the tendentious quality of evolving Canadian society. He opined: "It may safely be affirmed that the Press of Canada shows
advancement rather than retrogression...in the freshness of their intelligence, in the fullness of their reports...each year shows signs of improvement and the future may be reasonably held to be full of promise."[112]

With respect to the depiction of Canada's Indigenous peoples, as evidenced by the 1869 and 1873 *Globe* and *Gazette*, he appears to have hit the
mark. Not only was there more news about Aboriginals in 1873 but the news
itself, in good measure because of more numerous reports emanating from
the west, had become more comprehensive. In this way, the damnation of
Natives had also become deeper and wider. From a colonial perspective,
then, improvement had indeed occurred. Still, the increased volume and
breadth of coverage did not improve Native stature in the press; instead, it
became more pronounced as the papers frantically added layer upon colonial layer. Yet this *news* was not *new* at all; it was the same old colonial regur-
gitation of a teleological world view. As sociologist William Stahl writes,
"Progress is perhaps the most powerful myth of our time, today's version of
eschatology."[113] Yet the *Globe* bathed in the glory of the discerned influence
of the press: "One cannot help remarking what an enormous influence must

be exerted by so large a portion of printed matter being regularly taken into so many quarters of the country."[114]

So, too, the opening of new lands gave the press the chance to compare and contrast Natives east and west. While the east prevailed, in the expressed views of the *Globe* and *Gazette*, the Natives of neither region can be said to have won credit or praise of any kind. For example, the *Globe* reported in August 1873 that "the Indians of Ontario and Quebec are acknowledged to be in every respect in a far superior condition to those in the other Provinces."[115] What separated them, the narrative explained, was treaties and the "Indian schools" that devolved from treaties. Of course, the residential school system that emerged from these early forays was an unmitigated disaster.[116]

Given the clearly higher stakes in play by 1873, one might expect the colonial rhetoric to have been ratcheted up a notch. And that is precisely what happened. The popular desegregationist ideal, common to the later twentieth century and central to some conceptions of the value of Canada's so-called cultural mosaic, which holds that stereotyping diminishes when people of different backgrounds mix, appears to be without merit at all. White-Aboriginal contact in the west, as reflected in news reports, seemed only to reinforce the colonial mentality, not undo it.

It is worth remembering, too, that Natives and Métis are on occasion guilty of the same sorts of crimes that litter mainstream society in Canada and the United States, including murder, larceny, assault, rape, pillage, theft, and so on. Sometimes, too, these crimes are committed under the influence of alcohol. And indeed some Natives are alcoholics—in the same way that some whites also are alcoholics. Our point is not so much to dispute the existence of the particular behaviours reported but, rather, to draw attention to the larger framing of the behaviours. This includes accounting for them in cultural terms. And it is here that the prevalence, constancy, and consistency of the images take their toll.

The two papers tended strongly to smear all Natives with an innate absence of corporeal diligence, the lack of cultural and biological strengths that might engender resistance to temptations of the flesh (e.g., violence, killing, warring, insurgency, alcoholism, wildness, unaccounted bouts of dancing and shouting, and such). In this way, the mere allusion to the behaviours was easily invoked in a code that was transparent to the same degree that it lacked in subtlety—with obvious words such as "savage," less obvious but no less damning terms such as "red man." In short, by 1873 the reader of either of the newspapers in question would have searched high and low for examples of Native humanity on par with white Canada. In this way, the *Gazette* and the *Globe* helped maintain colonialism's chokehold on the Canadian imagination. Herbert Spencer captured the sentiment aptly in the *Globe* when he chastised those without the "capacity to observe" the world as it really is. Lest there be any mistake about the absence of reflexivity of and the redolent hypocrisy inherent in Canada's colonial mind, Spencer erases them. "Judgments distorted by emotions and hatred or admiration will prevent us seeing things as they really are," he proclaimed.[117] In short, Canada's normative white cultural core existed independently of and beyond "culture," which was what Others did or were.

The papers defined what it meant to be white in Canada by juxtaposing it with its opposite. Imagined Natives served as a foil to the white, male, Protestant ideal. In so doing, the very possibility of Native humanity became a logical impossibility. Correspondingly, in news reports of whites warring upon Natives (the American frame), in fact they were fighting a defensive war. Or when whites usurped Aboriginal lands and fretted about the possibility of Native uprisings in response to it (the Canadian frame), whites likewise engaged in a defensive struggle in the name of civilization. They were pitted in a teleological struggle to vanquish barbarism (as signified by everything Native).

The antithesis of the Aboriginal in "the present age of progress," as the *Globe* laid it out before readers, stood like this:

> 1. The farmer must possess nature's greatest gifts—a healthy mind in a sound body. 2. He needs, in the highest degree, patience and perseverance, not alone for days or weeks, but for years in succession; 3. He must be a thoroughly trained botanist. 4. He must understand zoology as far as applied to the domesticated animals of the farm... 6. He must have studied natural philosophy and meteorology... 7. He must be a practical chemist, able to analyze his soils... 8. He must have traveled to some extent.[118]

Clearly, scant few of white Canadians could have measured up to such a demanding and diverse set of talents. But notice, more importantly for this book, how the farmer, that paragon of virtue upon whom Confederation depended, is by definition a white Protestant male. Here point-by-point, or more generally as detailed by the voluminous evidence presented in this chapter, the *Globe* and *Gazette* depicted the imagined Aboriginal as the complementary binary to him. To begin with, the papers make it abundantly clear that the Native had neither "a healthy mind" nor "a sound body." Instead, Aboriginals were cast as unhealthy to the points of depravity and moribundity. Second, the Native was uniformly cast as being without "patience and perseverance," especially the Métis. Subsequent points, while no doubt flattering the white farmer, champion the sort of education that the Native was incapable of receiving because of an espied lack of intelligence, lack of patience and perseverance, lack of initiative. The model Canadian, after all, and by this the press meant white Protestant male, not female, exemplified "pluck...of the truest British kind,"[119] a virtue that would serve the country well in 1885 when Louis Riel again seized centre stage.

Did grounds exist for optimism? Clearly, the press imagined that the stakes were high. "The watchword of humanity is still onward and upward, and the march of civilization is ever in the same direction," the *Gazette* limned. But the very same paragraph added that "the nature of the Indian...seems to be incapable of eradication."[120] Whereas, on another day the paper claimed, "He is untamable."[121] Put more bluntly, the *Globe* offered, "A nation to be great must have great thoughts; must be...a light to the dark places of the earth; to rule inferior races mercifully and justly; to infuse them into a higher life."[122] If measured by material success, there seemed to be some truth in this for Canada. Canadian-style colonialism, according to news reports, was set to profit mightily in the old Northwest at the same time as the country had become blinded by it. The logical result was that Natives must cease to be Natives. And within ten years the federal government would begin to implement this policy in the form of the residential school system.

But why bother to school a people on the verge of extinction? The press reported eagerly that Natives were on the whole moribund yet continued to push the idea that Canada had to do right by them and strike treaties that would effectively strip them of their land and to make arrangements to civilize them via education. A contradiction? Not quite; it is more apparent than real. The depth of the Canadian Christian sense of duty should not be underestimated. Canada was all too willing to sacrifice morally, if not economically, to embody its colonial ideals with respect to Native education. The best example probably comes from the residential school system. For example, by the early twentieth century it had become abundantly clear that widespread abuses and neglect plagued the system but a penny-pinching federal government chose to do nothing.

In the 1873 press it was not so much that Natives had lost all agency. They had never had agency in the press. Their relative absence may be counted as a necessary expedient to justify the continuation of English-style imperialism in North America, but this should in no way suggest that settler Canadians were not heartfelt in their sense of entitlement and superiority. Real Native people were simply invisible. When the *Globe* reported on the population of Manitoba in June 1873, Natives simply were not counted because they did not figure as real human beings.[123] Thus the land was ripe for the taking. This was the Canadian way in 1869 and in 1873.

CHAPTER THREE

"OUR LITTLE WAR" [1]

The North-West Rebellion, 1885

Riel Revolt
A General Uprising of Indians
Imminent.
BATTLEFORD CAPTURED.
Five Hundred Cree Indians on the
War Path.
READY TO JOIN THE REBELS.
Troops Hurried to Quell the Indian
Rising at File.
SETTLERS IN GREAT ALARM.
Archbishop Tache Issues a Pastoral
Counselling Peace.
THE SIOUX AROUSED.
War Fever at its Height Among the
Citizen Soldiery.
—HEADLINE IN THE OTTAWA *CITIZEN*, 31 MARCH 1885

The Métis leader Louis Riel was hanged to death for treason on 16 November 1885, in Regina, Saskatchewan. Recreated, the event, especially Riel's passionate address to the Protestant jury, has become a minor tourist attraction in the city every summer as actors restage some of the drama of Riel's trial. Audiences are then left to decide: guilty or innocent? Scholars and other writers have also waged a spirited debate on the topic.[2] Naturally, it is rife with ideology. Still, certain facts are beyond dispute. For example, an armed resistance to Canadian colonial authority occurred in the Northwest Territories in 1885, the area today consisting of the provinces of Manitoba, Saskatchewan, and Alberta. Dozens of lives were lost. The conflict, comprised of resisting Métis and Aboriginals, on one hand, was quashed by government forces. Riel and some others were hanged.

Beyond this things get murky. Was it a rebellion? An incipient revolution? An uprising? Or just a thuggish "riot," as the Conservative organ Montreal *Gazette* put it?[3] Was Riel responsible for all of it and all of the actions taken by all participants on the losing side? Or just some? And if some, how many and which ones? Or none? Or perhaps the resistance was justified and the government, eager to flex its muscle and firmly establish law and order as understood by Canada's colonialist mainstream, was at fault because it repeatedly ignored important petitions from the west that required immediate attention? Perhaps the government deliberately ignored petitions in the hope that a crisis might ensue, which it could then use to political advantage (which included crushing the Métis and eliminating Riel)? Or maybe the fault was shared? If so, how? Maybe the events are best laid at the door of incompetent government officials? Or maybe Riel was mad and/or megalomaniacal? And so on.

At any rate, a jury found Riel guilty of treason and he was hanged. His offenses had been clear—refusing to fully embrace Canadian sovereignty as it was understood in Parliament and threatening to establish a sort of parallel governing body in the west, not to mention the killing of Thomas Scott in 1873 and the uprising of 1869–1870. Canada's press heartily, in some cases rabidly, endorsed the decision and sentence.

These guilty-as-charged pro-Canada boosters fully endorsed the central unifying Canadian cultural project at work in the west: colonialism. Seldom known directly by its name, euphemisms such as *civilization* (occasionally juxtaposed in binary fashion: *civilization* versus *barbarism*), *law and order, pluck, our boys, gallantry, sobriety, Christianity* (that is, of the Protestant variety), and such, stood in for Canada's emerging raison d'être. And the ineluctable benefits of colonialism were signified, it seemed, veritably everywhere in Canada's press. Not surprisingly, the press framed the North-West Rebellion of 1885 not as democratic, but as subversive. Hence the war. Hence Riel's lynching. Also not surprisingly, the press held that Aboriginal populations required tending and herding and domination. Key papers from provincial capitals and Ottawa made these points relentlessly throughout 1885. Yet before engaging that discussion, one so deep that it reaches into the very marrow of what Canada *is*, it bears noting that Canada was hardly unique in its endeavour to solve its percieved Aboriginal "problem."

Spurr refers to such congruencies as "unexpected parallels" among "common genealogies that united...apparently disparate occasions of discourse."[4]

"SECOND CONQUEST"

The latter half of the nineteenth century saw countries across the Americas attempting to "quiet," to borrow the *Globe*'s euphemism, Aboriginal populations. Neo-liberal capitalism, fixated with modernization, swept the hemisphere, and Aboriginal lands suddenly appeared more attractive than they had since the initial European invasions centuries before, what some scholars have aptly termed the "second conquest."[5] Colonialism, in its various guises, justified the usurpation of these lands. And on the whole, the subsequent grand theft of Indigenous lands was neither wanton nor unpremeditated. With new vigour, governments adhered to philosophies that championed modernization; and Natives stood in the way. The result, in all cases, found nationally bound hegemonic orders Othering Natives in order to justify the actions taken to secure the land. In practice, this took an assortment of martial forms, from outright genocide to less systematic but no less lethal assaults.

For example, after the American Civil War concluded in 1865, the country redoubled its long-standing efforts to militarily conquer its Native population, launching the so-called Indian Wars (though, in fact, since the arrival of the Puritans, Americans had been at war with Natives).[6] The white order framed this as a defensive struggle—that is, as Aboriginals fought tenaciously to protect lands they had inhabited for millennia, whites cast themselves as victims while casting "Indians" as the aggressors, who always, as in Canada, fired the first shot.[7] In a struggle that pitted civilization with savagery, the Natives fought unfairly, in which "skulking" in the dark featured prominently, and "in the wildest and most unprovoked manner."[8] In other words, turning empirical reality on its head, white America averred that it was victimized by Native aggression.[9] Thus, in the name of civilization, it had to fight back. While the struggle was punctuated with countless small skirmishes, perhaps the most dramatic and public occurred when a group of Sioux and Cheyenne famously laid waste to George Armstrong Custer and the 7th Cavalry in late June 1876 in southeastern Montana. The outcome only intensified America's determination to crush the various western tribes. The press aided and abetted this project, careful recent research has demonstrated.[10] The results were spectacular, violent, and inevitable after Custer's demise—the United States declared something akin to total war on Natives.

Mexico, too, engaged in a similar activity. Curiously, the land grab began at the hands of a Zapotec Indian president, Benito Juárez, in the late 1860s and then intensified during the Porfiriato, the thirty-five-year period (1876–1910) during which Mexico was dominated by the war hero and self-proclaimed liberal Porfirio Díaz. It is worth remembering that proportionately Mexico had a much larger Indigenous population than the United States or Canada. The result is that relatively more land had been occupied more densely by more Natives. Further, one could argue that Roman Catholicism had been nominally kinder to Aboriginals than had the Protestant churches dominant in the U.S. and Canada. At any rate, during the late nineteenth century Mexico systematically and ruthlessly pushed Natives from their traditional lands. This effort was nominally legal as the equivalent effort was in the United States. For example, in the 1880s laws were passed ostensibly to protect all landowners as well as to promote modernization. Yet while "Indians" had occupied the land for thousands of years, they had no paper documents to substantiate ownership. In this way, the land was made available to those wealthy enough to purchase it. The government also simply turned a blind eye to extralegal land seizures (as was likewise common in the United States). Another key legal means by which to seize Native lands occurred when a law allowed for surveyors of previously unsurveyed lands to lay claim to one-third of the property in question as a kind of payment for the work. Overwhelmingly this land was Indigenous land. Over time the effect of such policies so profoundly traumatized Mexico that they contributed importantly to the outbreak of revolution in 1910.[11]

A similar situation unfolded in Guatemala. Mexico, unlike its neighbour, had abundant natural resources that were readily exploitable during the colonial period, such as gold, silver, and hemp. One result is that Mexico became relatively more ethnically mixed and arguably more hispanicized. In this way, Mexico had increasingly become a *Mestizo* nation, a rough Euro-Native corollary to Canada's Métis, yet proportionately far greater in size. Yet a sudden demand for coffee in the industrializing world, which began more or less around the time of the American Civil War and has never abated, transformed the way of life of Aboriginals in Guatemala. The Central American republic proved to be an exceptional location for growing coffee and other exportable agricultural products such as bananas.

But coffee was king. And, again, an emerging neo-liberal hegemonic order surveyed the potentially rich agricultural lands in question, found that they were occupied by Natives, and set about usurping the lands as well as, in a fiendish subplot driven at least in part by demographics, forcing the Natives to work in near slave-like conditions.[12]

When Mexico opened the door to foreign investment as a means of modernizing its economy, the country was sufficiently large not to fall into the hands of a single or even a handful of foreign corporations. Guatemala did, however. In time the United Fruit Company of Boston, Massachusetts, came to dominate Guatemala's economy and thus the politics of the country. So the circumstances vary considerably—size of the country, fraction of the country that was Indigenous, natural wealth of the country, and the pace of ethnic mixing. Yet, in both countries, the pressures deriving from the late nineteenth-century "legal" usurpations contributed to revolutionary movements.[13]

A pattern emerges. In Canada, the United States, Mexico, and Guatemala, Natives were stripped of their traditional lands.[14] For the most part, it was entirely legal. But in none of these countries did Natives have basic legal rights until well into the twentieth century, let alone any voice in the decisions made to forcibly remove them, until well past the point of no return. So we must understand the law in cultural and hegemonic terms. Whites in these countries coveted the land and white cultures provided similar lines of reasoning, codified into the law, in which it was appropriate for the lands to be appropriated.[15] This idea, which consumed news analysis of things Aboriginal in late nineteenth-century Canada, was in fact hemispheric in scope. And Riel's dramatic story, in this way—an Aboriginal struggling with land reform against an intransigent and violently racist colonial metropol—was played out all over the Americas.

Argentina's Native population mixed over time to produce something equivalent to the *Mestizo* or Métis, the *gaucho*, a Euro-Native hybrid. The *gaucho* became and endures today as a symbol of a more romantic, manly time, a South American *vaquero* or "cowboy." Yet empirical reality stands removed from this imagining. Like the Northwest's Métis, *gauchos* were renowned for their horsemanship, their tenacity, their durability, their marksmanship, their close connection to nature. Yet when the lands they occupied became attractive in the late nineteenth century to the emergent neo-liberal order in Argentina, they were systematically obliterated.

The reasoning employed bears close resemblance to the examples already noted: the *gaucho* was retrograde, stood in the way of progress, violated not just cultural norms but the law itself. That is, insofar as the law incorporates and expresses culture, the *gaucho* became an outlaw by virtue of his very existence.[16]

Enter Louis Riel, devout Roman Catholic, Métis leader, French "half-breed." In the press Riel occupied a liminal, illicit status by virtue of his renegade identity, as a latent criminal, much like the *gaucho*. A propensity to commit murder or engage in treasonous behaviours were merely aspects of what the press expected, even demanded, from a "half-breed." News reports from 1885, taken from ten dailies across the country, argued this ferociously throughout 1885. Riel, from the Liberal left, Conservative right, and points in between, emerges from a discursive context in which damnation figures centrally and from which guilt then derives more or less in knee-jerk fashion. In other words, Riel was guilty by virtue of embodying and personifying the aboriginality of *métissage*. Put in Platonic terms: to exist as a Métis was to engage in heinous criminal behaviour; Riel was Métis; therefore Riel was a criminal.

"RIEL MUST PAY"

We explored the contents of ten newspapers in their entirety from key centres in each province for 1885. Four of them, which we label politically Liberal, expressed the view that the Macdonald government was squarely to blame for the North-West Rebellion. These include the Calgary *Herald*, Halifax *Citizen and Evening Chronicle*, Toronto *Globe*, and Manitoba (Winnipeg) *Free Press*. The four that held that the Conservative Macdonald government was blameless for the conflict and laid the onus elsewhere we have identified as Conservative. These include the *Daily* (later Victoria *Times-*) *Colonist*, Charlottetown *Examiner*, Montreal *Gazette*, and Ottawa *Citizen*. Two publications we have labelled independent by virtue of a dearth of coverage or because the war elicited relatively balanced colonial reportage. These include the St. John's *Evening Mercury* and the Fredericton *Maritime Farmer*.[17] Within these categories the respective views, the tone, the nuance, the bombast, varies significantly. No two papers were identical, though they often shared stories verbatim.[18] Yet the partisan fault lines remained clear in a basic way—either it was the fault of Macdonald's government or it was not.

The papers flew their political stripes proudly and sometimes aggressively before and, especially, during the conflict. If one were to measure the vituperation of anti-Macdonald sentiment, surely the Halifax *Citizen and Evening Chronicle* led the charge. Comparing the conflict morally to the American Revolution the daily acknowledged legitimate "half-breed" grievances in the North-West: "The half-breeds have been justly irritated at the hands of the Canadian (MacDonald) government. Surely, as a civilized and ostensibly Christian people, we owe it to ourselves to see that the cause of irritation is removed before punishing the acts to which such irritation has given rise."

To do less would be "cruelly unjust and almost murder," the paper intoned, responding to calls in the Tory press for the hanging of Riel.[19] The Conservative Ottawa *Citizen* put it plainly: it was a case of "LAW VS. TREASON," noting elsewhere in the same day's paper, "If law and order are to be maintained in Canada; if authority is to be respected...Riel must pay."[20]

The Halifax daily also lashed out at its political rivals, claiming the Tory press was exaggerating the "enormity of the crime of rebellion" for naked political aims, which included obfuscating government culpability for the war in the first case. Instead, it asserted that readers should pity the "half-breeds who have been by us reduced to the verge of starvation" and "who have for years demanded their rights and received only neglect."[21] On other occasions the paper employed a common rhetorical strategy of printing sermons on the topic of the war so as to bolster the paper's claim to moral authority. For example, a late April sermon lamented the insufficiency of Christian evangelizing on the Prairies: "If Christian churches had done their duty this Indian war might have been prevented."[22] And while the paper was careful not to endorse taking up arms against the government, it strongly pressed the case for "criminal negligence of the men who drove them to rebellion."[23] In particular, Indian Commissioner and the appointed Lieutenant-Governor of the Northwest Territories, Edgar Dewdney, was "among a horde of greedy political supporters...insolent officials...and petty tyrants." Dewdney had deservedly earned "the hatred of all sorts" of inhabitants in the North-West.[24] Not surprisingly, then, the paper counselled "noble self-restraint" in treating the rebels as the war neared its conclusion.[25]

The other three Liberal organs agreed in the main with these positions. The Calgary *Herald*, for example, rigorously criticized the administration of Indian Affairs during the war in Canada. "Under these circumstances," the paper asked, "it might be well to inquire if the Indians would not be fools if they did not rise."[26] The problem, as the paper saw it, was basic incompetence on the part of government officials and unrepentant eastern party politics played at all costs by Tories.[27] It also blamed the "east" and its Tory press for playing politics in the Northwest, especially those who had the political goal of discouraging emigration (for unstated reasons) to the region.[28] Still, it also demanded that the rebels be severely punished.[29]

The Manitoba *Free Press* mostly concurred, though it presented a relatively less obstreperous tone toward Macdonald's regime. That said, published in Winnipeg, this organ chastised the Tory press's take on the conflict as mere "unbounded veneration for the Tory Government"[30] and a veritable "scream."[31] It assailed the Macdonald government for laziness and basic incompetence, citing it for being "too pre-occupied with plundering the country and feeding their political pets."[32] Ultimately, the paper found the Macdonald government "guilty" for the crisis.[33] The logic of its core position was straightforward: "Why did the half-breeds take up arms if they had no grievances? Do men usually risk their lives, their all, without cause?"[34]

Unique among the ten papers explored here, one story in the *Free Press*— remarkably, given the normal racist cant—raised the matter of racial discrimination as a potential factor engendering the armed conflict, noting how the "half-breeds… felt that they were looked down upon and treated with contempt by the new settlers."[35] It also blamed Christian churches for lax missionizing, repeating the same article (quoted above) in the Halifax *Citizen and Evening Chronicle*.[36] And it too endorsed hanging for the Aboriginal instigators of the war, including Riel, as did the Calgary *Herald*.[37] The Conservative *Daily Colonist* captured the feeling that "Riel and his followers have placed themselves beyond mercy."[38] The *Free Press* also offered a significantly greater amount of coverage of Aboriginals than the Halifax, Calgary, or Victoria dailies. This tended to lend a greater breadth and depth to reportage. For example, the paper was more likely to consider historical antecedents in the buildup to war. To this end it claimed that the original sale of Rupert's Land in 1869–1870 had been a deliberate fraud, a spectacularly unjust land theft that had in turn sown the seeds for later armed resistance.[39] Still, it too called for the noose.

Canada's leading daily newspaper, the Toronto *Globe*, also sharpened its Liberal talons on the war, attacking the Macdonald government with much relish. As elsewhere in the Liberal press, part of the problem was seen as a basic Tory unwillingness to address legitimate "half-breed" grievances about the arrogation of Aboriginal lands.[40] It went so far as to claim that even "many Conservatives" were turning against the government for its poor handling of the events leading up to and the conduct of the war.[41] "Not until the Half-breeds were on the verge of rebellion did the Government take any action in reference to their grievances," the *Globe* reported on 21 April 1885.[42] Another day the paper cited the "Government's fatal obstinacy" as the real culprit.[43]

Not surprisingly, the Tory press disputed all of the Liberal allegations. The *Gazette* captured the sentiment precisely: "That the Indians have any real grievances we do not believe."[44] Moreover, "No half-breed has ever been deprived of the land upon which he was located."[45] The *Citizen* dismissed the Liberal press's claims as "fictitious."[46] The Macdonald government had acted, in fact, above reproach in its conduct of Indian affairs, the *Gazette* argued.[47] Dewdney and his colleagues were great men, outstanding, sympathetic, empathetic, deeply professional, and even heroic.[48] Moreover, the government had specifically gone to extraordinary lengths to treat fairly "half-breed" land gripes. For the conservative press, the political problem lay in Grit malfeasance and the Grit press's inability to understand empirical reality.[49] The real culprit though, the evil driving force behind the conflict, was Louis Riel and the Natives and the "poor misguided half-breeds" whom Riel swindled and bullied.[50] Still, the Tory *Daily Colonist* supported Macdonald, yet criticized the government's unwillingness to take the Métis land claims complaint seriously. Mostly this stemmed from an orientation derived from land claims issues unique to British Columbia where treaties had not been struck; thus provincial land claims issues remained in the forefront, and the paper identified a basic lack of interest from Ottawa.[51]

Punishment as pedagogy emerged as a key plank of the Tory press's position. On 30 November 1885, the *Gazette* argued that Métis rebels should be taught "a lesson which they will not soon forget.... Hanging is too good for them.... The Indians need a lesson."[52] But then all ten of the papers agreed that Riel deserved to swing. "We will insist upon Riel being hanged," the *Daily Colonist* perorated.[53] The *Free Press* reinforced this view by naturalizing the hegemonic order: "The first lesson he has to learn is that there is a power in this country so much greater than his own that he need not dream of resisting it, but that it is a power that will protect the honest, the peaceful, the industrious."[54]

In one sense we return to where we introduced this section: Liberal papers blamed Conservatives and the Conservative press responded by blaming Liberals and the Liberal press[55] for what the *Gazette* termed "our little war" and the Ottawa *Citizen* and St. John's *Evening Mercury* termed a "regular Indian War," and the *Daily Colonist* called "the war excitement."[56] Yet, despite the venom expressed, a common ground existed because the stakes were high—as the *Free Press* put it, "the Northwest must either make or mar the Dominion."[57] First, the Grit and Tory and independent press agreed strongly about the inherent inferiority and savagery of all Aboriginal peoples. The *Gazette* captured it neatly: "Fear or expectation of favour keep the red-skins in subjection, but the moment the opportunity seems to present itself for a general uprising they fling aside the cloak of amity, and become the reckless, murderous devils which nature has made them in their native condition....Sooner or later it was inevitable that the red-skins would make an effort to regain control of the country, massacre and pillage the settlers." The *Citizen* agreed: "Sooner or later half breeds and Indians were bound to try their strength with the whites."[58]

Riel was no match for such historical inevitability, and in fact, he fits squarely into the recipe, personifying for the papers a wild Aboriginal, a slithery, charismatic, and conniving polymorphous enemy run amok. In the press these arguments were presented typically with little attribution and often with nothing more than hearsay to back them up, journalistic behaviour that by today's standards might be illegal and would, at the very least, be considered by the industry to be unethical.[59] Second, the presentations were often framed so as to champion Canada not simply as superior to all things Native but as morally superior to the United States, as exemplified by its allegedly more civilized conduct in the regulation and administration of its Indigenous populations in the west. Moreover, third, a teleological context pervaded the triumphal struggle of civilization over savagery, with white Canada exemplifying the former while all things Aboriginal characterized the latter. In this way, aboriginality became moribund. Fourth and finally, the presentations invite Patricia Seed's analysis back to the discussion because the papers delivered observations about the need for whites to exploit invitingly rich agricultural lands that Natives had proved unwilling or unable to develop, in what the Tory *Evening Mercury* referred to as "our sister colony."[60] Put simply and in terms that would appeal to racist sentiment, according to the *Gazette*, Native behaviour amounted to "evils that call for strong intervention."[61]

"WE'LL HANG LOUIS RIEL"

In general, the press obscured the lines between "Indian" and "half-breed," though on occasion drew attention to the "mongrel crowd" of Aboriginals living in the west, into which the breeds fit.[62] Meanwhile, when the press sought to champion civilizing efforts in the west, the papers tended to play up the European fraction of the "half-breed." This was artificial and problematic in many ways, not least of which was because it implied an equal ethnic mixing when many "breeds," including Riel (who was technically one-eighth Indian), were nothing of the sort. Further, the premise upon which the Métis land claims rested stemmed from the observation that they constituted a distinct people in their own right. Yet the papers sought easy answers—binaries usually sufficed—and avoided complications at every turn. So more typically, and certainly during the conflict, this pretence of beneficial European admixing was evaporated and the "half" that was Indian took over.

So what then did it mean to be an Aboriginal, and this includes Riel, according to the press in 1885? The press provides thousands of pages of examples, obviously too many to quote or cite. Instead, we offer a summary of the normative treatment. Where we have employed the terms "Native" and "Aboriginal" and "Indigenous" as rough synonyms for persons of Aboriginal background, the press in 1885 daily substituted monikers such as "savage," "heathen," "pagan," "redskin," "redman," "children of the plains/forest" to equate with "Indian." Of course, the press also applied a wide collection of synecdoches, as in "red skin," and so on, in the same way as "our boys" and "pluck" represented white civilization more generally.

The Ottawa *Citizen* proffered the greatest quantity of coverage, though not necessarily in depth of vitriol aimed at Riel and Aboriginals. Like a number of papers, it reported favourably in late January 1885, just weeks before the conflict began, that "Indian matters have on the whole maintained their normal satisfactory condition."[63] This view, an endorsement of Tory governing, also augured an unwillingness to take the war seriously at first. Instead the paper tended to dismiss the possibility of escalating armed conflict as highly unlikely because, as noted, things were "normal." The paper inclined to champion tendentious stories such as one heralding the success of limited educational initiatives among the Cree and Blackfoot. These exemplified, the paper reported, "an all important element of national growth and progress."[64] Not to be outdone, the paper trumped its own gleeful prose on the subject days later, noting the "progress" for the "benefit of these wards of the nation in the establishment…for the active duties and the responsibilities of citizenship."[65] Yet the *Globe* ruefully judged that "Indians" simply "are not making the progress towards civilization that is desirable."[66] The *Daily Examiner* agreed in early May, commenting "that they are as minors, in a state of tutelage, is a state of fact."[67] Such a view, that Natives were children who needed to be taught the rudiments of civilization and, as well, that the country was marching evermore toward greater progress, reinforced the idea that war was unlikely. Children may misbehave, but war is for grownups.

But the war came anyway and papers duly reported it. Early Ottawa *Citizen* headlines, for example, termed it the "Riel Insurrection,"[68] "the Riel Trouble,"[69] "the Riel Rumpus,"[70] "the North-West Riot,"[71] "Riel Troubles,"[72] "the North-West Difficulty,"[73] obdurately determined to term it less critical than it in fact was. Early reports also highlighted the paper's own war news as "terribly exaggerated."[74] The *Citizen* asserted that "the general impression here is that the whole affair is merely a piece of bravado on Riel's part,"[75] and chided "the ambitious designs of the disturber Riel,"[76] continuing to dampen the seriousness of events at the same time as introducing a key Conservative gambit: the fault, however large or small, was Riel's and his alone. Ever partisan, it warned readers to beware "opposition journals" that would surely attempt to "make it appear that the natives have been treated unjustly"[77] by the Macdonald government. The Toronto *Globe*, for example, knew "neither patriotism nor honour" because of the way it attacked the Macdonald government over the war. Worse, and probably well beyond the point of credulity, the *Citizen* went so far as to claim that the *Globe* had actually "incited an uprising," and wilfully inflamed the passions of "semi-savages" in the Northwest.[78]

When it became apparent that war was in the offing, the *Citizen* tackled it head on: "a crisis has been reached in the history of the country which demands prompt and energetic action on the part of the Government in the vindication of authority."[79] This refrain that "law and order," as the *Globe* phrased it[80]—what the *Daily Colonist* called "the law of the land" and "the only law for the Indian and the white"[81]—must be respected at all costs translated into support for the most severe form of corporal punishment, ultimately death by hanging. In late March the *Citizen* printed a brief ditty: "We'll hang Louis Riel; to a sour apple tree; as we go marching along."[82]

Riel became the focus of all blame, but the *Citizen*'s aim was direct only on occasion. For example, in late March it was Riel "the agitator, delivering inflammatory speeches" supported by "malcontents."[83] The heat of this rhetoric increased as the struggle wore on into May when it charged that "the ruffian be made to pay the penalty for his crimes on the soil where he has caused murder, massacre and plunder to take place."[84] As was usual practice for the period, no source was identified nor was any explanation presented of the alleged crimes. By this time, mid-May 1885, the press had long since passed verdict and assigned a sentence. At the same time Riel was smeared as a "breed," as a leader of "breeds," and as (partially) Aboriginal. In this way, the context for understanding his framing as a mere "agitator" becomes heightened; he had in a sense always been guilty. Curiously, the press constructs Riel as a sort of lone wolf; yet his actions are thoroughly stereotyped to the imagined community to which he belonged, the "half-breed" Aboriginal.

"IT IS THE ABSOLUTE TRUTH"

In 1885 Natives had virtually nothing to recommend them, according to the press. The epithets flew fast and furious and became unremittingly predictable. For example, in one paragraph the *Free Press* described the Cree chief Big Bear as "adventurous and uncontrollable," engaged in "pillage" and "massacres," leaving "bloody traces" of his "evil" work, full of "rage," murdering "innocent women and poor children," and otherwise leading "barbarous peoples" enabled by the "thirst for blood."[85] In similar fashion, the *Herald* offered this advice: "Let any eastern man, no matter how enthusiastic on the Indian question, live for six months among them, see them beg, see them steal, sell their women and lie around, too lazy and shiftless to make an effort to earn the slightest part of their own living....This may sound like strong language, but it is the absolute truth."[86]

Indian males' primary activity was fighting or horse theft.[87] The women, unintelligent "squaws" on virtually every occasion mentioned, tended to bear resemblance to "a hideous set of hags" and were invariably whorish and sometimes "crazy."[88] Further, females were "dirty" and likely infested with fleas like dogs.[89] This framing squares with Elizabeth Bird's analysis. She notes that North American popular culture has tended historically toward presenting females in binary fashion. For Native women, burdened both by race and gender, the constructed "squaw" was the most common result. Bird notes that "the squaw...is a drudge who is at the beck and call of her savage Indian husband, who produces baby after baby, who has sex endlessly and indiscriminately with whites and Indians alike."[90] Equating Canadian and American Indians, the *Daily Examiner* noted an inherent Native "joy in war for the sheer sake of plunder and slaughter."[91] The *Free Press* averred that "their love of mischief" was "inborn,"[92] and circulated widespread stereotypes: "The flour may be musty, the canned meat tainted or the fruit sour; it may be a dead horse or even a dead dog, our Nitchie [an apparent bastardization of the term Anishinaabe] will eat it and cry out for more. Cleanliness with them is a negative virtue, and dishwashing is not enforced."[93] Aboriginal neediness and corresponding government largesse was an ongoing refrain.[94]

The conflict itself brought out near hysterical reportage. In all the newspapers stories of "massacre," "mutilation," "Indian depredations," "scalping," "deviltry," "cannibalism," "intense horror," became common.[95] Suddenly Canada's Indians, "bloodthirsty," "diabolical," "murderous hordes," were on the "warpath,"[96] a label normally associated with American Natives. Reports of "raiding" and "burning" and "pillage" "and "thieving" are simply too numerous to mention. Probably for readers the most frightening feature of the imagined Native predilection for violence was that it was fickle, arbitrary, random. Stories abounded in the press about unprovoked and especially vicious Native violence often culminating in murder, especially during the months of April, May, and June of 1885.[97]

After one military engagement, two white women were taken hostage for several weeks by rebel forces. The press ran wild with the tale, printing groundless stories about their murder. A *Citizen* headline read, "MRS DELANEY TORTURED TO DEATH."[98] Nine days later the *Citizen* reported that the body of the other murdered woman, a certain Mrs. Gowanlock, had been mutilated, that her "breast had been cut out."[99] The *Gazette* pronounced the mutilation of her body an "intense horror."[100] The women had also been raped, a foregone conclusion "too terrible to think of," opined the *Evening Mercury*.[101] The *Globe* had long since reported on the Native predilection for raping and torturing women and torturing children.[102]

But then it turned out that the women had not been sexually assaulted, let alone killed, "as we imagined they would be," the *Evening Mercury* admitted with ironic candour, echoed almost word for word by the Montreal *Gazette*.[103] In fact, upon release the two women reported that they had been well provided for.[104] Nonetheless, the Natives did not deserve any real credit for the unexpected self-restraint. Instead, the "civilized" treatment the woman had received, the *Gazette* averred, stemmed directly from the effects of earlier Christianity and colonization upon the Indians.[105] The trouble was, the *Herald* opined: "They are not content with merely killing a white man, they delight to torture him to death by inches, and to tear the body apart and burn it afterwards. Their treatment of prisoners, especially women, is shocking, and Mrs. [George Armstrong] Custer was in imminent fear always of falling into their hands."[106] The Halifax *Citizen and Evening Chronicle* noted that is was common for women and girls to be raped and then murdered when in captivity. Their bodies might also be "slashed with knives."[107] Yet the paper also noted that Delaney and Gowanlock had been freed unharmed but only after having been purchased by "half-breeds" (a rare case where the European fraction trumped the Indigenous) "to save them from the Indians."[108]

While the strong tendency of the press was to lump all peoples of Indigenous background together, on occasion a publication would draw attention to the specific alleged attributes of the Métis. The *Globe*, for example, noted: "they have...inherited all the bad points of their dusky progenitors.... Possessing the shifty disposition of the Indian they are the most accomplished liars imaginable, indeed the immense fertility of their imagination is only equalled by that of the country they inhabit....[They] are poor farmers...a result of their dislike for hard work, and their ignorance....The half-breed will not fight in a square stand-up fashion unless they are in overwhelming numbers... [they] swagger and bluster...[but] will become cringing and submissive."[109] Yet on another occasion the *Globe* opined that the trouble was that the groups had interbred to the point of blurring distinctions.[110]

"Throughout the course of their history, the half-breeds have shown much jealousy of English-speaking immigrants, and a disinclination to settle down peaceably to the routine occupations of an advanced civilization," the *Gazette* noted, neatly encapsulating Seed's argument and presenting it as undistilled common sense.[111] The Winnipeg *Free Press* observed that the "French half-breeds are hunters, not farmers."[112] The Calgary *Herald* observed that "the Metis mind is exaggeratedly simple."[113] Yet it was complex enough to have incited the Indians to savage violence, the Halifax *Citizen and Evening Chronicle* said.[114]

"CANADIANS WILL NEVER TREAT THE INDIANS AS OUR NEIGHBOURS HAVE DONE"

The direct comparison of Indian policies in Canada and the United States occurred frequently and always favoured the former in a way that clearly contributed to the emergence of chauvinistic press nationalism, despite the reality that Canada, like the U.S., waged war on its Aboriginal population.[115] In fact, by framing the respective Indian policies as disparate—the Canadian approach as ethical and practical and peaceful and the American version as the violent and vindictive "cowboy"[116] variety—the press was able to frame Canada's war against its Indigenous population as a benign, thoughtful, necessary, and wholesome undertaking (the American press, meanwhile, used the North-West Rebellion as evidence that Natives were essentially the same in Canada and the United States[117]). In this way, claimed the *Free Press*, Canada's tack had partially "softened" the "savages."[118] The American way was the cowboy way, as personified in Western film and fiction. In this long-standing myth whites went to the frontier and were there transformed, importantly through the use of aggression and war. The ensuing white conquest both required and engendered those characteristics typically associated with mythical cowboy behaviour—individualism, honesty, cleverness, sobriety, perseverance, attractiveness, and self-control.[119] Canada's frontier myth, at least as played out in the press in 1885, was similar (and will be discussed further in chapter 4). As in the U.S. version, whites were victimized by Native aggressions when they (reasonably) went to the frontier. Yet the response differed—in myth, if not necessarily in reality—wherein the Canadians displayed considerably greater self-restraint, articulated in the press as pluck, bravery, loyalty, duty. The Canadian version should be seen as a response, at least in part, to the American frontier myth because it framed Canada as different from and morally superior to the United States, as countless news articles proclaimed throughout 1885. Despite this perceived difference, scholars have found that the United States press portrayed Riel in ways similar to the treatment he received in Canada.[120]

The framing worked something like this, as the *Gazette* summed it up pithily: "It is only when the quietude and comparative contentment that reign throughout our vast Northwest regions are contrasted with the wars and massacres, which have spread desolation through the Indian peopled country of the United States, that we begin to perceive how much reason we have for our thankfulness." Such were the benefits of Canada's "practical work of progressive civilization, as far as it is possible."[121] The article champions Canada, Canada's Indian policies (in which lies buried a reminder of the Indian propensity for savagery), and the value and inevitability of progress, while at the same time noting the likelihood that it would never bring equality among the races because the Indians were not fully capable.[122] Even the United States press secretly agreed, the *Citizen* claimed.[123] The key was to treat Aboriginals with firmness, to cow them into subjugation, the *Gazette* counselled.[124] That is the premise upon which the claim that they were "our Indians" was made, thereby stripping them of autonomy and agency and reducing their humanity by claiming ownership of them, as if they were property.[125] In short, while the impetus was couched in moral terms, to do the right thing, the practical aim was pragmatic, to ensure peace: "We all remember Sitting Bull and poor Custer...Let us hope that Canadians will never treat the Indians as our neighbours have done," the *Globe* reported.[126] The spectre of the 1862 Minnesota Massacre, committed by some Sioux who later took refuge in the Northwest, was also used as an ongoing reminder of innate Indian savagery, though typically such stories provided neither context nor any semblance of journalistic balance. In this way, the story, like many, resembled a fairy tale, full of imagined monsters and rife with the warning to stay the course.[127] It is important to note, too, that while the stories of Aboriginal excess punctuated news reports throughout 1885 and were thereby employed to champion Canadian nation building at the expense of the United States, in Canadian newspapers Canada's Aboriginals received largely identical framing as American natives received, especially after the war began.

Evidence of the alleged unsavoury outcomes of American policy earned charged headlines from the *Gazette*, including "Apaches on the Warpath," "THE SOUTHERN INDIANS; More Murders and Outrages," "More Slaughter by the Raiding Apaches," "Bloody Fight with Indians," "The Indians Up in Kansas," "The Indian Raiders," "Indians Massacred in Montana," "Massacred by Indians in Arizona Territory," "The Indian Rising in Arizona," "An Indian Scare," "Another New Mexico Massacre," and "How the Apaches Massacred the Cavalrymen." A story headlined, "Terrible Outrages by Apache Indians," related how the Indians took a Mexican child, bashed its head in by swinging it by the feet against a wall and then hanged the corpse on a meat hook.[128] By contrast, *Citizen* headlines abounded in ways that prefigured the glory of white Canadian conquest during the war. For example, on 11 May 1885 the *Citizen* ran the following series of headlines: "VICTORY; For Our Brave Volunteers at Batoche"; "A PLUCKY FIGHT"; "The Most Decisive Blow of the Campaign on the Insurrection"; "A DARING DEED"; "The Enemy's Entrenchments Gallantly Carried by Our Forces"; "Riel Declares Himself Prophet of the Half Breeds."[129] Here we encounter a Canadian discursive code for empire, championing the daring of white Canadian heroes, winning intrepidly, while the Métis leader sank evermore into madness. Notice, too, the claim of ownership by use of the pronoun "our," as in the headline, "GALLANT BEHAVIOUR OF OUR BOYS."[130]

"BROTHERLY CONSIDERATION FOR THE WEAK"

That humankind—"mankind"—partook necessarily of progress was a fact, not an ideological proposition, the press suggested. The *Gazette* simply called it "the history of the advancement of civilization."[131] Thus a key problem, the *Daily Examiner* waxed, was that the Aboriginal "knew nothing of the doctrine of survival of the fittest or of natural selection; but he knows that sentence of death had been passed upon him [by progress], and his heart is heavy with anger. Civilization, which ought to provide for him in his last hours, simply starves him...The Indian knows he is doomed."[132]

The *Globe* printed an eloquent sermon on the nature of the relationship between white Canada and its Natives:

> We all know that priority of occupation is regarded as a special claim to protection against all appearances of encroachment from the new settler representing the dominant race. They are the weaker section of the community, and by the same instinct that makes us feel tenderly towards the woman and the child because of their weakness, we must be disposed to feel tenderly towards those poor, weak, and dependent people smarting under what they believe to be unjust dealing towards them. These reflections will help to maintain our minds firm in the duty towards our civil rulers, and the cause of the Dominion, whilst at the same time tempering our loyalty with sentiments of mercy and brotherly consideration for the weak and dependent, thus combining vigour in the advance against rebellion, with peaceful disposition towards the vanquished.[133]

And so the *Globe* differentiated among three options: feed and clothe them "as long as one of the race survives"; "exterminate them," which would be popular in Canada; or "put them in a way of taking care of themselves" so as to overcome "ignorance and idleness." The paper recommended the third option.[134] Again, the issue of pecuniary practicality came into play. A common line held that it was cheaper to feed than to fight the Indian. Putting a price tag of Christian charity was common.[135] "Aside from all notions of economy, it was prompted by a feeling of kindliness and sympathy," the *Daily Examiner* opined. Still, the paper held, the government "must either feed or fight the Indians."[136] The Winnipeg *Free Press* rephrased this oft-cited either/or option in a headline, "Civilization vs. Shooting the Red Man."[137] In an attempt at humour, the *Free Press* offered: "The Indian is progressing. He is fast becoming civilized. An Indian shot and killed his squaw last week, and then blew his brains out."[138] Perhaps the Montreal *Gazette* put it most elegantly in a simple headline, a symbolic observation that aptly summarized colonial teleology, "IN THE LAND OF THE SETTING SUN."[139]

A vital idea in the promulgation that human society was improving over time, that is, "progressing," was built on several assumptions. First, as discussed earlier, rightful ownership derived from behaving like the English and using the land in the ways that conferred legal and a moral authority based on English tradition. Additionally, the idea required some level of acceptance of Aboriginal humanity. While associated with and demeaned by their association with lower forms of life and base instincts, Aboriginals were considered to be human beings. But of what sort? The answer, because the press eschewed such complications, was not presented with specificity. What is clear is the sense that Aboriginals were of a lower order of humanity. The *Globe* summed up the prevailing view by noting that Aboriginals were "comparatively low down in the scale of humanity."[140] How far they might progress was anybody's guess. For example, the *Gazette* speculated that "if the Indians can hear the jingle of dollars in their pockets, they may follow the sound into the promised land."[141] In other words, by superimposing a common enough white Canadian everyday idea about the innate greed of all human beings, inside every Indian, it was assumed, a capitalist struggled to get out. In fact, unsavoury and dangerous characteristics, according to the press, struggled to get out of Indians all the time and the job of white Canada was to prevent it. Treaties earned praise in this regard. Treaties, the *Gazette* reported, "diminish the offensive strength of tribes, gratifies their attachment to their homes, gives them a market, and offer opportunities to the industries to attain a position of independence."[142]

As a result of "humanizing" influences in the Northwest, the Liberal *Globe* noted, murder and violent crime and mutilations were on the decline and "squaws have in no respect been the furies of former days."[143] Yet the *Herald* reminded readers to keep steadfast: "Learning to eat potatoes instead of musk-rats and gophers does not render a mind less dangerous."[144] The irony, of course, is that Natives had introduced Europeans to the potato in the first place.[145]

The Calgary *Herald* mocked attempts to provide Natives with a modicum of education: "Let future Indian agents chatter away about the progress the poor savages are making in kindergarten." The solution, the daily held, was keeping them in check so as to prevent any future outbreaks, effectively grant-ing the federal government a blank cheque to deal harshly with Aboriginals.[146] It went so far as to endorse genocide in the case of the Blackfoot, "thieves and murderers" all.[147]

"BLESSINGS OF OUR CHRISTIAN CIVILIZATION"

Spreading the word of Christianity, especially Protestantism, to shine the light of the "blessings of our Christian civilization"[148] into what the *Free Press* called "heathen darkness,"[149] figured prominently, as already noted. The virtuous benefits of agriculture and the construction of an agricultural infrastructure in ongoing possession taking were many and were obvious to the press. Chris-tianity and farming blended.

"There could be no higher triumph of missionary zeal and of enlightened enterprise than to see as their results communities of peaceful industrious Indians dotting the plains of the Northwest," the *Gazette* dreamily exhorted.[150] The *Daily Examiner* extolled the missionary work as "philanthropic and self sacrificing."[151] The "boys," the "heroes" who fought Riel and his forces, mean-while, also exemplified a "loyalty to Christ."[152] Further, ultimately, Indigenous religion did not really exist, as the papers portrayed it. Whatever spiritual enterprise in which Natives engaged was comically stupid, according to the *Gazette*, all "idolatry" and worship of "old Sol."[153] And Riel's own Catholicism was confused and inconsistent, barked the *Daily Examiner*, though he had studied at a seminary.[154]

The *Herald* complained bitterly about Indian indifference and resistance. After all, the paper exaggerated wildly, the "white man...came to this country for the sole purpose of shedding his beneficent and Christian influence on the life of the poor heathen."[155] The English surpassed all other Europeans in this regard. "The Englishman does not emigrate but expatriates himself for a special purpose, and when his object is achieved his home is fixed in the new land," the *Gazette* added.[156] The Anglo settlers had accomplished nothing less than "reclaiming a barren wilderness," the *Citizen* concurred, although from whom or what it had been reclaimed was not stated.[157]

"The half breeds…should be impressed with the necessity of settling down in fixed localities and directing their energies toward pastoral and agricultural pursuits," the *Daily Examiner* recorded.[158] The *Gazette* noted in early February that "the Indians who were induced to remove north of the international boundary line have settled upon reserves and are now making fair progress in farming." Then it applauded the fact that "The sanitary condition of the Indians throughout the territories has, on the whole, been satisfactory." Such stories abounded, stuffed with ideological signifiers packaged as plain common sense. Note how the forced movement of Natives is presented as a passive gesture, how farming is framed as self-evidently worthy, and that progress, as evidenced by farming, is desirable, even ineluctable. Also note how the reader was called upon to remember "Indian" filth and approve of how farming somehow had a hand in cleaning it up. The article then went on to note the positive appearance of new permanent construction and the "repair or improvement" of existing buildings.[159] The basic trouble with "Indians," in this regard, as the *Globe* captured the prevailing sentiment, was that "they all like fighting, plunder, and horse stealing better than farming."[160]

Civilization and colonization and Christianity, as portrayed by the Canadian press in 1885 were one and the same. "There are few things more difficult than to transform the savage into a civilized man," the *Gazette* stressed.[161] In the meantime, Natives would remain "wards" of the state, for their own good but also for the good of the country as a whole.[162] Thus it made perfect sense for Canada "to pursue the same" imperial policies that had marked British rule, the *Daily Examiner* encouraged.[163] Evidence abounded in the west, the *Daily Colonist* declared, to show how the effects of Christianity and education lifted the Indian to a higher level.[164] Further, the *Citizen and Evening Chronicle* argued, a failure for all white Canadians to rally round the idea of the Dominion, "would mark a sad deterioration of our race." Thus, "that half-breeds and Indians should possess the sovereignty of any portion of this country is insupportable."[165]

"I SHALL BE KING OR DIE"

In the press, Louis Riel began, in 1885, as something like an "infamous rascal," but shortly became a stereotypical Aboriginal savage: a murderer warranting death by hanging, a *Gazette* article expressed the prevailing sentiment.[166] He was a traitor to Canada, the *Citizen* argued.[167] Worse, he was certifiably a "freak" and "demented."[168] "I must rule or perish. I shall be king or die," the *Citizen* quoted Riel, casting him as a megalomaniac,[169] but on another occasion claimed he was only pretending to be insane so as to escape the noose, a gambit he had employed previously, reported the *Globe*.[170] Whereas the Tory press preferred modesty in all things, for Riel "vanity is inordinate—his ambition uncontrollable...He wants to be a ruler, an absolute dictator."[171] He was a bully, "a cruel, heartless monster," excessively prideful,[172] said the *Citizen*, and he intimidated "half-breeds" and "Indians." Such a framing suggests further that all Métis and "Indians" were willing dupes, easily swayed by an unbalanced savage. The *Herald* charged them with "behaving as if they owned the country."[173] Toward that end, the *Citizen* cited Riel's "cunningness" and "tyrannical" behaviour as means by which to sway less than stalwart Aboriginals.[174] And like an "Indian" he was "bloodthirsty," added the *Daily Examiner*.[175] Indeed, while Natives' mental aptitude was identified as severely limited, they nonetheless exhibited a remarkable predilection for "shrewdness and cunning"[176] when behaving criminally, thereby rendering a mostly pathetic creature as simultaneously canny and dangerous.

Riel was smeared by both Aboriginality and Frenchness.[177] He was not, according to the *Gazette*, a trustworthy friend prior to the war and his conduct during the war was "treacherous."[178] He was a "coward" and "responsible for the horrible murders committed, and for the outrages that have been perpetrated."[179] Importantly, too, he remained unpunished for the murder of Thomas Scott in 1873, which the *Citizen* claimed was sufficient grounds for hanging him.[180] "The manner in which Scott was butchered to death by drunken ruffians who were the tools in the hands of the cowardly, bloodthirsty Riel is well known," the *Citizen* commented in June.[181] Never does the paper provide more than hearsay evidence. Regardless of any other details, the implication here is that Riel must be guilty if the signifiers are accurate—and they were, at least in the view of the press in Canada in 1885. To put it baldly, the *Citizen* asserted, "the state is bound by the law of self-preservation to crush him and all who are associated with him."[182]

While the press called for a quick end to Riel, it also identified the Indian as moribund. The *Daily Examiner* claimed that the Indian knew that "he is doomed."[183] One result of the civilizing process meant the death of the Indian "race." This might be assessed in one of two ways. First, there remained the commonly held view that they were physically dying off in the empirical world because they were simply destined to die off,[184] or possibly because they would starve because the Sioux had killed off all of the buffalo, as the *Herald* claimed,[185] though the *Globe* cautioned that there was simply "no use attempting to exterminate them."[186] An uncommonly generous appraisal offered by the *Free Press* granted that the "poor devils....must steal or starve," so ill-equipped were they for emerging modernity.[187] Second, there existed the idea that, as we have seen, to some extent the Indian was ripe for improvement. In this way, the Indian might be killed culturally in order to make way for the universal, essential man, as government policy at about this time embraced the idea and sought to institute it operationally in the emerging residential school system: kill the Indian in order to save the man.[188]

The resulting reportage tended in one of two directions—lay blame for the war at the government's doorstep or absolve the government of any wrongdoing and lay the blame elsewhere; typically this meant the former Grit government of Alexander Mackenzie (1873–1878) and Natives and Riel. This too allowed for a range of opinion. For example, the Halifax *Citizen* attacked the Macdonald government with an intensity unmatched by the other Liberal publications while the Calgary *Herald*, nominally Liberal, by condemning the operations of the Indian Affairs Department rather than explicitly attacking the Macdonald government, provided coverage that bore resemblance to the Tory publications' general position (i.e., blame the Liberals, blame the Indians, blame Riel, even blame administrative incompetence—blame anybody but Macdonald). In this respect the *Herald* points to an important feature of coverage in 1869 and 1873, that is, that the political right and left in Canadian newspapers, on the topic of the country's "Indian problem," were far more similar than they were different. As a consequence, it is all too easy to overstate the partisan bickering. To be sure, the question of blame for the war is of considerable historical importance; but the nature of the content of the coverage with respect to Aboriginals, despite partisanship, was largely indistinguishable. While the papers disagreed vehemently about the causes of the war, they expressed a basic worldview that fully endorsed Canadian colonialism, especially its triumphal teleological aspects and the almost gleeful condemnation of all things Aboriginal.

In sum, Canadian newspapers had discovered nothing new about Natives by 1885; instead they had uncovered more of the same old, same old. Still, one substantive difference from 1873 was that the west had become somewhat settled by immigrants and, fortunately for this study, more publications had thereby been established nationwide but particularly in the west. Second, and this establishes a pattern that will re-emerge throughout the remainder of this book, the intensity and quantity of the anti-Native coverage increased dramatically as result of a flash point, in this case war, only to decrease after the conflict. It is predictable, of course, that a domestic war is sure to gain wide coverage. Meanwhile, the level of the intensity of anti-Native feeling expressed is best explained by the fact that the conflict, portrayed as the unsurprising expression of inherent Native proclivities, directly challenged the very reason that Canada existed, thus the severity of reaction stood in direct proportion to the espied seriousness of the war. The stakes were high because it was a war on Canada *qua* imagined community.

All of the papers in question decried "Indians" and "half-breeds" as cut from the same soiled cloth. The only substantive difference is that in 1885 Liberal publications tended to evince slightly greater sympathy for Natives' discerned plight (for which they blamed the Tories; and to which the Tory press responded by blaming the Grits and their alleged wide-eyed naiveté in dealing with things Aboriginal) and to endorse less violent means to instruct them in the ways of civilization, especially after the war concluded, though this did not extend to pardoning Riel. Generally, the distinction made between "half-breeds" and "Indians" during the war tended to favour neither group because the "breeds" in question were half French, a delineation that the publications tended to disparage. In other words, on balance the white fraction, the potential bleaching agent, of these groups tended to be undone by the fact that they were cast unflatteringly as stereotypical French. English and Scottish "half-breeds" were framed inconsistently as slightly improved by virtue of their more sober and industrious and Protestant British heritage.

A small article in the *Gazette* from late July provided a hint of another difference about 1885. It was headlined, "RELICS OF THE REBELLION." It goes on to describe a variety of "curiosities brought home" by the eastern soldiers who had fought in the conflict. "One is a war club, a terrible looking weapon...On the stone are several stains of blood." It was last employed "against that gallant American, the lamented Custer."[189] The article stresses the importance of keeping a memory of the past alive as a reminder to remain steadfast; but it also optimistically hints that these troubles are behind the country now if it stays on track and eschews the immoral American strategy, exemplified by Custer, employed to "quiet" Indigenous peoples.

There exists the key element of Canada *qua* being derived from not being the United States. Press coverage makes this abundantly clear: mainstream Canada defined itself by what it was not—and it was *not* the United States. Much of the important proof lay in how Indian policy was effected. The American policy was of the Western film variety wherein the only good Indian was considered to be a dead Indian. Canada preferred, instead, to laud its moral high road, which the *Gazette* termed "the philanthropic work of trying to improve the condition of the Indians,"[190] not by killing them directly (unless warranted in the eyes of the law) but by maiming them with a fatal kindness, a murderous forbearance reflective of the Brits' "white man's burden." In this way, the continued physical existence of Natives in Canada served the ends of nation building vis-à-vis the United States as well as providing an ongoing reminder that in this Indian policy Canada was asserting itself as itself. For these reasons, the press's Riel deserves credit as a great, if ironic, Canadian nation builder. He enabled Canada to champion itself by clearly differentiating itself from the United States, at least with respect to the treatment of Aboriginal peoples. That this was neither honest nor accurate is beside the point. Further, he—or his press image—allowed Canada to gain its own legs by being required to act in its own right in a major crisis; the war after all threatened the very fabric of what Sir John et al sought to build. Finally, Riel caused the Protestant nation to engage in community-building and, further, crush the competition (to the extent that it was competition—Natives and French and "half-breeds"), to rally round the metaphorical flag. As the St. John's *Evening Mercury* put it, "the effects of the rebellion will be highly beneficial to the Dominion.... With the blood of their sons the provinces of the Dominion will seal the compact made in 1867."[191] The war became in the west a sort of Canadian equivalent to America's foundational call to arms, its injunction to *remember the Alamo*.

CHAPTER FOUR

THE GOLDEN RULE
The Klondike Gold Rush, 1898–1905

AN ABBREVIATED DIALECT FAVORED BY THE INDIANS:

'Well, so Lagus Perryman was a sly old coon and
was made Wolf Warrior hide out up to Okmulgee.

'Hotgun, he say, "Well, so how he do it?"

'And Tookpafka Micco he say, "Well, so they had was
a big fight over the last bone?"

'Then Hotgun he say, "Well, so what Chief Porter
do when they was get into it?"

'And Tookpafka Micco he say, "Well, so he was just set off to one side
and watch the wool fly and glad he was not had a hand in it."

'The Hotgun he say, "Well, so what about Charley Gibson?"

'And Tookpafka Micco he say, "Well, so he was
load his rifle and say nothing."

—*DAWSON RECORD*, 16 SEPTEMBER 1903

When the cry of gold was uttered, leading to the remarkable Klondike stampede that began in 1898, many thousands poured into Dawson City and its
environs. It was famously difficult to get there and few struck it rich; but
some of those few became extremely wealthy. The community, which had
up till that point been little more a speck of a trading post along the Yukon
River, swelled to a saloon-laden population of 40,000 seemingly overnight.
It did not last. The easy money was quickly scratched and rinsed from the
ground and by 1905 almost all the fortune seekers were gone.[1]

Most of those arriving in the Dawson area were Americans, and Canadian control of the territory "seemed under attack again." The North West

Mounted Police (NWMP), forerunner to the Royal Canadian Mounted Police (RCMP), strengthened its numbers and worked forcefully to halt the "spread of American-style frontier development...and vigilante justice" from polluting Canada's north, according to historian Kenneth Coates.[2] Still, United States national holidays took precedence over Canadian celebrations and the Klondike was "for whites only; natives were welcomed only temporarily, as curiosities or suppliers of provisions and furs."[3]

During those brief few years the press quickly established itself in the Yukon Territory. News coverage framed the Klondike story as the opening and preliminary conquest of simultaneously vacant and savage territory, much as the press had earlier depicted Rupert's Land in 1869, the initial effort to settle the Prairies in the early 1870s, and the west more generally during the 1885 North-West Rebellion. Each case presented an old-fashioned frontier tale, not unlike a Canadian-style version of the Hollywood Western. News coverage from the Klondike relied on several common tropes of the mythical frontier tale, including land conflicts, frontiersmen, unsettled territory, regeneration through violence, and the inevitability of human progress.

First there was the basic struggle for land and its potential treasures (in this case, gold!). This theme has been central in Hollywood Westerns, too, whether in *Shane*, where ranchers battle settlers,[4] or *Dances With Wolves*, where the settlement encroaches on Indian territory and is violently endorsed by the United States military.[5] In the Yukon, of course, there was no real struggle as such because there seemed to be plenty of land for all and, more importantly, because the government foreclosed conflict with the scripted arrival of the mounted police force.

Second, the key players were the classic colonial pairing of frontiersmen (usually, but not always, cast as cowboy types) and Indians. The former exemplify a wide variety of positive attributes—strength, kindness, decency, sobriety, honesty—whereas the latter serve as binaries that, at least in part, serve to champion the frontiersman.[6]

Third, the geographic setting was obviously a "frontier civilization," as the *Yukon Sun* put it,[7] one of the many sparsely populated expanding edges where civilization met, fought, and conquered savagery in the name of evolution yet packing a cross and Bible.

In this way, fourth, the Natives' very existence presented an invitation to colonialism. Here the inherent violence of the colonial project served to regenerate the culture in a way similar to how the North-West Rebellion of 1885 and the subsequent hanging of Louis Riel served to contribute so importantly to the nation-building exercise of Canada as a nation-state and correspondingly as a cultural sign packed with ideology and emotion, and thereby resistant to rationalism.[8]

Finally, fifth, the myth embodies the familiar teleological assumptions about the desirability and inevitability of human progress—"evolution," which sometimes was interpreted to require the moribundity of Natives.

The most common and best evocation of the mythical frontier tale was delivered first as a scholarly paper by the young historian Frederick Jackson Turner, at roughly the same time the initial discovery of gold was made by prospectors near Dawson City.[9] Turner's essay brilliantly vetted and endorsed a long-standing vision of American historical "evolution."[10] Beyond its considerable influence on American historiography, Turner's thesis provided a sheen of academic integrity to the popular notion of the wild frontier, which suffused the novels of James Fenimore Cooper[11] in the early nineteenth century and the countless Western dime-store novelists of the later nineteenth and twentieth centuries[12] and the hundreds of Western films made in the past century. These latter works did not often articulate the thesis clearly or even consciously, but they spoke to the enduring mythical power of the Western genre, which derives its ideological essence from the frontier tale.[13]

You likely already know the story. It goes something like this. A white man goes off to the frontier located somewhere in the imagined wild west. Think John Wayne,[14] though you might also consider Jimmy Stewart,[15] Tom Cruise,[16] or Harrison Ford,[17] even Richard Harris.[18] Think mountains, cactus, desert, horses, severe weather, saloons, sagebrush, and such. The significant point to remember is that the frontier posits a dangerous yet potentially bountiful garden—"It used to be a desert and now it's a garden," a line from John Ford's *The Man who Shot Liberty Valance*—what with the wild animals, cruel Mother Nature, and, of course, savages ever ready to pounce. Our hero is tested here on the frontier, as heroes necessarily must be, and he (again, not she) prevails violently in the encounter. In so doing he is re-made, a process Turner called "perennial rebirth."[19] In so doing the man is stripped of his eastern cultural baggage and transformed into a rugged, democratic, peace-loving, gun-slinging individualist because of the experience of the frontier and in particular its violence. Turner wrote: "To the frontier the American intellect owes its striking characteristics. That coarseness of strength combined with acuteness and inquisitiveness; that practical, inventive turn of mind, quick to find expedients; that masterful grasp of material things, lacking in the artistic but powerful to effect great ends, that restless, nervous energy; that dominant individualism working for good and for evil, and withal that buoyancy and exuberance which comes from freedom—these are traits of the frontier, or traits called out elsewhere because of the frontier."[20]

Successive waves of this process, the myth holds, populated the United States and fashioned the country into the unique country it is today. Again, Turner stated: "The frontier is the line of most rapid and effective Americanization. The wilderness masters the colonist. It finds him a European in dress, industries, tools, modes of travel, and thought. It takes him from the railroad car and puts him in the birch canoe. It strips off the garments of civilization and arrays him in the hunting shirt and the moccasin...In short, at the frontier the environment is at first too strong for the man. He must accept the conditions which it furnishes, or perish.... The fact is, that here is a new product that is American."[21]

This serves as a secular creation story for the United States. In this way it has been and arguably retains an astonishing cultural currency. Popular culture, from the Marlboro Man to Dirty Harry, from the Jeep Cherokee to *Raiders of the Lost Ark*, from the Dallas Cowboys to self-appointed mavericks running for the White House, the signs are omnipresent in American history and culture. For that matter, think no further than the cowboy stylizing of George W. Bush or even Pierre Trudeau's gunfighter pose of the 1970s. North Americans respond favourably to mythical cowboys and to the violence they promise and deliver, hence the reason that the Western has been the most popular of all movie genres and that John Wayne was the most popular movie actor in the twentieth century.[22]

But Canada was not the United States either, the press constantly reminded readers in the 1860s, 1870s, and 1880s, as we have seen, despite the similar ways in which the press in each country portrayed Aboriginal peoples. The American Indian Wars lasted many decades and cost many lives on both sides. Canada's settling of the west was more deliberate, somewhat less violent, and ultimately equally successful; yet it too, as subsequent reportage of the North-West Rebellion illustrated, required the use of arms and stringent regulations, born of hostility, fear, and reproach, regarding the movement of Aboriginal peoples as well as a policing force to cow and bully Natives into submission. Aboriginals were inherently, savagely violent, the press had long and widely held; apropos, the Canadian government matched and then overmatched this violence during the 1885 war, as the press cheered it on. In other words, the similarities between American and Canadian Indian policies outweigh the differences. As the *Dawson News* had it: "He [the Canadian Native] is here what he is in every part of the United States—shiftless, lazy and a vagabond—and so long as he can whip his klootch [female] and live on her earnings and fool the credulous white man, so long will he work his graft."[23]

In a carefully researched study Elizabeth Furniss details and demonstrates the reach of the frontier myth in a typical Canadian small town, what she terms a "frontier cultural complex," in the community of Williams Lake, British Columbia.[24] The book is instructive for considering how the Yukon press in the Klondike era, 1898–1905, portrayed Natives because it provides a clear and compelling case study of how the frontier myth operates in the day-to-day lives of Canadian communities, from casual conversation to local politics to the news media. The printed press, Furniss argues, serves as but a single point of colonial iteration. To turn this around, the press, by virtue of embodying and expressing the community, models the prevailing social norms.

Furniss writes that the principal difference in the ways that the two countries envisioned the frontier myth stems from Canada's disinclination to glorify violence, an approach which she refers to as "conquest through benevolence."[25] Roger Nichols, who penned an excellent history comparing Indian policies in the two countries, agrees that Canada's policies have been marginally less violent.[26] Yet our research discovers no discernible rhetorical difference in the ways the press of each country portrayed Natives. Instead, the news of American Aboriginal violence in Canadian newspapers served the dual purposes of sanctimoniously promoting Canadian-style exceptionalism (that is, nation building) at the same time as fudging the quotidian reality of Canadian colonialism by naturalizing a discourse that is mythically and rhetorically the very "frontier complex" that Furniss unpacks in Williams Lake.

As the Yukon press expressed the basic elements of the frontier myth in a Canadian context, it employed what Furniss identifies as a kind of metaphorical mythical reasoning.[27] In this way, for example, the espied innate character of the "Indian"—the whoring, the drunkenness, the violence, and so on—served as a justification for usurpation of the land. Because "Indians" did not use the land according to the English (or American) style, as exemplified by their ignorance or rejection of Canadian (or English) cultural norms, the land was essentially empty and available for the taking. Or because "Indians" were savage, they invited correction in the form of corporal-based schooling and aggressive proselytization (in Canada *and* the United States).[28]

In another case, to provide a stamp of approval upon the alleged "benevolent conquest," "Indians" were imagined as moribund. They were dying off anyway so, again, the land really was available. In short, and as we have seen in the earlier chapters, the newspapers focussed primarily on providing overwhelmingly negative portrayals in ways that enriched a self-satisfied affirmation of the rightness of colonialism or, in this case, on the oft-tagged "last frontier."

The vast territories of the north (Yukon) or the far west (Prairies) had been occupied for thousands of years by Aboriginal peoples. Both Natives and whites throughout the north had long exploited established trade routes. Yet press accounts not merely heaped scorn upon Natives for alleged racial, cultural, and moral inferiority, but rationalized the seizure of the overwhelming majority of the land, and the attendant physical and psychological abuse of its owners—the so-called "red man," the "children of the forest," or simply "hostiles"—as the necessary and just actions of white Canadian Protestantism.

The press content we have chosen to examine in this chapter reflects the dates of the Klondike gold rush, 1898 to 1905, as well as the extant availability of the various newspapers. The publications include five from the then-capital Dawson City (Whitehorse became the capital in 1954), the daily *Yukon Daily Morning World* (1904–1905); the daily *Dawson News* (1899–1905); the daily *Dawson Record* (1903); the semi-weekly *Klondike Nugget* (1898–1902); the weekly *Yukon Sun* (1900–1903); and the then-weekly (now daily) *Whitehorse Star* (1901–1905), the only paper still in publication.

In its inaugural editorial address to readers, the *Dawson Record* heralded a "new era in the history of the Yukon journalism" where "subjects will be treated strictly on their merits." Sharply demarcating those merits, however, the publication endorsed a key frontier norm in the capital of the territory: "No pain will be spared to make of this paper a gauge of public conscience, a criterion of public conduct, a conservator of all that is best and most enlightened in the community...everything will be done to encourage and stimulate the mining industry.... The Canadian Yukon offers a field hitherto unequalled in colonial possessions."[29] As the *Dawson News* explained, "the cruelty of the Indian is inborn and inbred, and it clings to him through his life."[30] On another day the paper quoted a certain Chief Johnson retelling a story from days of yore: "So we bound him hand and foot to the bank of a river, dug a hole in the sand and buried him alive."[31] The *Dawson News* called Aboriginals "hostiles," "vindictive," "warlike," "dangerous," and identified "general debauch" wherever Natives dwelt.[32] "The torture of human beings gives him more pleasure than any other act of his life," the paper reported. Likewise, the *Dawson Record*, the *Klondike Nugget*, and the *Whitehorse Star* supplied many similar accusations.[33] In short, the alleged Indigenous appetite for violence allegedly knew few bounds.

These six publications were not merely regurgitating established stereotypical constructions of Native people. Rather, the apparent driving force of benevolent conquest was economic—that is, fuelled by a lust for gold—and Aboriginals stood in the way. Yet, ironically, two local Natives, Tagish Charlie and Skookum Jim, along with American George Carmack, together discoverered the inital gold strike at Bonanza Creek.[34] Nevertheless, cast in moral terms, Natives stood in the way of the light of civilization—in "darkness," as the *Klondike Nugget* expressed the story of civilization versus savagery.[35]

"AN INORDINATE AMOUNT OF SUPERSTITION"

Natives were identified by all six publications as inherently violent and often criminally so. Consider a perusal of common headlines and what they imply: "INDIANS IN JAIL," "SKOOKUM CHARLEY ON THE WARPATH," "AN ALASKAN HORROR; Greedy Indians Murder and Rob Prospectors," "The Terror of the Sioux," "DEATH FIGHT OF THE YAQUIS" (no distinction between Canadian and American Aboriginals), "INDIAN IS BURIED ALIVE," "ARE ON WAR PATH; Yaqui Indians Looking for Scalps," "INDIANS REPORTED ON WARPATH," "INDIAN TRIES TO KILL SQUAW," "INDIAN HANGED AT KAMLOOPS," "INDIAN CRUELTY IS NOT ERADICABLE," "Two White Men Murdered by a Koyutuk Indian," "Indians Murder Man Near

Nulato," "MURDERED BY INDIANS," "INDIAN WOMAN IS SENTENCED," "Indian Thieves," "ONCE AN INDIAN CAPTIVE IN B.C.," "THE INDIANS DISLIKE WHITES," "Trouble With Indians," "U.S. INDIANS ON WARPATH," "AWFUL MURDER BY INDIAN BOY OF HIS GIRL PLAYMATE."[36] These headlines only scratch the surface yet instructively, as headlines are designed to do, provide a measure of predictability as to content of the accompanying news stories. Notice, too, that some of the stories reach far beyond the Yukon, from Mexico through the continental United States to Alaska, yet none of them distinguished among groups, applying and reinforcing the idea that all Aboriginals were essentially the same.

It is not that Natives did not commit crimes. Theft, for example, was a common charge.[37] But the news insisted on racializing the stories by weaving the reported violence and the crimes with alleged innate Indigenous characteristics. Culture cross-pollinated with nature to contribute to alleged Native inferiority, the papers all agreed. In a classic rhetorical appeal to authority, the *Yukon Sun* summed it up this way: "The Indian agent at Edmonton says that during his forty years of experience he has never met an Indian who was a Christian. He never met an Indian who would not lie, steal, and be immoral."[38] Yet, overall, religion figured mostly tangentially in the Klondike press but it was not exactly invisible. On the one hand, the championing of white civilization normally included some nod to the primacy of Protestantism. The flip side, Indian paganism, served as an easily constructed binary, as in the report in the *Nugget* about how witchcraft led straight to murder and incarceration.[39] Such was the result, the *Dawson News* argued, when Indians worshipped, among other deities, a "war god."[40] These stories were presented in such a way as to demonstrate the futility of autonomous Indigenous spiritual life and that Christianity would necessarily conquer the Indian or the Indian would die in the trying. The vexing issue grew out of the observation that "Indians by nature possess an inordinate amount of superstition," a claim made by the *Yukon Daily Morning World*.[41]

The *Dawson News* also found that savagery lay at the core of Native religious practice, as in the "fiendish" case where an Alaskan medicine man had murdered two prospectors, whom he then dismembered and threw into a river. When the perpetrator subsequently grew frightened that white authorities might capture and punish him, he ordered his people, who lived in the Yukon River valley, to relocate. They did so willingly because "the slightest disobedience of his commands would result in swift and terrible punishment."[42] Such was the reported debased quality of Indigenous religious practice.

The *Dawson Record* celebrated Christianity by noting in several stories that Geronimo, the famous Apache leader, had converted to Methodism. His life served as a kind of morality tale, then, but the case was complicated, the paper reported, because despite a sudden contrition ushered in by his conversion, "the wicked chief" had much blood on his hands:

> A pathetic story is that of Geronimo the old chief of the Apaches who has now espoused the cause of Christianity and joined the Methodist church. When the wicked chief was captured the second time it was the universal opinion of the eastern press that he should be executed for the cruel murders he has committed. It having been decided that he was to spend his life in imprisonment there was disappointment and apparently for good cause. The Indian had earned death on the gallows as much as any murderer ever earned it. He knew the difference between right and wrong and he knew the murders and rapine he committed were not in the name of warfare or even savage. He invited his own death and his execution would have been a grand lesson to his followers and the members of other tribes.

Still, the publication granted that the conversion had "subdued" him and left "nothing more to fear."[43]

A story placed directly below offered up the usual stereotypes. Geronimo was a "decrepit warrior," "defiant," "the Apache scourge," "a man who had slaughtered innocent women and children, ambushed the luckless paleface," and "a grim old warrior who had terrorized the southwest for years" who had frequently mutilated whites. That said, the paper recorded with measured satisfaction that he had been led to see the light. He had decided "to walk with Jesus." Salvation, in short, was possible for anybody, no matter how debased. Moreover, the stories made clear that Geronimo's conversion displayed the futility of resistance to white conquest.[44] This was a far cry from Indians described earlier in Dawson newspapers who stupidly and superstitiously mistook cave bats for "evil spirits" or believed in reincarnation.[45]

"HEAP OLD MAN! THE YOUNG SQUAW! BOTH CRAZY"

The Yukon press found Aboriginals comically vapid.[46] For example, it not infrequently mocked their inability to speak grammatically correct English. In a dissolute tale where a ninety-year-old Aboriginal man took a sixteen-year-old girl for his wife, the paper queried their chief about how such a marriage occurred: "'Don't know,' was the laconic response. 'Old Pop [the groom] he heap funny man. Makeum no love. Tellum nobody. He just wal-kum up to little squaw, about so big,' indicating a height of five feet or there-abouts, and say: 'You my wife! Callum in missionary and marry. Ugh! Heap old man! Too young squaw! Both crazy!'"[47] On another occasion a story that began as a routine report of "squaw beating" [48] morphed into pathos when the *Yukon News* followed it up with more Aboriginal pidgin English. The key explanation for the violence? "'Me don't like. Squaw makum heap big fool sometimes. Keepum home now.'"[49] Likewise, the *Yukon Sun* offered:

> What promised to be a sensation in Moosehide camp developed into
> a rather tame squaw-beating incident yesterday afternoon. The report
> wa[s] brought to Dawson by Chief Issac's son that a woman was in a
> dying condition at the camp as a result of an assault with a clubbing by a
> Tanana brave.... It was found upon investigation that the squaw was not
> in a dangerous condition though she had received a hard beating. Her
> assailant, Silas Horse, was taken into custody.... It is said the trouble
> was brought about through the squaw's chastisement of one of Mr.
> Horse's children. This made the fond father so angry that he grabbed a
> club and plied it over the lady's head with considerable vigor.[50]

Though infrequent, pen and ink drawings played up the Native as comi-cally ugly. In one case, an Indian, presumably a chief because he is adorned with a headdress common to the Prairies or Plains, stares at a grotesque, large-headed fish in a fish tank. The joke is that each character—Indian and fish—has the same response, as if looking into a mirror: "Each—'Ugh! If I looked like that I'd quit the business!'"[51] Even Indian names were portrayed as moronic and backward—"uncouth, un-American and uncivilized."[52]

Other espied Native ritual behaviour fell into a liminal space between humour and mockery. For example, a reported Native predisposition to lascivious dance and lewd, boisterous singing was common. The particu-lar variety common to the Klondike, the *Dawson News* explained, "was characterized by the participants yelping and howling like dogs as they danced. Even the dogs in the house joined the chorus."[53] Likewise, the *Whitehorse Star* observed, without attempted humour, a "big pow-wow." It featured "their dancing and weird festivities."[54]

"Pathetic," showy, and vain "Indian" behaviour juxtaposed sharply with mainstream white national chauvinism, what the *Yukon Sun* termed "manifest...loyalty to our country and to our king." Such sentiment itself was "emblematic of a greater power, a nobler, a greater and a grander civilization....nobility of character, a steadfastness of purpose and a dauntless spirit of purpose and resolution that laughs at difficulty and hazard that wins honorable success."[55] When a baseball game was struck between white and Indigenous youths in Whitehorse the outcome was predictable because the former displayed the "vim and vigor of their race and spared no effort to crown their attempts with success." The latter team, consisting of "sons of the forest," compounded their defeat with humiliation, the paper crowed, by refusing to offer a rematch the following day.[56]

Not just in baseball but in other ways alleged inherent superiority of whites was measurable, as implied in international news coverage. In the body count recorded when American white soldiers squared off against Filipinos, 2000 of the latter were killed and 2500 were scared off. Meanwhile, "our loss, two killed and 12 wounded."[60] The two key features are the exaggerated numbers, by turn implying weakness and strength, inability and ability, death and life, and the curious use of the pronoun "our," as if laying a claim to partial ownership in the community of American imperialism in the Philippines.

Another way to measure Natives was to assess those signifiers of civilization that remained shockingly absent from their material culture. What was missing, the *Dawson News* asked? The answer: "Their tribes possess none of the accessories of civilization. They have no houses to adorn, no beds to make, no dishes to wash, no sewing machines to sew their primitive garments together."[61]

The *Yukon Sun* opined, "contact with twentieth century civilization has been more or less disastrous" for Aboriginal peoples.[57] The white man, after all, the paper proclaimed, was "destined to make of the country what it is now and wrest from the bosom of the earth the wealth."[58] Perhaps that is why a "benevolent" social organization was struck in

Dawson City, the "Improved Order of the Red Men," though none of the members was Aboriginal.[59]

"DYING OFF LIKE A FLOCK OF SHEEP WITH THE ROT"

Klondike newspapers deduced that Natives were dying off and, indeed, were intended by evolution to die off—even if the papers periodically reported that scientific study disproved this widely held late nineteenth-century view. The *Whitehorse Star* explained, for example, that "Indians...have no idea how to cope...[they] are rapidly disappearing before the unequal struggle for existence side by side with white men."[62] The "average" Indian, the *Star* said, could only "mourn for the future of his race."[63] The *Yukon Sun* offered the observation that "Indians are dying off" in spectacular fashion and went on to cite "horrors beyond description among diseased natives."[64] The *Klondike Nugget* concurred, observing simply that "civilization is death to the red man." The *Nugget* also presented an ink drawing that symbolized the moribund status of Aboriginals. In it, a young man stands nobly near the forward end of a beached canoe, paddle in one hand, as he gazes at the sun setting. His face is hidden. Would the expression show resignation, anger, or surprise? Yet his stance says enough: he is faceless and his day is done. The sun is literally and figuratively setting on him. More than this, the particular problem the Yukon's Natives faced was that they had been thoroughly cross-bred with Russian traders, the paper continued. The result rendered them increasingly more susceptible to disease, leading to the conclusion that "Indians have been dying off like a flock of sheep with the rot, and the race is destined for extermination." The social-Darwinist principle at work, the paper explained, was "the law of the survival of the fittest,"[65] a phrase also employed by the *Dawson News*.[66]

Still, the *Dawson News*, contradicting itself, negotiated between the two positions by arguing that while overall Native numbers probably were not diminishing, the "Indian" as a pure breed was in fact disappearing because admixing with whites inevitably and invariably washed away the retrograde Aboriginal blood. The result was not the Métis of 1885 reportage. Instead, the paper held that "one cross [with] white blood on Indian is enough to offset and destroy fully eight tenths of the Indian character and disposition." Anything less than continued miscegenation would lead where it always had, to a "home full of whiskey and disease, and meaner than they were before...more perverse and stiff-necked."[67]

A lengthy article citing an expert in "Indian" education claimed to provide first-hand evidence of this phenomenon: "Among the pupils [at a school
in Arizona] there is only one who has any white blood, yet it is startling to
see the difference it makes in intelligence."[68] Yet on another occasion the
same paper reported that "half-breeds" "are just as ignorant as Indians with
whom they mingle."[69] The paper also claimed that to the extent that population decreases were attributable to warfare waged with American whites,
such reductions paled in comparison to the kinds of genocide Indians had
inflicted upon one another prior to the arrival of whites.[70] Further, the oft-
repeated contention in the press that Natives were starving, and that such
a condition might be employed as evidence of their moribund state, the
Dawson News dismissed as so much "sentimental rot." Instead, the paper
averred, "it is their own fault and the result of their own indolence and
inherent laziness." Yet mostly the fault lay with Aboriginal men, who summarily avoided work; and the women simply could not do it all.[71] The results
were "indeed pitiable," opined the *Whitehorse Star*.[72]

A third manifestation of Aboriginal moribundity emerged in the way
that the news froze Natives in time. This is striking in the context of the
frontier myth because at the core of the frontier idea rests the proposition that whites evolved whereas Aboriginals did not and, in fact, could
not. Stories narrating distant past events served this purpose effectively
(a practice continued in the Canadian press through the twentieth century). For example, the *Yukon Sun* featured a long tale of a captivity narrative set in Kentucky on a Saturday in February 1785. Four boys had
gone off hunting waterfowl when darkness suddenly fell upon them.
Hardy lads, the progeny of soldiers and scouts, they were well equipped
to build a temporary structure for the night, even though it snowed. The
next morning they woke to the sound of "Whoop! Whoop! Whoop!" as
Indians "burst in upon them." The boys survived by acting bravely, "as
coolly as did Daniel Boone."[73]

The boys' "pluck" and cleverness soon found them adopted in to the
tribe—over the wishes of "squaws...ready to kill" them. One boy was
adopted out to another tribe, never to be seen again. The three others assimilated in a highly effective way, mastering the "savage sports and amuse-
ments." Yet, too, they played at "a deep game." That is, they bided their time,
watchfully waiting, preparing, making ready for escape and return to civilization. In the autumn, "that chance came at last."

One day the men of the tribe went off hunting while the boys were fishing away from the main camp under the guidance of an "old Indian and his squaw." The couple "had been kind" to the lads but they had to die in order to effect the boys' escape. So the boys killed them "while they slept." If that sounds harsh, the paper instructed, "it must be remembered that these boys had been taught since their infancy to kill an Indian was a commendable action. Besides, the father of two of these boys had been killed by Indians,"[74] so the murders sort of evened the score. Yet since Indians plotted to kill whites in their sleep, the story was termed a "horror," by the *Dawson News*.[75] At any rate, twenty-one days later the three lads were home, triumphant, elated, and with "no lack of listeners to their thrilling story of adventure."

The story is instructive because it portrays Indians of the late eighteenth century in the American South as largely identical to turn-of-twentieth-century Yukon Natives: stuck in time, unable and/or unwilling to change or advance, murderous, wanton, decrepit, and vicious (especially the women). The hardy white lads were all frontiersmen in the moulding, too, being compared favourably to that archetypal frontiersman, Daniel Boone.[76]

Historical reminiscences in which Aboriginals fared poorly were not uncommon. A lengthy tale in the *Dawson Record* spun a tale of a "thrilling" 1872 battle, pitting Pawnee against the Sioux. It too reminded readers that the "Indian" was basically immutable, not given to evolution. It called this the "old time spirit of savagery" that remained wont to return whenever events triggered a lapse into atavistic "Indian" predilections—such as "the chase." The Native's love of violence was ingrained.[77] To wit, the *Dawson News* reported an American military officer warning, "'There is considerable danger of the Sioux breaking out at any time.'" Why? Because "'They are among the fiercest and most warlike.'"[78]

Another captivity narrative, reported by the *Whitehorse Star*, told of how a "half-breed" girl had been abducted by "Indians" who then spirited her away. She had been cynically drugged "with the juice of herbs."[79] Yet another captivity tale, reported in the *Dawson News*, centred on a war between Yukon tribes in which the victor kidnapped females and then subjected them to slavery. The importance of several bodies found at an excavation site where a new fire hall was being erected in Dawson City could not be overstated, the paper pressed, because it "has added a new chapter to the unwritten early history of the Yukon valley,"[80] yet it remains unclear how the evidence of slavery was adduced from the remains. Nevertheless,

slavery was not uncommon among Natives, the paper sought to demonstrate, recording a story which described how a white explorer among the
"Esquimaux" (Inuit) had been offered a man's wife and children in exchange
for a "shining knife."[81] Aboriginal women, in short, amounted to drudges
and idiots in the Klondike press,[82] fungible, cruel, and engaged in marriage
practices that were explicitly racist toward whites[83] as they also were toward
blacks.[84] "Eskimos," meanwhile, were dismissed by the *Yukon Daily Morning World*, as "not of a high intelligence."[85]

Possibly nothing would have shocked Yukon newspaper readers. The
Yukon Daily Morning World referred to Aboriginals as "ill-smelling and
foully be-smeared...Poor ignorant lot...[with] slow minds...low on the ladder" of civilization.[86] The charge of alcoholism was ubiquitous and often
snidely inferred core immorality,[87] "general debauch," as the *Dawson News*
had it, as was the case with a "dusky maiden" who earned herself two months
in prison, or a "drunken orgy" among Ontario Indians.[88] Sometimes it was
linked with whorish female behaviour, as in the case of a woman "whom
Pocahontas would disown."[89] Among reservation girls in the United States,
the *Dawson News* claimed, "there is scarcely one who remains virtuous."[90]
"In many narratives," writes anthropologist Elizabeth Bird, "Indian women
are portrayed as bloodthirsty, lazy, filthy, and prone to drunkenness, the
occasional acts of kindness being interpreted as out of character or abnor-
mal for Indian women."[91] Even the best Aboriginal females received little
better treatment. The Tagish wife of Skookum Jim, co-discover of the initial
Klondike gold strike, was described as "a stout maiden of about 22 cold sea-
sons, with a beautifully flat nose, fine round face and voice like the gurgle
of an overturned bottle of liquor."[92] Elsewhere, the *Klondike Nugget*, like
the *Dawson News*, found Aboriginal "dusky" women given to drink and
whorish behaviour.[93] They could be fiendish, too, said the *Dawson News*. For
them, "the torture of a human being is an active, exquisite pleasure." It typically led to scalping and mutilation and the death of "babes whose brains
had been beaten out against walls or trees."[94]

Apart from frequent references to Natives in the United States, some of
which have been noted, the Yukon press had relatively little to say about
non-Canadian Aboriginals. Apaches, for example, were described as
"marauders."[95] While not always consistent, the press assumed that readers understood that races existed hierarchically. For example, in an article
about the hopelessness of attempting to educate Natives, the *Dawson News*

reported that "when it has been said that our wild savages are among the lowest class of savages, the simple truth has been expressed."[96] At best, the Indian was "just reaching for the first rung on the upward move," the *Yukon Daily Morning World* commented, "low though they be on the ladder" of races.[97] North American whites, by contrast, stood as the "dominant race of the continent." Turks, on the other hand, the same article explained, were "semi-civilized" as were "so-called Spaniards in Cuba."[98] What opinion it did offer about Aboriginals abroad was uniformly derogatory. Mexico's Yaqui Indians, for example, were dying off—yet somewhat nobly. They were fierce warriors, doomed by the advance of civilization— "perishing fast"—and its attendant superior military force.[99] The *Klondike Nugget* reported no such Yaqui nobility or martial talents, instead focussing on their "weak resistance."[100] But the Yaqui were not entirely routed, it turns out, because they were returned to the "war path" more than two years later, the *Nugget* later reported. Worse, the *Yukon Daily Morning World* indicated that after taking to the "warpath," the Yaquis began attacking targets in the United States.[101]

The Klondike was not, as imagined by the press, the mythical American frontier that stripped easterners of culture and rebirthed them as prototypical rugged individualistic democrats. Instead, here, based on news reports, miners, would-be miners, and the service industry that grew up around them, driven by the lust for gold and the opportunity to take advantage of the lust for gold, brought mainstream North American culture with them. We see this in the pointed similarity from the ways in which Yukon press portrayals resembled those from the Northwest in 1885 and of the Toronto *Globe* and Montreal *Gazette* in 1873 and 1869.

In other words, Yukon publications did not invent colonialism so much as they brought it with them. The images fit neatly with Furniss's evocation of the "frontier complex," featuring "conquest through benevolence." All of the Yukon newspapers endorsed it and championed it. In sum, mythical frontier imagery vis-à-vis Natives was central to Yukon newspapers.

CHAPTER FIVE

POET, PRINCESS, POSSESSION

Remembering Pauline Johnson, 1913

THE EDUCATION OF GIRLS

In such a utilitarian age as this, the education of a girl should never be considered as complete or even half completed, until she thoroughly studies and comprehends the science of bread making and has become a thorough adept of the art.

She should be able to cut, fit and make her own dresses...

She should know how to keep a daily account of all the money received by her...

She should know how to select the best meals and vegetables and fruits of all kinds...

As every true woman calculates on getting married sooner or later, she should learn beforehand the art of keeping her husband rather than of getting one...she should sedulously cultivate purity of character, self-respect, control of temper, equanimity, integrity, truthfulness in all things.

—MONTREAL *GAZETTE*, 13 JANUARY 1873

The English took possession in the new world in ways strikingly similar to how Anglo-Canada claimed Rupert's Land. This included the erection of fixed and permanent domiciles, fences, bridges, roads, and gardens. Canada thus became preoccupied with boundaries and boundary markers, as witnessed in treaty making or in the Riel imbroglios. Basically, it came down to taming the land by planting and tending gardens and building infrastructure to aid and abet the process. This equalled, signified, and asserted possession. In short, the story of Canada has been a story of domestication and control. Natives played a key part in this Canadian metanarrative because they ultimately, too, became possessions of the state; and the state eagerly and aggressively sought both to domesticate and control them.

Of course, the state both failed and succeeded in its efforts. It failed insofar as Natives simply bore no particular resemblance to what the colonial imagination demanded of them. As a result, residential schools, for example, failed in spectacular fashion. Yet, too, the state succeeded by relentlessly sticking to its script. A savage is a savage and a "squaw" remains a "squaw." End of story. In short, if in the empirical world Aboriginals existed outside the perimeters of Canada's colonial vision, it made no difference. In this way, the various imagined Native stereotypes and archetypes endure. Possession is thus unavoidable because the Native has been constructed by Canada and for Canada. Fair is fair: you build it, you own it. In this way, Native bodies themselves became scripts upon which colonialism etched itself, ongoing palimpsests. A good illustration of this occurred in 1913 in the ways in which Canada's English-language newspapers covered the death and funeral of mixed-blood poet E. Pauline Johnson, Canada's consummate Indian princess.

Pauline Johnson died in Vancouver on 7 March 1913 at age fifty-two after a three-year battle with cancer. The Vancouver *Daily Province* published the news of her death in the evening edition: "Her death was not unexpected, as for the last fortnight she had been slowly sinking. She had however, rallied several times during the last year from similar acute attacks, and it was not until Tuesday that it was recognized that she could hardly live through the week.... The funeral arrangements will be announced later. It is believed that these are in the hands of the Women's Canadian Club."[1] Subsequent press reportage in effect claimed and reterritorialized her body as a Canadian possession. Johnson, or Tekahiowake (her Mohawk name), was a peerless Indian princess, news reports proclaimed. To begin with, she was in fact a real princess. Her pedigree derived from her Iroquoian chieftain father being a "Blood Royal, a scion of one of the fifty noble families which composed the historical confederation founded by Hiawatha upwards of four hundred years ago," according to the Vancouver *Daily Province*.[2] The Iroquois, it was reported, were best known and fondly remembered for their loyalty to the British crown.[3] The *Province* explained that her unique position of importance derived from her colonial ties in that she was brought up on land granted to the Mohawks by the British after the conclusion of the

French Revolution and the War of American Independence. "It was inevitable," the paper argued, "that the loyalty to Britain and Britain's flag which she inherited from her red ancestors as well as from her English mother, should breathe through both her prose and poetic writing."[4]

Mikhail Bakhtin argues that every nation necessarily views "its own language as the verbal and semantic center of the ideological world."[5] With respect to empire, David Spurr carefully demonstrates that colonial discourse ineluctably frames Natives as living in a state of nature. This colonial monologue also grants "dominion over the earth to more advanced peoples" and correspondingly naturalizes the process of domination.[6] In similar fashion, Canada's press employed the occasion of Johnson's death to utilize her body and words to personify the perceived truth of the imagined Indian princess. In other words, the memorialization of the poet offered an opportunity to unleash the rhetoric of Canada's imperial ideology.

Newspapers melded Johnson's poetic language with media reports that reinforced and bound an ideological position of patriarchy over Aboriginal peoples to the discourse of nation building. Reports paired poems such as "As Red Men Die,"[7] "The Lost Lagoon,"[8] and "C.P.R. [Canadian Pacific Railway] Westbound No. 1"[9] with details of her death and burial at Stanley Park in Vancouver. Her poetry, represented in obituaries and memorials in Canada's newspapers, well served the aims of the imagined nation. The Regina *Leader* printed the "Lost Lagoon" in full while the Toronto *Star* and Edmonton *Journal* offered these lines from "As Red Men Die":

> I carry the brave and bold—
> The one who works for the nation's bread,
> The one whose past is a thing that's dead.

The words assumed suddenly more poignancy when placed within the context of her colonial memorialization. The alleged moribundity of Aboriginals still maintained currency.

"DISTINGUISHING CHARACTERISTICS OF THE PROUD AND CAPABLE TRIBE"

In a 1981 biography, Betty Keller takes exception to the manner in which Johnson had been framed earlier. Keller argues that the "saccharine and virtuous Indian maiden poetess" depicted by W. Garland Foster in *The Mohawk Princess: Being Some Account of the Life of Teka-hion-wake*

(E. Pauline Johnson) (1931) belies the self-directed and sometimes aggressive but "utterly charming part-Mohawk woman" Keller found.[10] The title of Foster's biography alone positions the poetry as secondary to her racial identity. Keller attempts to reacquaint Canadians with Johnson who, Keller argues, had slipped into obscurity and was known in 1980 only as "that Indian poetess who wrote 'The Song My Paddle Sings.'"[11] Keller succeeds in part only. While she tries to set the record straight by engaging in copious research about the poet's family history on both sides, the book also casts Johnson's Mohawk roots as exotica. More recently Charlotte Gray's *Flint and Feather: The Life and Times of E. Pauline Johnson* and Veronica Strong-Boag and Carole Gerson's *Paddling Her Own Canoe: The Times and Texts of E. Pauline Johnson, Tekahionwake*, in addition to a small number of articles and book chapters, have all attempted to explain Johnson's complex self-positioning.[12] Feminist scholars Strong-Boag and Gerson in particular adopt a revisionist tone, advancing the idea that Pauline Johnson "talked back" to dominant culture.[13] They argue that Johnson "was a complicated, contentious, and passionate personality whose life blurs the borders of what it means to be Native, a woman, and Canadian."[14] Gray agrees that Johnson increasingly became a symbol for both nationalism and Indigenous causes that became more polarized after her death.[15]

On the whole, then, the biographies have tended to paint a sympathetic portrayal. On the other hand, Daniel Francis describes her fake Indian costuming and her cloying romantic poetry as evidence of her compliance to serve as the "White Man's Indian."[16] Janice Fiamengo, most recently, in a 2008 essay that analyzes a press interview in the *Globe*'s 'Woman's World' section of October 1886, argues that Johnson continues to confound scholars and popular writers because Johnson's role in Canadian literary and cultural history satisfies a variety of positions related to racial identity from princess to pawn to self-possessed promoter of Aboriginal culture.[17]

"She was a princess, one of Canada's native royalty," proclaimed the Vancouver *Daily Province* on 10 March 1913. Press reports and editorials following her death evinced no hesitation in attempting to position Johnson as Canada's Indian Princess. While much coverage centred on her partial Mohawk roots, the press, in a disciplining role as champion of and cheerleader for colonialism, offered readers an uncluttered vision of Johnson. She was Canada's Indian poetess princess—she belonged to Canada.

Emily Pauline Johnson was born in 1861 to George Henry Johnson and his Quaker wife Emily Howells, from Ohio, whose family had immigrated from Bristol, England, in the first decade of the nineteenth century. She was the youngest of four children. George Johnson was a Mohawk from Six Nations of the Grand River First Nation near Brantford, Ontario. He was both elected Teyonnhehkewea—a senator in the Iroquois Confederacy—and also appointed as an interpreter for the Canadian government. As an employee of the Canadian government he dressed according to the white standards of the day—in a suit. On special occasions he donned Mohawk ceremonial regalia. Keller writes that "the romance of a chieftain's costume was irresistible" as Johnson straddled "both worlds, looking upon himself as a spokesman for the Mohawk people while leading a white man's life."[18]

Despite resistance from both the Howells and the Johnsons over the mixed-blood union, the poet's parents married and built a large middle-class home they called "Chiefswood" near Brantford, where Johnson was raised with her three older siblings. Strong-Boag and Gerson describe how Johnson's family was part of a "mixed-race aristocracy" that had emerged in North America and contend that mixed-race individuals in Canada were often close to the centre of resistance to settler society's dismissal of Native virtue.[19] Peter Jones and Louis Riel were two such male champions, though the authors argue that a number of women were involved in resistance at a local level. Johnson outshone them all because she reached a national audience.[20]

Johnson was for two years instructed by an English governess who lived with the family. A Montreal *Gazette* news report titled, "THE EDUCATION OF GIRLS," published in 1873 when Pauline Johnson was twelve years old, offers a glimpse of what a Canadian girl's education might have involved at that time. Cooking, cleaning, and husband-hunting were key lessons to be learned. For her formal training, Johnson was enrolled in the local reserve school for a short time before turning to her mother as tutor and then ultimately completing her education at Brantford Collegiate.[21]

Keller describes an enormous library that belonged to the Johnson family and that Johnson drew upon as the basis for her education.[22] Gray adds that Johnson and her siblings used to sit captivated at their grandmother's kitchen table listening to stories about spirit-healers, medicine men, and ghosts, told to them in the Mohawk language—the language they never spoke but nevertheless understood fluently.[23] Johnson wrote her first full-length poem in 1879. In 1884 her father died and the family was forced to rent out Chiefswood. They moved into Brantford and became part of Brantford society. She began publishing poetry in the local *Brantford Expositor* and soon began giving popular local recitations of her poetry to raise money to publish a book of poetry.

In 1886 Johnson took on the name Tekahionwake, interpreted as "Double Wampum," or double life.[24] The name befits the structured performances Johnson delivered during the fourteen years she toured as a poet and performer. Francis says that the name had belonged to her great-grandfather and somewhat cynically helped engender an exotic image sought by audiences.[25]

Johnson's public debut as a performer and poet did not occur until 1892 when, at age thirty in Toronto, she read during a literary event sponsored by the Young Men's Liberal Club at Toronto's Academy of Music.[26] A *Globe* reviewer excitedly responded to "A Cry From An Indian Wife" and "As Red Men Die." In the same breath that Johnson was cast as an authentic Aboriginal voice speaking on behalf of all Natives so too did the reviewer speak for a long-held Canadian vision of Natives: "It was like the voice of the nations who once possessed this country, who have wasted away before our civilisation speaking through this cultured, gifted, soft-voiced descendant."[27] And so began Johnson's meteoric rise to fame; straightaway she undertook a busy touring schedule that began in Ontario and quickly expanded to American cities such as Boston and New York. Critics everywhere raved. Gray explains the reception by noting that "crowds love uplifting patriotism and a great outfit."[28] The Indian princess outfit Gray refers to was only part of the costumed spectacle Johnson delivered to audiences.

Margaret Atwood interprets Johnson's brand of entertainment as that of a performance artist, though explains that in her time Johnson was prized as an elocutionist, meaning that she gave readings coloured by dramatic effect in drawing rooms and theatres.[29] The use of costume—guise, not regalia—in her performance promoted assimilation. Johnson almost always changed her garb midway through a performance.[30] Typically, she began in a fringed buckskin dress, which she had purchased at the Hudson's Bay department store, embellished with silver brooches, buckskin leggings, moccasins, and an ermine-tail necklace that was topped off with an "authentic Huron scalp inherited by her great-grandfather" tied at her waist.[31] Then at about the midpoint in her emotionally charged performances she slipped into a

Victorian-style gown. The effect served as an effort to visually affirm her cultural evolution (and reify the central tenets of Canada's colonial dream): the transformation from Mohawk princess to patriotic Canadian.

Her choice of poetry coincided with the performative aspects of the event, in tone and content mirroring the none too subtle teleological implications of her costume change. She would begin with charged poems relating to her princess persona; poetry in the second portion evoked images of Canadian national pride and Iroquois loyalty to the Crown.[32] "A Cry From An Indian Wife" published in her collection *The White Wampum* in 1895 offers an indication of the introductory portion of her reading, with its opening lines:

> My forest brave, my Red-skin love, farewell;
> We may not meet to-morrow;
> Who can tell what mighty ills befall our little band,
> Or what you'll suffer from the white man's hand?
> Here is your knife!
> I thought 'twas sheathed for aye.
> No roaming bison calls for it today;
> No hide of prairie cattle will it maim;
> 'Twill drink the life-blood of a soldier host.[33]

A poem like "Canada" demonstrates the shift in tone to flag waving found in the second segment of Johnson's performances:

> Crown of her, young Vancouver; crest of her, old Quebec;
> Atlantic and far Pacific sweeping her keel to deck.
> North of her, ice and arctics; southward a rival's stealth;
> Aloft, her Empire's pennant; below, her nation's wealth.
> Daughter of men and markets, bearing within her hold,
> Appraised at highest value, cargoes of grain and gold.[34]

Not surprisingly, Strong-Boag and Gerson contend, it was Johnson's performances as much as the poetry itself that attracted large audiences.[35] Fiamengo cites a number of newspaper reviews of her performances that illustrated a recognition of protest against "the wrongs of her race"; yet Mohawk literary scholar Rick Monture indicates that the deliberate choices of costume and sentimental poetry enacted in the second portion of the readings "negated any reality of Native oppression—all was forgotten by the audience with the assimilationist rhetoric embedded in the finale.[36]

After touring extensively in Canada, the United States, and Britain, Johnson chose Vancouver as her permanent home in 1908. There she turned her attention to serious writing. Gray relates that Johnson's mother disapproved of her daughter's interest in the public spotlight and adds that her sister Evelyn, who remained their mother's caregiver, was jealous of her sister. Gray also outlines the poet's struggles with money. Despite her fame, Johnson lived on limited funds in a modest apartment. Later she suffered from cancer, which ultimately killed her. Chapters of the Imperial Order of the Daughters of the Empire (IODE) and the Women's Canadian Club meanwhile adopted her and helped support her financially during her final years. Keller likens these groups to "efficient, hard-headed and aggressive" organizations who viewed Johnson as an ideal object for their attentions.[37] Evelyn Johnson tried to convince Pauline to return to Brantford or at least agree to be buried there, but the sisters inevitably clashed and Pauline Johnson wrote a detailed will that ensured that Vancouver and the Women's Canadian Club would be in charge of her funeral and burial details. After her sister's death, Evelyn telephoned her brother and cousin while her doctor alerted reporter Isabel MacLean at the Vancouver *Daily Province*. From there, the news of her death would soon spread across Canada.

"IN THE HANDS OF THE WOMEN'S CANADIAN CLUB"

The claiming of Johnson's body in news stories, both literally and figuratively, fixed her within a discourse of assimilation and conquest. It seemed the death of the Indian poetess became an opportunity for advancing a unique formulation of identity politics that simultaneously celebrated her whiteness *and* Indianness as a hybridized object. Canadians learned from reading evening papers on 7 March 1913 that funeral details were being jointly orchestrated by the competent and efficient Women's Canadian Club of Vancouver, City Hall, and the Department of the Militia (that controlled the land in Stanley Park where her ashes were interred), thereby allying the poet with the social elite. National news coverage of her death territorialized her body as a colonial possession taken over by governmental and cultural institutions. For this chapter we examined coverage of her death, funeral, and subsequent interment in fifteen daily newspapers from across the country from 7 to 14 March 1913 to more fully explore the notions of identity construction surrounding Johnson.[38]

Only four newspapers mentioned her death on 7 March, including the Toronto *Globe*, the Edmonton *Journal*, the Victoria *Daily Colonist*, and the Vancouver *Daily Province*. Because Johnson had been ill for an extended period some of the dailies, employing a common newspaper practice, had obituaries at the ready. The *Daily Province* included a stock profile headshot of Johnson dressed in her Indian princess costume alongside "an Account of the Life and Work of a Remarkable Woman." The ensuing two-page story of her life made it clear that Johnson belonged to the settler nation. It explained, for example, that although her sister Evelyn had been dutifully at her side until the end, funeral arrangements would be left, "in the hands of the Women's Canadian Club."[39] Entrusting funeral arrangements to Vancouver's social upper crust rather than to her own family served as a way for the *Daily Province* to lay claim to Johnson on behalf of the country. Johnson left specific details that included no flowers at the funeral and no viewing of the body. Neither request was honoured as the society invited a local artist to fashion a death mask and arrangements of flowers overflowed Christ Church Cathedral in downtown Vancouver.[40] Still, by designating full authority for her funeral to the Canadian Club, Johnson ostensibly gave her blessing to be taken as a possession.[41]

Rather than focus on her importance for and contributions made to Canadian poetry, after a short description of Johnson's waning health over the past few weeks and acknowledgement of her three-year struggle with cancer, the *Province* quickly launched into an enthralling and lengthy description of the poet's racial pedigree, as an excerpt from the Edmonton *Journal* illustrates:

INDIAN POETESS IS DEAD; AFTER YEAR'S ILLNESS
Pauline Johnson, of Six Nation Group Dies in Vancouver Hospital

VANCOUVER, B.C., March 8 - Pauline Johnson, Indian poetess, died at 11:38 yesterday at the Butte street hospital.

E. Pauline Johnson (Tekahwiowake) was the youngest child of a family of four born to the late G.H.M. Johnson (Onwanonsyshon), Head Chief of the Six Nations Indians, and his wife Emily S. Howells. The latter was of English parentage, her birthplace being Bristol, but the land of her adoption Canada.

Chief Johnson was of the renowned Mohawk tribe, being a scion
of one of the fifty noble families which composed the historical
confederation founded by Hiawatha upwards of four hundred years
ago, and known at that period as the Brotherhood of the Five Nations,
but which was afterwards named the Iroquois by the early French
missionaries and explorers. For their loyalty to the British crown they
were granted magnificent lands bordering the Grand river, in the
county of Brant, Ontario, on which the tribes still live.

It was upon the reserve, on her father's estate, "Chiefwood," that
Pauline Johnson was born. They loyalty of her ancestors breathed in
her prose, as well as in her poetic writings.

SCHOOL WAS LIMITED

Her education was neither extensive or elaborate. It embraced neither
high school nor college. A nursery governess for two years at home,
three years at an Indian day school half a mile from her home and two
years in the Central school of the city of Brantford, was the extent of
her educational training. But, besides this she acquired a wide general
knowledge, having been through childhood and early girlhood a
'great reader, especially of poetry. Before she was twelve years old she
had read Scott, Longfellow, Byron, Shakespeare, and such books as
Addison's "Spectator," Foster's Essays and Owen Meredith's writings.

Much was made in this initial obituary of the unorthodox upbringing to which
Johnson allegedly owed her elocutionary career; for example, to the training
she gained by reading to Chip, her childhood dog.[42]

The brief mention of her death in the *Daily Colonist* described her as
endowed with the "natural dignity and eloquence which have been the distinguishing characteristics of the proud and capable tribe."[43] The *Journal*'s front-page headlines announced that she "Was Daughter of Mohawk Chieftain"
and "People of Edmonton Specially Interested Through Daughters of Empire
Appeal."[44] Describing Johnson as "proud, with the blood of a great and honorable Mohawk chief in her veins," the *Journal* report praised the local chapter
of the nationalist IODE chapter for its efforts to raise funds on the poet's behalf
during her extended period of illness.[45] The Toronto *Star* paired, "Passes to
Happy Hunting Grounds After Long Illness" and "VISITED BY THE DUKE" in
its headline, conflating both her otherness and her colonial importance.[46]

Unlike the other noted newspapers, the *Globe* framed its report mostly around Johnson's literary contributions and printed "C.P.R. No. 1, West-bound," a patriotic Johnson composition that glorifies Canada's settling of its frontier. The poem pays tribute to the possession-taking of the colonial project, celebrating the railroad, agriculture, and hard work of the settlers:

I swing to the sunset land—
The world of prairie, the world of plain,
The world of promise and hope and gain,
The world of gold, and the world of grain,
And the world of the willing hand.

I carry the brave and bold—
The one who works for the nation's bread,
The one whose past is a thing that's dead,
The one who battles and beats ahead,
And the one who goes for gold.

I swing to the "Land to Be,"
I am the power that laid its floors,
I am the guide to its western stores,
I am the key to its golden doors,
That open alone to me.

Casting her as the interpreter of "the thoughts of the dying Indian Race," the *Globe* foregrounded her racial makeup before it turned to describe her literary career. Johnson's legacy, the *Globe* concluded, would be treasured because of its "individuality, virility, and for its complete expression of love for the red men and their free life, the grandeur of Canadian scenery and for various noble elements in our early civilization."[47] In this way, her life and her poetry become one—an expression of the utterance of empire set to the cadence of clunky verse.

Like other obituaries, the *Globe* could not resist the titillating details of the mixed-blood union of her parents: "There was real romance in the marriage of the Indian Chief and the white girl." The *Globe* creatively claimed that Johnson's mother came from Ohio as a missionary and explained that the two parents fell in love, "despite the degradation it meant for the Chief's tribal ambitions."[48] The two-page report repeatedly stressed events in her life that gave shape to a narrative that championed assimilationism.[49] The *Globe* included, for example, a personal recollection by "Mrs. Denison (Lady Gay), the well known society writer," about how the two had been childhood class-mates and that some of the girls at their school, "showed aversion to associat-ing with an Indian," until Denison pointed out "that Miss Johnson was a real Princess."[50] More than a month later, on 18 April the *Globe* printed a letter to the editor written by Evelyn Johnson responding to the comments made by Denison in the obituary. Evelyn's letter stated that her sister had known of Lady Gay's claims since they had appeared in a Vancouver newspaper a year earlier. But according to Evelyn, her sister had never attended school with the society writer nor had she been introduced to her until later in her career. The letter clarified also that Johnson had never "met with any aversion to herself as 'an Indian.' Why should she?" asked her sister.[51]

"By the death of Pauline Johnson Canada loses a great daughter of the flag," bemoaned an editorial in the *Province*. The text framed Johnson's passage to the "happy hunting grounds" within a bifurcated, stereotypical rhetoric—she was an "Imperialist," and "in spite of her English mother she was Indian to the core."[52] The Toronto *Star* similarly employed the term "Happy Hunting Grounds" to lament Johnson's death and described her poems as "mostly of a passionate nature, breathing the fine and ardent heroic spirit of the Indian race."[53] Johnson's poem "The Happy Hunting Grounds" was published as part of *White Wampum* in 1895 and romantically illustrated her conception of a "Red-skin" afterworld:

> Surely the great Hereafter cannot be more than this,
> Surely we'll see that country after Time's farewell kiss.
> Who would his lovely faith condole?
> Who envies not the Red-skin's soul.[54]

The Regina *Leader* (a forerunner to today's *Leader-Post*) devoted two pages on 8 March to remember Johnson's many contributions to Canada.[55] In contrast, the Windsor *Evening Record*, Victoria *Daily Colonist*, and Calgary *Herald* only printed short reports, mostly excerpted from the Vancouver *Province*. The *Leader*'s coverage included an illustrated homage to Johnson in its "News of the Week in Cartoon by John McNaughton," which symbolically placed a tipi donning a memorial wreath next to a smoking camp fire before a setting sun with "Tekawionwake" written across the bottom.[56] The cultural icons would have been easily understood by a Saskatchewan audience. The tipi, for the west, served as a synecdoche for Indianness—even though Johnson's Mohawk tradition had no connection to tipis. The accompanying wreath read as an important European memorial symbol. Together the two images illustrated a potent image of hybridity. The setting sun and smokey ebbing fire confirmed moribund cultural references supported by the text. The companion story described Johnson as a figure who acknowledged her links to a "noble dying" culture but also, importantly, recognized her allegiance to both the British and Canadian governments. For example, the front page outlined how the Duke of Connaught, Canada's governor general and King George's representative in Canada, was an honorary chief of the Six Nations, a lineage, according to the newspaper, established by the Mohawk chief Hiawatha. It reported that Connaught had both visited the poet in the hospital in Vancouver and had sent a telegram expressing his grief at her death. A number of other publications, including the Toronto *Globe* and Toronto *Star*, also situated the Duke of Connaught at the centre of this story.[57]

The *Leader* continued its coverage with a quarter-page stylized illustration titled the "Canadian Scene and Sentiment." It depicted an Aboriginal male paddling a birchbark canoe overlaid by Johnson's poem "The Lost Lagoon." The creation casts the world of Natives as dying off gently; they had prospered during a time of a "golden moon," but now that time is over.[58] A photograph of Johnson in her princess garb next to the drawing further blurred the distinction between fantasy and reality as it portrays her as archetypically frozen in time.

Johnson's role as Canada's Indian princess did not demand racial purity. Her English bloodline and the fact that she had benefitted from the instruction of an English governess as a child had aided her successful assimilation into Canadian society, noted the *Leader*.[59] As a "half-breed" she illustrated the inevitability of Native biological extinguishment; and as an assimilated breed she personified an ideal colonialized success story. Preserving her Indian princess status, however, was important because the story remained viable only so long as the body of the narrative—not its conclusion—remained alive. Thus she was simultaneously a process as well as an end product. Accordingly, the *Leader* story also exclaimed that "not to live out of doors at her will was probably the greatest trial Miss Johnson could suffer," though by all accounts she had been raised in a middle-class Canadian way as much as anybody had.[60]

Another regional connection in the *Leader* coverage included a memorial written by "one who visited the Qu'Appelle Lakes with her." Johnson held a special place in the hearts of Saskatchewan residents because of a poem she had penned about the legend of a dying Indian princess. The work, titled

"Legend of Qu'Appelle," related to a local landmark northeast of Regina. The poem tells how a princess, lying in her tipi, called out to her lover who shouted back in French, "qu'Appelle?" ("who calls?"), as he vigorously paddled his canoe across a chain of Saskatchewan lakes trying to reach her. The remembrance boasted how Johnson had "shed a tear" when she heard the story that had then inspired her to write the poem.[61]

Johnson's approval of the level of instruction given to First Nations youth at the nearby Lebret Industrial School, interpreted as a sanctioning of the residential school system, was also advanced in the remembrance. "The young generation of Western red men always looked forward to a visit from one of the noblest of their race," explained the story, because "she missed no opportunity of manifesting her interest in the education of the little Indians."[62]

Like the *Leader*, the Edmonton *Journal* also creatively framed Johnson's death around her poetry and her role in nation building. A report under the headline, "Pauline Johnson Sends Last Message to Women of Edmonton," included a facsimile copy of a handwritten letter of thanks by Johnson to the Edmonton chapter of the IODE and an excerpt of her poem, "As Red Men Die," that described a "savage yell" as a brave "leaps to Happier Hunting Grounds."[63]

Newspapers in both Hamilton and Windsor, Ontario, noted Johnson's death; though perhaps surprisingly, given the proximity of the two cities to her ancestral home, neither paper included the sort of emotional outpourings found in the Regina *Leader*, the Edmonton *Journal*, or in the Vancouver *Province*. Still, Windsor's *Evening Record* on 10 March described Johnson as "one of the truest interpreters of that dying race and all that it stood for," though the structure of the report clearly viewed Johnson's mother's family as a genetic basis for her literary prowess: "Miss Johnson was born near Brantford, Ontario, inheriting the red man's love of nature from her father, who was a Mohawk chief, and the interest in literature of the cultured pale face from her mother, who was related to the present dean of American letters, William Dean Howells."[64]

Unlike other news reports that romantically stressed her Mohawk pedigree, the *Evening Record* simply identified her father as a nameless Mohawk chief. "Her best verse," according to the paper, "is that which deals with the Indian and that which was nearest to him—Nature," and explained that she also wrote of the "miserable present" and the glories of "his distant past."[65] The Hamilton *Spectator*, located closer yet to Six Nations reserve, voiced a clear colonial posture in its report, next to a story that proclaimed "Drunkenness Can Be Cured."[66] The *Spectator* also outlined the success of Johnson's early poetry but claimed that her later work demonstrated a social evolution in its own right, one that had established Johnson in national literary circles: "But Miss Johnson did not spend her days lamenting a glorious past. Her poetry will be remembered quite as gratefully for her epics of Canadian life and scenery in the broad outdoors of the north and west…what more redolent of pioneer life than the exquisitely lyric, 'The Song My Paddle Sings?'…As the years passed on one feels in Miss Johnson's verse an increasing consciousness of the results of national development and civilization."[67]

Such assimilationist progress appeared to have been irresistible to the press, serving as confirmation of Canada's influence on Aboriginal peoples.

"SHE WAS A PRINCESS"

Descriptions of the poet's funeral further secured Johnson's body for Canada. The *Province* and the *Daily Colonist* discussed her final resting place at Ferguson's Point in Stanley Park as a permanent landmark—serving as one of the "expressive acts" described by Seed as a cultural sign utilized to legitimate dominion.[68] The *Province* offered a detailed story about her funeral with a photo of the location in Stanley Park where a stone memorial to the poet would be situated. The headline proclaimed that "Hundreds of All Classes and Creeds Bowed in Tears Before Casket," and explained in minute detail how respectfully she was treated by the citizens of Vancouver.[69] As if to assure readers of Vancouver's progressiveness, the story confirmed that the mayor and several aldermen had attended the funeral and representatives from almost every public organization in the city also were present. The newspaper described the many gifts of flowers and crosses (even though Johnson had asked that no flowers be included) by such notable groups as the Daughters of the Empire, the Royal Canadian Society, and the Vancouver Art and Historical Society displayed in the "impressive Church of England's" Church of Christ where her funeral took place.[70] The report devoted much of the page to detailing the types of flowers found in each donated arrangement, rendering the generous contributions by Vancouver's high society more central to the event than the poet's legacy. For example: "At the head of the coffin lay a wreath of laurel tied with a purple ribbon. She was a princess, one of Canada's native royalty… A magnificent wreath of sturdy oak leaves of a lustrous purple shade, was the gift of the British Columbia Society of Fine Arts… The ashes, at the express request of Miss Johnson, will be buried in Stanley Park, near Siwash Rock, a spot at which she spent many a quiet hour while living here."[71] The report documents the poet's preference for Vancouver over her childhood home as a final resting spot, though a sidebar story below the funeral coverage noted that the Mohawk Church "on the reserve" had also staged a memorial service for her.

Coverage in Ontario and the west far eclipsed the limited mention received in the Atlantic region. The Fredericton *Daily Gleaner* on 10 March devoted roughly a column inch to announcing Johnson's passing, sandwiched between a much longer story about the death of James Ready, a successful brewer in the province, and news of an Ottawa fire that damaged a woodworking plant. Johnson was described erroneously as the daughter of the "head chief of the Sioux Nations Indians" and Emily Howells, a native of Bristol, England.[72] The paper also mangled the spelling of her Indian name. The following day, however, the *Gleaner* included two photos under a headline, "Historical Hilltop is Consecrated to Memory of Red Men," with coverage of a different memorial, an American ceremony near Fort Wadsworth, New York, to commemorate the "departed glory of the Indian race."[73]

Calgary *Herald* editors stripped Pauline Johnson of her Indianness in their 11 March editorial, explaining to readers that it was not her Indigenous roots that brought Johnson renown, but "because of God's gift of a lyric soul and an heroic spirit that placed her beyond any limitations of race, or class, or creed...tutored by nature's voice and led by nature's call. Expressing, the truth of nature's God."[74] The Christian connection—her mother's English-Anglican influence—had seemingly protected the poet from the pagan influences of the "loyal chief of the Six Nation Indians' race."[75] In her biographical study Gray confirms that although Johnson's views on religion were varied, "in the end, her Christian faith had prevailed."[76] An *Evening Record* editorial argued that her death "is somewhat a reflection on our civilization, for when this woman of parts was forced to take to the lecture platform in order to eke out a bare existence, her reward was a broken constitution."[77] In an unrelated story, the *Evening Record* boasted the following day that its exclusive coverage of an "Indian Maid Who Warned British of Pontiac" earlier that week had inspired the United States Steel corporation to rename a municipality "Ojibway" from "Pontiac" in her memory, illustrating an unwavering support by that newspaper for Indian princesses, generally.[78]

After its 8 March obituary the Toronto *Globe* narrowed its coverage of Johnson's death to a terse news item that reprinted a telegram from "His Royal Highness at Ottawa," the governor general to Major G.J. Smith of the Indian Department, expressing condolences to the "Chief of Six Nation Indians" regarding her death.[79] A saccharine response by the Six Nations council to express its appreciation of the "thoughtfulness" and sympathy extended by the Duke of Connaught in connection with the death of Pauline Johnson rounded out its coverage of her death.[80]

The Sudbury *Star* chose not to report on the death of Johnson. However, the paper continued its routine coverage of stereotypical constructions of Aboriginals. On 12 March, for example, it announced, "the liquor men of Sudbury experienced a regular field day on Monday afternoon when Indian Agent Cockburn of Sturgeon Falls had four of the local hotels or their bartenders on the carpet for selling 'booze' to two of his 'Red Men.'"[81] The paper's usage of "his red men" echoed the possessive force of colonial rhetoric found in the memorialization of Pauline Johnson and draws attention to the binaries present in press coverage.

In 1913 Canada, as it always has, struggled to shape its national identity. The press laboured tirelessly in this national pastime and, as we have seen, frequently employed an imagined Native to help with the work. In death as in life, E. Pauline Johnnson contributed to the effort. News of her death and funeral offered Canada's print media an extraordinary opportunity to send the beloved Indian princess off to the happy hunting grounds of its colonial dreamscape. Her status as racial hybrid worked in her favour, too, because it granted an ideological victory for Canadian readers; they could bask in the glow of a comfortable, sanitized image they could claim as part of their nation's belongings.

By claiming her as a possession, Canada could, in effect, lay further claim to land over which it had long taken control. The death of the "Indian Poetess" provided Canadians with yet another ceremony of possession. In addition to her hybrid racial makeup and her allegiance to patriotic organizations such as the Canadian Club and the IODE, the language of her poetry exerted a powerful force. Obituaries, editorials, and coverage of her funeral, in tandem with her poetry, generated a Canadian ideological perspective through language that celebrated the success and progress of a white Canada.

CHAPTER SIX

DISROBING GREY OWL
The Death of Archie Belaney, 1938

Action to establish her claim that she is the legal wife of Grey Owl, noted naturalist, who died today, is probable by Mrs. Angele Belaney, Temagami Indian, following Grey Owl's death in Prince Albert today. Press services list Grey Owl's survivors as his wife Silver Dawn and their six-year-old daughter. Mrs. Belaney, however, claims she married Grey Owl in 1910 and that he actually was a full-blooded white man named Belaney. Over long distance telephone three separate eyewitnesses to the wedding today described it to the *Nugget* and said they were positive the man they knew as Belaney and Grey Owl were one and the same.

—NORTH BAY *NUGGET*, 13 APRIL 1938

The mythic story of Grey Owl has inspired a passel of authors, comic-strip artists, and even Hollywood directors.[1] Even today, his books, which were best-sellers in their day, abound.[2] Parks Canada continues to extol his virtues, though its website carefully avoids noting that he was a fraud. In 1988 Prince Albert National Park celebrated the centennial of the birth of its "most famous citizen" with a "lively schedule of events."[3] In short, the would-be Indian may have died seventy years ago, but the fertile narrative surrounding Grey Owl and his place in the Canadian imagination endures.

He became a poster boy for Canadian colonialism. Grey Owl, at least before he was outed as a fake upon his death in 1938, had become the country's most famous Native son. As a noble savage par excellence Grey Owl seemed to personify everything the Canadian colonial imagination sought in its Aboriginals. Embraced by the nation as more real than the actual Indigenous peoples living in Canada in the 1930s, he was in fact "hyper real," in the sense used by French philosopher Jean Baudrillard. Baudrillard's application of the term "simulacrum"—a copy without an original, seems apropos.[4] Roland Barthes calls it a "second-order" sign, where the signifier has become unhinged from its source.[5] But this is misleading because the source of Grey Owl's sustainability was not so much of empirical reality as it was in the projection of Canadiana's need to justify the colonial project. Grey Owl served that function to near perfection. Not surprisingly, the press loved him.

That said, our interest in this chapter considers how the press processed and presented the news that he was a phony. Grey Owl was in fact Archie Belaney, a British-born immigrant who simply and effectively went Native. How could the world, for he was an international sensation—and Canada, a country that purports to know Natives well—be so completely taken in by a charlatan who lived among the beavers in Prince Albert National Park north of Saskatoon? The press, popular culture, identity politics, colonial discourse, and Archie Belaney himself all played roles in the construction of the hyperreal persona that Grey Owl exemplified.

Elizabeth Bird has noted that "for most White Americans, to live in a media world is to live with a smorgasbord of images that reflect back themselves." On the other hand, she continues, "American Indians...do not see themselves, except as expressed through a cultural script they do not recognize."[6] By the time Grey Owl came along, Canadian newspapers, as we have seen, had long since naturalized Native stereotypes, always preferring the imaginary to the empirical. In *Cannibal Culture*, art historian Deborah Root argues that Grey Owl's popularity thus derived from the fact that Belaney simply told non-Natives what they wanted to hear, the idea that "Native people did not actually concern themselves with politics and indeed were quite content with the colonial status quo."[7] Grey Owl defanged the savage. A stereotypical shaman/charlatan like Grey Owl paradoxically had greater credibility posing as a noble savage than he could have as a White man espousing the same message. For example, in 1934 the New York *Times* noted that watching over beavers "is a task assigned to a half-breed Indian who goes under the name of Grey Owl... Now he is studying how Canada can best save from extinction the animal whose skin was once 'the coin of the realm.'"[8] Grey Owl's notoriety stretched to England, also, where his outing sparked a number of news reports. The London *Times* praised him as the "Ambassador from the

Wild," reporting that he gave a short talk on "Indian customs and animal lore" for the royal family on his second visit to Buckingham Palace in 1937.[9] The London *Daily Express* uncovered links to his childhood home in Hastings, England, reporting that his schoolmates recalled how even as a boy "he used to come to class with snakes and lizards in his pockets, rubbed sticks together to make fire, whooped round the playground with Red Indian feathers round his head, whirling his tomahawk."[10]

Pretender or not, Grey Owl has his supporters. For example, Anishinaabe poet Armand Ruffo and comparative literature scholar Albert Braz view Grey Owl in a favourable light.[11] For Ruffo, Belaney's embrasure of Anishinaabe traditions makes him an attractive and credible character, while Braz contends Belaney's writings merit critical engagement because they offer a more complex reading of his identity than an automatic knee-jerk rejection, because of the fraud, normally earns him. Unconvinced by Ruffo or Braz's arguments, historian David Chapin posits that Grey Owl held tight to the stereotypical persona he forged as a youth despite being acquainted with a number of Indigenous people in Canada. Via his sartorial deception and his various popular writings he positioned himself as a liminal figure operating fluidly between civilization and savagery, precisely as he would claim in his own right.[12] Literary scholar Marjorie Garber has termed Grey Owl's use of straddling cultures as "the transvestite effect," arguing that he serves to illustrate complex layers of identity construction that eclipse facile notions of the binary.[13]

American cultural historian Philip Deloria cautions that stereotypes function as too simplistic an expression for analysis. He calls for an understanding of identity construction within a matrix of more complex terms such as discourse and ideology. In other words, stereotypes must be placed in cultural and historical context to be understood. The body of accepted knowledge about Aboriginal peoples relates closely to cultural terms of *expectation*, according to Deloria, situated within a backdrop of colonial and imperial relations of power and domination.[14] The ways in which the press fawned over Grey Owl supports this idea with some precision. With respect to Grey Owl, *expectation* was, in a sense, everything. Expectation, in fact, went so far as to trump empirical reality even after Grey Owl's death, while as the press, after some considerable unwillingness, accepted the fact that Grey Owl was not Aboriginal, it continued to promote the legend. In this way, Grey Owl remained a noble savage at the same time as he was not Aboriginal at all. In other words, settler society expected an imaginary Indian and Grey Owl comfortably performed the role.[15] In doing so, Canadian expectations of this noble savage—the comparatively good Indian, which is really a colonial oxymoron—produced and reinforced a discourse of colonial exclusion and racism, one confirmed by the press.

The press in the main unquestioningly embraced Belaney's exotically constructed identity as a mixed-blood Native whose mother was, according to Belaney, Apache. Adding mystery to his upbringing, Belaney fabricated for himself a birth at an Indian encampment near Hermosillo, Mexico, far from the Anishinaabe in Ontario or the Cree groups in Saskatchewan near whom he later lived and with whom he claimed close affinity. For a father, Belaney conjured up a story of a Scots-American guide—drawing upon the cultural resonance of a kind of Indian princess/Pocahontas fairy tale—to satisfy any questions about his Anglo features. In sum, his alien pedigree easily convinced adoring fans and the press alike.

When admixed with a long, glistening ponytail, rugged buckskin attire, and fluid loquaciousness Belaney secured himself a carte blanche to become Grey Owl—an identity unquestioned so long as it conformed to the stereotypical notion of the noble savage. Bird frames Grey Owl within the stereotype of the wise elder who "spoke with the accumulated wisdom of the people," a construction that was crucial to his acceptance.[16] Iconic conventions signified his nobility, long spoon-fed to Canadians in novels, Hollywood film, and other forms of popular culture, argues Daniel Francis.[17] His deep spiritual attachment to nature, his sage wisdom, his prowess in knife throwing, his uncivilized relationships with women (including a common-law coupling with an Ojibwe woman), his penchant for alcohol (he was actually an alcoholic), and his remarkable ability to spin a good story, all reinforced for Canadians what they believed were "authentic" Indian traits.

Shari Huhndorf's *Going Native* demonstrates that Belaney's success at fabricating a Native identity was not unique and she outlines a number of examples of American mainstream culture's interest in all things Native since the late nineteenth century.[18] Francis sketches a similar case about one Sylvester Long who stylized himself as "Buffalo Child Long Lance."[19] Chief Long Lance, who gained international fame in the 1920s when his fabricated autobiography became a best-seller, was then feted, according to Francis, in New York high society as a "Noble Savage in white tie and tails" whose message was akin to that of an "Aboriginal Horatio Alger."[20] Even as recently as 2003 the city of Regina, Saskatchewan, saw a similar masquerade unravel. A certain Charlie Smoke, self-professed Cree, turned out instead to be a non-Aboriginal white American citizen with a criminal record. He was deported.[21] In 1905 J.W. Schultz, the inspiration for the lead character in the Oscar-winning film *Dances with Wolves*, also attempted an identity transformation, according to Huhndorf.[22]

Arguing that although images of Indigenous peoples continued to serve as civilized society's "inferior 'other,'" Huhndorf finds that increasingly in the early twentieth century Natives helped the United States fashion a unique national identity separate from Europe.[23] Of course, the Western film and literary genre had always served that purpose in the United States. Questioning how race and nation have intertwined in American culture, Huhndorf views the 1893 World's Columbian Exposition held in Chicago a pivotal moment for intersections of race, nationalism, and imperialism in that it put Indigenous cultures from the American west on display for popular consumption and featured the delivery of Fredrick Jackson Turner's seminal Frontier Thesis.

Grey Owl similarly fits within a discourse in Canada that demonstrates a juncture that coalesces race, nationalism, and imperialism. Grey Owl served as an opportunity for Canadians to celebrate the imaginary noble savage. News coverage of his memorialization and subsequent outing reveal clearly a Canadian need to embrace the imaginary Indian.

"OUR BELOVED GREY OWL"

Grey Owl's connection to Saskatchewan began with his hire by the Dominion Parks Branch of Canada. As the Parks Branch's first Indigenous naturalist—first naturalist at all for that matter—Canada and the Parks Branch granted Grey Owl an institutional forum from and through which to express himself. He travelled extensively across North America and Europe, and even met with England's King George VI to discuss his ideas, all the while masquerading in buckskin and braids. Yet it was not Grey Owl's position as conservationist—though this clearly benefitted Parks Canada—that interested his fans; instead it was how flawlessly he played the noble savage, that imaginary colonial Indian archetype. Saskatchewan print media reports embraced Grey Owl as a local hero in the inital reports surrounding his death. The *Leader-Post* explained that he "filled an important niche in Prince Albert and community,"[24] while Saskatoon's mayor offered that his death "was a distinct loss to this Province and to Canada,"[25] referring to Belaney as *"our* beloved Grey Owl" (emphasis added), in short, a possession—Saskatchewan's special trophy Indian.[26]

Born in Hastings, England, in 1888 and raised by his aunts, Archibald Stansfield Belaney grew up captivated by press coverage of the travelling Buffalo Bill's Wild West Show and a romantic vision of Canada's Indigenous peoples.[27] He arrived in Canada in 1906 and quickly and adeptly styled himself as a Native. His cover gained credibility as he befriended a number of Native people in the Temagami region of northern Ontario. Plus, he was married twice to Native women. Thus Belaney begat Grey Owl.

Grey Owl, first a trapper and then a widely disseminated voice for conservation, began writing in an effort to protect the Canadian beaver. Articulate to a Western audience, he eloquently pitched his cause. Of course he had a distinct advantage in anglophile Canada. His English schooling far outmatched Canada's residential school system reserved for Natives. Initially he sold a number of stories in 1930 and 1931 to *Canadian Forest and Outdoors*, a Canadian Forestry Association publication, and later went on to publish a number of best-selling books about beavers and conservation. Editor of the *Canadian Forest* Gordon Dallyn found Grey Owl's beaver articles especially compelling, according to historian Donald Smith.[28] Dallyn forwarded the articles to James Harkin, then-Dominion Parks Branch Commissioner. Recognizing a golden marketing opportunity when he saw it, Harkin hatched an inspired plan that would make Grey Owl a household name in Canada at the same time as promote Canada's fledgling national park system.[29]

Working to protect the wood buffalo, musk ox, and caribou in various national parks, Grey Owl's writings and promotional efforts to protect the beaver immediately attracted Harkin. He sent the Parks Branch's publicity director J.C. Campbell to meet Grey Owl in Cabano in Témiscouata County on the New Brunswick border, where he had been living since 1928, trying to establish a beaver colony while he wrote.[30] Campbell pressed Grey Owl into action in aiding the production of a short 1929 film about Jelly Roll and Rawhide, two beavers, explaining that such a film might benefit both their aims to "provide a living argument for conservation."[31] Grey Owl agreed, and thus began the relationship between the Parks Branch and the imaginary Indian.

Harkin's next step was pure marketing genius. In 1931 he decided to bring Grey Owl west and to employ him as a naturalist.[32] What better way to attract tourists and needed money to Canada's national parks than with such a compelling personality? Years later, Harkin confirmed his motivations. "The providing of a position for Grey Owl," he wrote, was entirely to serve our purpose of securing publicity for the National Parks and for wild life conservation by using Grey Owl's beaver and Grey Owl's personality as a spear-head in that connection."[33]

Early in 1931 Grey Owl accepted Harkin's offer and moved with his common-law Mohawk wife, Anahareo (sometimes called Silver Dawn) nee Gertrude Bernard, and his beavers to a cabin in Riding Mountain National Park in Manitoba. However, conditions were not ideal for the beavers, and soon Harkin moved them to Prince Albert National Park in Saskatchewan.[34] The 5000-square-kilometre area of boreal forest had only become a park in 1927. In an effort to sell Parliament on the potential profitability of parks, Harkin had opened Prince Albert National Park for summer car tourists. Housing Grey Owl there would, he hoped, spark the traffic needed to secure greater government funding. This move strategically benefitted Harkin's aims and brought celebrity status to Saskatchewan's new park. Grey Owl became a spectacle, and his story titillated Saskatchewanians, as it did fellow Canadians, who flocked to the park to meet their adopted celebrity Native son.[35]

Major James A. Wood, superintendent of the Prince Albert National Park, located Grey Owl at Ajawaan Lake and had "Beaver Lodge," his all-in-one cabin with attached beaver lodge, built to meet Grey Owl's specifications, complete with an indoor beaver run. The site quickly became a popular visitor centre where Grey Owl welcomed sightseers interested in wildlife. He performed his role so marvellously that Canadians and the world came to follow the quirky life of this exaggerated fellow. Thus, Grey Owl became a fixture of the park and Canadian society as a figure who satisfied the Anglo-Canadian desire for colonialism to work. And who better to play the role than Grey Owl, an Indian with British sensibilities.

A province with a wide variety of Indigenous groups including Dene, Cree, Saulteaux, Dakota, and Assiniboine, many of whom were signatories to Treaty 4 in 1874 or Treaty 6 in 1876, Saskatchewan had a long and problematic history with its original peoples, including two rounds of trouble with Louis Riel and his supporters.[36] The clashes between settler populations, Métis, and First Nations predictably began with immigration, as whites moved westward to take up trapping and farming.[37] Twentieth-century relations were not appreciably better.[38]

Saskatchewan became a province in 1905, and the dominant provincial narratives centred on agriculture and immigration. By the early 1930s John Tootoosis, from Poundmaker First Nation, emerged as a strong uniting force among the Cree. When Grey Owl moved to Saskatchewan, Tootoosis was already travelling throughout the province strengthening membership in the nascent League of Indians of Canada, attempting to challenge the federal government's Department of Indian and Northern Affairs (INAC) behaviour and policy.[39]

Grey Owl's relocation to Saskatchewan was not personally motivated—he did not choose the province—yet local newspapers rallied around him because he seemed to fulfill the desire for evidence that colonialism was working. When, for example, in November 1936 Grey Owl spoke at the Hotel Saskatchewan in Regina on his way to a book fair in Toronto, Ontario, the Regina *Leader-Post* championed Grey Owl's ability to attract international attention to the province—Dutch scholar Professor Van der Steen and Canada's governor general, Lord Tweedsmuir, had both visited Grey Owl in Prince Albert Park that summer, after all. The report forged ties between the Royal designate, Saskatchewan and Grey Owl: "When Lord Tweedsmuir visited the cabin this past summer, he was greatly interested in being shown the territory and tramped through the brush with Grey Owl."[40] For an unglamorous province easily overlooked, such news served as a form of much wanted boosterism.[41] In short, Grey Owl drew attention precisely as Harkin had hoped.

"A REAL FLESH AND BLOOD INDIAN"

It remains difficult to assess how Grey Owl viewed his place within Saskatchewan's Indigenous population. In 1984 John Tootoosis's daughter Jean Goodwill with Norma Sluman interviewed the elder Tootoosis who told a story that helps provide some degree of context for Grey Owl's sense of identity. In 1936 while in Ottawa on government business, Grey Owl met Tootoosis unexpectedly at a Chinese restaurant. Neither planned the meeting but both knew of the other and, according to his interlocutors, Grey Owl approached Tootoosis's table and asked him if he was an Indian. Ironically, it was Grey Owl who sported braids and buckskins and looked the part while Tootoosis, though swarthy skinned, was dressed in Western garb and had short, black hair.[42] After the Cree chief acknowledged his identity and explained he was from Saskatchewan, Grey Owl said he, too, was an "Indian" from Saskatchewan.[43]

The two men soon became friendly, write Goodwill and Sluman, and when Grey Owl discovered Tootoosis was in the city alone and did not have a hotel or contacts, he generously invited the Cree leader back to his hotel room. Tootoosis recalled that Grey Owl declared him his brother and said, "I am going to call you Brother from now on."[44] Grey Owl then explained to his Cree "brother" that he was Ojibwe (not Apache). When Tootoosis noticed his host's hand drum in the hotel room, Grey Owl offered to play and sing for his guest. Tootoosis confided that as soon as he heard Grey Owl sing an Ojibwe song, he knew Grey Owl was no Indian. Tootoosis explained that he had always kept this knowledge to himself, however, because he respected the efforts Grey Owl had made in promoting conservation in Saskatchewan.[45]

While Tootoosis fought tirelessly for treaty rights and better treatment for Indigenous peoples in residential schools across Canada, a struggle that fell largely on deaf ears, Grey Owl apparently felt no such pressure as an acknowledged Aboriginal of considerable influence. Unlike Tootoosis, who was constantly haunted by his twelve painful years in residential school, his Saskatchewanian "brother" performatively inhabited a radically different racial space—one constructed in response to and enabled by mainstream colonial amnesia, unfettered by untidy empirical reality.[46] Grey Owl was thus free to focus on conservation issues, nonthreatening matters the Canadian public had an interest in hearing about from a noble savage.

In sum, upon the eve of his death in 1938, Grey was famous, even adored in some quarters. Nowhere in the news was there a suspicion evinced that he was a fraud. In a report that identified him as a "well-known Indian naturalist," Grey Owl maligned non-rational, Indigenous observational practices. "GREY OWL NOT IMPRESSED WITH THOSE WHO FORETELL FROM ANIMALS" explained that he believed that observing the activity of animals to predict weather involved " 'a great deal of hooey'."[47]

Given his fame, Grey Owl's untimely death on 13 April 1938 did not go unnoticed in the local, national, or international press. What happened first was that accolades filled Canadian news dailies from sea to sea.[48] Photographs of Grey Owl in buckskins, long braids, a stoic stance, and a lone eagle feather headdress accompanied most newspaper stories, emphasizing those visual signifiers that unmistakably read "Indian." Textual references were no less obvious, such as the Lethbridge *Herald*'s characterization of him as "a child of the forest and streams."[49] Headlines shouted, "Death of A Noted Canadian Indian," and "Grey Owl Dies True to Indian Teachings."[50]

Not surprisingly, it was to the Parks Branch that the press turned for official word about his death. Superintendent Wood became the key quotable, credible source in the reports of Grey Owl's passing that ran throughout Canadian newspapers on that day. He explained that a recent six-month tour with stops in England, the United States, and selected cities in Canada had "apparently robbed him of resistance."[51] Relying on the wire service for the structure of the news item, most daily papers from Halifax to Victoria included much of the same basic information, framed largely around Wood's expert testimony.[52] Many papers then added additional information to the basic storyline in efforts to personalize the event for their particular readerships, such as the Windsor *Daily Star* report that included a photograph and short description recalling Grey Owl's recent tour of Windsor where he met with children from the local John Campbell School.[53]

Editorials published in Canadian dailies the following day provided ample evidence of how the press viewed Grey Owl. The descriptive language thoughtfully chosen to honour this icon illustrates a combination of praise and pride, tempered by an acknowledgment of his inferior savage, albeit noble, status in civilized society. On 14 April 1938 a romantically poetic editorial titled "A Gentle Indian Goes," appeared in the Ottawa *Citizen*: "He has gone now...it seems that the rigors of a traveling lectureship undermined his resistance. If this theory of his fatal illness is correct, it proves again that men used to living a simple and primitive existence in the wilds are under a great handicap when they follow 'civilization's' paths."[54] Descriptors such as "simple," "primitive," "in the wilds," reinforced the construction of the noble savage but also the moribund Native who was destined to die off. It seemed as if civilization, precisely as the press had long prophesied, had indeed been too much for the man. He died at the age of fifty.

The Hamilton *Spectator* ran a similar editorial that day. "To Grey Owl," it reasoned, "the halls of civilization were probably a dream, gaudy and incomprehensible. His real story remains as silent as the forests—the forests where creatures, inarticulate and pleading, will come to find a friend who has gone."[55] Such romantic drivel, extolling Grey Owl as it marginalized him as if he were the idiot spawn of nature, situated the man as attractive but firmly inferior to mainstream Canadians, and dredged up the very same signifiers Belaney had so artfully employed.

In similar vein a Windsor *Daily Star* editorial called the "great Indian" a "friend of the animals,"[56] while the Winnipeg *Free Press* wrote an editorial that cast the "lover of wild life" as someone who "belonged" to the forest. The *Free Press* voiced an opinion that surely confounded Canada's colonial sense of order. "He was an Indian but taught whites,"[57] the daily remarked.

An Edmonton *Journal* editorial about "a Great Indian" proclaimed, "while he had had little schooling, he had the great gift of expressing himself clearly and pleasingly."[58] The paper concluded, "The world of Canadian letters has suffered a real loss in the death of this native son who held that the good Indian had as fine traditions behind him as any the white man can boast."[59] The Vancouver *Province*'s editorial boldly compared Grey Owl to Snow White, but noted that "Grey Owl was no animated figure from a Walt Disney picture, but a real flesh and blood Indian from the back country."[60] Given Belaney's elaborate charade, the *Province*'s comparison of Grey Owl to Snow White may not have been altogether misplaced, though Disney's *Pocahontas* seems the better referent today.[61] A want of civilizing graces, lack of formal schooling, his spiritual relationship to the forest, the emphasis on him as a "good Indian" and perennial outsider, Grey Owl's ability to interpret the wilderness for Western civilization, all helped explain the figure imagined by the press.

Closer to his adopted home, the Prince Albert *Daily Herald*, the Saskatoon *Star Phoenix*, and the Regina *Leader-Post* issued a remarkably callow Saskatchewan perspective on the events surrounding the death of Grey Owl—local boy makes good. These three papers demonstrate a loyalty to the man echoed by other papers in Canada, with an additional twist—the Saskatchewan papers proudly claimed ownership. And, as papers across the nation exploited the titillating details relating to his subsequent outing, the Saskatchewan news remained solid supporters of Grey Owl well after evidence to the contrary seemed to have carried the point.

The Prince Albert *Daily Herald*, the paper closest to the park, mourned his loss with a banner headline and story, complete with several photographs of the naturalist and his beloved beavers.[62] The Saskatoon *Star Phoenix* devoted nearly a full page of coverage news of the demise of the "famed Indian naturalist" on 13 April 1938.[63] The story ran next to an unconnected story, headlined "First Scalp for Mounties," a tale about a recent RCMP prosecution of a local man for unlawfully operating a private automobile as a taxicab.[64] While the report may have been unrelated to Aboriginal issues, the use of "scalp" as a signifier promulgated an image of savagery, and the juxtaposition served to heighten Grey Owl's stature by way of comparison. The cover page provided a laudatory account of Grey Owl's recent six-week British tour where he met with King George VI.[65] The paper's obituary quoted Grey Owl, "'I started as a poor frightened savage on a stage in a theatre in London in 1906 with Buffalo Bill and I ended up talking to King George in Buckingham Palace.'"[66] With pride bursting, the Saskatoon broadsheet forged the famed impostor's provenance to Saskatchewan: "His tour, lectures and introductions to the prominent people of Britain and the United States appealed to Grey Owl but not as strongly as Saskatchewan's timbered north country...Grey Owl hurried back to Beaver Lodge."[67] The *Star Phoenix* coverage concludes by recalling a statement Grey Owl made to an eleven-year-old while on his latest tour: "Indian lad who had just had his leg amputated and said to him, 'Have courage, my boy, you have a lot to live for but above all never forget that you are an Indian.'"[68] In this way, as with other editorial commemorations of his death, Grey was remembered initially—fondly, almost reverently, and without suspicion—precisely as he had been in real life.

An adjoining report offered readers a further local connection to the dead celebrity Indian. It was announced that during a joint conference of the Prince Albert and Saskatoon Boards of Trade, Saskatoon's mayor R.M. Pinder stated that the "death of the famous Indian naturalist was a distinct loss to this Province and to Canada. He had spread the message of Prince Albert National Park throughout the Empire."[69] In short, Grey Owl's unique brand of tourism marketing had worked well for the province, and the province was grateful for it.

On 14 April the Prince Albert paper called Grey Owl's death "A Severe Loss to Indians" and explained how, because of his influence, regular assemblies had taken place between regional Cree First Nations in Saskatchewan and that later in 1938 a third assembly was planned that "would see a move towards consolidating Indian thought here, under his guidance."[70] The story, which obviously endorsed his racial legitimacy, did not provide support for this position by local Cree leaders. No mention of his "brother" John Tootoosis or the work he had done in creating assemblies among the Cree found its way into the story.[71] The headline and story do, however, provide a context for understanding settler considerations of Grey Owl as a chosen spokesman for Indigenous peoples in Saskatchewan—as well as on a national stage.

In step with the Prince Albert *Daily Herald*, the Saskatoon *Star Phoenix* ran a headline that day that read, "Grey Owl Champion of Indians: Considered Himself as Link Between White and Red Man."[72] Prefacing the article by stating that Grey Owl's death was "believed to have involved a severe loss to the Indian people of Western Canada," the staff correspondent from North Battleford reported: "Less than a year ago, Grey Owl wrote to a friend here: 'I am taking very seriously the responsibility that seems to have come to me as a connecting link, an intermediary between the whiteman and the Indian. I have an unparalleled opportunity with my Indian mind, training and experience, and my lucky entry into the public life of the civilized world to act as interpreter for both.'"[73]

All three Saskatchewan dailies stressed Grey Owl's leadership role perhaps in the hope that his noble savagery might rub off favourably on other Saskatchewan Indigenous peoples who were less tractable than the colonial poster boy. The possibility that Grey Owl occupied a liminal space as some kind of evolutionary missing link seems moot, despite his quoted musings, however, considering that he was a fraud.

The Regina *Leader-Post* confirmed Grey Owl's importance to the province in its 16 April coverage of Grey Owl's funeral by quoting Canon Strong, the Anglican minister who presided over the event. "Grey Owl had filled an important niche in Prince Albert," said the minister, who conceded that Grey Owl was skeptical about Christianity.[74] "But the happy hunting grounds of the Indian braves could easily be compared with the meaning the Christian church entertained of a hereafter," interpreted the clergyman as he easily assimilated noble savage type spirituality into a Christian context.[75]

"A BIT THICK"

It was the North Bay *Nugget* in northern Ontario that outed Grey Owl when, upon receiving the wire report of his death, it ran an article the paper had sat patiently on for three years, waiting until Grey Owl died before publication. The article, with photographs, encompassed the entire front page of the *Nugget* on 13 April 1938. Shockingly, it stated that one Mrs. Angele Belaney, his Anishinaabe former first common-law wife, claimed that Grey Owl "is not an Indian but a full-blood white man, probably of English descent who settled in Temagami in the early days of the district."[76] Ed Bunyan, the editor of the North Bay *Nugget*, had honourably protected the famous conservationist and kept the story under wraps until his demise. As newspapers across the English-speaking world pounced on the story, Grey Owl was being treated to a respectable burial next to his beloved Beaver Lodge on the shores of Ajawaan Lake.

While some western dailies took little note of the sudden and remarkable twist to Grey Owl's narrative, including the Halifax *Herald*, the Winnipeg *Free Press*, the Calgary *Herald*, and the Victoria *Daily Colonist*, the Ontario press, including the Sudbury *Star*, Windsor *Daily Star*, and the Toronto *Star*, excitedly followed the unfolding events, providing a surfeit of items both to prove and to disprove his Aboriginal provenance. Within the week the story had become a sensation in Ontario. Headlines pointed in a variety of directions: "Who Was Grey Owl? Controversy Grows," "Grey Owl Really an Englishman, Old Friends Insist: Made Himself Indian in Body and Spirit Fulfilled His Dreams," "Documents to Show Naturalist Run-Away High-Born Britisher," "'Grey Owl No Half-Breed' Says Man Who Nursed Him," "Toronto Publisher Sure Grey Owl's Mother Indian," "Grey Owl in Kilty Outfit: War Veteran Tells How He Met Belaney in Folkstone: Mexican Blood," and "English Wife and Mother of Belaney Found."[77] Depending on what you read, he was either British, an Aboriginal, or a Mexican.

Meanwhile, both the Regina *Leader-Post* and the Saskatoon *Star Phoenix* initially resisted reporting the controversial news from North Bay, until 16 April. However, along the bottom edge of the Prince Albert *Daily Herald* front page on 14 April ran an inconspicuous yet startling headline, "Grey Owl Was English, Not Indian, Says Guide." The story provided an abbreviated report from the North Bay *Nugget* explaining for the local Prince Albert readership that a certain William Guppy had known Grey Owl as Archie Belaney: "In 1906 when I first met him in Temiskaming [northern Ontario], Archie Belaney was a young Englishman, just doing nothing among all the others who were swarming into that country about the time of the Cobalt gold rush...The next thing I knew he was Grey Owl...but we will never forget him as the young Englishman whom we liked very much."[78]

Two days later, under the headline, "Friends Declare Grey Owl Really Was Part Indian," the *Star Phoenix* refuted the veracity of the *Nugget* scoop. The paper sought to shift the story's focus from Ontario back to Saskatchewan where "local friends," it reported, "still insist that the naturalist was not sailing under false colors in claiming to be part Indian."[79] The paper contended that Grey Owl had deliberately fooled people into thinking he was English so as to facilitate permanent residency in Canada. The reasoning held that he did not want to return to the U.S. after touring with the Wild West Show and instead wished to come to Canada and remain there.

Taken completely by surprise, Park Superintendent Wood also officially decried the *Nugget*'s revelation. Wood, a close friend, defended Grey Owl's claim to Native heritage and stated that the park naturalist had fooled editor Guppy into thinking he was British because he was an adept mimic. "He [Grey Owl] had no difficulty in putting the cockney accent on a bit thick,"[80] Wood told the *Star Phoenix*, though this hardly explained the affair. Wood's best defence of Grey Owl's Aboriginality was deeply ironic. He deployed the noble savage, a colonial shell game in its own right, in order to prove his friend's authenticity. For example, he recalled Grey Owl's prowess in knife throwing as convincing evidence of his Indigenous identity: "I remember once last summer that Grey Owl stood at one end of his cabin and with unerring aim he picked off the knot in the logs in the opposite wall with his knives. He had often demonstrated his ability in this fashion to friends who visited him."[81] Apparently, only a real Indian could throw knives like that. Two days later the *Star Phoenix* offered additional evidence by Wood under the headline, "SQUATTED LIKE INDIAN."[82]

As more details of Belaney's double life surfaced, contradictory theories about the twentieth-century Hiawatha filled papers.[83] But the *Star Phoenix* and the *Leader-Post* refused to budge, solidly supporting Grey Owl's bogus identity. Likewise a letter to the editor in the Toronto *Star* under the headline, "An Indian Lament," attempted to counter the *Star*'s coverage of Belaney's double life. Signed by "Big White Owl," who called himself Grey Owl's "brother," the letter expounded upon Grey Owl's virtues, wrought in stereotypical prose that was filled with symbolic references to the noble savage:

> Some people say that he was a white man. I don't care if he was! He loved us so much that he gave his entire life to us. All too soon his mellow voice was broken. But the echo of his appealing voice will continue to resound and sing to us from books for moons to come...Whenever I walk down the aisles of whispering pine, stately maples, mighty elms and graceful birches, I shall feel his presence there because he was like a real grey owl flying across the sunlit sky...Brave warrior and great romancer, he fought the good fight.[84]

On 19 April, the *Star Phoenix* maintained that naturalization records provided by Grey Owl attested to Mexico as his birthplace. However, the article oddly also conceded defeat, admitting that the weight of evidence no longer supported this position.[85] But the next day a Regina *Leader-Post* story kept hope alive by citing quotes from Grey Owl's estranged second Aboriginal wife, Anahareo, who was recuperating from surgery in a Regina hospital when Grey Owl died. "Grey Owl Indian, Says His Widow Denying 'Gossip,'" shouted the front-page headline. While the story may not have carried the argument, it served well as testament to the observation that local press invariably experiences crises more conservatively, because of vested emotional interests, than does its more distant kin. The article continued, "Added to the controversy over the birth and race of the famous Saskatchewan naturalist is the voice of Silver Moon, his widow...Mrs. Grey Owl, nee Yvonne Perrier...is a graduate of a Roman Catholic convent, an educated Canadian girl, and a rather attractive brunette, with laughing eyes...The stories have fired her Indian blood for Yvonne Perrier's paternal grandmother was a full-blooded Montagnes Indian."[86] Here the *Leader-Post* stressed "Silver Moon's" (on 16 April the paper identified her as "Silver Dawn") own Indigenous heritage as if they might somehow buttress Grey Owl's identity by association. Playing to the noble half of the savage brand, the paper also emphasized her Christian roots, noting that she and Grey Owl had been married by a United Church minister, in an effort to reassure Saskatchewan's settler readership of the couple's credibility and their impending assimilation into mainstream society. The passage also casts her as a classic sexualized female, calling her a "rather attractive brunette, with laughing eyes," and noting that her "Indian blood" had "fire" in it.[87] Later that summer Anahareo admitted she knew of Grey Owl's false identity, according to the *Leader-Post*.[88]

"I DON'T CARE WHETHER HE WAS AN ENGLISHMAN, IRISHMAN, SCOTSMAN OR NEGRO"

Unlike the other two provincial dailies, the Prince Albert *Daily Herald*, the paper closest to the epicentre, did not discount the news of Grey Owl's counterfeit identity; in fact, it devoted much of its front page to the controversy on 20 April, but gave the story a local twist. Accompanied by a large photo of Grey Owl and Anahareo at an Ontario bird sanctuary, with Grey Owl dressed in fully beaded regalia, a single eagle feather rising from his head, the paper confirmed reports of his English heritage that the *Leader-Post* and the *Star Phoenix* had vehemently denied. Identifying the local Prince Albert informant as one Mrs. Ross, widow to former Mountie Harry E. Ross and a "local aged confidante" she had been, according to the paper, bound to secrecy by Grey Owl. His death, thankfully, had "released her from the bond."[89] In the report Ross explained that she once confronted Grey Owl about his physical appearance: "'Indians don't have blue eyes,'" she claimed to have said, and to have received the reply, "'That's right, I am not an Indian. I was born of English parents, had a fair education.'"[90] Quizzing him further, Mrs. Ross stated in the article that she had asked Belaney if he could dance like the Indians, to which he replied, "'Sure I can'... and he got up and did a Sioux dance and chanted the accompanying refrain as well as any Sioux could do.'"[91] This local angle did not make the Canadian Press wire service as the North Bay *Nugget* story had, nor was it mentioned in the *Star Phoenix* or the *Leader-Post*. It did, however, afford local residents their own independent credible source in outing the celebrity.

In the ensuing days the *Star Phoenix* resistance began to crumble under the weight of its own reportage. It ran wide-ranging claims concerning Grey Owl's identity, with his birthplace ranging from Mexico to Manitoba, Montreal to England.[92] Then on 23 April it attempted an exquisite colonial pas de deux. It asked readers whether Grey Owl's background really mattered: "Whether Grey Owl was an Englishman living as an Indian, or a Scot, or a Canadian or a Mexican, it is not disputed that he was a naturalist, a conservationist and a lover of nature, whose life work has been of value to Canada."[93] The paper concluded that Grey Owl had served Canada well, and with that readers were encouraged to forget that the man had hoodwinked them. Yes, it was better by far to suppress reality and continue to valorize him rather than concede a nation's gullibility, a credulity itself built upon a monument to the colonial imagination. And the stakes seemed especially high, after all, for the province that had shown him much love.

Similarly, the Regina *Leader-Post* on 25 April implored readers to "Forget Petty Things" regarding Grey Owl, as it quoted Major Wood's unflagging endorsement: "Grey Owl was a great man...If Grey Owl was a faker and a bounder my respect for him as a literary man and as a naturalist would have been lowered as the years passed. But every year that I knew him my respect for him deepened."[94] In other words, to reject Grey Owl was to reject the major, to reject Canada itself. Thus Wood, in seeking to protect his own park's reputation, and in effect, Canada's stature, nonsensically contended that Grey Owl had fought for the "rehabilitation of the Indian to their old-time dignity, independence and pride of race." Wood's comments reinforced Canada's wish to remake Aboriginal peoples from their childlike state into stereotypical manifestations of the noble savage.[95]

But it was not only Saskatchewan news editors who wished to preserve Grey Owl as a frozen-in-time Indian. A 21 April editorial in the Calgary *Herald* defended his presumed identity by denying the empirical truth. "Now that Grey Owl has passed to the Happy Hunting Grounds the point raised may never be fully settled," said the *Herald*. But more important anyway is his life work and the valuable legacy he left to the world."[96] The paper concluded that "whether he was part Indian or all white is a matter of little consequence to him who sleeps in the northern wilderness near the beaver lodges he loved so well."[97] The St. John *Telegraph-Journal* printed a similar editorial on 26 April that attempted to make sense out of the media blitz it painted unflatteringly as "a quite unexpected storm in a teacup."[98] The editorial indicated the paper's ongoing support for the imaginary persona, asserting that Native origin was not the issue:

> At last the late Grey Owl is showing signs of getting off the front page…Frankly, what does it matter whether he was pure Indian, pure English, or half-breed? He chose to give out that he was an Indian. There has been no shadow of suggestion by those who now furnish him with another name and another race that his alleged misrepresentation was in any sense fraudulent…He furnished inspiration and entertainment of a sort…Let us leave Grey Owl's work and record to speak for him. He himself kept his two identities separate, and it is to his life as Grey Owl that the world gave recognition.[99]

But "frankly" it did matter; it had always mattered. Grey Owl's legitimacy derived from his professed Aboriginality. To claim that he was not a fraud in the same breath as acknowledging that he was a fraud while insisting that it did not make any difference suggests a deeper psychological game of denial at work, common to Canada's colonial project.

Once it became no longer tenable to deny the evidence that Belaney had duped Canada, the press responded in unison by saying that it did not care. The new argument held that race had little to do with Grey Owl after all. Wood eventually adopted this stance as he sought to valorize his poster boy by summarizing the man's work in a tribute published in the summer of 1938, titled *Green Leaf: A Memorial to Grey Owl*. Wood wrote, "I care not whether he was an Englishman, Irishman, Scotsman or Negro. He was a great man with a great mind, and with great objectives which he ever kept before him… He will be remembered for his courageous stand in regard to blood sports, and finally, he will be remembered for his efforts to rehabilitate the Indian, to the point where he would again possess some of his old-time dignity and independence."[100] Clearly, if he believed in the "old-time dignity and independence" of Native people, Wood had not been reading Canadian newspapers since 1869. Even as publications ultimately agreed that Grey Owl was little more than a mere English-born Canadian, they tended to maintain his cover—and their own. If Grey Owl was no longer Indigenous surely Canadians could preserve his memory as a crusader to help move other Aboriginals closer to a noble savage construction that everyone seemed so much more comfortable with. In short, without Grey Owl, the noble savage had little currency in the press.

Weeks later when Canada's newspapers had turned their attention to other business of the day, the *Leader-Post* printed a letter to the editor on 9 May that in almost guileless perfection expressed the sentiment that illustrated the source of Grey Owl's enduring support. Referring to "our beloved Grey Owl," Mrs. O. Ryan wrote:

> A name which will go down in the hearts and minds of Canadian people for decades to come. A name to ride along with that of Pauline Johnson, another part-Indian who will live as long as Canada herself...It seems to me that only a mixture of blood such as he claimed could produce a person with so romantic a nature, such endurance to accomplish his achievements, such patience and perseverance, mixed with the pluck to put his ideas across alike from pauper to 'their majesties'...In my opinion he deserves the credit of a hero. A hero who mingled with and was loved by the commonest of people, namely, the Indian, and yet he was entertained by lords, ladies, and royalty.[101]

The letter writer conjures a colonial dreamscape where Natives had become tractable, softened by Canada's imperial project. And she was quite right to prophesy that Grey Owl's masquerade "will live as long as Canada herself" because the colonial dream is Canada's imagined community. Without it, Grey Owl, Canada's noble emperor of the forest, would indeed have become buck-naked.

Disrobing Belaney, which challenged and thus disturbed the press's role in the promotion of colonialism, ultimately was solved by palatable amnesia. As a cultural construct, Grey Owl not so much eased a guilty conscience as he provided direct evidence that colonialism worked. The press also loved him because it had part ownership of him, as all Canadians did. By ignoring Belaney in favour of Grey Owl after his fake identity was confirmed, Canadians were able to preserve the national fantasy as they eschewed the embarrassment of being outed themselves. In the end, as in the beginning, it was a frozen-in-time noble savage that the press sought and *expected*. Packaged in buckskins and braids, the Englishman, in a predictable stereotypical garb, fluidly captivated and convinced the media. For shy and awkward Saskatchewan, adopting the internationally famous noble savage as its Native son was almost too good to be true. Accepting the fact that they had been duped was not an easy pill for provincial papers to swallow and so they mostly chose to disregard the claims for as long as they possibly could. The furious backpedalling that later occurred—the about-face claims that Grey Owl's Native ancestry was of no consequence when earlier it had been his single claim to legitimacy—illustrates that identity for the press, as for Grey Owl, remained a malleable object to be shaped and reconfigured as needed.

Grey Owl furnished Canadians with something First Nations' leaders such as John Tootoosis could not achieve, a Native that white society could admire. Grey Owl was believable precisely because—only because—he was a phony, an empirical fake, yet a perfectly authentic colonial stooge. The press and the public alike were more at ease with his romanticized package than they were interacting with actual Indigenous people. Thus, despite claims by some newspapers that race did not matter, it clearly did. But it was caught up in fantasy. Belaney, the Englishman, counted for nothing. His manufactured identity, however, was invaluable; the central issue of race was simply rationalized away. In this manner, papers, after an initial hiccup, succeeded in preserving Grey Owl as their formidable noble savage, a figure Parks Canada still refers to as a "cultural treasure."[102] It required turning around the old colonial endeavour of killing the Indian to save the man; in the case of Grey Owl, the press chose to kill the man in order to save the imaginary Indian.[103]

CHAPTER SEVEN

"POTENTIAL INDIAN CITIZENS?"
Aboriginal People after World War II, 1948

Around the clearing the ring of pale faces pressed closer as Chief Poking Fire raised his scalping knife and laid its sharp point against Hiawatha's sweating temple. The brave threw some cedar boughs on the fire and it crackled into flame, lighting up the stern features of Poking Fire and the drawn face of his victim.

"Ugh!" said Poking Fire.

"How!" muttered Laying Fire, the Medicine Man.
Hiawatha groaned, wrestled with the thongs of deer hide that bound him to the scalping post...

"Is he really goin' ter cut the man's head off Daddy?"
asked a small, scared voice.

"Shucks, no son! They're just showing up an old Indian custom."

All day Saturday and Sunday Chief Poking Fire and his people made pow-wow and danced, and did a rip-roaring business in hot dogs and French-fries with the hundreds of tourists and trippers who came to see the show.

—MONTREAL *GAZETTE*, 23 AUGUST 1948

During World War II, thousands of First Nations[1] men and women joined Canada's armed forces and more than 200 lost their lives on foreign battle-fields.[2] In Saskatchewan alone over 440 enlisted in military service. When the war ended, Canada's First Nations had proven themselves worthy com-patriots. Like their comrades, First Nations veterans looked forward to returning home to enjoy the hard-fought-for benefits.

R. Scott Sheffield's *The Red Man's on the Warpath* charts modification in Canadian media representations of Aboriginals during the war, arguing that newly manifested depictions encompassed a wider range of imagery, mostly positive. Sheffield shows that stories of enlistment and tales of Aboriginal patriotism began to permeate media reports and that by 1941 the negative contemporary image of the violent Indigenous criminal had begun to wane in favour of a positive "Indian-at-War" image, though not one necessarily free of stereotyping. This newer and more respectable construction carried through the end of the war and led to a national impetus for improving conditions of Aboriginal peoples across Canada, he concludes.[3] Our reading of Canadian newspapers shows that by 1948 any wartime honeymoon period with regard to Indigenous representation had come to an abrupt halt in the English-language press. If, as Sheffield argues, war news had effected more positive portrayals of Aboriginals based on "empathy" and "pity,"[4] coverage in 1948 remained remarkably consistent with what had come in earlier decades. Yet Sheffield's conclusion has an analogue to this study in that, as shown, the 1885 war elicited near-hysteria in depictions of all things Aboriginal, a tone and pace engendered by the espied seriousness of the conflict. Once the crisis passed, coverage in a sense righted itself. We will witness a similar phenomenon in chapter 9, around coverage of the so-called "Bended Elbow" uprising in Kenora, Ontario, during the summer of 1974. What Sheffield identifies, then, as an improvement would seem to be one side of a durable piece of currency.

Upon victory abroad, Canada turned its attention to a reconsideration of the Indian Act, an attempt to try to altruistically evaluate Canada's "Indian Problem." Miller contends that an awareness of Aboriginal substandard living conditions arose after the war. "In the midst of a war against institutional racism and barbarity," writes Miller, "it was impossible not to notice that the bases of Canadian Indian policy lay in assumptions about the moral and economic inferiority of particular racial groupings. The horrors of war seriously discomfited Canadians when, on rare occasions, they looked at the way in which they treated the Aboriginal peoples of their country."[5]

Systemic racism and an archaic bureaucratic administration system that did not accommodate First Nations considerations led veterans' organizations and church groups to mount a campaign that resulted in a Special Joint Committee of the Senate and the House of Commons (sJC).[6] The sJC formed in the spring of 1946 to examine broadly issues of enfranchisement, treaty rights and obligations, taxes, the operation of residential schools, and any other matters related to the social and economic status of First Nations peoples and their advancement.[7] The report was completed in June 1948, though it was not until 1951 that any changes were made to the Indian Act. The sJC final report envisioned a utopian future relationship between Canada and its Indigenous peoples that Sheffield describes conceptually as the "potential Indian citizen" but that Aboriginal leaders of the day criticized. Olive Dickason claims that James Gladstone, an Alberta Blood who later became Canada's first Native senator (in 1958), argued that the first draft of the report would further erode special rights rather than improve relations.[8] Even after additional consultation with Aboriginal advisors the report maintained its assimilationist goals.

In this chapter we have chosen to examine press coverage related to Aboriginal peoples from 1 July to 30 September 1948 by analyzing fourteen regional dailies across Canada, including the Calgary *Herald*, Edmonton *Journal*, Fredericton *Daily Gleaner*, Halifax *Herald*, Hamilton *Spectator*, Montreal *Gazette*, Regina *Leader-Post*, St. John's *Evening Telegram*, Sudbury *Star*, Toronto *Globe and Mail*, Toronto *Star*, Vancouver *Province*, Victoria *Daily Colonist*, and Winnipeg *Free Press*. Given the shift in press representations accorded Aboriginal people during the war period, we queried whether those changes were maintained after the war. Additionally, given the lofty goals of the sJC report, this period seemed like a constructive point from which to gauge changes. Would this process and final report have affected press content? Or were the positive war images and the sJC report dismissed by newspapers that had long sustained stereotypical representations?

While printed material in the summer of 1948 occasionally mentioned Aboriginal veterans, mostly the coverage applauded Canada's commitment to First Nations and lauded assimilationist efforts that could be categorized within Sheffield's conception of the "potential Indian citizen." However, negative imagery commonly printed prior to the war vigorously reappeared with stories of savage violence that overwhelmed positive depictions found during wartime.

"INDIAN VETERANS CAPABLE FARMERS"

Reportage referencing the war period lingered in the summer of 1948. For example, the interment at the Kanesatake cemetery near Montreal of a Mohawk soldier killed in Germany while fighting for the U.S. army was cause for a short news item in the Montreal *Gazette*. The leading sentence—"Thunder of an approaching storm sounded over the tiny graveyard in the Indian reservation"—set the stage for a mundane report that noted the presence of members from the American Legion as well as U.S. army and navy veterans in the second interment ceremony held at the reserve that summer.[9] Elsewhere, a Regina *Leader-Post* headline proclaimed "Indian Veterans Capable Farmers" and outlined the industriousness of the veterans and the generosity of the Veterans Land Act that provided grants to "Indian veterans" who took up farming.[10] No information on the difficulties First Nations veterans had in securing those land grants was discussed.[11] Another *Leader-Post* story, from its headline "Native Lead in Enlistments," appeared to be on topic but the report outlined that 730,625 men enlisted in the Canadian army during the Second World War were "natives of 48 different countries."[12]

News reports of contemporary Native success stories in 1948 were mostly framed within narratives of assimilation or intervention by a benevolent father/government to make the lives of Aboriginals equitable with other Canadians. As Sheffield argues, "the essential nature of the relationship between Canadians and the First Nations remained. At the base of this common sense rested the deeply rooted assumption that English Canada's race, society, and way of life were superior to those of the 'Indian.'" [13] A laudatory *Leader-Post* report of a dam, irrigation project, and canning factory to be built at Piapot First Nation, north of Regina, attributed the identified advances to efforts by a white Mormon missionary who had worked on the reserve for two years and confirmed, "The actual work on the dam will be done by missionaries."[14]

Literature on the topic of Aboriginal veterans remains scant. While Cree newspaper columnist Doug Cuthand has written about it in the Saskatoon *Star Phoenix* and the Regina *Leader-Post* on a number of occasions (mostly around Remembrance Day celebrations) little scholarly attention has been given to this topic.[15] Ronald Haycock's characterization of portrayals of Aboriginals in popular magazines between 1930 and 1960 is limited in relation to wartime constructions. He lumps the pre-war and postwar periods together and does not detect differences in the image of the Native in media after the war.[16] Jean Goodwill and Norma Sluman note in their biography of John Tootoosis that because of the wartime experience, Aboriginal veterans added new energy into Indian and Métis organizations, which supports Sheffield's analysis.[17] Canadian Aboriginal historian Laurie Meijer Drees, in a study related to the history of the Indian Association of Alberta, concludes that after the World War II experience, Canadians pushed government to improve conditions and rights for Aboriginals.[18] A comprehensive study of Saskatchewan Aboriginal veterans was undertaken as a master's thesis by Robert Innes in 2002. His analysis, which spans the period 1945 to 1960, concludes that Aboriginal veterans first served as passive catalysts for change and eventually as engines for social and political change in the 1960s.[19] In a subsequent journal essay Innes deals specifically with Aboriginal veterans in 1945–1946, using media sources to frame his argument.[20] Like Sheffield, he finds press reports had applauded Indigenous peoples for enlisting in the war, and, similarly, Innes suggests that the media "advanced the idea that Indians had 'progressed' to a stage where they were ready to be treated as equals."[21] Innes cites two *Leader-Post* reports in the fall of 1947 that acknowledged contributions of Aboriginal veterans during the war. The *Leader-Post* admitted "the Canadian Indian proved himself a loyal citizen and a good soldier."[22] However, Innes challenges Goodwill and Sluman and Meijer Drees and Sheffield, arguing that little evidence exists to justify a linkage of postwar political activities to veterans' immediate wartime experiences.

Alison Bernstein's *American Indians and World War II* details the impact of the war on American Indian life to assess its consequences.[23] In doing so, Bernstein mined the press for images of American Indians during wartime. She argues that during the war period images improved but that the postwar years "did not live up to white expectations that Indians would happily join the white world and abandon the tribal way of life. By the same token, these years demonstrated to Indians that winning more control over their own affairs was only a first step towards overcoming genuine economic and social deprivation."[24] Instead, she notes that American assimilationists naively assumed the war had turned American Indians into patriotic Americans when instead they began to organize politically to challenge mainstream policies. American Indian veterans, like their Canadian counterparts faced bureaucratic roadblocks after the war as they attempted to return to live on their home reserves and to collect benefits accorded to veterans.

"DON'T NEEDUM"

A large number of news items related to Indigenous peoples found in news dailies during this period amounted to demeaning fluff—human interest stories that simply gave readers a good chuckle. Language that mimicked Hollywood Indian-speak served as a common device in such stories and headlines. Celebrations across Canada from the Calgary Stampede in Alberta in early July to the Killarney Bazaar in Ontario at the end of July provided opportunities to position Aboriginal peoples as spectacle on slow news days. Cultural theorist Guy Debord argues that spectacle represents the dominant power's model of life, reaffirming and representing "the constant presence of this justification."[25] Likewise, images and headlines that mocked and satirized the exotic Native Other clad in traditional regalia clearly reinforced and justified a marginalized role for Aboriginals in Canadian society.

Under the headline, "Races and Indians Among Attractions," a Sudbury *Star*'s front-page story about the Killarney Bazaar boasted that "many of the visitors, especially those from the United States, had never seen Indians in tribal regalia."[26] Exotic and primitive, Aboriginal peoples were, at best, oddities available for mainstream consumption and entertainment. The headline, "Wild West Comes A-Whoopin' as Stampede Starts," over a photo of a group of "braves" setting up tipis was front-page news in the *Globe and Mail*, propagating the well-travelled and frozen-in-time image of the noble savage.[27] In late August 1948, Montreal *Gazette* coverage of the antics of "Chief Poking Fire" in the busiest ceremony "in many a moon" organized to honour the historic figure of Kateri Tekakwitha further illustrated how spectacle serves as justification for Canadian colonialism. The *Gazette*'s description of a related photograph explained: "Poking Fire pounding the tom-tom while his Medicine Man, right, prepares to give Hiawatha, at stake, a close shave or should it be haircut?"[28]

Newspapers used humour to denigrate Aboriginals, revealing inadequacies and demonstrating a lack of preparedness to meet the needs of a modern postwar society. The Winnipeg *Free Press*'s "Don't Needum:

Indians Offer to Buy Wings" must have produced guffaws and seen heads shake with its short report of how "Indians" at Norway House in northern Manitoba were convinced that "airplanes no longer needed wings when they saw their first helicopter."[29] In Vancouver the story, "Indians Offer Peace Plan to War-Jittery Palefaces," began with "Indians of North America, who abandoned the warpath decades ago, have offered a plan for world peace to their paleface brothers."[30] Couched in dismissive terms, the newspaper portrayed as ridiculous a proposal to the United Nations that would recognize North American Indians as a distinct, sovereign entity, separate from Canada or the U.S.

A *Globe and Mail* report with the headline, "No Blue Suit for Chief Cheeky, So Chipewyans Go on Strike," reoriented a First Nation's frustration with untimely food distribution to poke fun at a leader with an unusual name.[31] Chief Cheeky's demands were lampooned and his request for a new blue serge suit to make him appear more like a mainstream politician was mocked as humorously frivolous. "The white man's ways have been adopted by Chipewyan Indians of Duck Lake near Churchill, who figure that if the paleface workers can get their demands by striking so can they," the paper explained.[32] The chief's requests for adequate rations for his reserve appeared as a minor concern.

Photo opportunities of mainstream political leaders donning war bonnets in public or being made honorary chiefs abounded in newspapers. They promoted the illusion that Canada's Aboriginals were more than willing to embrace Canadian politicians as their own chiefs and leaders but simultaneosly remained stuck with ancient and backward cultural traditions.[33] Frozen-in-time representations of chiefs in war bonnets reminded Canadians of the popular and endearing images promoted by Hollywood Westerns.[34] In fact, three reports related to "Hollywood Indians" confirmed interest in the stereotypical constructions found in the cinema. Headlines such as, "Are Cinema Indians Indians?" "Who's Columbus? Indians Ask As They Turn Pale in Technicolor," and "Indians Learn To Zipper Tepees, Don War Paint For Hollywood Movie," and their accompanying stories acknowleged cultural inaccuracies present in Hollywood film yet still championed stereotypes.[35] The headlines raised questions regarding authenticity and savagery, titillating for civilized viewers who preferred the "Hollywood Indian" to contemporary ones. The Calgary *Herald* deemed Hollywood the authority on all things

Native with regard to a local Indigenous group. "It has taken Hollywood to bring the Stony Indians up to date on their own customs and to give them a few new ideas as well...movie officials have had to teach the red-men how to put on war paint," proving that "Hollywood Indians" could outdo contemporary Aboriginals in their grasp of "traditional customs, the paper explained."[36]

"AGAIN INTO THE BUSH"

In September 1948, a story about the tracking skills of an Indigenous guide aiding in the search for a missing U.S. navy plane in northern Manitoba capitalized on the popular culture representation of the noble savage and thus gained attention when the story was reported by the Winnipeg *Free Press*, the Regina *Leader-Post*, and the Halifax *Herald*.[37] This narrative emphasized traits that harkened back to useful skills from a primitive past by Aboriginals who continued to live lives unfettered by civilization. Such coverage is typical of news reports that Innes explores, where he finds that in the 1930s only one article appeared in the Regina *Leader-Post* that described Natives in a twentieth-century context.[38] The front-page *Herald* report conjured up stereotypical notions of the stoic "Indian" at home in the wilderness like Grey Owl by explaining that an Indian guide "trekked off again into the bush" after giving scant information and "two other Indians were sent into the woods to bring back their friend for further questioning."[39] Such stories promoted pride in "our" Native past and help fashion a Canadian identity separate from Britain.

That same month, news of the erection of a monument to commemo-rate Crowfoot, an influential nineteenth century Blackfoot chief referred to as "a statesman in paint and blanket" was covered in dailies from Calgary to St. John's.[40] The story reads like a case study from Seed's *Ceremonies of Possession* as it details a dedication service organized by the Southern Alberta Pioneers' and Old Timers' Association with representa-tives from the Historic Sites and Monument board.[41] The Calgary *Herald* treated the event as a toast to the settling of the west. The report waxed on about Chief Crowfoot's success in keeping the Blackfoot from taking part in the North-West Rebellion. It quoted extensively from a letter writ-ten to the chief in the late nineteenth century by the mayor of Ottawa, which was read aloud at the unveiling. The reporter explained to readers that "the letter was written apparently with great pains to talk Crowfoot's language and make the chief feel at home in Ottawa." It read: "Great Chief of the red men of the North West. Your pale-faced brothers of the chief city of the Dominion where our Great Mother Victoria commanded the Council Fires of the People to be lighted...offer you the pipe of peace."[42] Was halting English filled with demeaning symbolism the language of Crowfoot? Portions of the letter were reprinted to reinforce the symbolic language of conquest. Explaining that the "buffalo is no more," the letter hailed the arrival of colonization for the west—"The land, the plough, the cattle, the Reaper, and the Threshing Machine—the iron horse, the steel road, the fruits of the soil." The story concludes as the letter did, with a threat: "Go and tell your people that our hearts wish that never again shall the scapling knife be unsheathed or the war whoop be heard in the boundless prairies of the great Northwest."[43] The story of the plaque unveiling, steeped in nostalgia, bears no relation to the veterans of Canada's most recent war.

Around the same time, depictions of the "moribund Indian" and the "contemporary Indian" clashed when a park was created to protect petroglyphs in Nanaimo, British Columbia. Local Indigenous peoples protested the transfer of this 384-acre sacred site to the provincial government, claiming prior ownership of the land. The event sparked a mostly sympathetic though patronizing debate in the press regarding land rights and creation myths. The Vancouver *Province* reported that Edson White, a spokesman and son of the local chief suggested, "the white man's claim to Petroglyph Park and its ancient carving was as if the Indians put in a claim for Bethlehem, the birthplace of Christ."[44] A local historian, one of a number of mainstream "experts" who contributed to a rhetorical effort in the press to discount contemporary claims by local Indigenous groups by surmising that the site was one used by ancient and "unknown groups," not necessarily related to the contempoarary Natives, noted during the dedication ceremony that he believed, "a prehistoric race once gathered in sun worship in the rocky area...the carvings are the handiwork of a vanished race." The paper reported that the "Indian spokesman" denied that the work was done by "unknown races" and "declared the petroglyphics are in reality the story of creation...we Indians believe man was originally created here, just as Christianity claims he was created elsewhere."[45] The Calgary *Herald* cast the event as being one "without honour" and stood as a shameless example, as "white men handed one of the last of the west coast native shrines over to another paleface delegation." The Sudbury *Star* printed a version of the same story with a headline that evoked a message of epistemological misunderstanding, "Indians Unable to Understand Whites' Claim."[46]

During the SJC hearings a number of Aboriginal organizations formed provincial bodies that provided input to the committee regarding policy direction.[47] The Union of Saskatchewan Indians (USI), precursor to the Federation of Saskatchewan Indian Nations (FSIN) dates to 1946 and the merger of the League of Indians of Western Canada with the Protective Association for Indians and their Treaties. Cree leader John Tootoosis, president of USI, was re-elected in August 1948, resulting in a boxed story under a full-length photo of Tootoosis in traditional regalia in the Regina *Leader-Post*. Potentially an opportunity to present the USI as a positive political development related to Indigenous-white relations, instead the brief news item offered little information and the photograph impressed a stereotypical Indian upon readers. The image of the Cree leader dressed in buckskin and a large feather war bonnet, looking much like his "brother" Grey Owl, offered a static image that belied his contemporary role in a provincial political group.

"A FEW MINUTES LATER SHE WAS CALMLY SMOKING A CIGARETTE"

When the SJC findings suggested that the "Indian Problem" could be traced to unhealthy conditions rather than "indolence," news reports related to health and prosperity peppered the dailies—especially in relation to "Eskimo" populations.[48] Miller argues that the Second World War dramatically changed matters in the north, not so much because Canada accepted more responsibility but because an influx of southerners in the area publicized the poor state of many Inuit communities.[49]

The year 1948 marked the beginning of a number of relocations of a nomadic Innu community to Davis Inlet that has as recently as 2002 continued to play out in the press. Dickason explains that the devastating story of Davis Inlet began when the Newfoundland government decided in 1948 that the caribou-hunting Innu, who had not been designated under the Indian Act, would be better off as fishers in a new location 240 kilometres from their traditional territory.[50] The tragic consequences of this move has plagued the community and resulted in shocking suicide rates and welfare dependency charted in the press. Since, however, these well-documented social problems have been generally attributed not to the move itself as much as innate Indianness. Headlines such as, "Tragedy at Davis Inlet: The Near-Suicides of Six Teens Promises to Improve the Community," in the Montreal *Gazette* in 1993 or, "Moved Far from Their Homes, Natives Seek a Deadly Escape," in the *Globe and Mail* in 1996 and 2002 national coverage of the latest relocations revealed Ottawa's failure to provide essential services for the Innu.[51]

On 10 September 1948, the St. John's *Evening Telegram* reported the "transfer of Indians" to Davis Inlet in a larger story that outlined Captain Earle Winsor's summer sailing to the north on the MV *Winnifred Lee*. The boat had carried cargo north and returned with 400 barrels of pickled trout, thirty-five casks of seal oil, and seven school-age children from Labrador to attend school in the south in accordance with the Department of Natural Resources "scheme for improving the condition of the people on the coast."[52] The news of the relocation followed an extensive section devoted to fishing conditions that summer. Presented as a humanitarian effort on the part of the Canadian government, a result of the depletion of game in the locality to "enable the Esquimaux to improve their conditions of livelihood," readers might have wondered how the Inuit had survived for thousands of years without mainstream intercession.

Reports of the devastating effects of tuberculosis and government efforts to combat the disease also celebrated Canada's humanitarian treatment in the north. Little consensus on the health of Canada's Indigenous populations was found in the news, however. While the Calgary *Herald* reported that "Eskimos Found Hard Hit by TB," the *Free Press* announced, "Eskimos Healthier," reporting that health conditions had been greatly improved.[53] Likewise with dental hygiene in the north. The Sudbury *Star* explained that "whiteman's food and modern eating habits are ruining the teeth of Canada's northern Indians" and the Edmonton *Journal* reported that an Australian dentist who had spent the past four summers helping in the north argued that "civilised Eskimos may assist in the development of the northland, but they present a real dental problem."[54] Another story told of a U.S. naval doctor who went ashore to treat an "Eskimo woman suffering from bad teeth" in Port Burwell on Canada's northeastern coast.[55] The doctor "yanked two of the offending molars with no preparation. A few minutes later she was calmly smoking a cigarette," suggesting that an animal-like stoicism had inured her to the pain.[56] Context provided for the health-related stories from the north supported the aims of the sjc and also the federal government's poster campaign to instruct "Eskimo mothers" about how best to use their newly awarded family allowance funds by the Department of National Health and Welfare.[57] Inuit mothers became some of the first beneficiaries of the nascent welfare state that Canada began to erect in 1944–1945, though the "baby bonus" had to be redeemed at the local Hudson's Bay Company store for goods from a government-approved list.[58] Altruistic efforts to assimilate Canada's Inuit populations remained embedded in reports, such as the Montreal *Gazette* story that detailed the approved southern-Canadian goods available to the Inuit housewife such as powdered milk, baby cereal, corn syrup, biscuits, powdered eggs and marmalade.[59] Assimilationist efforts to help the Inuit in the North and turn them into Canadians resonated in both government policy and news stories in the summer of 1948.

"THE INDIAN LIST"

Canada's daily newspapers reinforced not only images of curious, childlike, ineffectual, and needy Aboriginals, but darker pictures also emerged. Press coverage of Aboriginal violence, unruliness, and alcohol abuse overshadowed the former. These commonplace reports cast Indigenous peoples as both deviant and disposable. Coverage resurrected and maintained negative stereotypes prevalent in the news prior to the start of World War II.[60]

Alcohol served as a backdrop for much of the Aboriginal violence reported and it supported the long-standing idea that Indigenous peoples could not resist alcohol and then became violent when they drank. Further, news stories coupled an ongoing discourse related to government control of alcohol and Aboriginals with the illusion that they required parenting by the government. The 1948 alcohol reports also indirectly referenced proposed changes to the Indian Act by the sjc that included the withdrawal of restrictions on the sale of liquor and access to public drinking establishments for First Nations. An editorial from the Orillia *Packet and Times* reprinted in the Toronto *Star* questioned this prosposed change:

A committee to the House of Commons has proposed that the
restrictions on the sale of liquor to indians should be withdrawn, and
that they should be permitted to drink in public places licensed for
drinking purposes. This is to effect the elevation of the Indians to full
citizenship. There are many other privileges which might be accorded
the Indians of Canada which would be very much more to their
advantage, the white man's liquor having proved a curse to them as
to most of the native races among whom it has been introduced. We
have not heard of demands for this privilege from the Indian leaders,
though they are asking for the franchise and more self-government
on the reserves.[61]

This commentary follows a story published in the Sudbury *Star* where
a storekeeper was jailed for two months for selling four bottles of ale
to "treaty Indian" Angus Commanda. Commanda received a suspended
sentence for having liquor in his possession—a violation of the Indian
Act, section 94.[62]

Until it was formally repealed in 1971, section 94 made it illegal for
First Nations people to consume alcohol while off-reserve. The *Star* also
reported that a non-Native resident convicted of theft explained to the
court that he was not aware of his actions because of his drunkenness and
asked to be placed on the "Indian list," which recorded persons forbidden access to liquor in the province.[63] A more serious case reported by
the *Leader-Post* outlined an investigation into the death of Mrs. Paul
Whiteman's death by alcohol poisoning. An Indian agent was involved in
sentencing a man charged with "supplying liqour to Indians." Reported
details in the *Leader-Post* from the inquest noted Whiteman died at a
"homebrew party after a reservation sports day on July 10."[64]

Another report conjured up images of primitive, uncivilized, and gra-
tuitously violent behaviours triggered by the introduction of alcohol. A
fatal stabbing of a man "trying to act as a peacemaker in a drunken brawl
between several Indian women" in Leamington, Ontario, was front-page
news in the Sudbury *Star* and received coverage in the Montreal *Gazette*
and the *Globe and Mail*.[65] The *Gazette* focused the report on who had
supplied the "liquor, beer and wine secured by the Indians" before providing details of the death. The *Globe and Mail* chose to focus attention on the conflict directly: "At the height of the screaming argument"

between the "drunken Indian women," the paper explained, the police questioned "the principals one by one as they sobered up."[66]

Still, other stories from 1948 proved that alcohol was not always necessary for violence to erupt. First, in Toronto, according to the Sudbury *Star*, a "full-blooded Indian freight-handler" severely beat his girlfriend and blinded her in one eye because, according to the perpetrator, "'all she did was talk, talk, talk, so I got mad and hit her.'"[67] Second, the *Globe and Mail* told readers that in Brantford, Ontario, a man was stabbed and left with a long gash requiring thirty stitches when a different man escorting an "Indian woman suddenly turned around and swore" at the victim.[68] "He then pulled a knife and stabbed him" and when the police went to arrest the aggressor, "he appeared to be in a stupor and would say nothing."[69]

"INDIAN CHIEF IS CHARGED WITH MURDER"

Serious crime stories filled the papers that summer. Sensational reports of blood and violence, of course, always sell newspapers and there appeared to be no shortage of such activity. The image of the drunken and violent Indian remained an essentialized and normal component of these stories. Adding a sprinkling of murder to the equation provided further evidence that the savage was alive and well in 1948, that he had not been curtailed because of service to the country during the Second World War. Descriptions of drinking, fighting, and strangulation peppered the news stories along with other stereotypical narrative elements: alcoholism, promiscuity, and mental deficiencies.

The murder, for example, of a twenty-one-year-old "dark, attractive half-Indian girl, naked and in a pool of blood" in Blind River in northern Ontario on 24 July 1948 and the subsequent investigation and trial was reported widely in the *Globe and Mail*, Toronto *Star*, and Sudbury *Star*. The alleged murderer, Richard Rivers, the victim's brother-in-law, was reported to have the mental age of a twelve-year-old. "'I just don't think I done it,'" he recalled the events of the evening until he "passed out," the *Star* recorded.[70] The victim, May Rivers, according to her mother's testimony in the *Globe and Mail*, had been an illegitimate child and had borne two illegitimate children herself already, establishing a generational cycle of promiscuity.[71] In case *Globe and Mail* readers needed assurance of the scandalous nature of the situation, the newspaper drew attention to the moral depravity of it all: "Mr. Justice Gale took exception to two teenage boys being at the trial and after asking them their age asked court attendants to remove them from the court. He said it was improper for them to be present at this particular trial."[72]

Front-page stories in the Toronto *Star* and the Sudbury *Star* also reported that a man from the Six Nations Reservation near Brantford, Ontario, Edward Hill, had beaten his wife May Maracle to death in early August 1948.[73] Details describing Maracle's semi-nude body along with evidence of violence and drunkenness in a small two-room house on the reserve succinctly completed the picture. The drunken murderer gave himself up to the RCMP, who told reporters he repeatedly cried, "My May is dead," after admitting to beating her.[74]

The Maracle murder garnered little attention from the media, especially when juxtaposed with a murder one week earlier in Toronto that included several common elements such as the toxic combination of alcohol, a deadly beating, and a male, Aboriginal murderer. A common tale of brutal violence unfolded but it was different from the Maracle murder in two significant ways. First, the female victim was not Aboriginal and, second, the incident took place in urban Toronto, not on a reserve. Press coverage expressed far less tolerance for Aboriginal violence when it spilled over into the mainstream. This was front-page news. The *Globe and Mail* covered the death of Mrs. Gwendolyn Pine by Peter Powless, "who claims the title of Big Chief Eagle of an Indian tribe in Wisconsin" as a sensationalized front-page story on 31 July that continued on pages 2 and 3.[75]

The repetitive headlines, "Indian Charged with Murder of Woman in Widmer St. Rooming House" and "Indian Chief is Charged with Murder of Woman," guided interested readers from page to page as the story unfolded. Despite the *Globe and Mail*'s detailed treatment of the story, other Canadian dailies, with the exception of the Fredericton *Daily Gleaner*, ignored it. The *Gleaner* simply printed a photograph of Powless flanked by two Toronto police detectives under a headline, "Indian Faces Murder Charge," and a short one-sentence description.[76] The visual impact of discipline and control signified by the photograph of the criminal controlled by the official representatives of law and order would have provided Fredericton readers with some assurance that justice would prevail. A collection of seven documentary photographs included on the second page of the *Globe and Mail* enriched the details of the case for Toronto readers as a reinforcement of the textual narrative. A photograph of the obviously Caucasian Gwendolyn Pine positioned next to one of her alleged Indigenous murderer drew visual attention to the racial dynamic in this case.

Alcoholism, violence, poverty, and race combined to spin a cautionary tale: "In a shabby attic room on Widmer St. where empty wine bottles told of a drinking bout, the semi-nude and beaten body of Mrs. Gwendolyn Pine, 41, was found sprawled on the floor yesterday."[77] The opening paragraph and setting for the narrative required little further explanation as readers could readily interpret the situation. Terms like "shabby," "empty wine bottles," "drinking," "semi-nude," and "beaten" reiterated the savage.

The murderer was dubiously identified as a chief, a heavy drinker, and a wounded veteran from World War II employed as a labourer, but was also described as an Indian herbalist and called "a good tenant" by his landlord. The paper established that Powless had "picked up Mrs. Pine at Queen and Spadina...he had not known her previously."[78] According to the paper, Pine had grown jealous of Powless's interest in Elsie West, another woman invited to the drinking party, and Powless had then beaten Pine when she objected to his attempt to depart with West.

While racial identity made this a story worthy of public attention and cast Powless as a drunken savage, it also framed the female Caucasian Pine as a whore. Her estranged husband, in an apparent attempt to resurrect the *Globe*'s sullied image of his wife as a drunken prostitute, explained that she came from a moderately wealthy, educated Pennsylvannia family. He stated, "'She was Catholic, I was Protestant, but we got married. We had a very happy life until a few weeks ago.'"[79] Nonetheless, the combination of class and race positioned both Powless and Pine outside mainstream culture in this narrative.

Conceptions of race and space emerged in two other reports that blended Aboriginal violence with Canada's uncivilized northern frontier. An Edmonton *Journal* story, "'Sordid, Appalling Case': Neglect Caused Wife's Death, Indian Sentenced to Jail," reported the same week that a Fort Simpson, Northwest Territories, man had failed to provide necessities of life for his pregnant wife. "Charles Cholo, a 39-year-old treaty Indian...has been a hard worker and has enjoyed average success as a trapper," but left his helpless wife suffering from gangrene due to frostbite in an unheated tent in the remote Deadman's Valley in the Nahanni mountains until RCMP stepped in and flew her to hospital where she eventually died.[80] The presiding magistrate termed the case as "one of the most sordid and appalling he had ever been called upon to deal with."[81]

A second story of Aboriginal domestic violence in the North found its way into the Sudbury *Star* and the Vancouver *Province* in a Canadian Press wire report, reminding readers of the region's lawlessness.[82] The story, "Trapper Slain By Indian Wife After Beating," confirmed a culture of violence generally linked to the Yukon. The widow of a gold rush veteran, Mrs. Annie Hayden, would face trial for murder after she shot her husband who had severely beaten her. The Sudbury *Star* quoted her, "I got scared he was going to kill me—that's why I shot him."[83]

———————————————

The three-month period of news coverage from the summer of 1948 belies the optimistic notion that, as a result of World War II and as desired in the sjc hearings' final report, fundamental change had come in the ways in which settler Canada viewed Aboriginal peoples. That report asserted that Canada needed "to facilitate the Indians to become, in every respect, citizens proud of Canada and the provinces in which they reside."[84] But press coverage made no effort to portray Aboriginals as citizens. Instead, it relied upon and maintained stereotypes long held in popular culture. Thus, the promise of this "potential Indian citizen" seems without merit, at least with respect to press reportage and despite Sheffield's otherwise carefully reasoned argument. In the summer of 1948 the themes found in Canadian newspapers since Confederation continued to frame Canada's Indigenous peoples in ways Canadians recognized and expected, even demanded. In this way, it appears as if the shifts that occurred in press coverage during World War II had simply amounted to a temporary and unintended side effect of war rather than a fundamental change in the ways Canadians viewed Aboriginal peoples. In other words, the limited beneficial effects wore off. It may also reflect a certain ideological bias inherent in liberal discourse, that is, a commitment to tendentious ideas about history and progress and evolution. For Aboriginals in the press, the notion of citizenship faded with the final inking of the sjc report, and it was not until 1969 when the issue of citizenship would once again demand that Canadians confront these ideas.

In the fall of 1948 both the Edmonton *Journal* and the Ottawa *Citizen* printed stories about the incoming freshman class at University of Alberta that belies any advance in consideration of Aboriginal peoples that extended beyond stereotypes. After the headline, "'Indians' Will Prowl Halls of Learning," the stories explained, "freshmen will be sporting green and gold feathers and 'Indian' garb...when the University of Alberta tribe goes on the warpath to initiate its new braves and maidens."[85] The *Citizen* followed up with an editorial that wholly endorsed the project that was instituted to apparently halt more mundane hazing rituals. In "Lo! The Campus Redskin," editors called the freshmen "lucky" and explained how the "upperclassmen with guttural 'ughs' and 'hows' will be the envy of most of the small boys in the country. Every boy, at one time or another likes to pretend he is an Indian, but few are favored with so rich an opportunity...The decision to play Indian is a step forward in the growth of our academic life."[86]

CHAPTER EIGHT

CARDBOARD CHARACTERS
The White Paper, 1969

The barriers—constitutional, legal, social and economic—are to come tumbling down. The days of tutelage are to end. The Indians are to join the contemporary Canadian scene as our equals and partners.

And we, as well as they, are invited to rediscover their cultural distinctness and proudly welcome it whole into our already many-textured society.

This is the offer of the Canadian government in the White Paper tabled in the House Wednesday. It is a truly momentous move —no less so because government leaders, including Prime Minister Trudeau, had already brought us to expect it. Or because much the same offer had been made, but never followed through, a century ago.

But how deeply engaged will the Indians themselves be in planning and implementing the programs necessary to effect this transformation?

Who will be in charge now, and take responsibility until the promises become fact?

—OTTAWA *CITIZEN*, 26 JUNE 1969

The world recognizes Canada as one of a handful of countries that has attempted to construct a coherent, pluralistic society. In this endeavor Canada has been more successful rhetorically than by its actions—and it remains a work in progress. Former governor general of Canada Adrienne Clarkson reassured Canadians in 1999 that "it is a strength and not a weakness that we are a permanently incomplete experiment built on a triangular foundation—aboriginal, francophone, and anglophone."[1]

Conceptions of unity within diversity may be central to Canada's official policy of multiculturalism, yet Aboriginals present a paradox that continually tears at the shiny fabric of multicultural Canadiana.[2]

Definitions of citizenry for Canada's Aboriginal peoples have always been problematic.[3] The road has been complicated, bumpy, and uphill all the way. First Nations began in Canada as wards of the state and have been subjected to residential schools, as well as informal segregation and bleaching policies ever since. Then there are the countless Aboriginals who were not status and thus have lived in legal quasi-limbo, some of which has shifted in recent decades. While the Citizenship Act of 1946, which for the first time recognized the definition of "Canadian" for its citizens, conformed to Western liberal traditions of political emancipation, it was not until 10 August 1960 that the right to vote in federal elections was extended to First Nations. Political scientist Joyce Green argues that popular mythology in Canada has naively understood Canadian citizenship as neutral and inclusive, exclusionary of class, sex, race, and ethnic bias. However, even with enfranchisement for First Nations the issues of citizenship were not fully settled for Canada's original peoples.[4] The year 1969 stands as an important benchmark in the long struggle for Indigenous legal equality, to say nothing about the informal variety that prospered in newspapers.

Prime Minister Pierre Trudeau's so-called "White Paper" released on 25 June 1969 "proposed to absolve the federal government of its commitments by revoking Indian status, eliminating the department of Indian Affairs, transferring responsibility for Indian matters mainly to the provincial governments," writes Miller.[5] The announcement sparked a vigorous editorial debate in news outlets across Canada. Editorial cartoonists, in particular, had a field day, succinctly capturing the tenor of the issues in richly intertextual caricatures.[6] The White Paper controversy provides a fertile context for examination of ongoing issues of colonialism and the problematic constructions of citizenry for Indigenous peoples in Canada.

In this chapter we investigate how eighteen dailies from across Canada presented the White Paper and reacted to it. These include the Victoria *Daily Colonist*, Vancouver *Province*, Edmonton *Journal*, Calgary *Herald*, Regina *Leader-Post*, Saskatoon *Star Phoenix*, Winnipeg *Free Press*, Sudbury *Star*, Ottawa *Citizen*, Toronto *Globe and Mail*, Toronto *Star*, Hamilton *Spectator*, Montreal *Gazette*, Fredericton *Daily Gleaner*,

St. John's *Evening Telegram*, St. John *Telegraph-Journal*, Charlottetown *Guardian*, and Halifax *Chronicle-Herald*.[7] We follow the story from 25 June 1969 through 30 December 1971, more or less till the end of sustained public reaction to the document.

"DOWN THE GARDEN PATH"

Native Studies scholar Karen Froman humorously describes the 1969 White Paper as "the thing that wouldn't die.... It came from Ottawa, oozing its way out of the muck known as Parliament Hill. It was 1969 and Jean Chrétien, the minister of Indian Affairs, had a plan to solve the 'Indian Problem' once and for all."[8] The quick fix proposed in 1969 was not the first time the government had sought changes to the Indian Act. Miller identifies attempts of various levels of significance in 1876, 1880, 1884, 1895, 1911, 1920, 1922, 1927, 1933, and 1951.[9] The *Hawthorne Report* of 1966 had advanced the term "citizens plus" to emphasize how Aboriginal peoples have the same rights as all Canadians but also additional rights because of their historical and treaty status.[10] The report, according to political scientist Sally Weaver, offered fresh directions in the consideration of citizenship and First Nations peoples.[11] However, the report's findings were quickly eclipsed by a new direction advanced by the Trudeau government, just a year into its first mandate when the White Paper came down.

Although Trudeau had not written about the formation of Indian policy, his personal philosophy on French-Canadian culture and federalism strongly dictated his government's direction.[12] He famously promised Canadians a "just society," free of all state-sanctioned forms of discrimination. Trudeau did not believe in special status for racial or cultural groups and largely ignored the testimonies given during public forums about the need for Canada to honour the terms of existing treaties and recognize Indian rights to self-government. "It is inconceivable," Trudeau said, "that one section of a society should have a treaty with another section of a society. The Indians should become Canadians as have all other Canadians."[13] By asking for the abrogation of the Indian Act in the White Paper, Trudeau adopted a social Darwinist approach to society and culture, Weaver argues, advancing a policy of cultural assimilation to eliminate special status for Canada's First Peoples.[14] This plan represented for Aboriginal peoples an unapologetic return to a nineteenth-century assimilationist agenda, according to Indigenous studies scholar Joanne Barker.[15]

Prior to the release of the document Aboriginals stood as a largely unorganized minority. The White Paper, ironically, provided them with an impetus to unite politically. The document, which Aboriginals roundly rejected and the government subsequently withdrew under a firestorm of criticism, became a rallying cry for "Red Power" in Canada, similar to emergent civil rights movements in the USA,[16] and helped forge a political lever for Indigenous peoples. As a result, the National Indian Brotherhood (NIB), precursor to the Assembly of First Nations (AFN), emerged as an important collective voice. Its response was well articulated in the Alberta Cree leader Harold Cardinal's landmark book, *The Unjust Society.*[17]

Saskatchewan lawyer Donald Purich has argued that one constant in Aboriginal policy has been "the failure to consult native people in a meaningful way on matters affecting them. No better example illustrates this point than the preparation of the 1969 White Paper."[18] The 1969 story began proximately with a 1967 promise of cross-cultural consultation that would, according to Arthur Laing, the unpopular federal minister of Indian Affairs under then-Prime Minister Lester B. Pearson, "provide for the emancipation of Canada's reserve Indians."[19] A booklet distributed to every reserve in the country titled, "Choosing a Path," asked thirty-four questions about the course of action the government should adopt regarding the future of Indian policy. Following the election, Trudeau quickly replaced Laing with Jean Chrétien but continued the consultation process, giving the impression, at least, of a sustained interest in Indigenous opinion before making policy that advocated significant policy changes as outlined in the White Paper. Trudeau brought to power a new liberal ethos that valued fundamental change and, as part of it, turned public attention to the so-called "Indian Problem" and sought abrupt and fundamental alterations without meaningful consultation with Native peoples.

As evidence of the lack of commitment to the consultative process, as early as September 1968, Chrétien told a meeting of the Indian-Eskimo Association: "It is possible that the Indian people will decide that there should not be an Indian Act at all. They might decide they do not want special legislation. There would then be required some transitional legislation which would transfer federal responsibility for the land to the Bands and individuals. On completion of the process, the Act would pass out of existence."[20] This speech foreshadowed the content of the White Paper. Chrétien here clearly implied that sensible "Indian people" would choose to opt with the government's view that they did not require and certainly did not merit "special legislation."

"Choosing a Path," quickly labelled "Down the Garden Path" in Indian country, was suspected by prominent members of the then fledgling NIB, including Alberta's Harold Cardinal and British Columbia's George Manuel, as a moot exercise, the real intention of which was to effectively disguise a hidden government agenda that had already been decided upon.[21]

"WARPATH ANGERS"

The immediate mainstream media take on the release of the White Paper earned it kudos because it seemed to promise a new direction in Canada–First Nations relations, newspapers argued. Numerous reports linked the policy changes to notions of citizenship. For example, headlines optimistically announced: "Ottawa Plan to Treat Indians as Full Citizens," "Indian's New Deal: He'll be Treated like Everyone Else," "Full Equality for Indian Set," "Indian's New Deal: He'll be Treated like Everyone Else," "Plan Would Turn Indians Into Full Citizens...," "Indians Independent 'Within Five Years,'" and "Equality for Indians Aim of Federal Policy."[22] These augured a seemingly positive advance. Who does not like equality? News reports from dailies across Canada implied that Canada's Aboriginals, as defined by the Indian Act, amounted to non-citizens and it was Trudeau's heroic aim to change this. But it was also a bait-and-switch manoeuvre. The stumbling block to becoming full citizens meant embracing an assimilationist doctrine. In other words, the papers uncritically adopted the Trudeau government's paternalistic position that Natives needed to be absorbed into the body politic. This thinking was not in fact new, though the sheen of Trudeaumania perhaps suggested that it was. The ideas were as old as Canada. And the policy amounted to warmed-over colonialist table scraps, in the press not different from 100 years earlier. Notice, too, that Aboriginals were not meaningfully consulted, another common colonial behaviour, precisely as if they remained children unable to make basic decisions about how to live their lives.

Predictably, then, press reports soon revealed that the remaking of Aboriginals as full citizens would not come as easily as Chrétien had bragged at his optimistic press conference unveiling the document. The Ottawa *Citizen* reported, "Indians Fearful: Federal Proposals Rejected as 'Unacceptable,'" and the Winnipeg *Free Press* tempered, "Indians Get New Deal Offer," conjuring Franklin Roosevelt's policy to solve the Great Depression in the United States, with "Indians Reject Ottawa Scheme." Many other news outlets were filled with stories of apprehension about the plan by the following day.[23]

A telling front-page photo of Chrétien at the public unveiling with "Indian spokesman Kahn-tineta [sic] Horn" peering over his shoulder was picked up on the Canadian Press wire service and printed in a number of daily newspapers across Canada on 26 June 1969.[24] The image almost poetically expresses the hegemonic relationship—Chrétien, a white man in a suit, in front and in charge, facing the microphones as Indigenous commentator Horn is physically and symbolically blocked by him, peeking from behind. Significantly, Canadian Press news stories across the nation mostly eliminated Horn's comments. Notably, the *Globe and Mail* did not. "It will cost a lot more to keep us on welfare than it would to keep us on the reserves," Horn said.[25] It is unclear whether the remarks, which conjure up the image of the needy Native, were intended to suggest that Aboriginals were already plagued by government handouts, or that this would be the result should the proposed changes not move forward. It also serves a kinder, gentler version of the 1873 "feed or fight" arguments discussed earlier.

The Montreal *Gazette* inexplicably described Horn as "Princess Kahn Tineta Horn, of Gaughnawa,[26] a sometimes [fashion] model and militant Indian rights leader," [27] thereby reducing her by the application of two well-trodden clichés, the Native princess and the Native militant. Her observation, however, "Indians don't want anything to do with the provincial governments," sounded decidedly un-princess-like and potentially spoiled the celebratory mood. Horn's opposition to Chrétien's charge that the Indian Act would be abolished in five years seemed of little consequence to newspapers on a day that promised a new era in citizenship.

The federal government heralded the elimination of the Indian Act as a progressive step by explaining that "Indians would become full citizens of Canada."[28] Meanwhile, Indigenous leaders such as the NIB's president,

Walter Dieter, opposed the move, charging that "we fear the end result of the proposal will be the destruction of a nation of people by legislation and cultural genocide," the Winnipeg *Free Press* reported.[29] Clearly, notions of citizenship meant something starkly different to the Liberal government than it did to Aboriginal leadership.

Sandwiched between a report of Ontario premier Bill Davis's endorsement of the White Paper and a story about how the federal government was not serving Ontario's Native population as it should, was a short excerpt of the White Paper in the *Globe and Mail*.[30] After the headline, "A Plea for Dignity," the prologue of Chrétien's tabled document was reprinted as follows:

> To be an Indian is to be a man with all man's needs and abilities. To be an Indian is also to be different. It is to speak different languages, draw different pictures, tell different tales, and to rely on a set of values developed in a different world. Canada has been richer for its Indian component, although there have been times when diversity seemed of little value for many Canadians. But to be a Canadian Indian today is to be someone apart in the provision of government services and too often apart in social contacts.
>
> To be an Indian is to lack power—the power to act as owner of your land, the power to spend your own money and, too often, the power to change your own conditions.
>
> Not always, but too often, to be an Indian is to be without—without a job, a good house, running water; without knowledge, training or technical skills, and, above all, without feelings of dignity and self-confidence that a man must have if he is to walk with his head held high.
>
> Obviously, the course of history must be changed.[31]

The remarks began with good intentions, framing Natives as equal to all men (again, females are simply subsumed). And they are different. True, but how so? The first paragraph instructs us: they are like us yet "apart" from us because of their special status. This implies that the root of the problem is cultural, not biological, yet it fails to note that the conditions as outlined were fostered by government, and not by Aboriginals. Regardless, the point is that the situation is not fair and must be addressed.

The text illustrates the weakness of Aboriginal people. Simply put, they "lack power." To begin with, capitalism is apparently unknown to them because they have not the "power to act as owner of your own land." And again they are needy—they have "no power to spend your own money." Every mainstream Canadian newspaper reader would have already known that the money for Natives had flowed from mainstream tax coffers. And they have not the power to direct the course of their own lives, "to change your own conditions." Without possessions, money, or authority, they were, in other words, childlike. Furthermore, Natives are lazy ("without a job"), slovenly (without "a good house"), culturally backward (without "running water"), stupid ("without knowledge"), backward (without "training or technical skills"), and pathetic ("without feelings of dignity and self-confidence").

The ineluctable solution was assimilation. Nowhere on any occasion did any of the eighteen newspapers we examined note assimilation policy had largely caused all of the identified problems in the first place. No paper thought to ask, how will more of the same lead to a different result? One definition of madness is just that, to repeat the same behaviour and expect a different outcome. Yet Trudeau and Chrétien managed to deny any sense of responsibility for the conditions as outlined. In a way, Chrétien's proffer constituted a threat, painting a dire picture of hopelessness for contemporary Indigenous peoples who would not aspire to assimilation, who would not choose to embrace the White Paper.

Aboriginals appeared, from this view, to require a tough love approach that demanded assimilation and more money from the provinces. The press predictably cast mainstream politicians as father figures, responsible and thoughtful disciplinarians, while it framed Aboriginals as children who required control and stern guidance. Press coverage of these events mostly situated the federal and provincial leaders as trusted authorities even though federal and provincial politicians quickly formed separate camps concerning the White Paper. The press presented Indigenous opposition as both demanding and aggressive.

Under a headline, "Indian Nationalism is Reawakened as New Policy Related," the Sudbury *Star* explained, "the essence of the conflict seems to be that Mr. Chrétien intends the Indians to have the same status as other citizens, while the Indians see themselves as 'more than just citizens of Canada.'"[32] In this way, the *Star* dismissed Indigenous leaders' resistance to the White Paper by appealing to the stereotype of the needy Native.

A Toronto *Star* headline declared, "Indians fear new policy will lead to 'genocide.'" The accompanying story explained, "The aim of the new policy is to put Indians on an equal footing with other Canadians in terms of their responsibilities and the services they receive from the federal and provincial governments. It will see the repeal of the paternalistic Indian Act which has set Indians apart from other Canadians for generations."[33] Here the press operated in a mildly scolding, corrective role, disabusing mistaken Native perceptions at the same time as endorsing government efforts to control First Nations' behaviour. It drew attention to all of the "free" services available to Indigenous peoples and argued that Chrétien would find resistance from the Indians "who resent the fact that they would have to pay municipal taxes."[34] In short, whining, "special" children suffused with a sense of entitlement, commanded and demanded more rights than all other Canadians. This frame came finally to dominate the press portrayals in 1969. In a chiding boxed story titled, "Be Consistent, Indians Told," a *Globe and Mail* reporter described Aboriginal leaders as angry, confused, and unsure of what they wanted. The notion of special status was described as greedily wanting more than other Canadians, and the article ended with a hectoring reminder from Mr. Chrétien aimed at a First Nations Chief, "You're a Canadian citizen; Canada is your country and you're a part of it."[35]

The notion of a united Indigenous political voice conjured up memories of warpaths. The Montreal *Gazette* set aside a corner of its front section of the 8 July 1969 issue under the title, "Canada's Indians Say." It presented a number of inflammatory short reports from around the country that echoed old colonial tropes. Natives were, by turns, described as "militant," "advised to use force," "blocked traffic," "wanted compensation," and "used evictive force," all of which served to paint a picture of discord and violence.[36] A Calgary *Herald* report titled, "Indians Threatening Force," echoed the *Gazette*'s casting as it cautioned readers about threats of violence regarding the negotiation of the new federal policy. A 7 July story employed terms such as "force," "forcibly evict," "threat," "warning," "outbreak of violence," and in a front-page report on the creation of an INAC commission to poll Indians about the White Paper.[37]

Editorials surfaced in newspapers in July that addressed the new Indian policy. A number of publications professed cautious optimism regarding the objective but questioned the government's motives and asked that the federal government clarify its intentions, as the Charlottetown *Guardian*'s reaction demonstrated. "Certainly an essential point is that all misunderstandings be cleared up before the policy goes into effect," the *Guardian* observed.[38] Placed next to an essay that discussed the two faces of Trudeau—the social liberal and the economic conservative—the Halifax *Herald* responded to the controversy with a guest editorial written by Douglas Fisher and Harry Crowe, who concluded, "We think integration is right and inevitable and that it must be staged for 30 to 50 years; we think this line of preserving Indian identity is a 'con' game; we believe the Indians will recognize this and in the fierceness of their negative reaction destroy a reasonable consideration of the merits of integration."[39] Other news dailies questioned Chrétien's and Trudeau's intentions, pondering the trustworthiness of the minister of Indian Affair's motives while cautioning the provinces against supporting the White Paper.[40] An Ottawa *Journal* editorial reprinted in the *Daily Gleaner* admitted that the goal to bring "Indians into the mainstream of Canadian life and end their 'burden of separation,'" was laudatory but it pointedly questioned Chrétien's reasoning in proceeding with a weak plan that had unnecessarily and unduly upset Aboriginal groups and sparked "warpath angers."[41]

Then, with the founding NIB convention in Winnipeg on 17 July 1969, fears of outbreaks of Aboriginal violence loomed and the corresponding need for control arose again in news reports. A Winnipeg *Free Press* front-page report on the proceedings issued a threat to Chrétien, "Indians Lambaste Chrétien: Won't Guarantee His Safety If He Visits Reserve." The threat of impending hostilities seemed to stalk the gathering. Issuing warnings about the potential for rising Native aggression and demands for more money, the press constructed a queasy and unruly image for Canadians to digest, all about the danger posed by an emerging national unified Indigenous voice.[42]

A letter to the editor in the Montreal *Gazette* captured a common sentiment: "Will someone tell me why so many of them want to continue living like their ancestors or as public wards on a reserve? Does the white man want to go back living like his ancestors? I should hope not

... Indians, wake up! You are basically just as intelligent and resourceful as anybody else. But nobody will believe it if you are going to be satisfied living like a primitive."[43] The choice of a word such as "them" obviously distances the reader in classic binary fashion. Natives also remain willfully, stubbornly stuck in an undesirable past, the letter argued, though it is not clear whether they can escape it. Whites progress but Indians seem to be asleep at the wheel. The real problem boiled down to the final word—"primitive." Natives were stuck with it and in it.

At least one effort to report a counter-narrative appeared. Wilson Plain of the Chippewa Nation at Sarnia, Ontario, responded to *Globe and Mail* front-page coverage of the White Paper in a letter to the editor that attempted to clarify resistance to the federal position. Plain outlined how terms such as "just society" and "discriminatory" deflected attention from an obvious intention to shirk federal treaty responsibilities. Applying a nineteenth-century euphemism, Plain argued, "Great White Father is trying to conceal his lack of responsibility to the first inhabitants of this continent by his clever use of the English language in works such as 'special status.' I do not consider myself special, nor do I consider myself an ordinary Canadian."[44] The same day the *Globe and Mail* noted in "New-Deal Smoke Signals the Indians Read Clearly" that although Indigenous leaders viewed the White Paper as an assimilationist document, mainstream Canadians remained at best apathetic on the subject.[45] First Nations leader Harold Sappier's letter to the editor in the Fredericton *Daily Gleaner* lamented, "other Canadians do not understand the Indian way of life and a lot of them do not really care."[46]

The Edmonton *Journal* headline, "Red Power Alliance based on white-radical thinking," outlined in an extensive report how a group called the Native Alliance for Red Power (NARP) had met in a Vancouver headquarters decorated with posters of Geronimo, Che Guevara, Eldridge Cleaver of the Black Panthers, and Chairman Mao Zedong, to discuss future directions. The report explains that the NARP radicals "have been forced to adopt the tactics and ideology of white radicals and black militants. There is little that is truly Indian in the program of Red Power and the ultimate goal of armed revolution is not realistic."[47] The report defangs any potential threat from this group and indirectly dismisses organized opposition to government policy.

"I HAVE NO DESIRE TO BE A GREAT WHITE FATHER"

The federal government's position smacked of less than altruistic motivations, given its treaty obligations. Opposition to the White Paper did not only come from the newly formed National Indian Brotherhood or NARP, however, it also arose from provincial politicians. Over the course of the summer of 1969 it became clear to provincial leaders that by doing away with the Indian Act and federal financial responsibilities outlined by the treaties, the brunt of this proposal would be felt by provincial coffers and amounted to an off-loading of services. Therefore, while federal minister of Indian Affairs, and later prime minister, Jean Chrétien felt the heat of Native leaders over the plan he also had to sell the idea to provinces.

Caught up in federal-provincial squabbling as well as vocal Aboriginal resistance, the White Paper fell quickly onto the proverbial ropes. As early as 9 July 1969 the Edmonton *Journal* reported that "leaders of Alberta's 42 Indian bands began formulating counter-proposals to the newly announced federal Indian-White Paper." Harold Cardinal reportedly said, "We have finished studying the government paper which, if accepted, would lead to chaos on the reserves. The Federal document just doesn't offer the Indian sufficient protection of his lands against unscrupulous white men. This is once again a case of the federal government talking out of both sides of its mouth."[48]

While Chrétien explained to British Columbia audiences in mid-July on his cross-country tour to persuade Aboriginal leaders, "I have no desire to be a Great White Father to the Indian," and that the principal aim of the White Paper was to end discrimination by allowing Aboriginal citizens to accept provincial services like all other Canadians, the *Daily Colonist* reported that he was open to alternative options.[49] Yet, Chief Philip Paul of the Tsartlip First Nation was not persuaded by the minister of Indian Affairs. In a meeting of Aboriginal leaders from four Vancouver Island First Nations, he said, "What they are trying to do, and they admit it, is to assimilate us, to bring us into white society—and to do this by making it impossible for us to stay Indians. They speak of giving us equal rights, giving us title to our own land as individuals, and of course requiring that we pay taxes on it. That will mean that we lose our land—that our children have nothing to inherit.... And we will not be taken into white society, either. We will live on the fringe of white society, in the slums."[50]

Editorial pages in the summer of 1969 were filled with diverse opinions related to the White Paper and most felt little sympathy for the NIB's reasoning for rejection of the White Paper. Still, it was clear that Trudeau and Chrétien had miscalculated the wide-ranging dislike for the White Paper. Timing and the hurried nature of the announced changes were of most concern to editors of major dailies in Canada. A Sudbury *Star* editorial, "Timing Important on Indian Policy," lamented that while many Canadians sympathized with Aboriginals who "so steadfastly cling to the old ways, and for those of their race who are alarmed at the government's plan," it was time to move on: "The Indian can never gain full equality of opportunity with other Canadians so long as he remains set apart by law."[51] The Montreal *Gazette* editorial, "Indian Plan Needs Caution, Care," similarly endorsed assimilation but worried that the abolition of the Act was too radical an idea. "Freedom, for the unprepared, can be the cruelest gift,"[52] it observed. The Toronto *Star* echoed this position in August with an editorial that concurred, "Indians aren't ready," while admitting that "Making Indians 'Canadians as all other Canadians' is a sound ultimate goal. But it will take more than five years, and it cannot be achieved over the opposition of the Indians themselves."[53] The *Daily Gleaner* plainly argued in "Indian Wrath Aroused Unnecessarily" that the "planned transfer of responsibility for Indians to provinces without guarantee" meant that "the Indian will gain nothing." The editorial, a reprint from the Ottawa *Journal*, concludes, "if the tentative nature of the Government proposals had been made plainer, especially in prior meetings with Indians, the warpath angers reported on reserves would have been averted."[54]

"SALVATION OF HIS RACE"

By June 1970 substantive change had occurred as a result of the White Paper. A historic delegation of 150 Alberta Aboriginals arrived on Parliament Hill and that month presented the federal government with its "Red Paper" (officially titled "Citizens Plus"), an obvious response to the White Paper.[55] Despite the fact that the somewhat aggressive Red Paper, penned by Harold Cardinal, read as a line-by-line refutation of the White Paper, it was answered by the prime minister with an admission that the federal position had been "naïve," "too abstract," "too theoretical," and "somewhat hasty," according to the Regina *Leader-Post*.[56] The Edmonton *Journal* headline, "Give Ottawa Chance, Trudeau tells Indians," explained that the remorseful prime minister pleaded to 350 Indians and their leaders not to "accuse his government of speaking with a forked tongue any more ... we can't reach progress if you don't think we're honest people."[57] Trudeau's comments bore little resemblance to his statements less than a year earlier. The Vancouver *Province* confirmed that the prime minister was "behind the killing of the white paper," while the Calgary *Herald* reported that Trudeau recognized the "inevitable."[58] The St. John's *Evening Telegram* reported that Trudeau told the delegation that it had had a right to be suspicious because, "'some fast ones have been pulled' in such talks over the last 100 years."[59] The paper neglected to comment as to whether the White Paper should be considered one of those "fast ones." Thus, a startling shift had occurred in Trudeau's handling of the issue, as he newly embraced a conciliatory approach that distanced him from the policies of his own cabinet minister, Chrétien, and INAC. However, while Trudeau was publicly prepared to retract his assimilationist position, the press was less willing to step back.

Press coverage through 1970–1971 vacillated between pitching Aboriginals as violent and finding opportunities to praise and promote assimilation. A *Leader-Post* editorial, for example, painted a brighter picture for future negotiations as it expounded upon an imagined future period for Indigenous-settler relations. The "once apathetic and isolated Indian is now being asked to share in the formation of policies pertaining to his affairs."[60] Yet, only a few days prior the same paper commented on the topic of Indigenous education: "No Indian need fear education, because education—and assimilation—will be the salvation of his race."[61] Pairing salvation with assimilation staked a moral position that left little room for the assertion of traditional Aboriginal rights.

A Toronto *Star* story, "Indians Spend Too Much Time Blaming Whites, Indian Says," confirmed that frustration resonated with assimilated Aboriginals.[62] Cree lawyer William Wuttunee, one of the few public Aboriginal supporters of the White Paper and author of *Ruffled Feathers*,[63] explained in a Canadian Press wire service story that was printed across Canada, "Public money is handed out to Indians, without any ground rules, to satisfy the white man's guilt feelings. The white man has nothing to feel guilty about. Is it not possible that Indians themselves are responsible for the creation and perpetuation of their problems?"[64] Terms such as "guilt," "public money," and "handouts" to Indians combined to speak loudly to mainstream Canadians. The Halifax *Chronicle-Herald* paired its coverage of Wuttunee's interview with a blistering headline, "Indians Create, Perpetuate Their Own Problems, Cree Lawyer-Author Charges."[65]

The St. John *Telegraph-Journal* included a large photo of Wuttunee scouring papers at his desk, ready for business, dressed in a suit and tie. In the extended report where he was referred to as the "silver-haired lawyer," Wuttunee explained, "many Indians do not consider themselves as Canadians, but only 'as Indian people.'"[66] He continued, "In the meantime, they've been accepting the benefits of the administration of the Indian Affairs branch, the money of the federal government and the protection of the RCMP." His comments reflected a level of assimilation toward which the press clearly hoped more Aboriginals would aspire. In his book, Wuttunee specifically complained about the Association of Alberta Indians and one of its leaders, Harold Cardinal, and the paper afforded him the opportunity to refute Cardinal in the last paragraph of the story. However, unlike Wuttunee's opinions, which earned favourable coverage, Cardinal's words by contrast sounded bitter and sour. "They always managed to pull some brown human being out, who claims to be an Indian spokesman, every time they get in trouble," Cardinal was quoted.[67]

A week earlier the *Telegraph-Journal* had featured another assimilation success story when it reported that one Graydon Nicholas had experienced "an awakening social consciousness" that prompted him to become Canada's fifth "Indian" lawyer. He was pictured as such in a comforting photo of the upcoming middle-class professional and his wife and young son. The Halifax *Herald-Chronicle* declared that assimilation was the preferred route in its report, "Better For Indians At School Not To Speak Mic-Mac—Mother." It told of Jean GooGoo's claim that being forced to speak only English at residential school had helped her integrate into white society.[68] Her opinion, supported by an official of the Victoria County school board, may have been misunderstood in the report, however. The final paragraph noted that GooGoo "does not want to see MicMac children lose their native language, but recognizes English is necessary for education."[69] Given the headline and first several lines of the article, most readers would have been satisfied with the commentary that their "mother tongue" reigned supreme, even among Aboriginals. The article also spoke to the basic asymmetry of white-Indigenous relations in Canada, similar in many ways to how the Mexican essayist and poet Octavio Paz portrayed them in his native Mexico, as a pyramid with whites on top and Aboriginals, the mass of the form, beneath.[70]

"AGGRESSIVE NEW ATTITUDE"

Press coverage continued to champion assimilation as a corrective and thus positive forward step for Natives, even while Trudeau had steered away from it as official policy. News reports that highlighted resistance to assimilation were cast in simplistic binary fashion. Despite the fact the fledgling NIB met with success in negotiating an end to the White Paper, the media cast the outcome not as a victory for the assertion of Aboriginal political solidarity or the assertion of pan-Native sovereignty but instead as a direct threat to the country, auguring future problems. A *Leader-Post* headline warned, "Indians Adopting Aggressive New Attitude." Readers learned that "militant" Indians, "as the white man has so long been fond of saying, are on the warpath. It is symbolic of aggressive new attitudes among Western Canada Indians today that the very word 'warpath' tends to give them despair."[72] Language such as "militant" and "warpath" coupled with the organization of a national Aboriginal voice spelled trouble in the press. Quoting Cardinal, referred to as a prophet among young "militant" Aboriginals, the *Leader-Post* championed the very language it identified as problematic. Further, it reinforced links between the NIB and impending violence. "In many ways," Cardinal was quoted, "there's more discontent among us now than in the past and for a number of reasons...the social and economic situation hasn't improved that much but the entire awareness of what is possible has vastly increased. I think a lot of people are beginning to get at least an inkling of what place they should occupy in Canadian society."[73]

In November 1971, an opinion piece in the Toronto *Star* by Indigenous studies professor Howard Adams supported such claims with his comments that Indians and Métis would inevitably "use violence" if further sovereignty was not recognized.[74] The next month, a Toronto *Star* editorial, "From Passivity to Protest Indian Anger: A Symptom of Health," admitted that given the "excessive paternalism" Canada has shown its Aboriginal populations, the resultant anger is a healthy response.[75] Yet, in fall, 1971, stories in the Charlottetown *Guardian*, the St. John *Telegraph-Journal*, the Vancouver *Province*, and the Victoria *Daily Colonist* provided headlines that cast Aboriginals as belligerent—they "defy," they "oppose," they are "against," they "protest," and they "demand," even in cases where the ensuing reports presented more favourable framing.[76]

The Canadian mainstream print media covered issues related to the White Paper from a variety of perspectives. One challenged the federal government in strict constitutional terms: things Aboriginal fell under the domain of federal and not provincial responsibilities. In a way, this story transcended Native issues altogether because much of it came down to bickering about tax revenue. In a zero-sum game, any off-loading of federal responsibilities represented a net savings for the federal government and a net cost to the provinces. The provinces, and political positions that supported their views, were predictably set against any such federal policy shift—and the White Paper fit here. This reportage belies the strong undercurrent of anti-Native bias.

Stripped of the federal-provincial power struggle, news coverage maintained its by now familiar pace and tone. Thus, Aboriginals might finally merit citizenship only if and when they conformed to settler ideals and culture and assimilated into the mainstream. For Aboriginals to consider a form of citizenship other than this—say, citizen-plus—left the press cold, with little recourse but to explain the behaviours by reverting to the interpretive frames of old—thus the Native whiners, children, and savages endured. The difficulties faced by Natives were their own fault, in other words.

White Paper events continue to resonate in Canadian popular culture as a lesson in how *not* to negotiate. A 2009 editorial on Aboriginal governance in the *Globe and Mail* lamented that mainstream politics should not have continually to shy away from changes to the Indian Act simply because of the legacy of the White Paper. Yet, AFN still feels it must warn off the Stephen Harper government against another all-too-familiar top-down reform of INAC. The *Globe and Mail* rancorously portrayed AFN Grand Chief Phil Fontaine's resistance to the most recent efforts at reform as evidence, not of entrenched patriarchal posturing, but of the AFN's internal political discord—so much predictable confusion in Indian country. In this way the *Globe and Mail* promotes the federal government's ongoing assimilationist policy as plain common sense and the Aboriginals as bellyachers.[77]

The White Paper fallout also resulted in a more politically united Aboriginal voice that, for the press at least, disturbed the cozy colonial relationship that had served Canada for so long. Prematurely celebratory reports of Aboriginals attaining full citizenship that filled papers in 1969 have morphed since into a thirty-year political debate concerning self-government, with no end in sight. The press reacted to the Trudeau government's failure to erase Indianness and create the so-called "just society" with warnings of escalating violence by Aboriginals. Those media warnings would be realized in press coverage during the summertime standoff in Kenora, Ontario, in 1974.

CHAPTER NINE

BENDED ELBOW NEWS
The Anicinabe Park Standoff, 1974

This community is dependent on tourism and this
kind of thing can hurt tourism.

—KENORA *MINER AND NEWS* EDITOR KEN NELSON,
  QUOTED IN THE WINNIPEG *TRIBUNE*, 26 JULY 1974

When the Ojibway Warrior Society[1] seized control of Anicinabe Park
in Kenora, Ontario, during the summer of 1974, leading to a legendary standoff, nearly all racial hell broke loose, according to local press
reports.[2] On the one hand, armed Aboriginals[3] took control and laid
claim to the ten-acre municipal park, arguing that it had been effectively
stolen from them decades earlier.[4] On the other hand, the local Kenora
daily *Miner and News* represented the story as one of a classic struggle
between civilization and barbarism, a colonial encounter, with white
townsfolk cast in the blameless role of aggrieved victims while Natives
were portrayed in three basic streams. In keeping with news tradition
that dates back to at least 1869, the stereotyping made little distinction
between or among local Aboriginal peoples, members of the Warrior
Society, and/or the hundreds of other discrete Canadian Native groups.

The borders of each of the constructions we will explore in this chapter remained porous and frequently overlapping throughout 1974. However, local press representations of Natives in the months leading up to
the park's seizure were decidedly more moderate in tone than during the
standoff, which began in mid-July and lasted for six weeks. Then, in the
weeks following the peaceful resolution to the event (though not necessarily the various issues raised by it), local news coverage generally resumed
its paternalistically colonial pre-conflict character. This phenomenon

parallels 1885 reportage and provides a kind of mirror image to the temporary improvement of such imagery during World War II.

In the first instance, the newspaper cast all Natives—including First Nations, Métis, Inuit—as if they had stepped straight out of an old-fashioned Hollywood Western.[5] Second, the newspaper depicted Aboriginals as hapless, ungovernable drunkards. According to this portrayal they could no more govern their base instincts than they could effectively manage their day-to-day affairs living in the later twentieth century. A third casting portrayed Natives as exotic wraiths, frequently stoic, a child-like people simultaneously in need of correction and direction at the same time as being on the verge of dying off. Common to this stream was the notion that pitched Canada's Natives as a defeated, defanged monolithic race that did not have enough sense to know that its own culture was as good as dead.

These press framings open a window to how residents of this small town in central Canada imagined Natives as well as to how Canadian colonialism has been aided and abetted by the press. That is not to say that the local paper accurately or representatively reflected all white opinions in the town or that Kenora stands in for all of Canada. Yet what emerges from Kenora was hardly unique. Instead it was quintessentially, colonially Canadian. Kenora's daily newspaper coverage spoke to the endemic and systemic anti-Native racism woven into the fabric of the community since its inception as a political entity in the nineteenth century.

In the early 1970s Kenora resembled many white communities in Canada. Brimming with freckle-faced children, outdoor hockey rinks, and a Kinsmen-sponsored winter beard-growing contest, it radiated wholesome small-town mainstream virtuousness. Nestled in the Canadian Shield, it sits on the northernmost shores of the breathtaking Lake of the Woods, a vast expanse of water dotted with countless islands and many cottages. With a population of roughly 10,000, economically the town relied primarily on a few key sectors—a pulp mill, tourism, and government. The town perched importantly then, as it still does, along the Trans-Canada Highway. American fishers and hunters flocked to the area when the lake was free of ice, leaving with their trophies of walleye, muskies, and white-tailed deer. The local pulp mill generated hundreds of good-paying, steady jobs. Apparently placid and well-contented Kenora seemed average in nearly every way a Canadian town might be.

The Kenora *Miner and News* certainly suggested as much. The publication ran the predictable sort of pulp upon which small daily newspapers flourished (and still do). For example, in early January of 1974 one could read a triumphal tale about a man who had retired from the local paper mill after decades of service. This was front-page material, as was the story of a fender bender, another day in January. Another front-page story that month told of a driver who swerved to avoid crashing into a dog and instead collided, but not seriously, with another car.

The paper ran "Dear Abby" and offered "The Bee Line," a local gossip column. Classified ads pitched cars and snowmobiles for sale. A healthy sports section that focussed on local teams, in particular hockey, especially the local junior squad, normally took two or three of the paper's usual ten or fewer pages.[6] A local Christian feature, titled, "According to the Book," by local clergymen, ran regularly. In sum, the paper sketched and served an ordinary white Canadian town.

The *Miner and News* also typically featured a smattering of regional, provincial, national, and international news.[7] For example, 1974 was the year that Kenora built its shopping mall, a big local/regional story. Streakers were all the rage that year in Canada and occasionally drew mention in the local broadsheet. Meanwhile, internationally, the kidnapping of newspaper heiress Patricia Hearst earned a lot of ink as did the exploding Watergate saga. All these and more garnered coverage, normally via news services. Meanwhile, editorials, when not picked up from the wires, were infrequent and tended to reflect middle-of-the-road positions on non-contentious topics (e.g., the positive value of a shopping mall).[8]

All in all, the *Miner and News* reflected the Kenora that generations of tourists and white residents had come to know—an honest, hardworking, decent community. On the other hand, Kenora's white–Native race relations through the 1960s and into the 1970s have been likened to the segregated Jim Crow South in the United States, where in the public sphere whites thoroughly and completely relegated African-Americans to the status of inferiors.[9] So, too, in Kenora during the 1970s, where Aboriginals had endured a century of public ridicule, rebuke, and stinging prejudice. This racism was systemic and systematic, and the local "ordinary" paper alternatively reflected, fuelled, denied, and abetted it.

The explanations accounting for the three basic image streams employed and championed by the *Miner and News*, when it infrequently provided explicit rationale for such framings, tended to be presented as common-sensical, self-referential, and derive from the omnibus assertions that Aboriginals stubbornly adhered to a retrograde past,[10] clung desperately to childishness,[11] and were incapable of full social evolution,[12] all of which have been identified by scholars as culturally bound in North America.[13]

Research conducted for this chapter shows that the local news depictions remained ideologically consistent throughout 1974.[14] However, a distinct pattern emerged in the press once the Ojibway Warrior Society seized Anicinabe Park in later July and it became apparent that the group was not about to hand it back without concessions on the part of the town. The timbre, if not precisely the makeup, of the stereotypes employed, took a desperate turn,[15] donning a new and heightened sense of urgency and drama. For example, according to the press, Natives suddenly posed a clear and present danger to the community.

According to the *Miner and News*, the predilection for perfidy among "the once proud Ojibway"[16] dated to the earliest contact Europeans had with Natives on the Lake of the Woods. In a feature titled, "Our Yesterdays," an attempt at providing some local history as a sort of public service and type of boosterism, the *Miner and News* recounted the legend of Massacre Island, in which a number of French-Canadian voyageurs were dispatched in a violent confrontation with Natives on the lake during the eighteenth century: "Some reports indicate that the party [of voyageurs] was overcome by treachery. In a time when it was difficult to tell friend from foe perhaps a party of Indians has approached the island signifying peaceful intentions. After fraternizing with the voyageurs perhaps they turned on their hosts, slaughtering them in a few minutes.... The story of an Indian treachery seems to be confirmed by the fact that no Indian bodies were found."[17] Bald conjecture, as indicated by the word "perhaps," does little to lessen the central allegation here that Natives on that memorable day more than two centuries ago exhibited deviousness (they "signified peaceful intentions"), treachery (the signal was a ruse designed to stage an effective surprise assault), bloodlust ("slaughtering them in a few minutes"—though there is no way of knowing the precise sequence of events or how they transpired, as the passage itself indicates), and a violation of any sense of common decency (by leaving the bodies to rot).

On another occasion, in early July, the paper sketched a similar narrative of the same bloody encounter. In this retelling, "intrepid" voyageurs

were confronted by the "fierce tribal warfare continually being carried on in those days and in this sanguinary arena." Further, the paper
intoned, "As we know, the character of the Indian of today and which,
as we learn from the records of early explorers, was also the character of
their ancestors, they lived on the natural resources of the country. Fish,
birds, and animal life were prolific, and apart from their savage warfare
they led a communal existence."[18] Here again Natives emerge as "savage"
warmongers, tarred by their crude tie to the land[19] and smeared with the
Cold War stain of leftism ("communal existence"). Further, this passage
freezes Natives in time ("the character of the Indian of today was also
the character of their ancestors"). The appeal is to common sense as suggested by the authoritative and confidential beginning—"as we know."

Miner and News reportage held that Aboriginals revelled in gratuitous
expressions of vandalism.[20] In early January 1974, an article highlights
alleged Indigenous primitivism and proclivity for wanton violence.[21]
In another case, in mid-June the paper devoted a whole page to a story
titled, "Members of isolated community forgive man in double murder,"
which links alleged Aboriginal barbarism with an inability to withstand
the allure of excessive alcohol consumption. Taken together, the results
proved predictably violent and criminal. The article snidely implies that
the very notion of community forgiveness was hopelessly naive. The
paper reported, "A night of drunken revelry in the tiny Cree settlement
of 208 persons...ended with two men dead and one woman, 15, suffering
gunshot wounds in the face. The jury listened carefully, with consummate horror on their faces, to a story about a freakish occurrence."[22]

The trouble started, one reads, when the alleged killer and friends,
whom he shot dead, decided to get drunk and ingest LSD. "'I had no
intention of killing them,'" the paper reported the accused as having told
the court. "'I don't remember killing Billy and Gordon. I couldn't believe
when my wife told me in the morning.'" The message was plain enough—
Natives wallowed in violence, engaged in "freakish" behaviour, made
civilized people feel "horror," and washed it all down with alcohol (and,
sometimes, illicit drugs). They had always been this way.

According to the *Miner and News* in 1974, Natives fundamentally
lacked self-control. This allegedly gave rise to various expressions of
barbarism—sneakiness, treachery, explosive violence and criminality. It
also found vent in an alleged love affair with alcohol. Ongoing accounts

of alcohol addiction and alcohol-related violence can be found in nearly every issue of the *Miner and News* in 1974. In fact, so prevalent was this framing that one might argue that it constituted a near regular, though informal, feature of daily coverage—in a sense, as regular as "Dear Abby," and more predictable than the weather.

To begin with, court docket reports commonly sketched alcohol abuse by local Natives. For example, one issue described a fine of fifty dollars handed down to one Mary Eliza Keewatin, charged with causing a disturbance on a downtown street. The short piece offered a detailed account of how Keewatin, identified as a mother of eight from the Grassy Narrows reserve north of Kenora, had been drinking at the time of the fight with another woman, also from Grassy Narrows.[23] Yet a more serious assault charge reported in the court docket that day concerning a local non-Aboriginal man offered no details about his personal life or ethnic heritage. This pattern of clearly establishing the race of all Indigenous peoples charged with crimes typified court docket reportage.[24] On another occasion, local police, the paper reported, without a trace of irony, found it difficult to differentiate between a drunken Native and a mentally handicapped one.[25]

A second key theme of alleged Aboriginal lack of self-control derived from the charge that Aboriginals could not administer their own affairs in concord with Canadian mainstream norms. According to reports in the *Miner and News,* Natives were unable to govern themselves properly or effectively, to the point that they appeared to be inherently anti-democratic, a reader of the local paper would have been reminded.[26] They frequently violated the basic tenets of cherished Canadian-style democracy.[27] Kenora's own Progressive Conservative MPP, Leo Bernier, also minister of natural resources for the province of Ontario, agreed with this assessment. The minister talked to the paper about the difficulty of getting Natives to work productively. "Our own people are working with them, trying to motivate them," he explained. "It will take time," he stressed. "Only the ones that are ambitious do it [that is, work]." The paper opined that the problem, at least in part, stemmed from the fact that "the Indians struggle with trying to learn to adopt the white man's ways." But Bernier would have none of it, responding in classic political double-speak. "There is no real suffering [in Aboriginal communities]," he proclaimed, at one and the same time refuting the easily documented and glaringly widespread poverty in Ontario's reservations as well as dismissing any hint that government policy had played a hand in contributing to the conditions that it was actively engaged in attempting to combat (and simultaneously deny) in this very instance. To drive the point home, the minister added, "about 90 percent of the reserves get government assistance of one kind or another."[28] Natives were, in short, lazy, ungrateful welfare recipients, according the town's long-standing member of provincial government. It is interesting, further, to note that Bernier's comments are framed in such a way as to juxtapose the alleged indolence of Aboriginal people with the activeness of government employees.

Bernier was not the only local official who questioned Aboriginal integrity and charged them with churlish, immature motivations. Kenora mayor Jim Davidson, who would later play a key role in the talks that followed the seizure of the park and whom the local press would come to champion as a sort of elder statesman, charged local Aboriginals with reverse discrimination against Kenora's white population. According to the *Miner and News*, "he [Davidson] said Kenora has been accused in the past of discrimination and being intolerant, but he believes the situation is the exact opposite." It went on to quote Davidson. "'We're not going to be bullied by a group of drunks,'" he charged, affirming the stereotypical Indigenous proclivity for intemperance.[29] At the same meeting, Davidson's contempt for local Aboriginals drew support from a Kenora alderman, Clarence Dusang, whom the newspaper reported as citing an alcohol addiction among local Natives as more severe than ever before.[30]

"ADDRESS THE ROT"

As exotics, Natives were generally portrayed in two ways—first, as harmless, even amusing, frequently intoxicated curiosities, and, second, as representatives of a moribund race.[31] Most often it was characterizations of public events, in particular the pow wow, that elicited this kinder, gentler, yet no less pernicious or constructed portrayal.[32] Not simply a patronizing tone but assumed evidence of Aboriginal childishness pervaded *Miner and News* coverage in 1974.[33]

According to the press, and somewhat incongruously, given the allegation that they were volatile and criminally explosive, Aboriginals tended also to be passive and needed, even supplicated for, government assistance. The implication was that they were not capable of self-management, let alone self-control.[34] Aboriginals needed, even invited, forceful guidance, direction, and white control. Childlike, they were essentially incapable of effectively governing themselves bodily or politically.

More than that, even in apparently more gentle characterizations, the press depictions constantly undermined full Aboriginal humanity. For example, coverage of an "Indian Princess" competition offered a double blow, marginalizing Aboriginal females by virtue of their culture *and* gender. Among other rewards, the winner got to have her picture taken handing a trophy to the captain of an Aboriginal hockey team.[35]

Yet this conflation of stereotypes—gender and race—was more complicated. Aboriginal males were sometimes feminized, as in portrayals of effete pow wow dancers[36] or girlish artist impersonators,[37] while Native females took on non-mainstream traditional roles, such as when Madeline Skead became chief of the Rat Portage reserve, located on Kenora's southern borders, in March 1974. While Skead's election might be read as an affirmation of female assertiveness—and no doubt it was, in fact—the paper used the occasion to smear Aboriginals by suggesting that they were so confused that they had gotten their genders mixed up. After all, Skead's election could only occur if all of the Aboriginal males were unfit for office—which, of course, might have seemed possible if one were to accept the stereotyping at face value. Yet, on the other hand, tempering this conclusion with the application of a non-racial stereotype—and this also became a key feature of later coverage—females served as a civilizing influence on men generally, so it seemed reasonable that Skead might signify a natural sort of social evolution at work, especially given that the chief had little significant real-world political power, the *Miner and News* implied.[38]

The same coverage also raised the repeated tropes of Aboriginal neediness and alcoholism. And because, according to portrayals, Natives were fundamentally incapable, it was up to the good Samaritans such as Leo Bernier and others in government to make "modest attempts to address the rot," the *Miner and News* opined in early April.[39] A letter to the editor in early May cut to the heart of the matter and captured the tone and pith of the sentiment: "Leaving the Drop-in Center at 4 p.m. last Friday, a bus entering Hennepin Lane stopped across a walk while two natives rolled around. One was a partial cripple while the other, perhaps 30 years of age, was being kicked in the head and face by a teenager, who in turn was being semi-restrained. Everyday occurrence? Winos!!!"[40]

In early June the Kenora Chamber of Commerce asked the town to ban fortified wine from being sold in the provincial liquor store, which held a monopoly on the sale of spirits. The issue was termed by the *Miner and News*, the "problem of inebriates." Less circumspect than many articles that danced around directly identifying local Aboriginals with alcoholic vagrancy, this article called for "scheduled busing service to the reserves" to attempt to solve the problem. It also called on the federal government to pitch in and create an Aboriginal hostel so that drunken Natives might not litter the town's streets.[41]

In sum, prior to the seizure of Anicinabe Park local press representations of Indigenous peoples reflected standard colonial stereotypings. Well-established press and cultural patterns of alleged Aboriginal inferiority stressed three frequently overlapping themes of Natives as barbaric, intoxicated, and moribund.

"STEP INTO REALITY FROM YOUR DREAM WORLD"

The rhetoric related to the seizure of Anicinabe Park made its first appearance in the *Miner and News* on 27 June, fully three weeks before the conference held at the park that led directly to the conflict. A provocative letter to the editor from the Ojibway Warrior Society claimed that "racism, bigotry, and subtle discrimination is running wild in this town." The missive blamed the business community, churches, "general society," judicial system, provincial government, local police, and resort owners for collusion in aiding, encouraging, and participating in long-standing traditions of abusing local Natives. The upcoming July conference at Anicinabe Park, the letter continued, would constitute a first step in reasserting Aboriginal sovereignty and redressing the structural inequities visited upon Natives as a result of endemic, myopic colonialism.[42] Despite the immoderate tone, all in all the charges were accurate, judging by press coverage—though notably they did not include an attack on the local media. In a deeply researched and thoughtful historical account of the forced relocation of the Grassy Narrows reserve north of Kenora, Anastasia Shkilnyk argues that the white population of Kenora was mostly unaware of the internal problems that had developed on local reserves during what Eleanor Jacobson, author of the poisonous and inflammatory *Bended Elbow, Kenora Talks Back*, cast as a golden age for racial harmony.[43] Therefore, Shkilnyk argues, townsfolk reacted to the Aboriginal presence in town with censuring disapproval.[44]

Predictably, the Warrior Society's letter sparked an angry letter in response. Its author, Judy Parkes, did not mince words, and articulated clearly, forcefully, and rancorously the stereotyped images that the *Miner and News* specialized in. Further, her letter effectively introduced a shift in *Miner and News* coverage to a more exaggerated, even occasionally hysterical tone, once the seizure occurred—that is, in effect, auguring what amounted to a hardening of representation. In short, the first rhetorical challenge in the newspaper to Kenora's well-entrenched colonial behaviour elicited a spirited and immediate reaction. Yet it is important to emphasize that the basic themes of the overall coverage did not change but, rather, became magnified and inflated. Parkes's letter signals a ratcheting up of the volume, for here for the first time in 1974 the paper presented whites in the role of victim.

To begin with, Parkes indicated that she was very nearly physically violated by the Warrior Society's letter. She had been "filled with disgust and a general sense of nausea" by it, she wrote. Raising the specter of reverse discrimination, she pondered, "Why should you get more than I... just because your skin is brown?" Then she veritably erupted, denouncing Aboriginals as childish hypocrites, "You Ojibway are just as much to blame for any discrimination as anyone. You're too busy crying over it to get out and do something about it." She proffered a solution:

> If you want equality, seriously, then cut your ties with the government and their juicy grants and free houses; step out into reality from your dream world, pick up your load...You're so selfish...Can you name one group of people of any race, creed or colour in all of Canada who are given free education, free houses, free land, free medical, free dentistry and also don't have to pay income tax or any sales tax? And what's more they don't even appreciate it! Admittedly, Indians have a problem, a drinking problem. One which could be remedied if their hands were kept busy at work.[45]

While Parkes's letter constitutes an extreme position, none of the charges she levelled, apart from casting whites as victims, were unfamiliar to readers of the *Miner and News* in 1974. Many of the basic characteristics of the three streams of imagery emerge from this missive. She singles Natives out by race and charges that they unfairly receive special treatment, exhibit selfishness, resentfulness, laziness, behave like children, and are alcoholics.

In a way, from the outlook imparted by Parkes, it is little short of a miracle that "primitive" and "hostile"[46] Aboriginals could ever have existed without whites. Natives were in need of vigilant guidance, even surveillance, the paper argued consistently. Meanwhile, whites, unlike Natives, had been able to tame and improve nature as God himself had long since requested, according to English-Canadian culture.[47] For example, in early July another article championing colonialism in the region noted that early white immigrants had had to clean up the area otherwise "full of swamps and backwaters." Such laudable efforts, the story continued, were supplanted by the notable civilizing effects of the construction of a post office and railway terminal.[48] Likewise, Treaty 3 (1873), which covers a vast expanse of northwestern Ontario, played the important role of "tranquilizing a large Indian population."[49] Further, to dispel confusion, the article stressed that the Natives of the region had been fairly and completely compensated by the terms of the treaty. Characterizing them as essentially clueless without whites to tutor them, the story explained, "Of the terms of the treaty it may be said that the promises made to the Indians have been fully kept and many advantages of civilization have been freely given to the benefit of succeeding generations of Indians."[50]

On the eve of the conference the *Miner and News* published a remarkable full-page guest editorial, penned by a local high-school teacher, William Laffin. While the title of the piece suggests Aboriginals are at least as much to blame for their colonized position as whites ("Indian-White problem inflicted by both sides"), Laffin's views reflected a dramatic departure for the paper. In a clear attempt to provide a more balanced interpretation of white-Indigenous relations, Laffin argued, on one hand, "that the Indian community has much cause to be angry and frustrated"; but, on the other hand, he also held that the veterans of Wounded Knee, South Dakota, where a bloody month-long standoff had taken place the year before, were not generally welcomed by Kenora Natives at the conference.

In the main, however, Laffin concurred with the central allegations of the Ojibway Warrior Society's letter to the editor published a month earlier, that racism and bigotry on the part of whites had not only tainted white-Indigenous relations but had engendered materially deleterious effects on Aboriginals. Laffin acknowledged that Aboriginal public drunkenness vitiated the widespread ignorance and intolerance among Kenora's white population. "Society," he wrote, "tars them all with the same brush, just as the 'Wounded Knee Veterans' tar all whites with the same brush."[51]

Yet Laffin's long letter to the editor did not reorient the dominant pejorative, racist, and stereotyped *Miner and News* framing of Natives. For example, he also opined, "When you see so many Indians drunk and unkempt about the streets, laying in doorways, on the street, urinating on the busy sidewalks, keeping our jail full with drunken charges, it is difficult to see the clean cut, sober Indians.... A person would have to exceptional indeed, not to develop a negative attitude towards Indians."[52] The same issue in which Laffin's letter appeared also quoted Harvey Major, a technical advisor to the Ojibway Warrior Society and a veteran of Wounded Knee, who claimed that organizers of the event had already suffered harassment at the hands of local brigands.[53]

Three days later, the weekend passed, the conference concluded, and on Monday, 22 July, news coverage seemed set to resume its regular pace and normal volume. For example, the paper evinced mild surprise and some relief that the conference appeared to have gone off without a hitch. "Those in attendance," readers were reassured, "maintained an orderly and peaceful conduct, with police reporting a quiet weekend." The report implied that this may have been due in part to the mayor's urging citizens to "keep cool" so that "a spark would not set off any incident." That said, the paper also solemnly noted reports that gunfire had emanated from the park over the weekend. No surprise, then, that "a considerable amount of conjecture and apprehension surrounds the proceedings."[54]

For once, though, the daily's apprehensions may have been well founded, for the next day it reported extensively the news that the Warrior Society had "occupied" the park. Dangerous ("heavily armed") and ungrateful (after all, "officials had granted the park free of charge"), the Aboriginals now menaced the whole town. "Along with the clubs, knives, spears, sticks and baseball bats they have several high powered rifles, shot guns and at least a half dozen Molotov cocktails," the paper warned its readers.[55] And comments attributed to Harvey Major would not have reassured local residents: "'If just one of our Indian people is hit by a bullet, Kenora will go up in smoke.'"[56] A careful reader might have recalled that months earlier the federal Department of Indian Affairs was already

"at war" with Native youth.[57] In short, while the employment of a discourse of hostilities to characterize Aboriginal behaviour was not suddenly new (as also shown in the discussion of reports about Massacre
Island), its increased frequency was after the 19 July weekend.[58]

Yet the Warrior Society's own rhetoric undoubtedly worked against
its professed aims. Leader Louis Cameron was frequently quoted as
threatening violence against whites. For example, on 23 July the paper
reported that Cameron "described the Indians remaining at the park as
'Kamikaze's,' [sic] who are willing to die for their cause." Cameron, the
daily noted in the same story, had also been arrested and released on the
Monday after the seizure began, for "carrying a dangerous weapon," a
hunting knife. Major, too, was quoted on that day, lashing out against
white authorities: "'There's one way to get by a group of pigs [police] like
that ... by using guerilla tactics we can beat them.'" The paper went on
to explain that Major "would begin teaching women and inexperienced
men how to use high-powered rifles and how to make bombs (Molotov
cocktails) today."[59] On another occasion, a week later, as the standoff
continued, Cameron warned that "if they don't meet our demands ...
we'll take aggressive action to see that we mean business.... We might
even decide to turn northwestern Ontario into a war zone."[60]

A list of Warrior Society demands were published in the 23 July issue
of the *Miner and News*. They included a call for effective, efficient, and
accessible transportation to and from Kenora and seven area reserves;
that interpreters be hired at all government agencies with which local
Aboriginals dealt; fairer treatment of Native people by police; and a less
racially discriminating attitude be shown by local businesses and labour
unions when hiring employees. But the paper dismissed the demands by,
first, refusing to respond to them, and second, drowning them, as had
earlier been the fate of Laffin's balanced comments, beneath the roar of
normal pejorative coverage.

The following day the paper confidently asserted that the occupants
of the park had run afoul of the law and that they could be criminally
indicted for trespassing. Further, the same front-page article charged
that the Natives holding the park were maliciously and irresponsibly
contravening the law as well as good sense by maintaining open camp-
fires as "hundreds of square miles of timber [were] burning out of control" in the region.[61] The fear and potential criminality of open fires

received notice for the first time the previous day: "the white community in Kenora is beginning to polarize over the occupation. One woman told the *Miner and News* today that she is alarmed at open fires being started in the park despite a complete ban on such fires imposed by the Ministry of Natural Resources...The woman said she plans to approach the ministry and determine if she can lay a charge against Indians starting fires in the park."[62] Moreover, the "occupying" force now openly menaced the peaceful townsfolk by making no attempts to disguise their rifles, as photographs printed in the broadsheet showed.[63]

For the duration of the standoff, the paper characterized the Warrior Society, its supporters, and effectively all of Canada's Natives as dangerous, irresponsible, and unreasonable. For example, a front-page article of 24 July contains key elements that would come to characterize the near-hysterical *Miner and News* coverage of the seizure. The piece reports on preliminary meetings held between local government officials and representatives of the Warrior Society aimed at resolving the crisis. As ever, in the newspaper the Natives were identified as an uncompromising pseudo-military force; whereas the local mayor, Jim Davidson, and MPP Leo Bernier were described as responsible, sober, optimistic, and desirous of a quick resolution of the problem.[64] Next, the article spins a cautionary fable of how some white tourists' sense of decency and decorum had been assaulted by "six Indians armed with rifles and clubs." Readers were reminded that the Natives represented a peril to whites and, further, that they had pledged to do violence to anyone and everyone who might attempt to dislodge them from the park.

The newspaper also presented a variety of sources promoting the rule of law. The framing worked in two directions. First, depictions sought to make it clear that the Warrior Society had violated several statutes, an allegedly common Aboriginal tendency. But, at the same time, other Natives were invoked to champion an immediate end to the "occupation." For example, the controversial Saskatchewan Cree political figure, David Ahenakew, was cited as arguing that "they [Kenora Natives] certainly don't need outside help," a reference to the participation of members (e.g., Harvey Major) of the American Indian Movement (AIM).[65] And on 26 July the paper reported that an unidentified survey indicated that "as a whole...members of the Ojibwe people in the Kenora area do not approve of actions taken by the Warrior Society."[66] Similarly, without attribution, echoing William Laffin's letter to the editor, the *Miner and News* reported that "the majority of Indian people in the Kenora area do not condone the actions of the Ojibway Warrior Society."[67]

Although the news coverage tended to assume more exaggerated proportions during the park seizure, in the letters to the editor section a bona fide debate erupted between polarized positions. It pitted those who, like Judy Parkes, robustly and with prejudice embraced a muscular variety of the most glaring negative characteristics of *Miner and News* coverage, against those who, like William Laffin, decried easy stereotyping and challenged readers to take a hard look at the legacy of colonialism in Canada in an effort to gain deeper and more empathetic understanding of white/Indigenous relations and issues. Parkes's response to Laffin's letter laid bare the contours of the opposing sides.

In a rambling verbal attack she labelled Laffin "vicious" and took a broad swipe at his more progressive politics by implying that he was ideologically aligned with feminists. Further, she attempted to impugn his integrity by denouncing him as a newcomer to town (five years residence), which, according to her, did not give him the right to criticize local traditions, the roots of which predated his residence. Further, Parkes vigorously rejected the idea that she harboured any prejudiced feelings against Aboriginals. Instead, she argued, "this group at Anicinabe Park is a classic example of thrill seekers." Despite the Warrior Society's allegations that Natives had long suffered, in part, from institutionalized racism in Kenora, a point taken up and supported at some length by Laffin, Parkes held that "they are just out to get publicity."[68]

On the other hand, Parkes also issued a thinly veiled threat to local Aboriginals. "If they're not careful," she warned, "there will be an uprising, but one instigated by the white people who are losing their patience and their tempers." She then listed four "possible [criminal] charges against them," which included "inciting to riot; possession of dangerous weapons; breaking a fire restriction ban; and illegally taking control of a municipally-owned park."[69]

Despite her spurious claim that Kenora as a white community was prejudice-free, Parkes assiduously expressed the very racism and intolerance she claimed did not exist. "God knows what they hope to achieve," she continued. "I don't. It only makes people resent to an even greater degree and contribute to even more violent discrimination." She blamed the federal government for kowtowing to Natives' every childish complaint. "It stands to reason, if people are handed everything on a silver platter, they will never be satisfied and lose all interest in striving to achieve," she wrote.[70]

"IT'S HARD TO SHOW EMPATHY AND LOVE"

Ojibway Warrior Society leader Louis Cameron emerged unequivocally as the leader of and principal spokesman for the seizure. Cameron repeatedly criticized the town not just for endemic racism but for institutionalizing the racial prejudice in ways that materially denigrated the quality of life for the region's Aboriginal population. In a *Miner and News* report he described Kenora as being "unrealistic" and "corrupt," though stated hopefully that "the majority of local whites realize we are fighting for a cause.'"[71]

Yet readers of the *Miner and News* had been repetitively warned not to have faith in Cameron. As if to reassure readers that Cameron could not be trusted, the same article reported that tensions had flared the night before when white men carrying rifles had stationed themselves outside the park, though police had ended the situation.[72]

After the "occupation" began, Kenora mayor Davidson quickly emerged in the *Miner and News* as a strong, paternalistic, and unbiased leader. He initially adopted a tough stance regarding the seizure, warning residents that "'we can't be blackmailed like this into making decisions.'"[73] However, as the crisis at the park began to attract national attention—most of it unflattering, which raised hackles at the paper[74]—the mayor's public position on the takeover softened. On 31 July, the mayor was quoted as saying that positive results had come out of the publicity Kenora had received over the park issue.[75] He then attempted to portray Kenora as an enlightened community, shifting the blame for the interracial problems to provincial and federal authorities. When the Warrior Society surrendered its arms without incident on 18 August, a reinvented, newly benevolent Davidson was quoted as saying, "This is a symptom of a condition that should be changed, and I won't be happy until some of the conditions are changed that brought on the demonstrations such as we have had."

Yet, while he sought to downplay the park's seizure to the level of a mere demonstration, letters to the editor suggested that many readers were reluctant to adopt more conciliatory rhetoric. As one missive put it, "Why are these supposedly intelligent bodies of people wasting their time and our money trying to negotiate with this type of people?"[76] Another complained, "I, for one, can see why its [sic] hard to show sympathy and love etc., toward our Indian people, when we, the residents of Kenora have to put up with the drunks and filth and bad language... and get spit on."[77] Even an anonymous fifth-grade student wrote to the paper and complained, "I don't think it was fair of them to take over the park."[78] Probably the most strident among the various correspondents was Eleanor Jacobson, whose explosive prose was punctuated with the image treatment of Natives common in the *Miner and News*: "I have seen with my own eyes Indians all tanked out of shape making love on the Library lawn...in broad daylight. Now I ask you, is this natural? These people have no pride at all and they say that we don't respect them. How can we respect them when they act the way they do?"[79]

Still, the mayor continued to receive praise from the *Miner and News* for his efforts to demonstrate his, and by association, Kenora's good working relationship with local Natives. For example, when Davidson spoke at the Indian Homemakers' Association banquet on 21 August the paper reported that the mayor "hinted that people should not ignore skin color but learn to examine, admire and respect the difference between groups of different cultures."[80]

Meanwhile, the Warrior Society's list of demands continued to take a distant back seat to the coverage in the *Miner and News*. The 4 September front page typified this framing. Continuing to ignore the grievances aired by the Society, it focussed on the "willful destruction and vandalism" of the park rather than on any positive or hopeful outcome to the seizure, as promoted by Cameron and Davidson.[81] Photographs emphasizing abandoned cars, refuse, and discarded "sharp instruments" littering the now-abandoned park were sprinkled throughout the edition and drew attention to the core allegations about alleged Aboriginal recklessness, ignorance, lawlessness, filth, and untrustworthiness. As a letter to the editor assessed the situation two days later, "they turned a white man's park into a garbage dump."[82]

Despite the letters to the editor, once the conflict concluded peacefully, the regular inflammatory *Miner and News* coverage quickly resumed its earlier tone, offering a less aggressive vision of alleged Aboriginal inferiority and depravity in their various manifestations. In the only editorial offered by the paper on the seizure, on 1 August the *Miner and News* proclaimed its own objectivity while simultaneously heaping scorn upon the Warrior Society: "The media's role now is to keep the public informed on concrete developments at the negotiating table and not worry about militants waving firearms around and positioning gas bombs."[83] In this way, the paper ascribed to itself the right to determine right from wrong, truth from untruth.

Yet, in spite of the paper's modernist pretensions, throughout the fall of 1974 a battle continued to rage in the letters to the editor section. On the one hand, incendiary correspondence poured in while more tempered notes heaped praise on local officials, especially the mayor. Meanwhile, Kenora mayor Davidson apparently misread the public mood that fall. He narrowly failed in his bid for re-election in October after focusing his campaign efforts on the promotion of his role in the management of the successful and peaceful conclusion to the events of the Indian summer. He lost by five votes to the law-and-order candidate, William Tomashowski.[84]

Warrior Society leader Louis Cameron, at the same time, while at a pow wow at a local school in late September, told the paper: "the occupation of Anicinabe Park this summer brought Indian problems to the forefront.... This is one of the very few times when Indians and non-Indians have gotten together. It's one of the greatest victories of the summer; that there's now unity."[85] Clearly, the letters to the editor section of the daily broadsheet also suggested strongly that Cameron too had misread the public mood.

Cameron went on to lead a march to Ottawa in the early fall. The so-called Native People's Caravan garnered much local reportage about the new "militant" Indians. Significantly, a local editorial on 2 October used the occasion to deflect all blame for the Anicinabe Park seizure and standoff toward the federal government, echoing a commentary penned in early August by the publisher William Dempsey.[86] Speciously, Dempsey's argument employed the very existence of the Native People's Caravan as proof that the problems that contributed to the crisis at the park reached far beyond the reaches of the Kenora area: "One of the basic problems in Kenora concerning Indian-white relations is that many people can't see the real problem of the Indians for the drunks and filth on the streets. For years municipal leaders have hoped the problem would go away but it just got worse. Then their pleas for provincial and federal assistance brought nothing."[87] And so the paper itself took the bold step of making its own position representative for all of Canada. That is, Natives everywhere and whites elsewhere were to blame for Kenora's racial bigotry and institutionalized colonial behaviour. In this way, Kenora, the quintessential white Canadian community, according to its local daily newspaper, emerged as faultless. And the Natives? Here the paper hints at "real problems" but seemed satisfied with resorting to its past practice of conjuring up images of intoxicated and dirty savages.

Kenora, the paper averred, had tried to make changes (the precise nature and scope of which went unexamined), but the town's hands were tied by anonymous federal authorities. In fact, it was the federal government that ignored mounting problems and triggered the "occupation" in the first place, the paper argued: "As a result Kenora as a community will suffer, and suffer, and suffer, unless these decision-makers can really get plugged into what is going on and implement sound programs which produce results."[88] In presumptive and classic agenda-setting terms the editorial seeks to instruct and to reassure readers that Kenora whites had, first, been victimized; second, that Aboriginals presented a serious problem ("what is really going on"); and, third, it implies that assimilationist policies augured the best answer to the problem ("sound programs which produce results").

While the images discussed herein speak to a single newspaper's year-long coverage, with special emphasis on a charged, yet discrete, incident, the *Miner and News* depictions of Aboriginals typified (and typify) Canadian newspaper representations of Natives since 1869. As noted, scholars have identified the mainstream press as a central instrument in structuring and naturalizing colonialism. In short, then, one may argue that the *Miner and News*, in addition to serving its business masters and the local reading audience with the "news," also contributed to Canadian imperialism by promoting racist notions about the alleged inferiority of Aboriginal peoples. Further, that the images reflect the racialized image patterning common in other colonial societies, and that the press has been found to serve a key role in the promotion and affirmation of colonialism in such societies, shows that the "Bended Elbow" narrative, as news story, also very much served to add yet another brick in the wall of the Canadian colonial project.

CHAPTER TEN

INDIAN PRINCESS/INDIAN "SQUAW"
Bill C-31, 1985

Jennifer Williams had the opportunity she wanted last week. The British Columbia Indian princess was presented to the Royal Family. She was one of 10 Indian princesses from across Canada to compete for the Canadian Indian Princess title in Yellowknife. Miss Williams, 18, found the Queen 'very informal; she seemed to be interested in us.'

She also met Princess Anne but regretted having been unable to meet Prince Charles. The northern trip lasted one week, and, according to Miss Williams, 'We were entertained by the mayor of Yellowknife at the banquet and we in turn sponsored a fashion show, modeling suede outfits, including an evening gown.'

She is not the only princess in her family. Her sister, Debbie, was one of the Indian princesses crowned during this years Cowichan Corpus Christi festival.

—VICTORIA *DAILY COLONIST*, 14 JULY 1970

Joyce Green refers to Aboriginal women, marked both by race and gender, as proverbial canaries in the coal mine of Canadian inequality.[1] Even when the federal government attempted to fix wrongs as it did in 1985 with the passage of Bill C-31 it only succeeded in creating new problems.[2] Bill C-31 seemingly acknowledged and supported Aboriginal women. That watershed change to the Indian Act retroactively reinstated some women as Status Indians who had lost their rights because of sexual discrimination within the Act. For example, prior to Bill C-31 First Nations women who married white men lost their status; whereas white women who married First Nations men gained status. Still, the attempts to address inequities in the Indian Act have fallen short and the law is currently being challenged in the courts.[3]

Newspapers in Canada have long imagined Aboriginal women within the stereotypical binary of the Indian princess/Indian "squaw," and these essentialized images remain ordinary and ongoing in popular culture. Like Disney's Pocahontas, a sexualized version of the historical figure, the beautiful and virtuous Indian princess who aided the European explorer John Smith, illustrates a passive and sometimes eroticized framing of Aboriginal women. Meanwhile, the squalid and immoral "squaw" lurking at the margins of civilization and whose presence threatened moral order has been a constant from 1869 down to this day. Anthropologist Elizabeth Bird demonstrates such stereotypes continually resurface and are difficult to combat. Both Aboriginal males and females have become sexualized in relation to the white gaze, according to Bird, but in particular the Indian princess, as epitomized by Pocahontas, endures as white fantasy.[4] Serving as "agents of enculturation," the media promote bifurcated images of anonymous, whorish "squaws" or sexy, exotic princesses who desire and serve white males.[5] Both of these constructions resonate in press coverage related to the passage of Bill C-31. However, to consider these stereotypical representations only as simple binaries ignores the subtle and overlapping manifestations found in press coverage.

Everyone loves an Indian princess. The press knows this because a cursory glance at press coverage of newsworthy items related to Aboriginal women in the past 100 years confirms that such formulations have persisted, especially in human-interest stories. The princess image evokes a hopeful yearning for assimilation, as was the case in depictions of E. Pauline Johnson (chapter 5). After all, the passivity of the princess renders a malleable construct not just unthreatening but sexually attractive as a paternalistic and patriarchal construction.

However, the image of the prostitute, derogatorily inscribed early on as the "squaw" construction, also has tempered press coverage related to Aboriginal women. Existing as a negative corollary to the submissive construction of the princess in news stories, the "squaw" stubbornly, even recklessly, resists assimilation and conformity to Canadian ideals and thus remains anathema and threatening to the colonial project but also, importantly, serves as a reminder of just how necessary it is that assimilation takes place.[6] The stakes are high because nothing short of the moral order of society is at risk.

In order to fully contextualize press coverage in 1985 related to the passage of the bill, we must go back to earlier coverage in the press. The intractability of the "squaw" image runs the gamut from the lazy drunken drudge at the beck and call of her man to a corrupting sexual presence that incites white males to act violently (as noted in chapters 4 and 7) to the shrill activist working to change inequities for Aboriginal women in Canada related to the passage of Bill C-31.[7]

A legacy of racism and discrimination remains at the centre of this investigation. The initial drive to change the act occurred much earlier, with two cases that moved through the Ontario provincial courts and ended up being heard by the Supreme Court of Canada in 1973. This chapter investigates press coverage in English press regional dailies with most specific examples drawn from 1969 through 1973 and again in 1985 through 1987 on issues related to Aboriginal women. Three specific episodes from this period reinforced the popular cultural manifestations of the Indian princess/Indian "squaw" in a variety of guises that ultimately contextualize the dearth of reportage concerning Bill C-31.

First, during the late 1960s and early 1970s images of the Indian princess appeared in newspapers frequently, directly and indirectly related to national Indian princess competitions. Second, the murder of Helen Betty Osborne in The Pas, Manitoba, in 1971 and the subsequent murder trial in 1987 reveal extreme racism and sexism found in Canadian communities and illustrate how the "squaw" remains fungible currency in Canada. Third, beginning with the Supreme Court challenge to the Indian Act launched by Jeanette Corbiere Lavell and Yvonne Bédard in 1973, the princess/"squaw" construction that serves as an interpretive rubric for Aboriginal women aligns itself neatly with well-established patterns of Native representation in the press since 1869, as already discussed.

LEGENDARY INDIAN PRINCESS

The chaste princess mimics stereotypical framings of mainstream females but with added Aboriginal baggage related to mythical images of the Hollywood Indian: fringed and beaded buckskin dresses, feather headdresses, passive, and, crucially, docile. As shown throughout this study, Canada's English-language newspapers have served up an array of such images. Equally simplistic constructions of Indigenous males as the noble or garden-variety savage support and provide context for the Indian princess in the press. For example, in reports in the Calgary *Herald* in 1939 of the noble savages clad in beads and feathers and paraded before visiting royal dignitaries, the Indian princess typically trailed a few steps behind her chief, demurely and passively objectified for public consumption.[8] Such constructions in the news affirmed notions of Canadian identity as a settler nation that had subdued its Indigenous population.

North Americans generally have jealously coveted the imaginary Indian princess in an attempt to confirm its unique identity—signifying difference from Britain and Europe, even as Canada has continued to play the same old colonial game. Disney's Pocahontas and Mattel's "Native American" Barbie dolls still capture the imaginations of Canadian and American girls who dress up and role-play.[9] Additionally, the historical figure of Pocahontas has reached mythic proportions since her 1616 trip to Britain.[10] For example, a 1948 news story in the Montreal *Gazette* illustrated an allegiance to the romanticized Pocahontas in a Grey Owl-like penchant to "go native" by a British aristocrat. The *Gazette* reported that the "British Earl Mountbatten of Burma's wife" claimed to be a descendant of Pocahontas. The story presented the aristocratic blue blood as an unlikely candidate for red blood lines but found the claim amusingly exotic: "The tall, blonde Edwina Ashley was once considered the wealthiest heiress in England, being the granddaughter of Sir Ernest Cassell, fabulously rich English financier, and was goddaughter of King Edward VII...Countess Montbatten claims descent from the Indian princess Pocahontas from her father's side, and from the princess of ancient Israel...The countess is an excellent golfer and ardent traveler."[11]

The report offers no evidence to support the countess's claims unless one considers her prowess as a golfer as a signifier of athleticism derived from her alleged Aboriginal pedigree. However, seriousness and Indian princesses have never had much in common, and news stories related to this subject satisfied human interest with little expectation for "hard news."

Stories and photos of princesses were not really part of the daily news. Rather, they appeared as a pleasant antidote to the paper's newsworthy offerings. They nonetheless served the serious purpose of commodifying Aboriginal women, in the best case, as shallow, empty, vapid, and nonthreatening. In this way, photographs of buckskin-clad beauties dotted newspapers in the 1960s and 1970s.[12] One seemingly lighthearted report of Alberta's acting premier trading a bicycle and a catskin (allusions to romantic historical trades of ponies and beaver pelts) in exchange for "Running Water, legendary Indian princess, to take up residence" in his tipi during the annual Louis Riel Pageant in Edmonton exemplifies the stereotypes pitched as harmless humour.[13] Yet, how funny was a story that saw a mainstream political figure symbolically buying himself a whore as part of a public festival?

"MEMORIES OF A NOBLE PAST"

The creation of a national Indian princess competition complicated the typical depiction of the princess because the events were undertaken seriously by Indigenous females and thus moved beyond simplistic genderized Othering. The ongoing regional and national competitions across Canada served as positive opportunities for numerous Indigenous women within the cultural practice of pow wow. However, the agency inherent within pow wow competitions was lost to mainstream audiences.[14] Press coverage mostly provided little context for the competitions, which tended to ensure the presentation of an imaginary construction allied with romantic associations of the past.

For example, a June 1969 Calgary *Herald* report described a travelling pow wow group as "Indian warriors in feather head dresses and buckskins," who had "invaded" Paris, France. And the paper called the 1968 reigning national Indian princess, Vivien Ayoungman, also on tour, a "beauty queen."[15] Between June 1969 and July 1970 a number of stories relating to the annual national Indian princess competitions surfaced in newspapers across Canada that sometimes shifted coverage from the human interest spin to newsworthy reports, making it a useful time period for analysis.[16] Judged like contestants in any beauty pageant on the basis of their physical appearance, poise, and conversational ability, the Fredericton *Daily Gleaner* explained, Indian princesses were additionally adjudicated on their "Indian" dress and knowledge of "Indian" heritage and culture.[17] With this added seriousness came particular language patterns that reinforced connections between assimilation and the culturally moribund—themes commonly found in news stories linked to Aboriginals—such as Princess Ayoungman "invading" Paris with "warriors." In 1969 testimonial statements from the princesses regarding the importance of education and helping others emerged and served as nods to the successful project of assimilation evidenced in the press stories and photographs.[18]

A 1969 Winnipeg *Free Press* photograph offered a visual primer to how the Manitoba contestants were chosen, without providing any textual description. The winner, Dorothy Campbell of Ste. Rose du Lac, posed next to runner-up Valerie Klyne of Camperville. Campbell's attire as that of the stereotypical princess beat out an assimilated modern woman.[19] Campbell's long flowing black hair, beaded headband, and her impressive traditional regalia met Canada's standard, whereas Klyne, in a mainstream version of a fringed leather jacket and skirt with a fashionably short hairdo, seemed out of place in such a competition.

An Edmonton *Journal* report of the selection of Alberta's representatives to the upcoming national competition reinforced familiar tropes. Paired next to a large two-column-wide photo of Amelia Crowfoot clad in beaded attire, a feature story of the event held in conjunction with Louis Riel Day was filled with colonial rhetoric that referenced the treaty signed with the "Great White Mother." "The colour during treaty signing between the 'Great White Mother' and the North American Indians was dull compared to the pageantry of selecting Princess Alberta,"[20] the *Journal* gushed. Historical allusions to a nineteenth-century power relationship between Queen Victoria and "her Indians" awkwardly introduced a contemporary topic and had seemingly little to do with the past except to instill for readers a colonial discourse. The following paragraph situated the event within the imaginary past through its use of descriptive language: "Drums reverberated, haunting chants envisioned memories of a noble past, as proud young costumed Indian dancers defiantly stamped their moccasined feet, beckoning the past in a victory dance heralding the 1969 Princess Alberta, 18-year-old Amelia Crowfoot...A Mountie in his red tunic, dignitaries from provincial and civic government and prominent citizens made for one of the largest head tables imaginable."[21] Phrases such as "haunting chants," "memories of a noble past," and "beckoning the past" reminded readers of a romanticized glory that no longer defined indigeneity in Canada. The terms "noble" and "proud" functioned as common descriptors in human interest stories depicting Aboriginal peoples but mostly served as signifiers for moribundity.

The quintessential image of Canadian identity—the Mountie in his red tunic—recalled the disciplinary and civilizing force of colonialism.

After a discussion of Crowfoot's accomplishments and her intention to attend Brigham Young University, the paper included a number of inspirational quotations by the princess to support the appropriateness of her selection. For example, she said, "I am not militant, but believe that my race can be a great race again."[22] Such a statement conveyed two important pieces of information to the reader. First, given the ongoing political challenges related to the release of the White Paper at the end of June 1969 and the National Indian Brotherhood's vociferous stand against it, her admission of not being militant would have assuaged Edmonton *Journal* readers' fears that she might pose a threat to Canada's dominant power structure. Second, in Crowfoot's acknowledgment of her "race" the paper reinforced mainstream dominance.

"A beautiful 18-year-old Indian girl from Vancouver, B.C., Evelyn Joseph won the coveted Miss Indian Princess of Canada title at the impressive national pageant," announced the Fredericton *Daily Gleaner* that summer.[23] Following a description of Joseph's height and weight, the report went on to explain the events of the pageant. Because the national event was held in New Brunswick, the *Daily Gleaner* printed five stories with coverage that framed the competition as a provincial marketing opportunity, naming local participants, judges, and tourist sites visited by the entourage—amounting mostly to regional boosterism.[24] The *Globe and Mail* also reported news of Joseph's national victory. However, an editor added a headline to the story that had little to do with the princess or the competition—"Heroic Sagas of Battles Against Whites." It must have left readers questioning what had gone on at the beauty pageant.[25]

News dailies across Canada also covered the 1970 national Indian princess competition. When Alberta crowned Laverna McMaster as its princess the Calgary *Herald* reiterated themes found a year earlier in the Edmonton *Journal*. The pageant's keynote address by well-known Native actor Chief Dan George became the focus of the news story. According to the *Herald*, the popular Indian chief/actor's speech "captured the audience with a reminiscense of the Indian life, past, and present."[26]

The 1970 National Indian Princess competition took place in Yellowknife to coincide with a royal visit to the territory. Positioning Canada's Indian princesses with British royalty, news dailies once again took notice of the ongoing regional competitions that led up to the national event. A large photograph of competitor Jennifer Williams, British Columbia's representative Indian princess, made the front section of the Vancouver *Province*.[27] Williams perched on a rock at the beach on English Bay recalled the bronze Little Mermaid statue in Copenhagen, Denmark. Barefooted, in fringed buckskin and beaded necklaces, the image dredged up the old romantic association with nature, which contrasted sharply with the high-rises of Vancouver in the background. The photograph spoke clearly of the noble savage frozen in a modern, civilized cityscape.

The Prince of Wales ultimately crowned Alberta's Laverna McMaster as the national princess and brought added royalty-sanctioned attention to the national event. Though little substantive information about the competition found its way into press coverage, an unfortunate photo showing McMaster with her mouth agape and her tongue flopped out as she faced a politely smiling Prince Charles was printed in both the Victoria *Daily Colonist* and the Vancouver *Province*.[28] The photograph indubitably juxtaposed the two "royal" figures in a classic savage/civilized binary.

The *Province* ignored the competition in its accompanying story but forcefully and not too subtly articulated narratives embedded within a larger negative imaginary of what indigeneity meant in Canada: "The royal tour party penetrated Indian country Thursday. While there were no hostile manifestations of Red Power, the Indian people did not turn out in the same numbers as the Eskimos had in the Arctic segments of the tour."[29] The prevalence of these inscriptive terms suggested a naturalized character fraught with violent and antisocial behaviours. First, with the phrase "penetrated Indian Country," readers could reconstitute an aggressive and symbolically sexual dominant action that endured between the British Crown and Canada's Indigenous peoples. Second, the next sentence implied an expectation of violence—"hostile manifestation"—linked to the emergence of Red Power since the Trudeau government had released the White Paper in 1969. Third, the press chastized Aboriginals for being less enthusiastic than their "Eskimo" counterparts for the royal tour. This commentary situated Aboriginals outside of mainstream Canadian cultural identity.

Coverage of the national Indian princess competition declined steadily in the news dailies after 1970, and, while the iconic princess lived on in popular culture, images appeared less frequently in press coverage.[30] The *Globe and Mail* included a large front-page photo on 19 July 1971 of two

Indian princesses enjoying cotton candy with a cutline description, "It's white man's medicine, but candy floss is good medicine by any youngster's reckoning. Cheri and Lana Hill of Cheektowanga, NY, take refreshment during a traditional border crossing by Indians at Niagara Falls."[31] Later, a staged 1971 photo was printed in the Hamilton *Spectator* of four eager Indian princesses from the Thunderbird Cultural Society of Hamilton dressed in braids and buckskin.[32] The caption explained that the princesses were collecting reading material to be donated to a James Bay community. The promotion of altruistic and assimilationist events captured by such documentary photographs returned princess representations to their more comfortable role—and merely sexist, rather than sexist *and* racist.

"KEEP THE INDIANS OUT OF TOWN"

Stories of violence against and sometimes by Aboriginal women have always provided fodder for the daily news in Canada. The theme gained attention, for example, after the story of Robert Pickton broke in 2002. More than thirty missing women, many Aboriginal, from Vancouver's Downtown Eastside were murdered on Pickton's pig farm in Coquitlam, British Columbia, between 1997 and 2001.[33] Amnesty International reported in 2004 that over 60 percent of Aboriginal women have experienced sexual violence in Canada and that First Nations women were five times more likely than all other women of the same age in Canada to die violently.[34] Cree columnist Doug Cuthand highlighted Amnesty International's "Stolen Sisters" report in "Aboriginal Women Face Abuse at Home, Too" where he argues that "we have picked up too many bad habits from colonialism. We can't continue to ignore the problems around us and blame it on outside factors."[35] The press tells this story, however, but only in snippets and short reports that belie the overwhelming pervasiveness reported by Amnesty International. In a Victoria *Times-Colonist* opinion piece four years later, law professor Constance Backhouse attributes a lack of action to the "legacy of misogyny and racism that runs through the heart of Canadian history." She details three specific cases of murder against Aboriginal women that have occurred across Canada since 1967 including Rose Roper, Helen Betty Osborne, and Pamela George, in addition to over 500 missing women cases that support her position. She holds all Canadians culpable for the ongoing atrocities and asks, "when will Canadians wake up?"[36]

According to historian Sarah Carter, violence against Aboriginal women functioned as a nineteenth-century settlement strategy of domination. In her research on captivity narratives featuring the abduction of white women and children by Aboriginal peoples on the Canadian Prairies, Carter finds that stereotypical constructions helped define the spatial boundaries between the settler and the Native.[37] She argues that powerful negative images of Aboriginal women as licentious and bloodthirsty served to propagate and justify the increasing legal regulation of Aboriginal women's movements and access off-reserve.[38]

Within a colonial framework the maintenance of power of social, economic, and spatial distinctions between dominant and subordinate populations abound. Aboriginal women thus became easy, attractive targets. Even as white Canadian women were relegated to second-class status, they also were made the moral and cultural custodians of mainstream culture. Thus, when the Indian Act imposed a patriarchal structure to the administration of Indians in Canada, Aboriginal women were two times damned—as females and as Aboriginal. In this way, they were branded as threats to colonial rule in mainstream Canadian culture. The tendency to portray Native females as simultaneously nobly chaste and whorish illustrates the point.

In the trial of a murderer of a Cree woman working as a prostitute in Calgary in 1889, described by Carter, the press contended that "Rosalie was only a squaw and that her death did not matter much."[39] This was typical and even predictable. Carter utilizes the nineteenth-century trial as an illustration of the negative threat Indigenous women allegedly posed to stable settler society. Rosalie's brutal murder garnered two trials after the judge refused to accept a not-guilty verdict rendered by the first jury. The judge charged a second jury to "forget the woman's race and to consider only the evidence at hand…. It made no difference whether Rosalie was white or black, an Indian or a negro. In the eyes of the law, every British subject is equal."[40] Although the accused was eventually found guilty of manslaughter, he received a light sentence, and Carter shows that the jury did not in fact "forget" the Cree woman's race. The Calgary *Herald* concluded: "Keep the Indians out of town."[41]

On its own, each case of violence against women reported in the press may appear as an independent act; and violence clearly occurs in all societies.[42] However, while criminal behaviour in the press is mostly associated with "deviants," as Frances Henry and Carol Tator argue, crime committed against Aboriginal women by white males has been treated differently and presents Aboriginal women as aberrant rather than as victims.[43] The murders and violence against Aboriginal women outlined in chapter 7 found in the press during the summer of 1948 support such claims.

Although no systematic study of sexual violence against Aboriginal women exists in Canada, the few critical analyses done suggest that the nineteenth-century perceptions of Aboriginal women as immoral and licentious endure, a trend press reportage exemplifies. In fact, reports of violence against Aboriginal women by white men offer yet another aspect of the Canadian story of conquest.

Nineteen-year-old Helen Betty Osborne of The Pas, Manitoba, was brutally murdered by two white men in 1971. Her story bears close similarity to other cases except that it eventually sparked a debate that forced Canadians to confront the stereotypical notions of Aboriginal women. Lisa Priest, a Winnipeg *Free Press* reporter, penned *Conspiracy of Silence* in 1989 to illustrate the shocking cover-up by the RCMP and corresponding whitewash by the press regarding Osborne's murder. Doing so brought national news attention to the now infamous case.[44] And not long after the murder became the focus of a 1991 Manitoba Aboriginal Justice Inquiry, where commissioners concluded that Osborne's attackers "seemed to be operating on the assumption that Aboriginal women were promiscuous and open to enticement through alcohol or violence. It is evident that the men who abducted Osborne believed that young Aboriginal women were objects with no human value beyond [their own] sexual gratification."[45] While the original murder had been largely overlooked by Canadian dailies, not considered a newsworthy item, today her murder may be viewed as a pivotal example of the racism and sexual discrimination against Aboriginal women that exists in Canada.

That said, in November 1971 only one brief story about the murder surfaced in the Winnipeg *Free Press*. No other daily in Canada reported the story. In the fifty-word *Free Press* report under the headline, "Girl Slain At The Pas," few details were given though Manitoba readers would likely have recognized that Osborne was Cree because she was from Norway House.[46] That same day another case made front-page news. In "Indians, Whites At Odds," the *Free Press* warned that "an Indian war could develop if Indians don't stop hunting deer at night on their land."[47] Both

stories were as old as Canada—the familiar narrative of violence perpetrated against a Native woman and the ever-present alleged threat of
Aboriginal violence.

When the Osborne case finally went to trial in 1987 Canada's daily
newspapers initially displayed little interest in the sixteen-year-old murder case. The *Free Press* ignored it completely and instead focussed that
day on a Cree community near The Pas that had more than a 90 percent
unemployment rate. It quoted local Chief Jim Tobacco. "Frustration is
so intense people turn to alcohol and that's the main reason for our high
crime rate," he said. "At the present time there's practically no respect for
law and order on our reserve."[48] Alcoholism, crime, lassitude, and a lack
of respect for Canadian law again eclipsed any positive efforts for change
presented. This story presented Aboriginal peoples as threats to Manitoba's mainstream, meanwhile the absent Osborne trial coverage supports
Henry and Tator's claims that the press is mostly interested in presenting
narratives that preserve dominant culture.[49]

Short notes in both the Montreal *Gazette* and the Charlottetown
Guardian reported that "sixteen years after the battered body of a young
native woman was found on the frozen shore of a lake north of The Pas,
a man was convicted of second-degree murder in the case."[50] The story
explained that Dwayne Johnston was sentenced to life in prison and a co-
accused man was acquitted: "Evidence at the trial indicated that Johnston, Houghton and two other men were drinking heavily the night they
picked up Osborne and took her to the lake, where she was beaten and
stabbed to death with a screwdriver."[51] Unmentioned in the press was
the intense racism that allowed sixteen years to pass before justice was
served and when, according to testimony, many townsfolk in The Pas
had known the details of the events at the time it happened yet had said
nothing. The absence of any investigative reportage regarding the details
or context of the murder supports a larger narrative that framed Aboriginal women as a threatening presence to the moral order of colonialism.

In 1988 the Manitoba government organized the Aboriginal Justice
Inquiry to examine the handling of Osborne's death and subsequent
murder trial.[52] The mandate of the inquiry, as stated in the commission's
report, directed that commissioners investigate and determine: "whether
there exists any evidence of racial prejudice with respect to the investigation of the death of Helen Betty Osborne. It has been suggested that the

delay in bringing the case to court indicated racism and that the police would have exerted more effort if the deceased had been non-Aboriginal. It also has been suggested that residents of The Pas were in possession of valuable information and kept that information from the police because the victim was Aboriginal."[53] Suddenly, the story became news after all. On 8 August 1989, the *Globe and Mail* journalist Timothy Appleby reported that at the time of Osborne's murder it was common knowledge that groups of white men cruised the streets of The Pas searching for Indigenous women in a practice known as "squaw-hopping."

The commission released its findings in the fall of 1991. "After hearing all the testimony and reviewing the evidence," it reported, "we have concluded that racism played a significant role in this case, but it did not cause any delay in the investigation of the killing or in the prosecution of those responsible."[54] The inquiry agreed that Osborne had been the victim of two circumstances over which she had no control—she had been born Aboriginal and female, a potentially lethal combination in Canada.

In an essay that considers gendered racial violence as a colonial encounter as recorded and encoded in court transcripts, sociologist Sherene Razack critically investigated the 1995 Regina murder of Aboriginal sex trade worker Pamela George by two young white males. The trial pitted an anonymous Aboriginal prostitute, a faceless "squaw," against two young university boys portrayed as merely sowing their wild oats, boys-will-be-boys style. For example, the account found in the *Leader-Post* did not adequately capture the extent of the violence to George's body, with characterizations of her injuries as "bruises, cuts or swelling," when trial transcripts describe that she suffered severe and brutal force.[55] In the end the boys were sentenced to six years in jail for the murder but, as Razack argues, a combination of race and gender diminished the men's culpability.[56]

Henry and Tator provide a discourse analysis of a 1999 case involving Jack Ramsay, a former Alberta Reform Member of Parliament and former RCMP officer, who was accused of sexual assault by an Aboriginal woman thirty years prior. They found that the *Globe and Mail* resorted to "stereotypes in its representation of Pelican Narrows [where the incident occurred] and the Native woman who pressed charges against Jack Ramsay" and that the mediated negative image of the Aboriginal woman as a passive, alcoholic, indigent remained familiar to readers within the dominant discourse.[57] Ironically, while Ramsay was found guilty of a serious crime, Henry and

Tator found that *Globe and Mail* readers "were provided with many strongly positive images of a White, middle-class, morally upright family man with a loving wife and daughters who contributed to the community for many decades."[58] Journalists covering this story presented a familiar narrative that validated a colonial discourse that rhetorically punished the "squaw."

Bridget Keating's 2008 master's thesis, "Raping Pocahontas," analyzed press coverage of the 2001 rape of a twelve-year-old Indigenous girl in rural Saskatchewan.[59] By examining provincial press imagery, Keating discovered many portrayals cast the child as a sexualized Pocahontas, an unsavory conflation of the princess/"squaw" that shifted press reports away from the sexual violence done to a young girl by a group of grown men to a framing of the events around an image of the child as a kind of Cree Lolita, a sexual aggressor who seduced adult men. As in the George and Ramsay examples, the press positioned the young men as victims. Keating casts this trial as an example of settler colonialism that binds and smears the unnamed girl with the lives and stories of other Aboriginal women—"squaws" one and all—who have been victims of brutality.

And so stories of violence continue, despite the findings of the Manitoba Justice Inquiry in 1991. Simply identifying racism and sexual discrimination against Aboriginal women in the press and in Canadian society appears to have been of marginal consequence. Margath Walker, a geographer, who has studied Mexican newspaper constructions of gender and difference along the U.S.-Mexico border, has concluded that in Mexico, as in Canada, the press tells stories of violence against Aboriginal women by constructing them as weak, backward, sexualized objects—anonymous, replaceable bodies—yet simultaneously aggressive.[60] Such press coverage, she finds, actually condones the disposability of the maquiladora (female border factory) workers. In Canada, the press has likewise policed the borders of a colonial imagination where Native females are reduced to two unpalatable creatures, Indian princess or "squaw."

"SHE HAS BEEN A CHURCH-GOING CHRISTIAN SINCE SHE WAS NINETEEN"

The official story of gender inequality for Aboriginal women began more than 130 years ago, in 1876 when Canadian Parliament amended the 1868 Indian Act to establish patrilineality as a criterion for determining

Indian status. With this amendment the Indian Act structured inter-marriage by making Indian women legally "white" and non-Indian women legally "Indian" depending on their nuptial choices. One result of this policy was that as many as 25,000 Indigenous women lost their status and were forced to leave their communities while countless white females became "instant Indians" between 1876 and 1985.[61] The patriarchal structure of the act further marginalized women on their reserves and made it difficult to challenge disempowerment inherent in the legislation. The Gradual Enfranchisement Act of 1869, for example, denied women the right to vote in band council elections and limited physical mobility via the pass system on western reserves that was not changed until 1951. Indigenous studies scholar Bonita Lawrence asserts that the Indian Act has fundamentally shaped the ways Aboriginal peoples have come to think of themselves, and because of the inherent gender discrimination embedded within the policy it has impacted Aboriginal women in disproportionately detrimental ways.[62]

Responding to the sexist structure of the Indian Act and the dominance of male-centric views within the NIB and band governments, two national groups advocating Aboriginal women's rights emerged during the 1970s. These organizations for the first time gave women a political voice and included Indian Rights for Indian Women (IRIW) in 1970 and the Native Women's Association of Canada (NWAC) in 1974. Both pushed for legislative changes to the discriminatory aspects of the Indian Act. In 1970, two pivotal cases came through the Ontario judicial system that challenged the displacement of Indigenous women. Jeanette Corbiere Lavell and Yvonne Bédard mounted separate charges to section 12(1)(b) of the pre-1985 Indian Act that would eventually be heard by the Supreme Court in 1973. In 1971 Canadian daily newspapers turned the provincial court successes and pending Supreme Court case into front-page news. Coverage of the women's plight proffered twenty-one stories in Canadian dailies, reflecting a heightened interest in the issue, most printed when the cases were respectively appealed to the Supreme Court in October and December 1971.[63]

According to press coverage, Canadian mainstream politicians viewed Lavell and Bédard as passive women who needed the protection of mainstream Canadian justice. Framed as Indian princesses, the women served as pawns in an ongoing rhetoric that championed the government's progressive treatment of Aboriginals. Such depictions promoted an imaginary princess who would ultimately embrace and endorse assimilationist policy.

In contrast, by framing Lavell and Bédard as licentious threats to traditional Indigenous culture and future efforts to secure autonomous strength with regard to the Canadian government, the two women also appeared as deviants in news stories across the nation. Media sources quoted NIB and band officials who argued Lavell and Bédard polluted Aboriginal culture and additionally worked to undermine efforts for Aboriginal self-government because the case served as legal precedent to change the Indian Act.

When Lavell, an Anishinaabe woman from Manitoulin Island and a journalism student at Ryerson Polytechnical Institute in Toronto, married David Lavell, a non-Native, she, like other Native women who had married white men, received a notice from the Department of Indian Affairs and Northern Development stating that she was no longer considered an Indian according to section 12(1)(b) of the Indian Act. The letter stated: "12 (1) The following persons are not entitled to be registered, namely ... (b) a woman who married a person who is not an Indian, unless that woman is subsequently the wife or widow of a person described in section 11."[64]

The Ontario Native Women's Association (ONWA), to which Lavell belonged, supported her as she challenged the Indian Act in court on the basis that it was discriminatory and should be repealed, according to the 1960 Canadian Bill of Rights. In June 1971, County Court Judge B.W. Grossberg ruled against Lavell. However, in October 1971, the Lavell case was heard in the Federal Court of Appeal, which ruled unanimously in her favour. Under pressure from the federal government and Native organizations, this decision was appealed to the Supreme Court of Canada. Then justice minister and later Prime Minister John Turner explained that he had asked the Supreme Court to hear the case "because of the importance of the case and because it meant the government and Indians would have to "devise policies and laws that will respect the legitimate claims of all concerned."[65]

Meanwhile, Bédard, a member of the Six Nations First Nation near Brantford, Ontario, had married a non-Indian in May 1964. Bédard, with her spouse and two children, lived together off the reserve until 23 June

1970 when they separated. She then returned with her children to the reserve to live in a house bequeathed to her by her mother.

Since Bédard had married a non-Indian, she, like Lavell, was no longer legally First Nations. Subsequently, the Six Nations Band Council passed a resolution ordering her to dispose of the property from her mother within six months, during which time she could live there.[66] When the band later demanded she leave the reserve, Bédard took the matter to court.[67] Bédard obtained an injunction from Ontario High Court Justice John Osler prohibiting her expulsion from Six Nations. He relied on the recent decision in the Lavell case as guidance in the decision. Both cases were then heard together by the Supreme Court of Canada.

Well-known civil rights lawyer Clayton Ruby defended Lavell and argued the Federal Appeal Court's decision resided outside the racial confines of the Indian Act. "We've made a significant, a very important breakthrough in Canadian civil rights. Sexual equality now means sexual equality and a federal court has said so," he said.[68] Justice Minister Turner and members of Parliament interviewed by the press considered the issue around the Canadian Bill of Rights and the universal notion of gender equality espoused by the Canadian government. Turner also viewed the Supreme Court challenge as one based on gender equality—thereby side-stepping the racial component that lay squarely at the heart of the debate.

The Saskatoon *Star Phoenix* reported that Turner called the case pivotal. "It is important with respect to women's rights and the status of women upon marriage," Turner was quoted.[69] In the same Canadian Press wire service report, MP Eldon Woolliams described the Supreme Court challenge as "most surprising" and stated that the government should have changed the Indian Act earlier to conform to civil rights law. Similarly, MP John Gilbert reportedly wondered why it had taken ten years to overturn a discriminatory section, while MP Rene Matte doubted that the government needed to take this decision to the Supreme Court at all as it was an "elementary principle of civil rights."[70] Given the strong endorsement from Canada's mainstream political establishment and the espoused discriminatory nature of the cases, the Supreme Court hearing appeared almost unnecessary. Canada's Bill of Rights would naturally protect the rights of Lavell, Bédard and all other First Nations women in the same situation.

Introduced as if this were a Hollywood movie trailer, one Canadian Press wire service report romantically situated Lavell as a classic princess: "A vivacious 28-year old Ojibwe woman's love for a white man and her pride in being a Canadian Indian have combined to force a major revision of the federal Indian Act."[71] Lavell later stated, "I'll always be an Indian person—no matter what the Indian Act says."[72] Under the headline, "Yvonne is an Indian...Again," Bédard echoed Lavell's sentiments by acknowledging, "I'm proud to be an Indian" and the report explained that "although she has been a church-going Christian since she was nineteen, she still attends the traditional ceremonies of the Long House religion occasionally."[73] After establishing their authenticity as "real" Indians, the press focused on mainstream political efforts to protect these women. The moral battle would ultimately lead to assimilation, if all went as planned.

"I DON'T KNOW WHY THEY DON'T MARRY THEIR OWN KIND"

The front-page layout of the 2 December 1971 Victoria *Daily Colonist* illustrates the complex frames used in this story. The story, "Woman's Indian Act Fight: Rights Case to High Court," began with a laudatory description of mainstream political support for the case, before it moved on to accounts of fractured Indigenous political positions. "Indians themselves have been sharply divided on whether or not women should lose their treaty rights as is the case now," it noted.[74] Without the aid of Canadian politicians it seemed Aboriginal women would continue to be discriminated against, forgetting that it was the Canadian government through the Indian Act that had instigated the discrimination in the first place.

A short boxed item, "Women's Rights Move Over," announcing that Prime Minister Trudeau had adjusted the cabinet portfolio, handling women's rights over to Labour Minister Martin O'Connell, also reinforced for readers the government's active resolve to fight tirelessly against sexual discrimination of all Canadian women.[75] The story implied an assimilationist strategy that equated Lavell and Bédard with all other Canadian females. A Supreme Court victory would bring the Aboriginal women one step closer to full Canadian citizenship. Thus, by implication, assimilation equalled human rights.

A third report next to the aforementioned news stories followed the headline, "'What Wrong Has B.C. Done?' Nishga [sic] Hearings Open in Ottawa." The opening paragraph stated that "British Columbia is 'an innocent bystander' in the Aboriginal rights battle between the federal government and the non-treaty Indians, the Supreme Court of Canada was told Wednesday."[76] Readers could presume from the linking of this front-page story to the other two that ordinary citizens need not concern themselves with ongoing Aboriginal issues. Together this set of related news stories encapsulated a posture that both privileged mainstream political thought and dismissed the importance of Aboriginal concerns.

A less palatable aspect of the court challenge that centred squarely on the nuanced complications of the patriarchal structure of the Indian Act found its way into news stories through comments by Aboriginal politicians, bandleaders, and by Lavell and Bédard. Unlike the unwavering support for women's rights espoused in comments attributed to mainstream politicians, newspaper stories on the whole were more restrained in offering such support. This played out structurally as the supportive politicians' comments were normally relegated to secondary importance by way of positioning them later in the narratives, in keeping with the inverted pyramid structuring of "hard" news. Reopening a debate related to the Indian Act, a plot that had festered in the news for almost a year after the 1969 release of the White Paper appeared of little interest to editors.

According to Joanne Barker, the NIB viewed the Supreme Court challenge as an attack on treaty rights that questioned special status rather than an issue of sexual discrimination.[77] While Lavell and Bédard identified three foes in their struggle—the patriarchal structure of the Indian Act, unsympathetic Aboriginal leaders who wished to maintain the status quo, and the sexist and colonial history of the Canadian government, male Aboriginal politicians identified only one adversary—Aboriginal women. If mainstream politicians claimed Lavell and Bédard as Indian princesses then for Aboriginal leaders they functioned, ironically, as a colonized binary—traitors who had abandoned tradition, married white men, and now attempted to undermine efforts for self-government by demanding equal rights.

An unidentified Aboriginal spokesman in a Canadian Press wire report explained that because of the court rulings in favour of Lavell and Bédard the potential for a large migration to reserves existed. The corresponding acquisition of treaty rights by gradually whiter generations of children would then imperil the country's "native culture."[78] Mohawk Chief Ronnie Kirby agreed that the issue was problematic for reserves. "On Caughnawaga [near Montreal] the band is pretty strong against marrying whites," he was quoted. Kirby continued, "There are enough men—I don't know why they [the women] don't marry their own kind."[79] Richard Isaac, chief of Six Nations and the claimant against Bédard, responded to the 1970 court decision: "We don't discriminate against anyone but when a girl marries off the reserve, her husband is responsible for her. This is common with any race—the man is responsible for his family."[80] Isaac's concern that reserves "will eventually be dissolved" completed the racialized argument that made Aboriginal females the enemy.[81]

In the Hamilton *Spectator* Bédard countered that the Canadian government was at fault on this issue. "Indians have sat too long and taken anything the white government has handed down," she asserted.[82] Aboriginal women's groups agreed with Bédard, though judging from press reports the NIB largely ignored this reasoning. Canadian Press stories also outlined responses to the Supreme Court challenge by Aboriginal women's groups. One featured Mrs. Gerald Dore, formerly of Kahnesatake (near Montreal), who was directly impacted when she married a white man and lost her status. As a result she organized Quebec's Equal Rights for Indian Women (ERIW), comprised of disinherited women from Kahnesatake.[83] A December conference held in Edmonton invited the vice-president of the ERIW to take part, and the Edmonton *Journal* announced the passage of a motion contending that the Indian Act protected men but told "women to go out and protect themselves."[84]

Not all Aboriginal women saw the case as an advance, however. Kahn-Tineta Horn, a female Mohawk rights activist also from Kahnesatake, sided against her Aboriginal sisters. She, like the NIB, interpreted the decision as a matter of Aboriginal sovereignty rather than one that upheld universal equality: "We are not citizens and this so-called Bill of Rights does not supersede and overrule our treaties and our Indian Act."[85] Frank Horn, described in the Vancouver *Province* as the brother of "fiery Indian spokeswoman Kahn-Tineta Horn," clarified that the case involved "a women's liberation group that needled Mrs. Lavell into taking action against the Indian Affairs Department...If her victory is allowed to stand, it means many thousands of whites or halfbreeds will be allowed to live on reserves and take control of the Indian land."[86] His comments succinctly framed a gendered and racial debate related to status reinstatement. Both sexist and racist in tone, many prominent band politicians chose sovereignty over Aboriginal women in this battle that had little of the romantic potential contained in the appeal to morality evinced by the quoted mainstream politicians. Rather than princesses, in press reports Lavell and Bédard emerged as traitors to their people and simultaneously as whiners.

The NIB and band governments lobbied against Lavell and Bédard, maintaining that the Indian Act was not required to conform to the principles of Canada's Bill of Rights. Barker finds that Lavell and Bédard and their supporters were accused of conspiring with the colonialist, assimilationist, and racist agendas of the Canadian government that undermined efforts for Aboriginal self-government.[87]

Lavell and Bédard lost their case. On 27 August 1973, a 5–4 Supreme Court decision held that the Bill of Rights did not apply to that section of the Indian Act. Joyce Green argues that this court decision "confirmed the racist, sexist status quo of the pre-1985 Indian Act as *de jure* equality, as all Indian women were equally subject to the offensive provisions."[88] Law professor Constance Backhouse agrees that Canadians have historically considered themselves to be mostly free of racial prejudice yet her study of six court cases in the early twentieth century provides overwhelming evidence of blatant racism enforced through the law.[89] In short, this ruling clearly contributed to the enduring preservation of racial and sexual discrimination against Aboriginal women in Canada.

Given the abundant support for the rights of Aboriginal women by mainstream politicians in 1971, it is surprising that the results appeared of little consequence to the news media in 1973. A short *Globe and Mail* report noted in July 1973, under the headline, "Woman Called Indian Act Semi-Apartheid Policy," that the co-chairwoman for the IRIW called the act blatantly discriminatory, arguing that "internationally it puts Canada in the position of being a country that supports a semi-apartheid policy."[90] Yet, beyond this sensational claim the paper provided little context or information for the remarks and made no attempt to reference the recent Supreme Court decision. News dailies largely ignored the decision, too. Put simply, the press abandoned the Indian princesses once the assimilationist fairytale promulgated by mainstream politicians was defeated.

"THEY KNEW"

When Canada's Charter of Rights and Freedoms went into full effect on 17 April 1985 (having been adopted in 1982), the story filled the front pages across the country. Editorials and regional reports of how the Charter would improve rights for minorities from sea to sea reinforced the celebration. One Toronto *Star* column bragged that section 15 of the Charter gave Canadian women unprecedented freedoms that resulted in cheers from U.S. feminist leaders such as the legendary Betty Friedan and National Organization for Women's president Judy Goldsmith.[91] Yet, while photographs in papers throughout the nation showed feminists toasting to the success of the passage of the Charter, Aboriginal women were decidedly absent in press images of this celebration.[92]

A search of seventeen regional daily newspapers across Canada for the month of April 1985 resulted in not a single story related to the struggles of First Nations women to exert change to the Indian Act—deemed by the Supreme Court to be exempt from following Canadian discrimination laws.[93] An editorial in the Toronto *Star* titled, "Another Bad Deal for Natives," accused then–Prime Minister Brian Mulroney of publicly endorsing self-government while working behind the scenes to cut off any progress.[94] However, the editorial made no specific mention of Aboriginal women or their efforts to gain equality. The St. John's *Evening Telegram* outlined multiple battle lines that would be drawn with regard to the equality rights section of the Charter, including women's groups and disabled organizations but did not mention Aboriginal issues.[95] A Regina *Leader-Post* story covering a Regina Native Women's Association workshop on 18 April made no mention of the passage of the Charter nor of any political efforts at hand by Aboriginal women's groups to convince Canada to change the Indian Act.[96] The report instead maintained a sharp focus on local fundraising initiatives to support local counselling programs.

Still, pressure from Parliament wanting all discrimination of women removed from federal statute when the Charter became law saw the AFN (formerly NIB) work towards a compromise with NWAC, despite political divisions entrenched since the 1973 ruling.[97] In an effort to move forward, the NWAC conceded to the AFN and agreed to changes that did not meet its wishes but allowed for at least some measure of status reinstatement.[98] The compromise resulted in Bill C-31, which received royal assent on 28 June 1985, but was signed retroactively into law to coincide with the full adoption of the Charter of Rights and Freedoms in April.

News dailies mostly ignored the legislation but the few stories that did occur expressed anger over the bill and framed those Aboriginal women whose status would now be reinstated as predators. While the Edmonton *Journal* celebrated the news of the passage of the bill with a small region-ally focussed front-page feature story about a local sixty-eight-year-old woman who had waited forty-five years for the change to the Indian Act that would allow her to return to her home community of Frog Lake—including laudatory comments from Jenny Margetts, president of IRIW, and support from other Alberta women applying to be reinstated—it left the bad news till the end. The final paragraph confirmed a lack of sup-port for the bill by the Indian Association of Alberta. News of a confron-tation on the steps of Parliament between Indian Affairs Minister David Crombie and the Alberta NIB leader was buried in the final sentence of the story. The NIB's Wilf McDougall was quoted as threatening, "Go ahead and pass your...C-31. We're not going to abide by it."[99]

The Calgary *Herald* opined that Bill C-31 would prove to be "cata-strophic" for the Sarcee First Nation near Calgary because of the lack of additional funding available to bands to accommodate the expected growing number of band members due to the bill.[100] Two additional short news items on 9 July 1985 noted that Bill C-31 was poorly received. One Canadian Press report explained that the Alberta Council of Treaty Women planned to ask the Supreme Court for an injunction to stop non-status Aboriginal women from regaining Indian status. The council chairperson, Helen Gladue, lamented, "To satisfy a handful of women they have opened the door to allow the government to change our rights."[101] The second Canadian Press story told that the Westbank First Nation near Kelowna, British Columbia, viewed Bill C-31 as a hard-ship for band enrolment because of added pressure for housing by newly instated members.[102] The scant news coverage confirmed that Bill C-31 had proven to be a thorn in the side for band councils and for the federal government as it prepared to accommodate growing numbers of women now entitled to treaty rights, and the few stories printed suggest a lack of mainstream interest in the events.

The *Globe and Mail* reported the following February that the Six Nations band council was split over the restoration of the rights of Aboriginal women and children. Ottawa had given band councils the right to determine membership in their bands as part of the negotiation to pass Bill C-31, and the news report quoted elected council chief Wil-liam Montour as admitting that despite the fact that almost every family was affected by the former Indian Act ruling, the reaction by many on the reserve to the change was not sympathetic. "What I'm hearing is that they knew from the time they were children that if they married outsiders, they would lose their status," he said.[103]

A 1987 *Globe and Mail* report followed up on the changes for women and reported that the legislation "appears to have placed between 50,000 and 100,000 native Canadian women in legal limbo."[104] The report monitored the plight of Jane Margett and her children who attempted to move back to Saddle Lake First Nation in Alberta. The paper included an extended commentary by Margett: "After 100 years of unfairness to native women nothing has changed. It is a real mockery of justice that white women can still vote and live on the reserve while our band will not even recognize that we exist. Yet we are the ones who speak our language and can teach Indian traditions and history to the young...Everyone should be aware that this business is not finished yet. We're prepared to go to court to protect our reinstatement rights but, if possible, we want to work with the bands to avoid this."[105] The *Globe and Mail* feature identified with Margett's frustration, though the media had done little in the past several years to apprise Canadians of the ongoing narrative surrounding Bill C-31 or rights of Aboriginal women. By 1985 when Bill C-31 finally forced changes to the Indian Act and reinstated some aspect of equality to Aboriginal women, female activists were mostly portrayed as harpies, shrill and aggressive, positioned in the press as threats even to other First Nations women. By depicting them as "squaws," newspapers dismissed them and the logic of their legitimate political and moral arguments.

"NEW DEFINITION OF INDIAN"

The battle for the passage of Bill C-31 pitted Indigenous male political organizations against female, often represented as the rights of Aboriginal women against treaty rights. The results led to bitterness and acrimony. Green argues that Aboriginal women found themselves "under attack" for seeking to defend Aboriginal and treaty rights, ironically, by an Aboriginal political elite in Canada.[106] Clearly, the impact of patriarchal thought, a palpable aspect of colonialism, had directly impacted Aboriginal women in untold ways, supporting Indigenous Studies scholar Bonita Lawrence's assertion that the Indian Act has fundamentally shaped contemporary Aboriginal identity.[107] The shift from pre-contact egalitarian societies to a colonized patriarchal monolith eroded traditional gender roles and those ideologies still affect Aboriginal women's positions within their communities today.

Nearly twenty-five years later the *Globe and Mail* argued that Aboriginal women have continued to fight against discriminatory aspects of Bill C-31.[108] In June 2007 the British Columbia Supreme Court agreed that Bill C-31 did not do away with all discrimination in the act. Sharon McIvor and her son Jacob Grismer launched the lawsuit heard by the court, yet the tenor of the *Globe and Mail* report focussed on the contentious notion of the legal definition of "Indian" rather than on issues of sexual discrimination. The report included input by lawyers, a spokesman for Indian Affairs Minister Chuck Strahl, and Justice Harvey Groberman. However, the story did not feature comments from the AFN or any Aboriginal women's groups even though the report warned, "Parliament has less than a year to craft a new definition of 'Indian' before Canadian native policy risks tumbling into chaos as the existing rules for determining native status are thrown out by the courts."[109] The *Globe and Mail* chose not to include information regarding Sharon McIvor, a prominent Aboriginal feminist and political activist who has worked for many years to evince constitutional change and improve the rights for Aboriginal women in Canada.[110] As a member of the Feminist Alliance for International Action (FAFIA), a Canadian-based organization dedicated to advancing women's rights internationally, vice-president of NWAC in the mid-1980s, and the plaintiff in the lawsuit against Bill C-31 referenced in this story, McIvor's perspective should be germane. However, McIvor does not conform to the lingering stereotypical construction preferred by popular culture and thus was silenced in the discussion.

While Parliament is now poised to pass Bill C-31 amendments in 2011, sexual discrimination remains entrenched in the Indian Act. No changes were made to inherent sexism. As a result, McIvor announced on 22 December 2010 that she will file a complaint against Canada at the United Nations in an effort to eliminate sex descrimination.[111]

Images of the Indian princess have functioned as diversions in Canada's press. Coverage of the national Indian princess competitions revealed an eagerness to embrace mainstream cultural norms that fixated on the female body, with an Aboriginal twist. Through Indian princess imagery notions of what constituted beauty were reinscribed upon female Aboriginal bodies to frame them as "exotic."[112] By taking part in beauty pageants patterned on popular mainstream ones, at least in press reports Aboriginal princesses entered an assimilationist arena, complete with paternal and patriarchal white regulation, oppression, and exploitation.

Lavell and Bédard also served as princesses and pawns of assimilation that afforded the Canadian government an opportunity to draw Aboriginal women into the larger debate opened up in 1969 regarding rights of citizens. In 1971 the Supreme Court case promised to smooth over discriminatory aspects of the Indian Act. Mainstream male politicians protecting Indian princesses delivered to readers a welcomed romanticized and unthreatening image. However, when male-centric Aboriginal political organizations such as the NIB began to employ classic colonial stereotypes of Aboriginal women as plotting to thwart treaty rights for all, newspapers began to lose interest in the story. After the case failed in 1973, Canadian politicians abandoned their Indian princesses, and the press did, too, instead smearing them as "squaws" and then dropping interest in the story.

"A squaw's eradication, like that of the male savage," according to historian Donna Barbie Kessler, "was necessary to create a safe haven for civilization."[113] And, dutifully, the Canadian press worked to eradicate the "squaw," in part, by keying on certain aspects of stories while ignoring others; yet the "squaw" also remained a necessary element of the savagery/civilization construct. In short, the press employed its imagination selectively and in keeping with long-standing news traditions in Canada. In this way and for these reasons it could ignore certain news stories, such as the outcome of the 1973 Supreme Court ruling or other efforts related to sexual discrimination in the Indian Act that contributed to the passage of Bill C-31. Yet, it had also promulgated the "squaw" construction when necessary as a form of absolution for Canadian men who inflict violence upon Aboriginal women and for the Canadian government that has treated Aboriginal women as deviant from day one. Thus, stories of violence against Aboriginal females have been continually recast to turn the victim into the aggressor. Scant coverage of Aboriginal women's fight for equality under the Indian Act illustrates a form of eradication or silencing needed to maintain patriarchal authority. It operates a kind of selective colonial amnesia.

Aboriginal law expert Patricia Monture, in an analysis of Supreme Court judgments, argues that ignoring gender in decisions on First Nations governance and land relationships is a result of colonialism of Canadian law and results from a lack of understanding about the centrality of gender in Native law.[114] However, Barker counters that gender is not silent in these judgments but rather its presence resonates in the affirmation of sexist ideologies and practices that "have established and maintained existing relations of power between Indian men and Indian women on the one hand, and between Indians and Canada on the other."[115] The same could be said for news coverage on Aboriginal women's issues in the press. Arguably, the passage of Bill C-31 marked a fundamental change for Aboriginal women in relation to sexual discrimination inherent in the Indian Act. However, press decisions to selectively and narrowly report on the issue affirmed entrenched stereotypical, sexist representations of Aboriginal women in the Canadian press.

As noted, Terry Eagleton remarked that "a nation is defined as much by what it forgets as what it remembers."[116] More recently, in 2000 Canadian literary scholar Stephen Bertman in his text *Cultural Amnesia* engages this notion with regard to American culture and a lack of memory associated with cultural events that might otherwise serve to alienate Americans from their imagined past.[117] Canadians smugly pride themselves on celebrating cultural milestones that promote a national commitment to the values of diversity and multiculturalism. However, a form of cultural amnesia nonetheless permeates understandings of Indigenous women. The characteristics the Canadian nation imagines itself to embody has little interest in reminders of the messy, patriarchal history wrought upon Aboriginal women. Conveniently rubbing out traces of gender-based inequities remains an enduring Canadian trait that has long plagued Aboriginal women. It is not these actions that make the treatment necessarily more palatable; rather, the press aids in rendering them invisible.

CHAPTER ELEVEN

LETTERS FROM THE EDGES
The Oka Crisis, 1990

Every person, I think, is proud of his or her heritage, but it
shouldn't reach the point of worship. There is not a person living
in Canada whose forefathers didn't at one time come from another
country and continent. If sovereignty was given to every group in
Canada, we would probably have some 50 nations within a nation,
instead of one nation.... Threats will only produce a stiffening of
attitudes and confrontation leading to warfare and death....
The present government of Canada must govern.

—LETTER TO THE EDITOR, REGINA *LEADER-POST*, 15 SEPTEMBER 1990

And then there was Oka.

Arguably, the Mohawk summer of 1990 marks one of those "paradig-
matic shifts" in thinking, one that led Canadians to a new way of seeing their world.[1] "The Oka crisis did more than interrupt the traffic and
economy of a large city. It created a deep dissonance within the national
symbolic order," according to Amelia Kalant.[2] In the spring of that year
Mohawks just west of Montreal barricaded access to a few dozen acres
that the small community of Oka sought to use for expansion of a golf
course. The Mohawks claimed the land as a sacred burial ground and
argued that it rightly belonged to them. A subtext included observations
that the Mohawks had never "surrendered" to Canada (and thus were a
sovereign nation) and, further, that Canada had systematically and consistently failed to deal with the Mohawks in an honourable way.

Meanwhile, Oka sought and was granted a court injunction instruct-
ing the Mohawks to desist and dismantle the barricade. They declined
to do so. So the province dispatched the provincial police, the Sûreté du
Quebec (SQ), on 11 July 1990 in a surprise and violent action to achieve

that end. It ended badly, with shots fired, a police officer dead, the barricade intact, and tensions ratcheted way up. A seventy-eight-day standoff
ensued. Meanwhile empathetic Kanesatake Mohawks nearby blockaded
a commuter bridge to Montreal in a sign of solidarity. Some local whites
reacted violently to this gesture, rioting, uttering threats, and screaming
racial epithets.

The days passed and the tension mounted. Eventually, in late August,
2500 members of the Canadian Forces were unleashed to replace the
police. This augured the beginning of the end for the siege as the soldiers
simply squeezed the Mohawks tighter and tighter. The standoff ended
peacefully yet chaotically on 26 September when the Mohawks decided
to lay down their defences and simply walk out. Most were arrested and
charged with various criminal offences, though only two were convicted
of minor charges.

While the military achieved the aim of ending the standoff peacefully, the symbolic winners at Oka were Natives everywhere. Suddenly,
Aboriginal issues were front and centre in the country as never before.
Many Canadians were appalled by the treatment they saw Natives receive
before their very eyes on the television news. It seemed that at long last
the tipping point had been reached in Canada's press—if not government conduct—where the colonial imagination was being shoved aside by
something more befitting a late-twentieth-century liberal democracy that
prided itself on its commitment to multiculturalism and racial tolerance.

But such a conclusion, upon reflection, given the copious evidence we
examined as well as the small body of literature on the topic, would have
been premature. Instead, indeed for the first time, a sustained counter-
narrative emerged, one which engaged and challenged colonialism fully.
But it was difficult to hear it amidst the roar of colonial-style reportage.
And the counter-narrative was curiously *not* the voice of the many who
cried racism and intolerance. Those voices tended overwhelmingly to
oppose racism and the treatment accorded Aboriginals yet also to champion assimilation. This is common posturing even today, for example,
as exemplified in the writings of *Globe and Mail* columnist Margaret
Wente.[3] Such coverage musters up "common sense," as if by denouncing
racism one simultaneously declared oneself free of the stain of ideology.
Bhodan Szuchewycz expresses the point well by noting that in Canada
the "denial of racism routinely appears as a semantic move of positive

self-preservation." In so doing, it operates on a less-than-subtle form of racism in its own right.[4]

Much reportage levelled harsh criticism at the governments in Ottawa, Quebec City and, on occasion, Oka, yet inclined strenuously to defend Canadian colonialism. Another strand focussed on the military and tended to heap praise upon it, again as a way of sanctioning colonial-style behaviour (despite the fact that the Canadian military was used against domestic civilian protestors) without necessarily directly attacking Natives. And then there remained the old-school colonialists for whom Natives remained mere savages, though the language used expressed a contemporary fear—"terrorists," as dubbed by then–Canadian Prime Minister Brian Mulroney.[5]

Meanwhile, spontaneous gestures of Native support for the Mohawks were reported all over the country, from New Brunswick to British Columbia. Road and rail blockades sprang up in nearly every province. But more than that, Oka re-energized land claims impetus across Canada, even in British Columbia, where successive governments had ignored the issue for more than 100 years.[6] Ultimately the media attention and consequent political pressure bore some fruit, leading the federal government to amend and improve its slow-moving land-reform efforts. Yet the results of Oka, according to scholars, remain unclear. And, to be sure, the surge of media interest certainly was shortlived as the press's fascination with Oka and Native affairs dissipated quickly. Olive Dickason has observed that "a decade later there was still no agreement on what had been learned from Oka."[7] The eminent scholar J.R. Miller has concluded that the crisis left "hard feelings" in an already bigoted Quebec but that "the aftermath was somewhat more positive" outside the province.[8] Less measured and more optimistic in his assessment, popular historian Daniel Francis has opined that the crisis earned Aboriginals "unprecedented political power."[9] Roger Nichols has evinced less optimism and noted that "many of the central issues here remain unresolved."[10] Part of the difficulty emerges from the sheer breadth and depth of the problem. That is, almost any real progress could only be at best partial, short of revolutionary change, because the problem–colonialism–is so intimately woven into the fabric of Canadiana, hence, in our view, the measured academic observations.[11]

The Oka crisis meanwhile has spawned a minor cottage industry in book publishing.[12] A number of participants from both sides published works, as did journalists.[13] For at least one then-teenage Mohawk, Taiaiake Alfred, the experience helped fuel an academic career and several important studies.[14] Naturally the crisis earned a key space in books related to Aboriginal history or white-Indigenous relations.[15] But the ripple effect has been even wider, and mention of the crisis has extended well beyond all too frequently hermetic academic borders, from studies of education to a guide book of Montreal to the art world.[16] Anecdotally, our experience with teaching university students has shown that precious few of them, apart from some of those with Native ancestry, indicate they have ever heard of the Oka crisis, suggesting it may be as removed from public consciousness as, say, what the average nineteen-year-old knows about Watergate or the October Crisis of 1970.

In 1990, Canadians watched it all unfold on the television news.[17] In fact, it dominated news discourse of all media. A number of journalists camped out with the Mohawk warriors and their supporters throughout the siege. One result is that Oka received "intense press coverage" unlike any other Aboriginal event in Canadian history.[18] Oka also represents the one historical case about which scholars and other writers have considered the nature and tone of media coverage, though it is interesting to note that this interest waned within a handful of years.

Press coverage of Oka has received a modest amount of study, not more than a handful of examinations. Most of it concludes that the English-language press portrayed the Mohawks as common Native savages, in so many words, bathing in violence, criminality, and other disquieting behaviours. This scholarship tends to be well informed theoretically, though some inclines toward the unreflexive and chauvinistic. Of course, theory is not everything. Yet its absence or paucity invites more or less immediate criticism and even possible rejection by those who would differ with the conclusions proffered. We stress this point because the scholarship, as with the coverage itself, gravitates toward an ideological cleavage somewhat resembling the contours of the colonial narrative and the corresponding counter-narrative. It stands in inverse proportion to the coverage itself: most supports the assertions of the counter-narrative while the rest, a small minority, sharply disputes it. We identify no discernible middle ground.

Rick Ponting has argued that the Mohawks, despite losing the military engagement, ultimately won the media war by focussing international attention on land claims issues in Canada.[19] And we agree; in fact, we found that this Mohawk victory was immediate and can be teased from examples of newspaper coverage in British Columbia. Marc Grenier's analysis of the coverage argues that the press presented the Mohawks in an "Indians versus us" binary, especially after the army replaced the sq.[20] Warren Skea generally concurs with Grenier.[21] Skea employs a content analysis, which offers the visual attribute of tables and statistical analysis of large amounts of information—for example, Saskatchewan and Manitoba newspapers he found to have exhibited the lowest proportion of "anti-Native" coverage.[22] But therein one also finds the central weakness of such an approach—the analysis bogs down in an over-consideration of tabular data and insufficient examination of discourse. For example, the analysis frames articles without much nuance, in an us-versus-them fashion, as either pro-Native or anti-Native.

Eliciting the ideas of Kulchyski's "totality" and Furniss's "common sense," Martin J. Morris has concluded that the state's communication strategy featured domination, intimidation, and coercion, all in the name of professional legitimacy.[23] "Violent disciplining of aboriginal dissent has been the rule rather than the exception in the history of native struggles," he writes.[24] Indeed, Charles Stuart found that coverage derived from government news releases disproportionately dominated the front pages and, further, that such reportage tended to frame government sources as more reliable than Aboriginal sources. In short, the media's coverage "reinforced the status quo."[25] Heather Smyth shows that "the Warriors were stereotyped by the English-language mainstream media as terrorists."[26] James Winter agrees and, in a study more aimed at electronic news than newspapers, carefully reconstructs how the Mulroney regime was able to propagandize an anti-Native agenda.[27]

On the other hand, spinning events in a sharply different way, in a simplistic, wordy, and unabashedly pro-army essay, Whitney Lackenbauer has characterized the military's media strategy as having allowed it to "win the media war."[28] And we agree on the narrow point that the military "won" in the sense that it encircled the Mohawks in an ever-tightening grip and ultimately arrested them; but such an outcome suggests no particular reason to heap praise on the military for doing its job competently. The author would do well to heed Skea's observation that "hegemony enables ideology sustaining the political and economic status quo to be latently published in newspapers without any skepticism by the reading public."[29] While the term may be tweaked in various ways, Jeannette Mageo and Bruce Knauft capture it effectively by referring to hegemony as "an ideology that presents itself not as a philosophy with which one might or might not agree, nor as a moral system that describes how things should be, but rather as the way the world *is*."[30] After careful consideration, Stuart too refers to Oka as a "hegemonic crisis."[31] Claude Beauregard's partial and awkward examination of the media coverage at Oka found the military's media efforts "exemplary." It makes an unfounded claim that Canadians came, as a result of the military's propaganda strategy, to sympathize with the soldiers. Further, it supports Lackenbauer's view that military propaganda was fully rewarded in the form of positive press portrayals, though it has little to say about how Mohawks were displayed.[32]

We have chosen in this chapter to explore letters to the editor printed in two daily newspapers from the day the sQ unsuccessfully stormed the Mohawk barricades until six weeks after the standoff concluded. This includes the Moncton, New Brunswick, *Times-Transcript*[33] and the Prince George, British Columbia, *Citizen*.[34] Letters constitute an important element of the daily newspaper. A 1973 study, *Principles of Editorial Writing*, noted the value of the letters feature. "A virile letters-to-the-editor column or reader's forum is a surefire circulation booster," it noted. "Surveys show it is the best read feature of the editorial page...Its importance is obvious...On the one hand it provides a public service...by being a clearinghouse for diverse viewpoints of readers. From the strictly mercenary point of view, by encouraging reader response, the newspaper keeps in better touch with public attitudes and questions and has some yardstick by which to judge the effectiveness of its own operations....Most people who write letters to the editor are against something and protesting."[35]

The Journalist's Handbook, a sort of rough guide to the world of newspapers, is less sanguine and notes that letter writers often "seem to have completely missed the point."[36] But that may partially *be* the point to such correspondence. Perrin and Vaisey note that "letters serve a dual purpose: they offer readers an opportunity to respond to the newspaper itself, and they offer a public forum for discussion of issues of the day."[37] Perrin and Vaisey also note that letters present an imagined public sphere, which promotes a sense of community and reifies faith in democracy.[38] The letters section is seen by many journalists as central to the "vitality of a newspaper," writes journalism professor and scholar Bill Reader.[39] His study draws related conclusions that the letters serve a basic democratic function while building or maintaining a sense of community, as Benedict Anderson famously argued for the media as a whole.[40] As we saw, letters to the Kenora *Miner and News* in 1974 inflamed the already heated local reportage. Yet Perrin and Vaisey argue that distance tends to engender a more contemplative letter because a reader has less personal stake in any outcome.[41] This raises interesting questions about the Prince George and Moncton letters. Moncton lies of course much closer to Oka, but was it close enough to effect a different kind of letter? It is well known that Canada's west has long felt alienated from central Canada and part of this feeling manifests itself in anti-Quebec sentiment. Would this have affected content? Or was the Oka crisis felt at such a deep symbolic level, à la Benedict Anderson's notion of shared "imagined communities," as to trump distance?

We first approached the forty-four letters—fifteen in the *Citizen* and twenty-nine in the *Times-Transcript*—by coding them into basic thematic categories that emerged from the letters. This included dispatches with clearly articulated positions: pro-federal government; anti-federal government; pro-Quebec government; anti-Quebec government; pro-Oka town council; anti-Oka town council; pro-army; anti-army; pro-SQ; anti-SQ. It included letters that made a host of allegations: Natives were guilty of reverse racism; Natives were demanding and/or greedy, violent, non-violent, primitive, culturally backward, uncivilized; Natives have more rights than whites; allegations of white racism; Natives were to blame for the death of the police officer/were guilty of murder; Natives were the recipients of government handouts; Natives were mere immigrants; whites were greedy; Aboriginals had an affinity for alcohol; colonialism was the root cause of the crisis; Quebec was intolerant; Canada was superior to the United States in terms of race relations. Some letters identified an irony that Quebec refused to acknowledge another nation's right to sovereignty while it claimed such status for itself. Some letters lay the blame for the crisis and its duration at the media's doorstep. Finally, some letters averred that Natives were un-Canadian or non-Canadian.

Many of the letters were no doubt edited for length or for the sake of clarity. We know this for two reasons. First, it is common newspaper practice. Second, the two publications we examined printed guidelines in which they stated that they reserved the right to edit letters as they saw fit. Letters also may be edited not merely for length but so as not to offend readers, not to stray too far from editorial opinion, for clarity, or simply to reflect the whim or mood of a given editor at the time of the editing. Finally, letters may be submitted and yet never printed. The reasons for not printing a submitted letter vary but may include a failure to identify the author (even if one requests anonymity), insufficient space, use of offensive language, employment of slanderous comments, and the like. Roughly 85 percent of U.S. newspapers require that names be printed with all letters.[42] That said, on average it is estimated that 90 percent or more letters received are printed. One authority cites this as evidence that "gatekeeping" is not a common problem[43] while another considers it precisely as evidence of gatekeeping, a phenomenon that poisons the democratizing effect of letters.[44]

We chose to read the letters by asking three basic and interrelated questions. First, does a colonial narrative surface or endure in the missives? If so, how? If not, what (if anything) appears in its stead? Our second basic query asks, does a counter-narrative (or narratives) emerge either to replace or to compete with the colonial narrative? For example, what about ideas such as multiculturalism or the melting pot? Do such notions surface? Finally, in the opinion of the letter writers, if colonialism does not explain the Oka crisis, then what does? In other words, how do the letters to the editor attribute motivations to the key players?

It is important to keep in mind that reading audiences in 1990 would not have approached the material at hand as if they were blank slates reading objective material. Rather, readers came culturally loaded, at the very least with the news as we have explored it from 1985, 1974, 1969, 1948, and, for those old enough, the 1930s and earlier. Remember, Canada's history and press is deeply tainted by colonialism. Szuchewycz summarizes the scholarly literature on the topic this way: "The historical and continuing prevalence of systemic racism has been documented in a wide range of Canadian social institutions, including the legal and criminal justice systems, immigration, education, and employment....A broad-based popular ignorance of Canada's history of discrimination and civil rights against visible and cultural minorities remains prevalent."[45]

"PLEASE WRITE"

Before we settled on Moncton and Prince George we explored the more general reportage of papers from five cities, which also included Regina (*Leader-Post*), Toronto (*Globe and Mail*), and Montreal (*Gazette*). While that work informs this chapter, the media coverage of the Oka crisis itself merits a much more detailed study that can be accomplished in a book chapter. We chose Moncton and Prince George from among them in part because they were about as far east or west as one could get from Oka and thus ideally might provide a sense of readers' thinking from disparate regions of the country. Further, more general reportage in two core papers—the Montreal *Gazette* and the *Globe and Mail*—have already figured in previous chapters, whereas letters to the editor, as a discrete yet compelling subject, have not.

Given that virtually all of the news about Oka came to these publications via the Canadian Press wire service, letters arguably provide the least filtered or mediated means by which to assess local and regional press reportage, keeping in mind that letters are neither perfectly unfiltered nor perfectly mirror reflections of the public mood. That said, the standing headline given to such letters by the *Times-Transcript* suggests that the paper may have seen the section as embodying the essence of its title, "Public Opinion."

Letters to the editor have received scant study by scholars. The best work argues that letters serve a basic democratic purpose in that they "enact a public sphere using technological mediation."[46] In other words, they promote and sustain common ideas about participatory democracy and the importance of individual engagement in democracy. Yet, too, any number of letters can no more be said to represent public opinion, which is itself mutable, inconsistent, and given to frequent and sometimes abrupt changes, than a comparable number of voices elicited by any other means.

Both papers provided guidelines to prospective letter authors. The *Citizen*'s "Please Write" panel invited readers to "express their views on topics of public interest." Writers were required to sign letters, though anonymity could be requested providing "there are good reasons" for it.[47] The paper indicated that all letter writers would be contacted so as to verify authenticity. Further, length should be limited to 200 words.[48] The *Citizen* meanwhile offered an "Electronic Mailbox" and would accept letters from "Computer owners who own modems,"[49] obviously a small cohort when compared to today. The *Times-Transcript* said letters "should be kept brief," no more than 500 words, though the publisher reserved the right to publish lengthier missives. Like the *Citizen*, anonymity might be granted but the paper required that all writers identify themselves in the first case so that the paper could verify authenticity before publication.[50] The *Times-Transcript* published 29 dispatches, 25 of which came from New Brunswick, two from Toronto and two from communities in Quebec. The *Citizen* printed 15 letters, all but one of which were local or regional (the exception came from Vancouver).

The most common themes in the *Citizen*'s fifteen letters included denunciations of the federal and Quebec governments (7), allegations that Natives were guilty of reverse racism (7), given to violence/demanding/greedy/backward/primitive/out of control/guilty of the murder of the SQ officer (12), and claims that Aboriginals unfairly had more rights than whites (6). In sum, employing charges that we have encountered again and again throughout this study, the letters were overwhelmingly critical of the Mohawks at Oka, though the reasoning varied. Only two letters, by contrast, expressed strong endorsement of the Mohawks. And one letter expressed strong ambivalence. On the whole, the results lent to the creation of a standard colonial image, the Native savage.

The numbers do not add up to 100 percent of the total number of letters because many contained more than one of the above elements and a few contained none.

To begin with, reverse racism was a common charge, that is, that the problem at Oka and, by extension, with all Natives, was that they were racist against whites, intolerant, undemocratic, and unfair. It was a double-edged sword because it simultaneously framed whites as tolerant, non-racist, democratic and fair. Evidence of this stemmed, for example, in the assertion that Aboriginals unreasonably demanded 100 percent of British Columbia's territory in a massive land claim while they constituted a mere 3 percent of the general population. "The rest of us—97 percent—are squatters," one letter charged. "They say we have squatters' rights and little else....Ridiculous...and I find demands based on race or ethnic origin unconscionable." Yet the author employs the very same gambit to affirm white rights as s/he uses to attack Natives.[51]

Native violence was also a common charge. "The native blockades are violent acts," noted a letter to the *Citizen*.[52] Perhaps they were best met with violence, another *Citizen* letter opined. It was addressed not to the editor, as is customary, but to "Fellow Canadian Taxpayers." It began, "I cannot believe the apathy of the taxpaying public in the face of the recent Indian demands and behaviours. Do citizens not realize that this movement can only gain momentum if not quelled?" While the threat implied by use of the word "quelled" is not developed, the letter goes on to complain about Native "greed." Canada had allegedly become so unequal that "today's Indians have more rights than other Canadians...and keep asking for more." There seemed to be no solution: "Is the taxpaying Canadian to be forever more held hostage by the aborigines here?"[53]

Violence was again the story of a 17 August *Citizen* letter that identified the "heavily armed" Mohawk "thugs" as guilty of "murder of a law enforcement officer." A reinstatement of law and order was thus vital, the letter explained, "to deal with this criminal element." The writer expressed support for a military assault on the Mohawk barricades yet noted that the responsibility for any "future bloodshed lies with those armed [Aboriginal] thugs."[54] The solution here, in other words, was to meet discerned Mohawk violence with even greater violence. That would be one way to "quell" the problem.

The immigrant theme and the idea of the greedy Native surfaced again at the end of August. A *Citizen* dispatch began by asking, "Whose Land? Whose Rights? Who knows who was here before the native Indians arrived...Who knows how many original inhabitants were massacred before they were taken over?" Whites had worked too hard to end up receiving such shabby treatment as Oka exemplified, the letter continued:

> Now we have a group of people who figure they can hold a government at ransom by their demands. They have been given advantages which are denied the white man.
>
> They have received payments from the government on a monthly basis to cover their living costs. The education of their children has been subsidized.

They no longer have to ride to the nearest trading post to exchange furs for groceries, but can drive their mechanized vehicles over highways developed by the white man...

Their ever-increasing demands are reaching a point which is close to the ridiculous. They have blockaded roads and railroads [a reference to gestures made elsewhere, including the Prince George region, in support of the Mohawks at Oka] in an effort to cripple an economy which is responsible for their very existence.

The letter concludes by identifying the Mohawks as practitioners of "primitive ways."[55]

The letter effectively expresses many of the key allegations levelled at Natives since 1869 in the press. Among the accusations, they are mere savage immigrants (they "massacred" those who were there before them). They have contributed nothing to the country whereas whites had done it all, from the introduction of industry to the building of roads. Further, they are needy and demanding and unreasonable. In fact, somehow they owed their "very existence" to whites.

Another letter the same day took the immigration allegation and reframed it as an appeal to authority. Citing a *Webster's* dictionary definition of the term "native," the author writes, "As someone who was born and raised in Canada, I think of myself as a native Canadian. Why is it then, that a native Canadian must pay for medical plan coverage... free medical and dental for life [for Aboriginals who]...are paid to go to school...received free land and subsidized housing?" Moreover, the letter asks, why is it that Natives can express racism against whites but not the other way around? "Status Indians, with so many benefits, demand so much...let them earn their equality."[56]

Days later many of these allegations surfaced in another letter. The author draws particular attention to alleged special rights that Natives received. "In the view of many," the letter contends, Natives "at one time" were recognized as "oppressed" but now at Oka they had simply gone too far. The result was that they "are now regarded as holding the upper hand as negotiations become a reality."[57] Such a conclusion may well have struck some as spurious given that the army would ultimately surround and outnumber the Mohawks by a factor of roughly fifty to one. On the

other hand, the Oka crisis appeared to have prompted the British Columbia government to agree to engage in treaty negotiations after 135 years
of stonewalling. Thus, the author called "for a more balanced approach."

The immigration issue resurfaced on 20 and 26 September. A fearful
letter noted, "To me, this means I am a native of Canada, as I was born
here. Who exactly does the word native or non-native stand for?....What
is the government hoping or waiting for—a war amongst the aboriginal
people themselves and this war spreading to involve all other people of
Canada." This missive was considerably more moderate than most of the
letters, smearing Aboriginals with martial instincts and defensively yet
angrily insinuating the special rights Native stereotype.[58]

The next instance of the immigration theme attacked Natives by
impugning their patriotism and unique treaty rights. Whites fought for
the very survival of the country in two world wars as well as in Korea "to
protect your house," implying that Aboriginals required white protection
and, possibly, that Natives were too timid to fight, or cowardly, apparently unaware that Aboriginals fought for Canada in those same conflicts. Further, Aboriginals were simply ungrateful: "Maybe, based on the
number of lives lost and the blood let by immigrant Canadians to protect
your rights and your house, we should be sitting down and asking you to
negotiate our land claims from you...for services rendered.... It's time for
the real majority to speak out... [or it] is soon to be extinct."[59]

A final immigration charge was bathed in childlike innocence. The
depths of supposed Mohawk chicanery elicited a letter from a schoolgirl,
a grade nine student. The letter recounted that the student had learned
"a fact that made the whole class think hard." Discrimination was illegal in British Columbia, the class discovered, the student reported. Thus
the student expressed perplexity at the news, taken from the *Citizen*,
that a local Native housing complex was under construction. "Are people who were born in Canada, who are native to Canada, not eligible to
live in these apartments or do native Indians only qualify?" The charge
became one of reverse racism and indirect damnation of the government
for allowing it to occur. "Am I missing something because the Human
Rights Act states that we must not discriminate against anyone?"[60]

A last letter, dated 22 October, champions the creation of the "United
Northern Citizens" group, a direct response to Oka and the land-claims
ripple effect Oka generated in British Columbia. The purpose of the

group was "to create public awareness so there is proper representation by responsible leaders of an informed public concerning land claims issues." This brush tars Natives and government alike with basic dishonesty. Further, the letter charges that members of the group, as a result of Oka, "have had our rights violated." Specifically, these rights included "the basic right of freedom of thought and the right to pursue a livelihood. Even to communicate to the public these fundamental views has been difficult because the media appears to be more attracted to sensationalism."

Of course, it is true that the media revels in sensationalism. Still, how Oka or its ripple effect "violated" white rights in Prince George, especially "freedom of thought," is anybody's guess. It is possible that the writer saw the "right to pursue a livelihood" threatened by land claims— that is, if one were to reason that any land claims in British Columbia, because they had the potential to increase Native landholdings and thereby reduce non-Native landholdings, marginally shrank access to the forest resource base. Even so, the vast bulk of such lands was unused Crown land.[61]

In sum, the letters penned to the *Citizen* adhered closely to colonial imagery. In particular, the letters engage the issue of land usage and ownership, perhaps not surprisingly in the hub of a resource-dependent region of British Columbia. Among the key ways that the east first claimed western Canada was upon the premise that Natives did not effectively employ its resources in ways corresponding to anglo-Canadian culture and legal norms. This charge emerged clearly in the *Citizen*'s letters, whether Natives had allegedly done nothing to build the country up, and thereby failed to earn and thus demonstrate ownership, or whether they signified their lack of ownership by virtue of receiving handouts. Finally, the core colonial assertion that Natives did not own the land emerges from the manifest and essential hostility to land claims at all. Aboriginals simply had no right to the land because they had demonstrated that they had not earned it in ways commensurate with English common law, which in turn has become a cornerstone of Canadian culture and law.

The charge that white rights had been abused serves as a way of reminding readers that Natives did not deserve rights because they had not earned them. Rights flowed from property. Instead, in classic colonial style, white rights were in fact under siege by violent Natives, as Oka allegedly illustrated. This posturing bears close structural resemblance to the late-nineteenth century's avowals that whites, as they pressed ever westward, were the victims of Native aggression. In short, white Canada's attack on Aboriginals and their lands was defensive, whether the year was 1869 or 1990. While it may strain credulity, it also continued to thrive in letters to the editor in Prince George in 1990. It turns empirical history on its head yet it resonates deeply in mainstream Canadiana because without it the conquest of the west has no particular defence.

Two letters stood in clear opposition to the views expressed by the majority in the *Citizen*. The first, on 16 August, levelled a series of charges, beginning with the claim that provincial and federal governments lay at fault for the Oka crisis. It termed this "the unprovoked assault by heavily-armed Quebec police on Mohawk ancestral land at Kanesatake." It further included the municipal government in its condemnation of all elected authorities "who have chosen the path of confrontation." It damned the federal government for "sitting on the sidelines" and the Oka town council for "greed." Ultimately, it attacked mainstream Canada: "The burning of Indian effigies at Chateauguay, the racist chants and the physical assaults on anyone who looked native showed how dangerously easy it is to fan the flames of racism in Canada." Indeed, the author might have used other letters written to the editor of the *Citizen* as evidence of the trend it identified and excoriated.[62]

Rejecting the contention that Mohawks and Aboriginals "across the country" were inherently violent, it averred that at Oka they "stressed they wanted [a] non-violent solution to the problem." It concluded with another broad swipe at Canadiana. "The incident at Oka is the consequence of an attitude in which rights of first nations are held in contempt," it contended.[63]

The second dissenting letter, on 1 September, written by a self-identified Métis, took issue with "racist undertones" in other letters. In its attempt to refute the contention that Natives had special rights, it concluded somewhat weakly that such "can only be assessed and judged in the eye of the beholder only." It claimed, further, that "the situation in the east would lead me to believe that the natives are the hostages."

A third letter ambivalently supported the Mohawks as the victims of colonial history and government chicanery yet dismissed Natives generally as drunken and pathetic recipients of government handouts—which they deserved. The author appears to make a genuine attempt to see the Mohawks as historical actors yet at the same time cannot escape the chains of common colonial signifiers.[64] For example: "introduction of liquor to native Indians has resulted in a tragic moral, physical, and spiritual decline unparalleled anywhere...these are some of the symptoms of a cultural identity crisis which the native Indians are suffering. Their sense of alienation is intense... The government gives handouts and certain so-called privileges to the native Indian. Don't resent it."[65]

"WE DO NOT NEED PEOPLE WHO BURN OUR FLAG AND USE IT AS TOILET PAPER"

The most common themes in the Moncton *Times-Transcript*'s twenty-nine letters included laying the blame for Oka on one or more levels of government (23), charges of mainstream Canadian racism (14), allegations that the root of the problem lay with the essential nature of Quebec, typically portrayed as racist or intolerant (8). Charges that Natives were guilty of reverse racism, common in Prince George, were comparatively infrequent (3), and, likewise, claims that Aboriginals unfairly had more rights than whites (3) were also less common.

The letters' recourse to employing colonial tropes mirrored the more common practice in Prince George. For example, a 17 August letter bashed Indians for being the ungrateful recipients of white handouts. "They have no right to be supported by tax dollars that the Canadian people dish out...It must be rough—paying no taxes, given housing and university education paid," the letter complained. The dispatch also resurrected old tropes of Native depredation: "To add insult to injury the aboriginals take a country hostage by terrorist action while still demanding funding. Who is the real victim here? Wake up...it's time they came into the real world and civilization and [sic] compete."[66]

A letter from 1 August 1990 raised the issue of Native special rights by characterizing them as receiving handouts at the expense of "the Canadian taxpayer...footing the bill." In so doing it also excluded them from "Canada," as other letters also commonly did. Plus, it admixes loathing for Quebec into its low regard for Aboriginals: "I do believe that all Canadians who are not supporters of a separatist movement should firmly take a stand and say enough is enough...Yes Canadians, we do not need people who burn our flag and use it as toilet paper." It is not clear here whether the latter jibe is aimed at Mohawks, Quebecers, or both. Taking aim at federal politicians, it added, "we do not need back-stabbing troublemakers in Ottawa."[67]

In another common thread, depictions of Aboriginal people get tangled up in anti-Quebec sentiment. No letters in Moncton evinced any support for Quebec while many deplored the province or its French-speaking majority. For example, one common gambit was to tie Oka to the failure of the Meech Lake Accord, Brian Mulroney's infamously ill-fated constitutional agreement, which died when a Cree member of the Manitoba legislature, Elijah Harper, effectively blocked it in a procedural vote that required unanimity. Thus, for one letter writer, the Oka crisis became a reflection of the "dark side of Quebec and Quebecers." In a unique and somewhat stunning allegation, the author claimed one could recognize French Canadians by their "physical" appearance. The specific person whom the author stereotyped additionally exhibited "brutal" sexist behaviour. All in all, the problem was the "double-standard" by which Quebec gained, even as it practised "racism," while everyone else in Canada, including Natives, lost.[68]

The same day another letter attacked governments in Quebec City and Ottawa for events at Oka. The respective political leaders, Mulroney and Quebec Premier Robert Bourassa, were "wimps" for failing to deal more strenuously with the Mohawks, though it is unstated precisely what a better policy might have entailed. The result? "We have a Quebec government in Ottawa."[69] Meech Lake and Oka were also garbled together (along with antipathy for Mulroney and the Goods and Services Tax) on 1 August in a letter to the *Times-Transcript*.[70] And on another day Mulroney and was what seem to be an intolerant and hypocritical Quebec were pilloried as the Mohawks were accused of deliberately trying to disguise their own "illegal activities."[71]

Perhaps the clearest evocation of such thinking was printed in a letter on 11 August. "I think that the persecution of native people in Quebec is carefully orchestrated revenge against them by Hull/Ottawa," the author wrote, "because MLA Elijah Harper stalled the Meech Lake Accord in the Manitoba legislature." Sharpening the attack, the author also called for an end to official bilingualism in favour of an English-only Canada. Further, "if Canada has any 'distinct society' it is our native people, and I protest their being pushed around by Quebec and Ottawa."[72] If Natives emerge at all favourably here it is only as the best of a poor lot, pawns in an old national tug-of-war pitting French against English.

Terming Quebec's observed intolerance for Mohawks a "malignancy," a letter in mid-August claimed the real problem at Oka was Quebec "chauvinism" situated in the "political, intellectual, and economic spheres and media of the province." This inured the province to the plight of Natives, a phenomenon it called "excessive blind nationalism." The results were two—first, racism aimed at Quebe's Natives, including the Mohawks at Oka, as well as vituperative anti-Anglo feeling; and, second, "the humiliations of Canadian citizens living in Quebec," though this latter charge only included non-Aboriginals.[73]

As in the case with expressed anti-Ottawa or anti-Mulroney sentiment, antipathy towards Quebec was not then necessarily a predictor of anti-Native sentiment. For example, another letter put it this way: the "problem in Quebec" was with, first, "stealing the land belonging to the Oka Indians." Thus, "the problem began with the Quebecois and should not be the Canadian taxpayer's problem or responsibility." Clearly here Natives are again positioned outside the definition of "Canada" or "Canadian." Yet anti-Quebec sentiment ultimately trumped anti-Native: "The sooner Quebec separates from Canada, the better."[74]

As noted, letters to the editor commonly framed Aboriginals as non-members of what they meant by the term "Canadian." For example, even an ostensibly pro-Native dispatch could not resist slumping into the use of this feature of colonial stereotyping. The writer recounted a youthful night spent at the home of a Mi'kmaq couple in Big Cove, New Brunswick. "It was a wonderful adventure," one reads. "The lady fed me some of the best pie I'd ever eaten." They were "wonderful, non-judgmental, peace-loving folk." As a group, the author continued, Natives have been "duped....lied to and cheated, placed on a restricted parcel of land." In this way, the author observes that the Oka crisis was in a sense the predictable outcome of "savage" historical mainstream Canadian behaviours. Yet, too, the author stereotypes the Natives s/he so acutely admires. Sounding like something penned by Rudyard Kipling, the author adds, "today the natives are restless." Calling Natives as a group "the proudest of the proud" and "the truly godly of the earth," s/he refers to non-Aboriginals as "we, the Canadians." In short, even this empathetic missive posits Indigenous people in an imaginary space where conflict is unknown and Natives are not actually Canadians.[75]

A letter written by a teenager eschewed ready classification. It blamed governments in general for Oka and presented Natives as welfare whores. "Forget about the privileges the Indians receive from the government," it began. The real issue lay with all levels of government for basic insensitivity in allowing for the construction of a golf course on a cemetery.[76]

Another letter that deplored government and empathized with the Mohawks suggested that a group of Mohawk leaders trade places with an equal number of members of Parliament for five years. Each group would gain invaluable insights into the thinking of the other group from the experience. "It would seem reasonable to believe that the MPs forced to live on a ghettoized reserve minus the glitter and trappings of their former hallowed halls, will see the comparative emptiness and hopelessness of their new digs," the author wrote. By contrast, the Mohawks in Ottawa would learn from exposure to "double-talking, back-room deals, badgering constituents, and pressure from lobbyists." While the author's suggestion may have been impractical, it served as a useful device to illustrate the uncommon position of a letter that at once found the federal government at fault for the Oka crisis but did not resort to stereotyping Natives. Meanwhile, it too jabbed, if mildly, at Quebec by noting its solution might resolve matters "toot-sweet."[77]

Four letters were penned by self-identified Aboriginals. All of these focussed on colonialism as the cause of the Oka crisis. Typically, these singled out historical patterns of mainstream racism, exclusionism, governmental duplicity, officially sanctioned violence against Natives, and mainstream efforts to disappear Native cultures through policies of assimilation. Aptly capturing this mood, a letter on 13 August 1990 argued: "I feel saddened, frustrated and angry. I see tensions rising and hear non-Indians show their hatred towards Indians. All of this shows how little the non-Indian understands about our struggle….It brings back memories of when I was growing up as an Indian and was faced with the prejudice and intolerance of those around me, when I sometimes had to fight just because I was an Indian."[78] The colonial tendency to blur distinctions among culturally disparate groups—to fashion a colonial monolith[79]—was one of the reasons cited by the author for supporting the Mohawks at Oka: "their struggle is my struggle whether I like it or not. Since I was born an Indian, it seems as if society has placed us all in the same boat anyway."[80]

An angrier letter was printed on 28 August. Written in response to a letter that the author felt portrayed Aboriginals as non-Canadians, it identified historical racism, bred mostly of ignorance, as the real culprit at Oka. Rejecting generations of government policy, it observed, "It's no wonder that we, the aboriginal people, chose not to be integrated and/or assimilated into such a society."[81] Of course, things are in fact more complicated. For example, the use of the English language and the forum of the letters to the editor section exemplify a certain level of assimilation.

Striking at the heart of the colonial project, a letter the next day charged that government behaviour at Oka, as represented by the authorities on site, would "in all probability be considered an act of hostile aggression if the lines were reversed." The author then stressed that it was important to remember that Europeans had invaded Indigenous lands in the first instance: "Let us not forget that their laws were imposed on us against our desire and with no consultation from us."[82] In sum, the author concluded that hypocrisy defined the colonialism at work behind the Oka crisis.[83]

Colonial hypocrisy coloured a similar letter on 11 September. Conjuring up Canadian common sense, the author claims that "when Indians go on strike the government just laughs at them, thinking that they are just Indians." The hypocrisy emerges from the observation that "we took you in and taught you the way of the new world—and this [Oka] is the thanks we get. First you take away our land, put us in reserves, kill off the animals and pollute the environment." The author proffered no specific solution but suggested that behaving with "peacefulness" in mind was the right way to start.[84]

Letters identifying colonialism at the heart of the Oka crisis did not only come from Natives. Two such letters expressed deep embarrassment over Oka. "I want to express the shame I feel as a Canadian for what we've done to the natives," wrote one author. Because of Oka "today my shame is worse," s/he added. Decrying the use of violence against a "brother," the letter displayed anger towards the various governments involved at Oka and chagrin that government policy at Oka seemed determined to "humiliate" the Mohawks and, by extension, all Natives in Canada.[85]

The second of these letters began, "I want to express my shame at the treatment of our native people by the governments of Quebec and Canada." The author threw the charge of Native "terrorism" back at the authorities, citing official Canadian and Quebec belligerence and aggression as the real culprits behind the crisis. Unusually, the letter framed the Mohawks as having had no option other than setting up a blockade. "Be honest," the letter continued, "was anyone listening before the initial standoff [that is, the first blockade, which the SQ stormed on 11 July 1990] at Oka?" Further, the letter claims that the media's very presence as witness "has kept the Mohawks alive." The final barb was aimed directly at Prime Minister Mulroney: "You have made me ashamed that I am a Canadian."[86]

A related dispatch referred to Oka as Mulroney's "undeclared war on native peoples" and charged the prime minister with dishonesty and criminal behaviour. Equally reprehensible and blatantly irresponsible, the author stormed, Mulroney had "put the Canadian army at the disposal of the Quebec Premier to invade land that clearly is Mohawk land."[87]

Finally, a similar letter chose to relate historical injustices visited upon the Stó :lo of British Columbia and the Nez Perce of the U.S. Pacific Northwest as evidence that Natives continent-wide had been denied "true justice." The author concludes by noting that "there may have been a time when white men could plead ignorance. That day is no more."[88]

Ultimately, these letters correspond to general press coverage of Oka, which has been seen as reinforcing Aboriginal stereotypes such as proclivity for violence and lack of control, which in turn fit neatly within historical patterns of press colonialism in Canada. A colonial narrative emerges again and again in letters to the editor examined in this chapter. The porousness of the stereotyping and the malleability of the archetypes in play made it possible to fit the clichés to match events as they unfolded. This included assertions of inherent Native violence and criminality but also allegations of special rights, lack of self-control, and childishness. Yet other common allegations—drunkenness, whorishness, thievery—received little notice. Nonetheless, the Native savage reared his head.

In some ways the depictions published in Prince George appeared more consistent than those from Moncton. But, then, letter writers may have perceived the stakes as higher. After all, within mere weeks and well before it ended, the Oka crisis spurred government action on British Columbia land claims, which may have been perceived as a threat, whereas successive governments prior to the Oka crisis had otherwise ignored these issues for more than 100 years. Of course, these actions were also engendered by symbolic actions taken in British Columbia to show support for the Oka Mohawks, also reported prominently in the *Citizen*, which included temporary rail and road blockades, for example.[89] As noted, much of the letters' content crackled with mainstream angst, anger, and resentment about land ownership.

In Moncton the land issue struck less of a chord, probably because the mainstream readership had no particular reason to fear land claims inasmuch as readers might simply have assumed they were long settled (however inaccurate this may have been). Savage imagery was also quantitatively less prominent in Moncton, at least in part because a greater proportion of letters was written by Aboriginal people, all of whom decried colonialism. Another feature in *Times-Transcript* letters that emerged disproportionate to *Citizen* characterizations was the matter of Quebec. Quebec played little on the minds of Prince George authors while Moncton letter writers frequently evinced deep hostility toward their neighbouring province, and sometimes the expressed antipathy for Quebec trumped anti-Native sentiment. Clearly, Oka in some cases simply served as a platform through which to lash out at Quebec.

In short, the answer to our second core question—does a counter-narrative emerge?—is yes, but barely. And it was difficult to hear it in the din of colonial-style reportage. Factor out Native letters—because one might assume Natives have always opposed, resented, and resisted colonialism—as well as the more rabid anti-Quebec feeling and you get a clear and unambiguous colonial tale in which homeless non-Canadian Natives play the violent aggressor to the innocent white Canadian. The 1990 letters bear strong resemblance to reportage of the late nineteenth century. Moreover, the very idea of attempting to quantify a counter-narrative is inherently problematic because it implies a structural moral consonance where authorship equates with some democratic ideal. To quote Ian Law, "it implies that portrayal of minority ethnic groups should conform with the pattern of portrayal of whites, and therefore places 'white' norms at the centre of the analysis and privileges these as given and unquestioned."[90]

That said, the mere existence of the counter-narrative stands in significant comparative contrast to the scenarios examined in every other chapter in this book. A mitigating factor, however, is that most of these letters, by a count of five to three, were written by Natives. Looked at another way, if one considers the way in which readers might have apprehended the letters, it seems probable that few would have been converted to the other side on the basis of the letters themselves. The two positions were simply too far apart. The result is that the counter-narrative dispatches, as with the colonial missives, preached to the converted. In this way the apparent numerical significance registered by a cohort of counter-narrative letters is partially undone because Natives across the country have always in large proportion opposed colonialism. No new converts there. That leaves a mere three counter-narrative letters from among the thirty-nine letters we examined—hardly a breakthrough in perception. Arguably, the counter-narrative at Oka amounts to little more than that expressed in letters to the editor in Kenora sixteen years earlier, as shown in an earlier chapter.

Still, for the first time Aboriginals used the press in much the same way whites always had. Should this be seen as a sign of empowerment and a kind of broadening of the democratic franchise? Insofar as letters to the editor constitute a forum via which to engage in democratic debate, however imperfectly, could this be seen as a hopeful sign? The answer is, not really. Here again we enter a mythical dead-end at the imaginary construct of Canadian democracy, every bit as unreal as alleged Native savagery. How many Canadian majority governments, for instance, have earned majority support from Canadian voters? Or what kind of democracy allowed whites to vote but would not extend the same right to First Nations till 1960? Why are women and minorities not represented proportionately in Parliament? How can a party with less than 40 percent of the popular vote govern with majority power when a party that earns roughly 10 percent of the vote fails to win a seat in Parliament? Yet the country lumbers onward because Canadians confer legitimacy upon it and because by doing so Canadians in turn reinforce their belief in the system. This particular closed circle provided special protection against Native inroads. In this sense, that part of the colonial imaginary that frames Aboriginals as aggressors to Canadian innocence is curiously accurate. Press content strongly suggests that the only way for Natives to break into "Canada" is to take aggressive action.

Ultimately, the Oka letters to the editor, despite the novelty of letters written by Aboriginals, largely reinforced the colonial status quo. Yet another compelling reason exists to suggest that this important symbolic step forward may be more apparent than real. Amelia Kalant writes:

> The question that may be too often ignored, however, is whether the lasting impression left by these moments slowly dissipates in the reasserted world of 'normal life.' The power of myths, after all, is not to be found in the simple act of their telling: rather, it is in their institutionalization, the repetition, and constant practice that shapes normal, regularized, social relations. And so the disruption caused by an event like Oka should not be heralded as a promise of lasting,

socially significant change. Alternative stories of the world need to be institutionalized to effect further change or they become sporadic expressions of frustration.[91]

This is precisely the case with newspapers in Canada. They promote myth, in the case at hand, that is, the Canadian colonial imaginary. It surfaces in the content of coverage but also then subsumes the industry itself, in turn reflecting systemic and systematic colonialism.

Szuchewycz observes that "the press and other forms of mass media circulate 'definitions of the situation' which contribute significantly to the formation, maintenance, and reproduction of a dominant popular consensus."[92] Seen in this light, the reportage, as represented by these letters, remained deeply coloured by the Canadian colonial imagination. Again Kalant captures the moment: "It brought to the blockade issues of Canada's relationship to Native peoples (and its second order natives of Quebec) and its own pretension to nativeness, Canada's myths of peaceableness, fairness, tolerance, love of wilderness, non-Americanness, as well as Quebec's relationship to Canada and to native peoples and its pretensions to nativeness and being colonized."[93]

Remember, this was 1990. A mere twenty-one years ago.

CHAPTER TWELVE

BACK TO THE FUTURE
A Prairie Centennial, 1905–2005

The 1840s and 1850s were a period of constant raiding by all the Blackfoot, young risked their lives for glory and gain, against the Crow, Cree, Shoshoni, Gros Ventures, and Nez Perce.... As chief Red Crow was always ready to defend Blood territory. In October 1871 he led 60 warriors in a strike on a Crow camp on the Upper Milk River, killing at least 60. In camp, however, life became more and more demoralizing as the Kinai were devastated by smallpox and pestilence of alcohol, which affected Red Crow as much as others, as he killed his own brother, Kit Fox, in a drunken brawl.... As the bison herds disappeared Red Crow began to see the value of the treaty for the future. He was proud, but he accepted reality. The bison were gone.

—EDMONTON *JOURNAL*, 1 JULY 2005

Canada staged a massive celebration in 1967 in recognition of its centennial. Poems and songs were written, pavilions constructed, massive government propaganda unleashed, and family treks undertaken in the station wagon to Expo '67 in Montreal. Though contrived, the country experienced a kind of nationalistic and heartfelt euphoria.

Then there was the 500th anniversary celebration of Columbus's "discovery" of the Americas. Stamps were issued, Hollywood movies released, galas planned, and in the end the quincentennial in 1992 also resulted in an opportunity for open dialogue around problematic notions of discovery and conquest. It provoked much debate in Canada and was marked by the mounting of two national art exhibitions of works by contemporary Aboriginal artists that challenged the whole notion of celebration.[1]

Canadian provinces also enjoy such occasions. For example, Alberta and Saskatchewan observed their first 100 years in 2005. Official ceremonies featuring premiers and mayors and members of legislatures abounded. People staged backyard barbecues, organized family and school reunions, launched parades, completed centennial school projects, and the like. Both provinces expressed much pride in themselves. As the Edmonton *Journal* put it in 1905, "Saskatchewan and Alberta are Provinces of unrealized and almost unexplored possibilities."[2] But why celebrate a mere 100 years? Why not a 10,000-year birthday party instead? After all, the provinces' first citizens have been around a lot longer than a single century.

But it did not happen that way. The obvious difference between celebrating a century and ten millennia is that, despite the rhetoric, the former proffered settler commemorations of mainstream significance— a way of saying that Saskatchewan and Alberta began to matter when they became officially sanctioned entities in part of mainstream Canada. Core Prairie Canadian culture was the thing to celebrate. The Aboriginal component of the observances as reported in the press in the summer of 2005 paled sharply in comparison, dredging up the familiar colonial discourse, and otherwise served as more of an afterthought to the festivities. In 1905 Aboriginals simply did not figure in the celebratory coverage of the birth of the provinces at all. Rather, the common view expressed in the Alberta and Saskatchewan press held that Aboriginals were, first, dying off and thus unlikely to survive another 100 years. Second, they were not worth celebrating for a variety of reasons that bore close resemblance to press imagery of Aboriginal people from the last decades of the nineteenth century.

That said, in 2005 key newspapers in each province diligently sought to incorporate Aboriginal peoples in the celebrations, much as they strenuously disparaged and ignored them in 1905. To assess how this effort was effected and to gain some understanding of how portrayals compare directly over 100 years, we explored the content of four dailies, the Regina *Leader-Post*, Saskatoon *Star Phoenix*, Edmonton *Journal*, and Calgary *Herald*, for the two summer months of 2005 during which most of the official events occurred. In order to make an enormous amount of material workable for this chapter we focussed on the week beginning with Canada Day, 1 to 8 July. We then compared and contrasted this content with similar examination of these same newspapers in their entirety for 1905, when papers were significantly fewer pages in length. Here we also included four weeklies—the Moose Jaw *Times*, *Saskatchewan Herald*, published in the Battlefords, (Fort) *Macleod Gazette*, and *Alberta Advocate*, published in Red Deer.

"PASSING OF THE RED MAN"

Augie Fleras and Jean Lock Kunz argue that Canadian-style racism has morphed over time from a colonial vestige centred on biological essence—"who they are"—to one more focussed on culture—"what they do."[3] Evidence presented thus far in this book only partially endorses this conclusion. To begin with, the press was little interested in parsing definitions in such ways. Further, as shown, the colonial imagination in the latter nineteenth century employed descriptions of alleged Aboriginal behaviour (that is, culture) at least in part to illustrate the truth of allegations that one might categorize as biologically racist (e.g., reports of bedraggled clothing, which signifies Aboriginal moribundity); but allegations of cultural backwardness and inferiority also stood in their own right in 1869. In fact, while it is impossible to quantify, espied Native behaviour, at least until the 1960s, would appear to have been categorized as much cultural as biological in nature, though we agree with Fleras and Kunz that since the White Paper most of the mainstream press framings have tended toward the cultural. Comparing and contrasting coverage of 1905 with 2005 seems to present an ideal case in which to consider nature versus nurture in press depictions, while keeping in mind that both are subsumed within a colonial ideology that was consumed in practice with power and not with arcane intellectual distinctions.

In 1905 Alberta and Saskatchewan were formally carved out of the Northwest Territories (previously known as Rupert's Land) and fashioned as discrete provinces. Basically, the territories had been till that time sparsely populated by whites; but in 1905 the federal government determined that a sufficient population had been established to create new provinces in the west. Thus, while the Canadian west only technically came into existence in 1869 and was only just opening up to settlement in 1873–74, by 1905 it was deemed, at least for the purposes of political representation on a national scale, to have become sufficiently full of Canadians (read: settlers; First Nations were not effectively enfranchised until 1960) to earn the status of provinces.

In 1905 it remained unclear on the Prairies whether or not Aboriginals were disappearing. The Saskatchewan and Alberta press equivocated on the topic. In no instance did the newspapers advocate physical genocide. Instead, they endorsed the common idea that Native people—not *peoples*, in keeping with the monolithic stereotype that all Aboriginals were essentially the same; for example, as the weekly *Alberta Advocate* suggested, all Aboriginals spoke the same language, simply called "Indian"[4]—would shortly fade away and die out, even as they infrequently reported that such notions were not borne out by real-world evidence.

The construction of the Native as moribund took several forms. The most obvious, intimately tying nurture with nature, was that as a group Natives were doomed because of backward culture unsuited to an ever-evolving world. The 1905 Saskatoon *Phenix* foresaw "extinction in the near future."[5] On another occasion it referred to the process simply as the "passing of the red man." The report drew attention to "Indian stoicism" in the face of ineluctable travel to "the happy hunting ground."[6] The Calgary *Herald* cited official reports from Ottawa that showed a decline in Canada's Aboriginal population from 1904.[7]

Yet the Saskatoon *Phenix* and *Alberta Advocate* noted an official from the Department of Indian Affairs had reported that Aboriginal populations were in fact increasing. "There was a general impression that the Indians were a dying race," the papers reported, "but the records of the department did not bear out that view."[8] In the space of three paragraphs in an *Alberta Advocate* story one learns, on the one hand, that "the Kitimat tribe is not decreasing" and that "the mortality of our Indians is decreasing" and that they represent a "vanishing race." The story explains the apparent logical discrepancy by noting that those who are not dying have been saved by Christian education.[9]

According to the *Phenix*, in order to combat espied demographic collapse, some British Columbia Native groups had resorted to purchasing white youths whom they then adopted and raised as their own. In one case, a five-year-old white boy was purchased for $4000, the *Phenix* detailed. He "was received with honor, elected a chief and allotted six wives...in order that extinction might be averted."[10]

The 1905 Regina *Leader*, published by the first premier of the province, Walter Scott,[11] argued, "the race is one which is liable to disappear. It was not apparently made for the conditions under which we live in this modern world, and fades away more or less under the influence of modern civilization."[12] And whatever might remain of them, that is, those fit enough to survive, would necessarily assimilate—in other words culturally evaporate, the paper opined. Likewise, the *Alberta Advocate* titled a brief story, "Indians Dying Off."[13]

On the other hand, the same newspapers pondered that perhaps Aboriginals were in fact thriving. For example, the *Saskatchewan Herald* published a report in which the Indian commissioner claimed that Natives were not disappearing. Instead there was "little destitution" for the first time in years. In short, he averred, they were diminished in comparison to whites yet not necessarily doomed. The article tempered such affirmations by reminding the reader that Natives remained "wards" of the state, legal children.[14]

The Edmonton *Journal* fashioned a somewhat different shading. Because Edmonton remained a fur-trading outpost in 1905, the paper was keenly aware of the ongoing value of Aboriginal trappers. Still, the Native was backward, readers would have learned, for example, because "money had no value to the primitive Indian in the wilderness. His knowledge of civilization is restricted to the little he learns by coming in contact once a year with a few traders and an occasional missionary."[15] Several dozen "superstitious" Cree witnesses to a sensational murder trial camped in tipis in the city in February and March. As the trial drew to a conclusion, the paper ruminated, "Imagine the feelings of surprise and wonder with which these simple people, many of whom had never been within three hundred miles of anything approaching civilization, must have surveyed the signs of the encroaching tide of whitemen."[16]

Related to such assertions, Natives, according to all of these papers, could not effectively feed themselves, echoing similar charges of the nineteenth century, though no discussion ever occurred to speculate how "primitive"[17] Aboriginals might have survived, and possibly thrived, the previous 10,000 years (or more) without European aid.[18] They remained "superstitious and very curious," explained the *Phenix*.[19] The *Saskatchewan Herald* contended that the best to be expected from Natives was that they might be taught to "raise a few cattle and grow a little grain." The paper concluded from this that residential schools were wasted on such "pagans."[20]

The *Leader* spun news of the identified general success of rudimentary education in mission schools in a slightly more positive light. To begin with, the white missionaries were doing laudable work, the paper said. Further, "the native race" showed aptitude "especially in drawing, writing, and singing."[21] On the other hand, in accord with the tenor of the *Saskatchewan Herald*'s assertions, the *Leader* lectured that ultimately Aboriginals were in fact intellectually limited and that the benefits of formal education had reached their apogee. The conclusion: "Indian people are as successful and contented as it is possible to make them."[22] Meanwhile, the Calgary *Herald* reported that a young Oneida woman in California was set to become the first Aboriginal female to study law: "She wants to learn law in order that she may go from tribe to tribe teaching her pathetic people their rights under the white man's law."[23]

In sum, the press identified biological weakness, which leaned toward physical disappearance, for Aboriginals. Yet it also simultaneously reported that physical disappearance was not supported by empirical evidence; in fact numbers were increasing. Not to be deterred by the facts, the papers also argued in favour of education, and, if not always precisely, assimilation. Some agreement existed that, though biologically weaker, Aboriginals might be taught to survive, if not necessarily prosper. In this way, nature and nurture walked hand in glove. On no occasion did any paper question assumptions upon which such notions were premised—inherent white physical and cultural superiority, or the obvious point that Natives had endured and even prospered without aid for millennia. With arrogant certainty the press in 1905 averred that Aboriginal culture was shrivelling away in the face of progress. Why? The reason was simple, the press argued: Christianity. Effective proselytizing was thus key. Missionaries were claiming victory at every turn in what they portrayed as the epochal struggle of civilization versus barbarism. So pronounced was the alleged mainstream advantage that those Natives who eschewed Christianity were paying for their hubris in the form of demographic decline and the punishment of creeping empirical extinction. In short, a cultural stubbornness earned biological demise. As the Edmonton *Journal* explained the common view, clerics generally worked for "the good of those poor human beings who appear to our advanced ideas so helpless when they come in contact with the white man's methods."[24]

Despite the good intentions and hard work of missionaries, the Calgary *Herald* expressed less optimism about the outcome of their efforts: "The close range view of the situation does not present the Indian in such an attractive light. Many pioneer characters who know the red man by close contact in other days when he was the savage monarch over all he surveyed, insist that civilizing influence has not improved this son of nature, to such a remarkable extent. Religion has certainly done much for the Indian but it has failed to make him appropriate the first principle of modern civilization—the perfection and elevation of womanhood."[25]

A key problem with Aboriginals, the *Alberta Advocate* explained, lay in their "superstitious" religious beliefs. For example, the publication dismissively explained that "the general belief is that the tribe is the miraculous outcome of the intercourse of some god with some animal, bird or fish."[26] How such an idea differed morally, theologically, or empirically from the Christian belief that some god impregnated an unsuspecting virgin was not explained. The Edmonton *Journal* flippantly added that Alberta Cree believed in a spirit figure, "Weetigo," who was a "man eater" and "cannibal,"[27] and literally had a "heart of ice."[28]

"DIRTY AND THOROUGHLY DEGENERATE"

And so the press had not warmed to Aboriginals on the Prairies in 1905. As a consequence, the tepid declarations of partial or potential Indigenous survival should be seen for what they were—a kind of colonial boosterism and not evidence of positive Native characteristics. Natives were surviving because of mainstream efforts to save them, the papers stressed. Left to their own devices, they would otherwise disappear. As the press had it, what remained of the Aboriginal population, despite the gilded sheen of Christianity, were Natives cast much as they had been since the sale of Rupert's Land.

Confoundedly, then, those who remained also continued to personify barbaric behavioural traits, the press averred. The papers made it clear that Natives remained heathen, childlike, dangerous, violent, crazy, volatile, stupid, and on occasion given to cannibalism. Such attributes called for sturdy and uncompromising Christian charity as well as hands-on government direction if Natives were to be redeemed.[29] To wit, beating an education into them, if necessary, was acceptable, even desirable. The *Saskatchewan Herald*, in an attempt at humour, for example, narrated, under the headline of "GREAT MEDICINE," how a hook-handed French

Canadian pioneer found it both necessary and useful to apply corporal punishment with his hook in order to teach Natives.[30]

The Saskatoon *Phenix* termed this process, "making good Indians."[31] Savages the world over—as well as women in general—simply had smaller brains than white men, the paper reported, which partially explained such deviant behaviour and the fair and measured response to it.[32] It took no particular leap of faith, then, to read and accept that Aboriginals also engaged in cannibalism, typified in a case where a man allegedly devoured his wife and their six children in mid-winter.[33] Again, the admixing of nature (e.g., brain size) with nurture (e.g., the cannibal made a conscious decision to devour his family). Elsewhere, violence-inclined Indigenous people were "murderous," "killed...without discrimination," for the *Saskatchewan Herald*, and murderous and "barbarian," for the *Alberta Advocate*.[34] One story reported how, apropos of nothing, an Indian agent had been shot in the eye by an arrow.[35]

Despite the effects of schooling and proselytizing, Aboriginals remained, according to the *Saskatchewan Herald*, essentially "base and dishonest" and had evinced such qualities since the earliest days of the settling of the West.[36] Horse thieving and larceny remained common as were other "ugly," "wily," and "debauched" behaviours, contributed the weekly Moose Jaw *Times*.[37] The Edmonton *Journal* saw the "pure" Native as "dirty and thoroughly degenerate" and on occasion given to cannibalism.[38] An insatiable affinity for strong drink was widely identified.[39] They were "crude [and] strange," claimed the *Alberta Advocate*.[40] Aboriginals could actually smell danger, at least in the commission of a crime, claimed the Moose Jaw *Times*.[41] Excessive alcohol consumption called out base instincts, which sometimes led to murder, as in the reported case in which one drunk "clubbed" another to death.[42] In short, self-control was almost unknown, as Natives all too predictably drank to excess, according to reports, which then often led to excesses of other kinds, especially violence and crime.[43] The *Phenix* told of a "brutal Indian" so debauched that after committing the worst of (unidentified) crimes he attempted suicide by slashing his knee with a shard of glass. But it did not work and he was apprehended. Once sufficiently healed he went to the gallows "half crazed by terror," yet to his credit ultimately "professing Christianity."[44]

In 1905, Prairie newspapers commonly devoted space to reprinting material from years and even decades gone by.[45] Such nostalgia took two basic forms. The first commemorated the twentieth anniversary of the 1885 North-West Rebellion by reiterating long lists of espied Aboriginal inferiority, as detailed in an earlier chapter of this book. These reports additionally championed alleged white superiority as well as the heroic qualities of the colonial authorities.[46] For example, the Regina *Leader* ran a regular feature titled, "TWENTY YEARS AGO," in which the war figured as the key theme. The language in such reports did not simply ape the reports from 1885 but, in fact, many of the earlier reports were simply reprinted. In this way, by dredging up near-hysterical tales of savagery and mayhem, the papers reminded readers to remain steadfast in support of colonial policy that reduced Aboriginals to a severely marginalized, degraded, and controlled status. More to the point, it reminded and encouraged readers to fear and loathe Natives. Undoubtedly, such reportage also contributed to ongoing informal racism and encouraged behaviour towards Natives that reflected the core colonial biases clearly evident in the news.

The second type of remembrance was less structured and included presenting tales highlighting Aboriginal savagery from earlier times, often reaching back centuries. For example, the *Alberta Advocate* painted "scenes of a famous Indian duel in Wyoming" as a picturesque confrontation among wild, brutal savages in which the victors ate selected body parts of the losers.[47] On another occasion, the paper began, "a thrilling incident, showing the influence of the Gospel among the Indians of Northern British Columbia, was related in Centennial Methodist Church, Toronto, recently." The narrative featured "savages" who "chanted war songs" but ultimately were dissuaded from all-out savage warfare because they had inadvertently scheduled their fight for a Sunday. The protagonist cleric was able cleverly to use their burgeoning piety as leverage to get them to lay down their arms entirely. It seems he had taught them well because "to them the Sabbath was sacred."[48] On another day, recounting the "Massacre of 1763," the paper identified Aboriginals as "blood-thirsty Indians" who "scalped" and took delight in "slaughter" and mutilation.[49]

The weekly Fort Macleod *Gazette* presented a kind of historical primer for its readers in mid-October. It captured brilliantly and expressed articulately much of the underlying sentiment of the 1905 press. It recorded, "The civilized era of the North West Territories began only in the latter half of the nineteenth century, but how long it may have been populated by rude nations of centuries past, will remain vague and dim to the present thriving North West...'The roaming hunter-tribes, warlike and fierce' hunted the bison in their vast hunting ground for many years before the white man endeavored to obtain the tract of land in the North-West."

Beyond making the standard conflation of civilization with whiteness, the report attempts to keep history tucked away in a metaphorical past, "vague and dim," so as to preclude any sense that Aboriginals were robbed of their land by whites. Indeed, the land was neither fought for nor stolen, it was instead "obtained" from "rude," "warlike and fierce," nomadic Aboriginals. The lengthy article goes on to relate the many supposed racial and cultural faults of the Métis, stressing their disloyalty and untrustworthiness, which culminated in the failed war of 1885.[50] On another occasion, two months later, the broadsheet referred to Aboriginals as the "noble red man," a term meant with derision, as the accompanying story detailed how after receiving treaty monies Blood Indians flooded the town of Fort Macleod, lurking "in the alleys, on the corners" like so many intemperate pests.[51]

Not to be outdone in reminiscing, the Edmonton *Journal* reprinted an article from the 19 July 1880 edition of the Saskatchewan *Herald*. It set about to undo a stereotype but instead reinforced it, to "prove that the stoicism and powers of endurance of the untamed Indian are not so mythical as some would have us believe."[52] With considerable economy of prose on another occasion the paper employed a common literary device that reads like the start of a fairy tale. "Some sixty or seventy years ago there lived in this valley a tribe of Cree Indians," it said. "They were wild, revengeful and barbarous, making war on the neighboring tribes and indulging in every sphere of vice and crime. Poor creatures! They knew no better; they were heathen. Some worshipped idols of wood, others worshipped trees, stars, or rocks, but most of them were utterly ignorant of anything higher than their own desires and passions."[53] In an unintended way the passage neatly summarizes 1905 reportage in Alberta and Saskatchewan: nothing had changed since 1869, neither nature nor nurture.

"EVERYTHING THAT THIS COUNTRY STANDS FOR"

By the centennial summer of 2005 a lot in fact had changed on the Prairies. After a hundred years the formerly rural provinces had become urban, though still tied economically to resource extraction. Populations had mushroomed to 3 million in Alberta and 1 million in Saskatchewan, of which Aboriginals counted as a small—though growing, especially in Saskatchewan—fraction. Two world wars had come and gone. Suffrage had been extended to white women in 1917 and to First Nations people in 1960. The last of the residential schools closed near Regina in 1996. The stringent pass system, instigated as a reaction to the 1885 resistance, which severely limited Native off-reserve travel, was long gone. A First Nations–inspired and –run university was created in Regina, with satellite campuses in Saskatoon and Prince Albert. And then there was Oka, which inspired Aboriginals across the Prairies to more urgently press for land and political reform.

Significantly, too, Canada had become officially multicultural. The country was now the world's leading immigrant nation. Given its colonial past and in an effort to cushion the blow of massive non-white immigration, it had adopted propaganda campaigns to convince Canadians that they were at heart a tolerant and racially empathetic people.[54] Officially, seemingly at every turn, politicians mouthed promises to alleviate stubborn Aboriginal poverty and the other various social ills associated with colonialism. In a word, in official rhetoric Canada had been reborn. In this newly minted Canada, racism was a thing of the distant past and Aboriginals were to be celebrated in their own right—a long time coming but a good idea nonetheless, many mainstream Canadians would today agree.

Such a sea change suggests that newspaper coverage in 2005 would then have dropped the colonial blinders of 1905 and have come to portray Aboriginals as it would portray white Canadians. Yet in several key respects this did not happen on the Prairies. In fact, coverage related to Aboriginals remained deeply cynical, often angry, typically disparaging, and gleefully resentful. The colonial tropes endured, moreover, and continued to reinforce long-established notions about alleged Indigenous inferiority. While use of the word "savagery" could no longer be found, much of the espied behaviour that had since 1869 signified Aboriginal inferiority, cultural or biological, remained intact.

To better examine this reportage we have chosen to consider three common storylines from the summer of 2005. The first concerns the trial of Cree veteran and Order of Canada recipient David Ahenakew, charged with inciting hatred as a result of comments he made in 2002. A key irony of this coverage is that it promoted hatred against Ahenakew, if one accepts the definition of the term as "prejudiced hostility or animosity."[55] Moreover, by framing Ahenakew as a colonialized archetype, by extension all Aboriginals were smeared by the reportage and somehow vaguely guilty of a variety of reverse racism. In this way, Aboriginals might be framed positively but only partially and only if their behaviour tended toward embracing assimilation; whereas evidence of Aboriginal non-compliance with the goals of assimilation automatically earned pejorative framing. Finally, we consider how the press framed Natives within the larger celebration of the centennial observances.

Ahenakew was charged with willfully inciting hatred as a result of anti-Jewish comments he made at a meeting in December 2002. Since, he was found guilty in a court of law, had his Order of Canada citation revoked, and upon appeal was found innocent of the charges in early 2009. The case generated a lot of coverage during the summer of 2005, especially in Saskatchewan, his home province, and in particular in Regina, where the trial was held.

Virtually all press commentary found Ahenakew's widely circulated comments highly distasteful. Yet the press also resorted to stereotyping Ahenakew to such an extent that the presentations came to promote a hateful view of him. The key framing posited Ahenakew as a twofold Native stereotype, ungrateful mooch and impetuous infant. He was cast as a whiner, ever ready with his hand out, demanding that he receive unfair advantages because of his status as an Aboriginal.

Almost all coverage judged him guilty before the outcome of the trial. He was invariably described as "disgraced" and that he "brought shame," that his words "denigrated" the honour of Canada. Identical articles in the 2 July *Leader-Post* and Saskatoon *Star Phoenix* framed Ahenakew and his lawyer as cowardly, immature, and lazy. Ahenakew was afraid to face justice. As a result he and his lawyer stalled for time in the case while the Crown had been "'ready to go' for two years." Tired of the nettlesome stalling tactics, which "irked," the case had reached "the third and final delay." Implying that God himself sided with the government, the paper reported the Crown attorney's observation that the "the courts have kind of moved Heaven and Earth" to accommodate Ahenakew. But to no avail. Further, the paper implied that letters to the editor written across Canada indicated that a majority of Canadians supported taking away his Order of Canada award and labelled him a "bigot." Probably nothing summed up the coverage better than the deeply ironic colonial lament expressed by a lawyer agitating against Ahenakew: "For the sake of everything that this country stands for, he should not be able to wear that pin."[56]

An editorial in the *Leader-Post* on 8 July took this one step further, claiming that "Ahenakew's name does not belong on the honour role of great people who have helped shape a nation noted for its tolerance and fairness."[57] In this way, the paper performed the double duty of reminding readers of the essential non-belonging of Native peoples as well as blatantly misreading the nation's history. An editorial the following day suggested that Ahenakew was stupid ("still doesn't get it") and mentally unstable ("twisted"). It concluded that "If a non-aboriginal public figure spewed similar venom against First Nations peoples, they'd justifiably be hauled before the justice system Ahenakew finds so flawed."[58] But a colonial press *is* a hateful press. A 9 July *Star Phoenix* editorial echoed the *Leader-Post*'s opinion and added, "First Nations people need every positive role model they can get."[59] The double complication is that the story ultimately also paints an unflattering, stereotypical view of Jewish people.

In the 9 July edition one banner news headline read, "GUILTY OF HATE. Despite verdict, Ahenakew lashes out at whites and courts." Of course, it is quite true that he was found guilty in 2005. And, indeed, the comments for which he was charged reflected basic historical ignorance and were morally reprehensible.[60] Yet the press also promoted hatred of Ahenakew. For example, the headline racializes the story. Nowhere in Ahenakew's reported comments is there a reference to whites, though he does express contempt for Canadian colonialism. Consider the language used in the accompanying story to describe him: "furious," "vowed to fight," "promoting hatred," "'I'm innocent,'" "'native people will never get good, solid justice in this country,'" "Lashing out," "Visibly angry," "his tirade," "defiant," "critical," and "'They will have to take it away [the Order of Canada pin].'"[61] The same day the *Star Phoenix* employed well-trod shibboleths to label Ahenakew as "still defiant," "convicted," "dehumanizing," a person who would "invite extremists," "extreme," displaying "arrogance," "outrageous," "obscene," "hateful," "abhorrent," "inappropriate," behaving in a "hateful way," and simply guilty of the "harm that [he] caused." Clearly, according to the descriptors, Ahenakew had trouble reining in his overzealous passions; he could barely contain himself, if the paper was to be believed—yet he childishly, stubbornly positioned himself as the wronged party, as the *Star Phoenix* put it in an editorial, "who blames everyone else for his woes."[62] In short, he was a big crybaby, reminiscent of an awkward 1905 *Saskatchewan Herald* attempt at humour where the weekly complained about the unfair payments received by treaty Natives in this way: "Wa-wah!"[63]

On no occasion does the paper take the time to note the incongruity between his terrible anti-Jewish comments and the lifetime of good works that had earned him the Order of Canada in the first place. Nowhere does the paper consider the irony that by repeatedly broadcasting the comments, the anti-Jewish diatribe reached a monumentally larger audience. For that matter, nowhere does the press consider that its framing of Jews in this story—as pushy whiners—is not so different from one of the ways in which Ahenakew is framed.[64]

"A GIFT FROM THE TWENTIETH CENTURY"

The goal of Canada's national Indian policy has concentrated on assimilating Aboriginals as cheaply and quickly as possible. For example, this was the core goal of residential schools and has been a key aim since missionaries entered Rupert's Land. The results have been mixed. On the one hand Christianity has thrived among Natives and the English language has become a first language in its own right for many. And while residential schools are rightly deplored for the behaviour of their many racist and predatory teachers and staff, less public attention has been paid to their goal of effecting the erasure of Aboriginal culture (sometimes known as attempted cultural genocide; an aim partially visible in the decline of Aboriginal languages and religious traditions). In other words, the government's assimilationist policies have met with some success, though the premises on which these have been based are ethically dubious, at best, and heinous at worst.

The press since Confederation has aided and abetted the promotion of colonial policies. For this reason, it should come as no surprise that the key newspapers in Alberta and Saskatchewan endorsed assimilation for Aboriginals in 2005. The typical framing in this coverage presents assimilation as an ineluctable good while casting Aboriginals as not fully capable of achieving it. In this way, 2005 reportage returns to the nature-versus-nurture matter of 1905. The idea of assimilation might seem to imply that all people are essentially equal. Yet the failure to assimilate, the failure to *have* assimilated after decades of assimilation policy *and* given the legacy of colonialism in Canada's mainstream press, leads to the common sense conclusion in 2005 that Aboriginals remain in fact racially inferior.

A business column in the Calgary *Herald* published on 2 July 2005 captures much of the prevailing sentiment without attributing it directly to nature or nurture. It begins by chastising then-Prime Minister Paul Martin for showing greater interest in addressing third-world poverty than in the "festering" Aboriginal problems in Canada. By turns, the article presents Natives as diseased, suicidal, lazy, uneducated, and poorly governed—"part of the reason may be that aboriginal groups seem reluctant to help themselves."[65] In other words, Natives need to demonstrate more initiative and behave more like whites, the column concludes. Further, it asks, "why should Canadian taxpayers [read: non-Aboriginals] support the construction of government-funded on-reserve housing? Shelter is a personal responsibility." So, again, a newspaper blames the victim of government policy for the results of government policy, the victim of colonialism for the effects of colonialism. The final sentence sums up this sentiment, as the author roasts government and Natives alike "for costing the Canadian economy as much as $10.6 billion a year." No mention is made of treaty obligations, let alone that Canada's wealth—its very existence—derives solely from the lands ceded to "Canada" by treaty or as the result of naked imperialism.

A typical *Leader-Post* article touting new government bursary money for Aboriginal students also stresses inherent Aboriginal neediness. Education has long been seen as key to assimilation. It was, in the quoted words of the Saskatchewan minister for labour, "a good opportunity for the aboriginal community to take advantage of some good opportunities."[66] The provincial minister's construction frames the government as having granted something to Aboriginals. It does not note that the federal government is required to fund Aboriginal education as part of a commitment to honour treaty obligations. That is, in return for accepting more than 90 percent of the territory of Saskatchewan the government of Canada promised to educate, as needed and as required, status Natives. The minister also declines to note that all non-Aboriginal Canadians also receive publicly funded primary and secondary education free of charge. Note additionally that the passage casts Aboriginals as "tak[ing] advantage," as if the government was somehow not morally and legally bound by treaty obligations.[67]

The remainder of the article continues in the same vein. For example, it draws specific attention to the failure of Aboriginals to assimilate. "More than 13 percent of the population in Saskatchewan is aboriginal," it continued, "and over 40 percent are under 15 years old…40 percent of that population lives in poverty. Post-secondary education is the way out of poverty….We deplore the fact that the poor and the aboriginal students of Canada are not represented in post-secondary institutions."[68] From this we learn that Natives are young, preternaturally fecund, poor, and ignorant. Yet, education is the only thing that can save them. But such was the cry 100 years earlier! What conclusion is one to draw from such "news"? Nowhere does the article attempt to explain the nature and source of such conditions. Again, can a typical reader be expected to be familiar with the scholarly literature establishing a clear linkage between colonialism and Aboriginal poverty and poor education? Common sense Canadiana already provides the answer. Would a story then surprise about a Métis blessed with "fishing in his blood...[as well as a] fishy stench"?[69] Repeated again and again, as Furniss stresses, the demeaning and derogatory images of Native people become nearly invisible because of their ubiquity.

A column in the 7 July Edmonton *Journal* reeked with such common sense. It tells the story of an Alberta Cree provincial cabinet minister who beat the odds of being born in poverty by sheer dint of hard work and determination. The piece quoted the minister: "'Everybody worked. Then the welfare system was introduced and the community fell apart and people didn't work.'"[70] The result? Again, we find the stereotype of neediness inherent in Aboriginal communities; the columnist calls it a "culture of dependency...which saps individual initiative and sets people up for a lifetime of failure and unmet expectations." While the conclusions drawn are not logical—one who aspires to welfare would not logically fail by receiving it, let alone be plagued by unmet expectations—they frame assimilation as the only salvation for Natives.

On 4 July, as part of ongoing coverage of a tragic story about a young Aboriginal girl's disappearance a year earlier, the *Leader-Post* sought to provide background information that might aid readers in contextualizing the story.[71] It came as a sidebar to the main story. Part of the problem, the paper cited a local police officer, was, "living in housing conditions that are below standard, that are not suitable for human occupation. But yet they're living in them." The article then continued: "Crumbling foundations, ceilings falling in, no running water and infestations of rodents and insects are just an example of what exists in some of Regina's most rundown houses. Some also contain evidence of drug and alcohol addictions.... 'Used needles, lots of those. Lots of evidence of solvent abuse. Those are the two primary indicators. We see lots of signs of intravenous drug use, as far as blood splatters on walls and ceilings. It's prevalent. It's there.'" What might a reader learn from this? That they are slovenly, unable to curb their historical love affair with substance abuse and alcoholism? That they remain violent? That the little girl's disappearance should not surprise readers? In short, the attempt to provide context in fact serves equally well another purpose, that of the colonial morality tale.

In 1905 media reports, such imagery drawing attention to how Aboriginal people had not assimilated would have been used as evidence of moribundity. The key difference found in 2005 coverage, as Fleras and Kunz have it, is that the reportorial gaze tends to settle on the behavioural. In this way, the article does not directly tell you what Aboriginals are; instead it tells you what they do, as well as smears them by association with filth, decay, and weakness. The article concludes by citing yet another expert, in a classic rhetorical appeal to authority, ostensibly to provide balance to the story: "Despair is the most destructive element there right now. It does lead to alcohol and drug abuse, it leads to crime and it leads to violence and it leads to neglect of children."[72]

"Criminal interference played a part in her disappearance," the police were quoted in the paper. "We've been unable to find any alternative explanation for the disappearance of this little girl except criminal activity, some kind of malfeasance," the statement, which also appeared verbatim in the *Star Phoenix*, continued. In short, it made perfect sense, once all other possibilities (not enumerated) had been exhausted, to assume that Aboriginal criminal "malfeasance" lay behind the tragedy.[73] Unacceptable behaviour that reflected an inability or an unwillingness to assimilate also featured prominently in stories about Métis elections that were not "clean" and had "Métis people screaming,"[74] as well as an ongoing narrative charting upheaval at the First Nations University of Canada (FNUC).[75]

The Métis elections, in particular, drew the ire of *Leader-Post* columnist. Murray Mandryk dredged up the symbols of an old Hollywood Western: "It's always tempting for a government to ride into town, guns a blazin', and announce it is cleaning up some mess in the First Nations or Métis community. Frankly, it's the approach most often demanded by the white majority." Lessons of "history" serve as one of his rhetorical strategies. So, too, does his common sense invocation of democracy—but while it suggests that the majority shall rule it also levels an implied threat that the majority will rule. This is a thinly disguised might-makes-right line of reasoning, a reductive and simplistic hegemonic appeal that conflates majoritarianism with nature—precisely one of the difficulties with colonialism in the first place. The "unnerving similarities" Mandryk discerns in the "electoral irregularities" and the "problems" at FNUC derive simply from the failures of assimilation policy, and thus, predictably, a "leadership that simply hasn't operated within any known accepted rules, procedures, or practices."[76]

Still, nature on occasion trumped nurture in 2005 press reports. "Aboriginal people have higher rates of chronic and infectious disease, lower life expectancy and heightened suicide rates compared to the non-aboriginal population," a 6 July report in the *Star Phoenix* calling for a "blueprint" to solve such problems stressed.[77] The article creates the troubling impression that Aboriginals are physically inferior to "non-Aboriginals," hence the statistics. Rather than provide any explanation for such phenomena, the article employs this material as context itself for why the government must spend hundreds of millions of dollars more on Natives. In this way, stereotyped needy Aboriginals themselves are to blame for their own poor health.

On Canada Day 2005 the Edmonton *Journal* employed a 1905 newspaper tactic, and remembered the past wistfully, as a headline indicated, "Red Crow Considered His People Equal to the White Men." Keeping the past alive in this way performed the obvious task of celebrating days gone by while keeping alive the colonial imaginary. By presenting the story as historical, there is no particular need for modesty. In this tale about the Blackfoot, we read that Red Crow was "noble," the Blackfoot inveterate criminal raiders, demoralized, given to drunkenness, murder, and stupidity. Fortunately, Red Crow "was proud, but he accepted reality." That "reality" meant surrender and capitulation to assimilation. This in turn made him "wise," whereas those Natives who chose another path experienced the "tragedy" of punishing demographic decline. In this context "equality" meant assimilation—that is, whites and Aboriginals were equal when and only when the latter gave up their culture and adopted the normativity of whiteness.[78]

Another article that day related how "a heavy-set aboriginal female" who "weighed about 240 pounds" assaulted a white teenage girl in Saskatoon, a story also printed in both the *Star Phoenix* and *Leader-Post*. Sidestepping the issue of slander because the attacker was not named, the paper had no compunction about racializing the guilty party. This was a savage Native at work. "'She took Josi's head and banged it against the asphalt 15 or 20 times... and started kneeing her in the chest area, the body, the face, kicking her in the back. She was kicking her like a rag doll. It was relentless,'" reported the mother to the paper, though she had not witnessed the incident.[79] Clearly, assimilation had passed the guilty party by.

On one occasion the Edmonton *Journal* directly took up the issue of assimilation and how it proffered the only viable solution for Aboriginal progress. The story involved charges that the RCMP "deliberately shot [sled] dogs in the

1950s and 60s as a policy to assimilate Inuit by keeping them off the land." The article provided a point-counter-point style of presentation—with a catch. The catch is that by the tone of the prose the writer makes it clear that the Inuit accusations are at best frivolous and that the reader should accept the RCMP investigation that found (before the results of the report were even presented) the charges as baseless. For example, the story begins by belittling the Inuit allegations as the work of canines—"Nunavut RCMP are preparing themselves for the political bite of thousands of dead sled dogs." Two sentences later the canine symbolism returns when one reads that Inuit were "demanding" a "public inquiry to sniff out the truth," as if accuracy were an odour. Later, "the finding"—that is, that the RCMP were faultless—"is sure to draw growls."[80]

Unlike many news stories, this one seeks to provide a context for the actions depicted. Yet it is unmistakably tendentious and may be summed up in a word: assimilationist. "A single generation was expected to leap from tents and igloos to the technocratic world of the 1950s Canada," the report continues. "There's no other group of indigenous people who went through so much change so fast…. As well, the Inuit were battered by famine and disease." In short, the Inuit need to put the distant past behind them and get on with blending in.[81] When this was achieved, as in the case of an Aboriginal activist who shared in the nomination of the Nobel Peace Prize and was born in a "tiny cabin" with neither electricity nor running water, "It's a gift from the 21st century."[82] Likewise, progress in Alberta would correct "rundown" reserve housing south of Calgary.[83]

"I LIKE THE COSTUMES"

The central trope to commemorating Aboriginal peoples on the Prairies focussed on highlighting the irrelevance of their past, according to press reports. For example, on 2 July the *Leader-Post* ran a story about how some Aboriginals celebrated Canada Day. A drum group performed at a downtown park. Such groups thrive in Saskatchewan; the tradition is thousands of years old. The report noted, "Their performance sent vibrations of nostalgia through the air as people imagined a time when aboriginal encampment like the one set up for the Canada Day celebrations, was a way of life. Three authentic tipis and horses decorated in war paint provided a back drop for the drummers."[84] The passage encourages readers to think of discrete Native culture, which they are encouraged to "imagine," as something that existed in the distant past.[85] The reference to authenticity confers not merely a sense of legitimacy to the proceedings but also one of control. And war paint reminds readers of the savage archetype, now long since defeated—yet, as the crime story about the 240-pound attacker suggests, the savage remains not merely latent but only a misstep away. Stressing that Aboriginals past and present represent nothing more than a single thread in the tapestry of Canadiana, the story quotes a local non-Aboriginal mother: "'Exposing kids to multiculturalism is very important to my husband and I.'" The woman's young daughter added innocently, "'I like the costumes,'" as if Aboriginal regalia constituted little more than a Halloween outfit.[86]

A Calgary *Herald* column celebrated Alberta's past on 1 July by reminding readers that once-savage Aboriginals had been defeated, defanged, and that Aboriginal culture was static (though it can be regulated and controlled). Leaving little room for ambiguity, the article begins, like yet another fairy tale: "There was a time in Blackfoot history when this many white men riding through Indian land would have resulted in bloodshed. Warriors, known as Brave Dogs, would have been blessed and painted and sent to kill the intruders and take their horses." Yet this section of the Prairies was only settled well after the sale of Rupert's Land in 1869, and despite the nineteenth-century portrayals of the Blackfoot as savage, no evidence exists for the central assertion that the Blackfoot "warriors" would have done any such thing. This is a return to a classic Canadian nineteenth-century colonial imagining, featuring Natives as inherently violent, aggressive, possessive, culturally backward, and thieving. Further, Blackfoot history is relegated to the junk pile. What remains can be measured by a few "religious artifacts" and "archeological sites."[87] Here the Blackfoot, like the Inuit, are associated with canine-like qualities.

Packaging up Natives and relegating them to a controlled, manicured, and patrolled past featured commonly in Calgary newspapers in early July. The reason is that Aboriginals served as an effective foil against which to assess the glowing wonders of southern Alberta's mythical cowboy history, especially as epitomized in coverage of the Calgary Stampede—billed as the "greatest outdoor show on earth." Some articles championed assimilation as the means to finish the disappearing of Aboriginal culture that cowboys began long ago. For example, a short piece about a Native artist commented on how Indigenous youth "straddle two worlds." While the advantages of the white side of the equation are referred to as "conventional," readers are reminded that the Native quotient "immediately evokes the issue of high suicide rates."[88] The next day the Calgary *Herald* ran a brief story about how the Canadian

Museum of Civilization in Ottawa "has donated" various "artifacts" to an Aboriginal group near the national capital. This constitutes a curious form of charity when the news story itself indicates that the materials were taken without consent by archeologists decades earlier.[89]

As part of a centennial series, "100 Years, 100 Towns," on 7 July the *Star Phoenix* focussed on Val Marie, a small community south of Regina, deep in cattle country: "Near where Val Marie stands today was the site of the last buffalo hunt in Canada. While American soldiers had killed off many of the buffalo across North America in hopes of wiping out the First Nations population, in 1885 a group of First Nations and Metis hunters rode into the plains and took down 482 of the beasts.... The area was first officially settled in the early 1900s when two French priests...." This short passage coughs up many by now standard refrains—Native culture is relegated to the past, Americans are reckless, American Indian policy was vile, and "official" history begins with the arrival of whites, in this case two prelates. The article continues with references to "cowboys" and a noted hockey star of the 1970s, Bryan Trottier, in a way a poster-boy for assimilation because he was Métis and played with great success for the New York Islanders of the National Hockey League.[90] And although the community has fallen on hard times in recent years, "it will never die." No mention is made about what happened to those Natives involved in the last buffalo hunt. Where are they now?

For the first week in July 2005, then, with two exceptions, news reportage with respect to Indigenous peoples was deeply pejorative and reflective of 1905 portrayals. The exceptions include, first, the standing columns of Doug Cuthand, a Cree commentator from Saskatoon, published in both Saskatoon and Regina. Cuthand's work tended to revolve around social and political issues related to Aboriginal peoples and the mainstream. The opinions offered provided the sort of balance one might expect, but would not generally encounter, in *Leader-Post* or *Star Phoenix* coverage. Notably, Cuthand's columns neither stereotype nor apply the colonial gaze that otherwise dominates coverage of Aboriginals and Aboriginal issues.[91]

The second exception includes printed materials stemming from non-traditional news sources. These are infrequent. For example, commentary in the *Star Phoenix* by a sociologist from the University of Saskatchewan took issue with the lack of clarity and absence of nuance in the way the media explained the news of the growth of Saskatchewan's Native population. The author illustrated how the press mistook and exaggerated Indigenous demographic trends, largely because the basic data about population growth was interpreted without an understanding of longer-term population trends reaching back several decades. Thus the conclusions, according to the author, were misleading to the point of inaccuracy.[92]

Nevertheless, with the notable exception of the columns of Doug Cuthand, during the first week of July 2005, virtually all of the news with respect to Indigenous peoples was bad news. Invariably, potentially positive depictions—such as cases where Natives embraced assimilation—were undone by the persistence of pejorative colonial imagery. One might counter this with the observation that news content generally tends to focus on the negative. And there is some truth to this. Yet the four papers every day during the same period printed much "good news" on a wide variety of topics with the exception of things Aboriginal.

The key differences in coverage between 1905 and 2005 are more real than apparent. The distinctions tend not to be apparent likely because we are conditioned to read the news in a way that is consistent with the "totality" of the core culture that dominates Canada's discursive landscape. That is the "real" thing. A result is that a steady diet of bad news about Aboriginals is swallowed up as natural, even predictable. For better or worse, readers tend to believe what they read in newspapers. In part, that is why they read them; they trust newspapers. Of course, no two readers digest anything in exactly the same way, which in turn belies the consistency and constancy of colonial reportage.

In 1905 the press continued the long-established practice of anointing Natives as savages, plain and simple. The identified behaviour spoke for itself. By 2005 such overt labelling was no longer acceptable, given Canada's commitment to the large-scale immigration of non-white peoples and a multiculturalism policy that included widespread propaganda to convince the country that it was racially tolerant to a degree unsupported by historical evidence. So it turns out that colonial imagery endured the centennial celebration. In fact, one might argue that the celebration itself was a party thrown in honour of colonialism; so it should come as no surprise that the press responded in kind.

CONCLUSION
Return of the Native

With its $24-million endowment, the Canadian Race Relations Foundation has become yet another player in our nation's vast, vigorous and mostly publicly funded racism industry. Although its stated goal is to eliminate racial discrimination, its real goal is to manufacture it. This it does by commissioning quantities of research projects that invariably turn up evidence of fresh atrocities. Often this discrimination is 'hidden,' 'systematic,' 'symbolic,' or 'subtle.' Only a trained eye can detect it.

—MARGARET WENTE, *GLOBE AND MAIL*, 8 NOVEMBER 2001

John Raulston Saul calls Canada's colonial mind "a marriage of self-loathing, humiliation, and adoration."[1] While sometimes overwrought, Saul makes a strong case. In newspapers the first two elements emerge historically as projections of the ways in which the Other is presented; something akin to homophobia and the commonplace wisdom that the root of fanaticism is self-doubt. The narcissism, meanwhile, has figured centrally in news imagery, as shown throughout this study. Newspaper portrayals of Natives swim in righteous mainstream self-veneration. No doubt Saul's three characteristics serve many psychological ends. For example, to label the Native as one with a thirst for wanton violence automatically situates the labeller at a distance—that is, the one who directs the gaze—as oppositional, which conveniently frees the labeller and may enable his or her own carnage.

Canada is an imagined entity—even federal Liberal leader Michael Ignatieff admits as much in the opening sentence of his 2009 book[2]—and newspapers, through their scripted colonial depictions of Aboriginal peoples, have contributed to it in important ways. The nation, writes Benedict Anderson, "is imagined as a community, because, regardless of the actual inequality and exploitation that may prevail…[it] is always conceived as a deep, horizontal comradeship."[3] News content across time illustrates this point with some precision, and indeed Anderson's observation is exactly right for Canada. Press imagery, from 1869 through 2009, has championed "inequality" as a means to promote the nation.

Media scholar Mary Vipond contributes to this argument. "In Canada," she writes, "governments have looked to the mass media to help create and express a sense of unity and identity to weld together a vast and disparate nation."[4] From 1869 through 2009 the English-language printed press endeavoured to exclude Natives from this "Canada." Curiously, the exclusion actually well served the purpose of cementing the nation's "deep, horizontal comradeship" by effectively affirming and lovingly espousing its core, if empirically nonsensical, tenets. The key element of this is that Aboriginals ironically played and continue to play a crucial and necessary role in nation building, but it works to their real-world detriment because it services an emotional need to elevate the mainstream by way of binary comparison. The outcome is never in doubt because the game is rigged by the compulsive desires and needs that reside in the colonial imagination.

In 1900 Canada had roughly the same number of newspapers as a century later, about 120. A key difference is that the former were owned independently whereas today a small handful of large corporations control almost all newspapers. Scholars rightly study this media concentration.[5] But in terms of the way Aboriginals have been portrayed it made no difference. The colonial imagination endured (and one might make a related argument, tearing a page from Noam Chomsky, that under such conditions the industry actually and necessarily prospered).

Much of this book explored press content taken from the decades when the mass media was dominated by newspapers. But then came radio, television, and the Internet. We focussed on newspapers in part for the sake of methodological consistency, in part because newspapers remain the bedrock upon which mass media has been constructed, and because we hoped to be able to assess what change, if any, occurred across 140 years. And it seems reasonable to assert that most Canadians, including many scholars, would expect that a good deal has changed.

The country, after all, has morphed from the days of horse and buggy to YouTube. Formerly not so tolerant, Canada is now assumed by many to be a racially tolerant land.

A variety of experts have concluded that the American press became "less blatantly racist" over the course of the twentieth century (but remained racist nonetheless).[6] We found scant evidence to support a similar conclusion for Canada. It is important not to confuse a minor change in tone with significant qualitative diminution. Miller and Ross demonstrate that even in liberal Massachusetts, home to the Kennedy political clan and John Kerry, the key Boston newspaper in the years 1999 to 2001 overwhelmingly portrayed Natives in strongly pejorative ways,[7] not so different from what Coward found for the latter nineteenth century and Weston found for the twentieth century into the early 1990s. Still, while it is probably not surprising that the Toronto *Globe* and Montreal *Gazette* of 1869 expressed yawning and risible loathing for all things Aboriginal, it seems fair to think that many Canadians would be surprised, some might even be shocked, to discover that newspaper imagery has not changed significantly since that time with respect to the application of colonialism as a lens through which to consider Indigenous people. In fact, the idea that Canada is a beacon of racial tolerance and multicultural acceptance plays a vital role in its imagined community today. In other words, the Canadian imagination warmly embraces the notion that Canada is a racially tolerant country (and sometimes avers, as many of our students invariably do, that it always has been). Newspaper reportage does not support this conclusion.

Indeed, our study shows a different outcome. The colonial stereotypes have endured in the press, even flourished. That the prose may have become less "blatant" however suggests that the audience has become more familiar with the genre conventions of colonial discourse. To put it another way: the nation has been built. Obviousness becomes somehow gauche once "common sense" takes over. This is the key to how genre operates. For example, think about how sagebrush and stagecoaches signify a Western, how certain strains of music set up a situation comedy on television, and how distorted or excessively tilted camera angles can indicate a horror film. How do we differentiate between a documentary and an action film? Between country music and hip hop? Between the good guy and the bad guy in an action flick? Between the *National Enquirer* and the *New York Times*? Actually, it is surprisingly easy to the trained eye or ear. But this cultural literacy first has to be learned. The same held true for Canada's early colonial imagination, very much an earnest work-in-progress in the decades after 1869. As literacy rates shot ever upward by 1900, so too had the nation's press become well schooled in the conventions and expressions of the colonial gaze. And in time, with practice and regular bombardment, they became second nature, common sensical, a kind of body language of colonial Canada.

As already detailed, in Kenora in 1974 the *Miner and News* meant "Indian" when it used the words "wino" or "drunks" in the same way that the term "Indian" could signify a variety of unpalatable images drawn from the well of the colonial imagination. From the coverage of Oka, "warrior" was understood as terrorist/savage. In 1869 or 1898 the term "child of the forest" meant culturally backward and mentally deficient Native. "Squaw" meant whore. And so on in seemingly endless tautological circularity. To be able to translate is to be able to speak Canadian. Of course it required a thoroughgoing informal education and social learning at which the mass media excels, but by 1900 most adult Canadians were literate colonialists and the memory of Louis Riel was little more than a cautionary waking dream.

That said, certain changes in the imagery have occurred. For example, the widely expressed idea that Natives were dying off, so common in the latter nineteenth and early twentieth centuries, itself endured a sluggish demise in the early decades of the twentieth century. Yet Aboriginals in other ways remain haunted by images of death and dying and disease, and their supposed cultural decline, a kind of ponderous departure in its own right, framed as benevolent and ineluctable assimilation, has been universally applauded in the press.

Coward and Weston each identify a trend in the United States that shows that Natives were sometimes presented favourably in the form of the noble savage. Yet our research suggests these findings are not applicable for Canada. It is not that the noble savage has failed to supplant more pejorative colonial ruminations. Instead, what we find is that the noble savage is not "noble" at all, and largely represents a false binary. For example, Grey Owl is often used as an example of the noble savage. Yet there was little "noble" about the way press cast him. He was perhaps portrayed as the best of a poor lot; but he never escaped Nativeness till he was outed as a fake.

Another key adjustment engages a conclusion drawn by Robert Harding in an analysis comparing and contrasting newspaper imagery in

British Columbia in the 1860s and the early 1990s. Harding found, first, that "the broader features of news discourse about aboriginal people have remained constant over the last century and a half."[8] Yet, second, he also significantly saw an opening where "the voices of aboriginal people, and many other voices that were formerly excluded altogether, have been selectively incorporated into discourse."[9] We agree but perhaps less optimistically. Where Harding may have seen an opening, we found a peephole. For example, Natives in 1969 registered vocal disagreement with the White Paper and the press duly reported it. But it did not amount to an independent voice. The tone and contours of the subsequent presentations were, as shown, cut from colonial cloth. Or in Kenora, 1974, the press frequently reported comments made by Warrior Society leader Louis Cameron, but this reportage could not reasonably be said to have given Cameron anything resembling an unfettered public voice. It may well have been the opposite. And, remember, newspapers reserve the right to edit content, though all we as readers are left with are the end products. The Kenora depictions reached levels of near hysteria. Oka in 1990 proved no better. However, both Kenora and Oka provided the only consistent opportunity for Natives to evince some public ability to speak, and it occurred in the letters to the editor section, which again may have been edited. Trouble is, this opportunity, though frequently stridently expressive, was drowned in the sea of colonial imagination that otherwise dominated the news, and even in the letters section those few pro-Native or anti-colonial missives were vastly outnumbered. In short, it may be tempting to identify an emergent "middle ground," to scrounge a term from Richard White's brilliant study of the Great Lakes region;[10] but the evidence simply does not support it.

The vivid sketching of Natives as savages, too, has transmogrified from a time when the news language left negligible room for ambiguity, to a situation in the early twenty-first century in which it may no longer be considered appropriate to apply such candid, distasteful monikers. For example, the press no longer refers to Aboriginals as "pagans" or "heathens" or "squaws" as it once did. This brings to mind an observation made by Fleras and Kunz. They contend that the framing has inclined in recent years to being couched in behavioural terms rather than biological essentialisms. Thus the savage becomes one who engages in behaviour that defines savagery but is not referred to openly as a "savage," an iteration of savagery-in-itself. This is a way of restating the point about genre. In this case the genre conventions are the words used to describe Natives—that is, their espied behaviours—that in turn signify the thing-in-itself—that is, in this case, the essential Indian.

To put it another way, if we are what we do, that is, if a person is basically defined by his or her behaviour, then it matters little whether you are called a savage or merely described as behaving like one. Arguably, in fact, the latter is more effectual because it requires evidence (again, empirical accuracy is not required), some effort, and at least the pretense of a line of argumentation. But there is something else at work here. The apparent substitution of nurture for nature provides a classic example of how genre behaves, and arguably represents the natural "evolution" of a genre, a way of compartmentalizing the world in order to see it better. For example, again, how do you know when you are watching a movie that is a Western? What would it take to convince you? Cowboys? "Injuns"? John Wayne? A dusty saloon? A ranch? Six-guns? Each of these elements can conjure up the genre once there exists sufficient public acceptance of what the genre *is*. It is not necessary to re-educate viewers on the meaning of what a horror film is, or a romantic-comedy, or a documentary, every time one is shown.[11] We know them because we have been exposed to them repeatedly. Miller and Ross call this "presupposition."[12]

A similar pattern holds with representations of Canada's Aboriginals. One knows them mostly because of popular culture, and the most reliable and informative and respected organ of popular culture has been the newspaper. It is not far off the mark to say that newspapers have created the Aboriginal Canadians know and they have done so nominally on Canada's behalf. And in the same way as with the Western, the imagined Native need not be reinvented every time one is deployed. When the Regina *Leader-Post* identifies north-central Regina in a crime story in 2009 it "presupposes" that a reader understands the neighbourhood as one overflowing with Aboriginals, with poverty, vice, and crime. As with any genre, once you are presented with the appropriate symbols or signifiers, you know it instantly. Hence the mere association of Natives and, say, alcohol in a news story dredges up the drunken Native stereotype as surely as the beating of tom-toms announces an impending "Injun" attack in an old Western.

The location of the historical events we have considered played an uneven role in press reportage. Proximity tended somewhat erratically to heighten the tone of coverage. The best example was Kenora in 1974. The local *Miner and News* coverage came to verge on the panic-stricken while the national reportage was more moderate, though notably not objective. On the other hand, Grey Owl's death in 1938 only partially supports the idea. Recall that two Saskatchewan papers, in Regina and Saskatoon, initially sought to refute the news that Grey Owl was a fraud. Yet the Prince Albert *Daily Herald*, geographically closer to the story, did not shy away from the shocking reports emanating from North Bay that Grey Owl was a phony. Other cases, such as letters to the editor about and during the Oka crisis seemed more resistant to the localizing tendency, likely because they spoke so directly to national mythology, though local issues certainly coloured the letters. Yet in no case did we find a newspaper that resisted Canada's colonial imaginary. Distance mattered, but only slightly, and concentration of ownership had no effect whatever.

"MY OWN FANTASY"

A fundamental way in which the old colonial shibboleths are kept alive is in the promulgation of colonial common sense and the related positivist or neo-liberal ideas that contend Canadian society is progressing and evolving. This difficult-to-quantify Canadian predilection makes the assertion that the press is less racist today than in days of old appear more reasonable than the evidence allows. Contemporary examples abound. Consider the writings on Aboriginal topics by *Globe and Mail* columnist Margaret Wente.[13]

Wente has written a column for the *Globe* since the late 1980s. Usually running somewhere around 1000 words in length, it specializes in the sort of outrage and indignation that helps sell newspapers. Frequently, it roots for the little guy/gal, especially children. Like many columns it also revels in the personality of its author, a self-absorbed columnist who is, predictably, always right. And like for many columns, the rules of journalism are relaxed.[14] Facts are usually what the author says they are. In the fifty-eight columns we considered it was rare to find any kind of attribution.

Wente expresses deep faith in an ideology that you might simply refer to as Canadian liberal pluralism of the latter twentieth century. Not the warm and fuzzy type of liberal pluralism and inclusionism that, say, John

Ralston Saul cherishes, but an edgier sort of belief in free enterprise, the inevitability of progress, and the idea that history represents in some sense a positivistic narrative of Eurocentric social evolution. Amidst this, the trouble with Natives, the columnist finds again and again, is that they stubbornly refuse to assimilate. And assimilation is necessary, she argues:

> People are inherently tribal, and are inherently inclined to believe
> they are exploited…The job of civic society is to overcome these tribal
> resentments and replace them with a set of values and aspirations
> that are shared. But our age is all about accentuating differences.
> We're supposed to not just recognize and tolerate differences, but to
> embrace and celebrate them. And so the gay-rights movement became
> the gay and lesbian movement, and the bisexuals wanted into the
> act, followed by the transgendered, the transsexual (and God help
> you if you insensitively confuse these two) and the two-spirited….
> My own fantasy is of a multiracial society, where we all become
> pretty much indistinguishable through integration, assimilation and
> intermarriage. (Imagine how much better looking we would be.)[15]

Wente presents the case for assimilation as an article of faith, that assimilation is necessary because it is, tautologically, inevitable. It operates as a self-evident truth, like the existence of God to a Christian. And it is as inevitable as the "evolution" inherent in history, that triumphal version where everyone else is marching in *our* direction. We use the possessive pronoun "our" because her stake claims ownership in the same way that the news on behalf of the Canadian nation claimed Pauline Johnson or Grey Owl or Rupert's Land. In this story Aboriginals remain stuck in an atavistic stage of evolutionary development. In short, what readers get is dressed-up late nineteenth-century neoliberal ideology: progress, measurable pseudo-scientifically, is foreseeable and desirable; all humans must pass through stages of evolution to arrive where the mainstream already is.

One day in 1999 Wente mocked "urban liberals" and lampooned Aboriginals for attempting to keep a centuries-old whaling tradition alive on the Pacific Coast. She scorned and begrudged Natives the use of modern technology—"The warriors finished off their prey with a .50 caliber armour-piercing assault rifle, then towed it to shore with a motorized fishing boat" and drank a Diet Coke "to wash down the whale blubber." The column stressed how "mystical" West Coast Aboriginals "defy" government, and smeared them with a reference to a teleological "missing link." The tenor of the piece holds that Natives must forget their old ways. To embrace them is pure folly. Moreover, Natives who hunted in ways less than traditional—with "motorized" boats and "Diet Coke" and an "armour-piercing assault rifle"—are plain hypocrites. The solution? She champions the efforts of one twenty-one-year-old who "isn't interested in killing whales." Instead, he labours in a place where Natives belonged, "working for the Neah Bay drug education program." In sum, in less than 1000 words we are reminded that many Natives remain stuck in the past, which is a pointless and wasteful spot to be, that Natives remain spiritually confused by adhering to "mystical" traditions, that Natives remain associated with substance abuse, and that sensible Natives embrace assimilation as the only way to progress.[16] For example: "But it's not hard to argue the business case for affirmative action. It has been embraced wholeheartedly by some of North America's oldest and most successful institutions, and some of its most profitable ones. The Bank of Montreal and Hewlett-Packard, for example, have given their shareholders some of the best long-term return of any companies in the world. They must know something."[17]

Three days later Wente termed reservations as "hopeless," rife with "outright theft" and general "financial mismanagement." The Stoney reserve near Calgary was an "oozing sore," a "slum," filled with uneducated suicide cases. Who was to blame? In part, INAC, she says, because the government simply threw good money after bad. But the government really was not most culpable, it was "only part of the problem." Aboriginal culture was the real issue. "What do we do when self-rule means self-ruin?" she asked. "Some cultures are too toxic to save. Maybe the Stoney reserve is one of them." The column also expectorated allegations of financial corruption, sexual abuse, lack of self-control, and the general mendacity of First Nations. In a way, it was simply distilled White Paper thinking—just get rid of reserves ("Abolish Indian Affairs and its programs," she pleaded) and assimilate those Natives "the hell out of there, before it's too late."[18]

Just five days later Wente's column suggested that the sins of residential schools had been overblown and that the country was better off, again, to simply forget the past.[19] Yet another day she belittled grant programs designed to aid Aboriginals.[20] Yet another day she found some evidence of assimilation working slowly to cure the "emotional, spiritual and material poverty" of life on reservations.[21] She ridiculed traditional medicine as so much "sweet grass and sweat lodges." A lot of good they do: "Canada's native peoples are the sickest in the country."[22] Fetal alcohol syndrome had run amok among Natives, she averred another day. That may be the case, but Wente presented little evidence. Instead, she explained herself by here asserting that Natives constitute a monolithic "culture in crisis."[23] Another symptom of it was those typical Native children who live "without goals or purpose or role models." The culprit? "Chronic, toxic, deadly boredom." In a rare admission, Wente said that the mainstream "bears some responsibility for these things." But it only goes so far. "Chewing over old wrongs won't help the children now," she warned. "Nor will nostalgia for the days of hunting and gathering."[24] In other words, this variety of the blame-game reproaches the victims of colonialism for its ills. She finds Natives at fault; in particular, she chided their stubborn adherence to cultural traditions that historical evolution, in her view, has wisely left well behind. In 2006 Wente wrote that "it's hard to see the opportunity all around you when you've been nurtured on so much grievance and injustice. The protestors were raised on an endless diet of stolen land, discrimination, evil residential schools and broken promises. Many of the injustices were real. But how do you move on? How do you make peace with the modern world when you are haunted by ancient wrongs and obsessed with a romantic version of an idealized past?"[25]

Wente's columns rely on every imaginable alleged Native shortcoming, from sexual depravity[26] to financial corruption,[27] thievery to alcoholism,[28] poor parenting[29] to childish behaviour,[30] receiving special rights[31] to reverse racism against whites,[32] inherent violence[33] to being stuck in dying cultures[34] without being smart enough to realize it.[35] Her fixation with "evolving" never wavers.[36] In this way, the columns fit the larger pattern of reportorial traditions as explored in the study. Wente's perspective on Aboriginal Canada is the rule, not the exception.

Canada's mainstream newspapers have aided and abetted the marginalization of Aboriginals in Canada. Overall, the results can only have been deleterious for the million-plus Canadians (today) of Aboriginal heritage, though it is impossible to tease out the specific media effects when the press operates as just one among many influences. Yet clearly the printed press has, since the sale of Rupert's Land, operated as a principal voice of and for Canadian-style colonialism. Accordingly, the resultant "news" has long identified and championed alleged Native inferiority on many levels, as this book has detailed. This includes, among a myriad of possibilities, permutations, and cross-pollinations, general charges of biological inferiority, cultural dissoluteness, and general haplessness. In media-bite fashion every Canadian knows them—the alleged drunkenness, criminality, whorishness, deviousness, lassitude, and so on.

Canadians, of course, have not envisaged themselves as continental imperialists. Canada does not abide imperialism. This, despite a history built on the usurpation of Indigenous land and the subsequent clumsy and lethal attempts to subjugate the original owners of that land. Put simply, buried somewhere in the Canadian imagination lies a kind of colonial amnesia. One way to fabricate such a shield has been for the press to consistently play that "thick" (in a Geertzian sense[37]) popular Canadian pastime of promoting Canada by denigrating the United States. With respect to Indigenous people this has served the obvious purpose of chauvinistic boosterism but additionally distances Canada from the allegedly worse treatment accorded Natives in "the States." The fabrication also appears to stem from divergent national creation stories—the United States famously has its frontier myth whereas Canada counters with, as Furniss has it, a frontier cultural complex. The United States, behaving like a rebellious second-born child,[38] has always championed its frontier experience, hence the popularity of the Western. But what is too easily forgotten here is the observation that each settler nation cut its primal teeth prior to independence by grappling with Native peoples. The result led to a good deal of anger, fear, hatred, and violence. Precisely there, it seems to us, is the rightful birth of Richard Slotkin's observation about "regeneration through violence." The fundamental difference that explains the divergence in creation stories between the two former agglomerations of English colonies derives from the manner of formalistic national founding. The United States was birthed in violence, actual (revolution) and rhetorical ("give me liberty or give me death"). This remains the drumbeat of U.S. foreign policy even to this day, its manifest destiny writ large.[39] Canada, on the other hand, had to be granted its independence through a process of negotiation. Canada was bestowed its right to be free from on high, hence one reason for the traditional Canadian deference to authority. The result is an imagined nation built first upon war with Aboriginal peoples but packaged since 1869 as the ineluctable duty of sober-minded patriots, imbued with self-righteous Protestantism and a determination to not be the United States. In other words, Canada is something like Frank Sulloway's identified first-born child, more conservative, somewhat anal, and identifying more strongly with the parent, as if to say, look here, we followed the rules and you did not.

Media scholar Paul M. Kellstedt has concluded that "media coverage of race has not been static" in the United States across two centuries.[40] But it never is, and that is one of the basic strengths of the Other—it is capable of taking on many shapes; and the many archetypes fit a wide variety of scenarios. Thus the sale of Rupert's Land found the stereotype of the wandering beggar a useful construction, whereas the Riel war preferred the savage, and Bill C-31 deployed the "squaw." Each case is different but the colonial toolbox is well stocked.

Colonialism has remained intact in the press. It appears as if in Canada it is the very malleability of the Native Other that lends weight to allegations of its non-existence. For example, another subtle amendment has occurred in Canada as the moribund Native has died a lingering death. That is, especially since the 1960s newspapers no longer often report that Aboriginals are a dying race. But nonetheless the idea endures in assertions about the value and necessity of assimilation. In other words, cultural extermination has trumped physical extermination. And it rules by common sense. In this view, Natives ultimately have to assimilate, all other things being equal. This is not so much an argument as it is a statement of fact in imagined Canada.

Canadian national identity remains firmly rooted in the constructed idea of the nation. Built upon the premise of an empty territory ripe for settling, Indigenous studies scholar Bonita Lawrence argues that "in order for Canada to have a viable national identity, the histories of Indigenous nations…must be erased."[41] Each chapter in this book demonstrates how Canada's newspapers have, over time, played an integral role in shaping the nation's colonial story. While the printed press has not fully rubbed out Native identity, it has instead moulded a number of stereotypical representations that cross-pollinate and naturalize, serving up for Canadian readers a primer for "seeing red."

NOTES

INTRODUCTION

1   See Olive Dickason, *Canada's First Nations: A History of Founding Peoples From Earliest Times* (New York: Oxford University Press, 2001).

2   In some ways the terms First Nations and Métis overlap. First Nations refers to status Natives, those who hold treaty cards. Métis refers to those of mixed European (most commonly French) and Aboriginal ancestry. A more restrictive interpretation of the term includes only those who can trace their ancestry to the Red River Settlement while a less restrictive one includes those who self-declare mixed ancestry. The overlap between Métis and First Nations occurs because many status Aboriginals also easily fit the term Métis, that is, they have some quantum of European ancestry. It is important to remember that the 'status' of status has been patrolled by Canada's colonial office governing and regulating the affairs of Aboriginal peoples, the Department of Indian and Northern Affairs (INAC).

   In this study we employ the terms Aboriginal, Indigenous, and Native as synonyms referring to persons of any Aboriginal background. In certain contexts we use the term "Indian" to reflect the diversity of terms used over time. While considered pejorative and outdated by some scholars it serves a number of aims, including the legal usage in the Indian Act. This is a common practice among scholars. But the other reason is that the mainstream press in Canada has tended not to distinguish among Aboriginal peoples, and typically has lumped them all together, and it is those particular images that constitute the key interest of this study. That said, we have left all direct quotes—which, as you will discover, are frequently imprecise—unaltered.

3   Mainstream values and culture derive from and are synonymous with white values and culture, sometimes referred to as settler culture. We use the terms "mainstream" and "white" interchangeably. Neither term includes all those who dwell permanently in Canada; instead, the terms refer synonymously to the dominant culture, what some would term hegemonic culture.

4   Mary Vipond, *The Mass Media in Canada* (Toronto: James Lorimer and Company, 2000), 2 and 133.

5   David Spurr, *The Rhetoric of Empire, Colonial Discourse in Journalism, Travel Writing, and Imperial Administration* (Durham: Duke University Press, 1993), 28.

6   Paul Nesbitt-Larking, *Politics, Society, and the Media, Canadian Perspectives* (Peterborough, ON: Broadview Press, 2001), 52.

7   See Benedict Anderson, *Imagined Communities: Reflections on the Origin and Spread of Nationalism* (London: Verso, 1991), 109–111 and 150.

8   We borrow the words from Benedict Anderson.

9   The seven-minute apology is widely available on the Internet. See http://www.youtube.com/watch?v=qAmUe17nUdY&feature=PlayList&p=08DD57E2D5EA374C&index=0&playnext=1 (accessed 17 April 2010)

10   For documentary films, see *Survivors of the Red Brick School* (Canadian Learning Company, 2000); *Circle of Voices* (Filmwest Associates, 2000); *The Nitnaht Chronicles* (National Film Board of Canada, 1998); *The Residential School* (Motion Visual Productions, 1997); *Sleeping Children Awake* (Magic Arrow Productions, 1993); *As Long as the Rivers Flow* (National Film Board of Canada, 1993). For government reports, in particular, see the multi-volume report, Royal Commission on Aboriginal Peoples (RCAP) published by the Government of Canada (1996). Book-length studies include John S. Milloy, *A National Crime: The Canadian Government And the Residential School System* (Winnipeg: University of Manitoba Press, 1999); J.R. Miller, *Shingwauk's Vision: A History of Native Residential Schools* (Toronto: University of Toronto Press, 1996); Celia Haig-Brown, *Resistance and Renewal: Surviving the Indian Residential School* (Vancouver: Arsenal Pulp Press, 2002).

11   Milloy, *National Crime*, 295.

12   Miller, *Shingwauk's Vision*, 427.

13   Gramsci famously penned his most enduring work while in jail. See Antonio Gramsci, *Selections From the Prison Notebooks* (New York: International Publishers Co., 2008). Also see David Forgacs and Eric Hobsbawm, eds., *The Antonio Gramsci Reader: Selected Writings, 1916-1935* (New York: New York University Press, 2000).

14   See Fred Dallmayr, "Modes of Cross-Cultural Encounter," in Anindita Balslev, ed., *Cross-Cultural Conversations* (Kennilworth, NJ: Value Inquiry Books, 1996), 211–236; Simon Gunn, *History and Cultural Theory* (London: Pearson, 2006), 85–87.

15   The quote comes from American Army Captain Richard Henry Pratt, founder and long-time superintendent of the influential Carlisle Indian School in Pennsylvania. American Indian vocational residential schools served as a model for the Canadian residential school system. Pratt's remarks were first delivered in an 1892 convention address, "Official Report of the Nineteenth Annual Conference of Charities and Correction," reprinted in Richard H. Pratt, *The Advantages of Mingling Indians with Whites, Americanizing the American Indians: Writings by the Friends of the Indian, 1880-1900* (Cambridge, MA: Harvard University Press, 1973), 260.

16   This point is made repeatedly, for example, in Karin Wahl-Jorgensen and Thomas Hanitzsch, eds., *The Handbook of Journalism Studies* (New York: Routledge, 2009).

17   Augie Fleras and Jean Lock Kunz, *Media and Minorities, Representing Diversity in a Multicultural Canada* (Toronto: Thompson Educational Publishers, 2001), vii.

18   Bhodan Szuchewycz, "Re-Pressing Racism: The Denial of Racism in the Canadian Press," *Canadian Journal of Communication* 25 (2000): 498. This is certainly not uniquely Canadian. "Race-thinking is still a dominant form of social cognition across the globe," writes Ian Law. See Ian Law, *Race in the News* (New York: Palgrave, 2002), 1. Also see John Downing and Charles Husband, *Representing 'Race'* (London: SAGE, 2005), 135–137.

19   See Elizabeth Bird, ed., *Dressing in Feathers, The Construction of the Indian in American Popular Culture* (Boulder: Westview, 1996).

20   See Robert F. Berkhofer, *The White Man's Indian: Images of the American Indian from Columbus to the Present* (New York: Vintage, 1979).

21   Elizabeth Furniss, *The Burden of History, Colonialism and the Frontier Myth in a Rural Canadian Community* (Vancouver: University of British Columbia Press, 2000). Also see Downing and Husband, *Representing 'Race'*, 2–4.

22   Paul Rutherford, *A Victorian Authority: The Daily Press in Late Nineteenth-Century Canada* (Toronto: University of Toronto Press, 1982).

23   See Stuart Hall, ed., *Representation: Cultural Representations and Signifying Practices* (Thousand Oaks, CA: SAGE, 1997).

24 The phrase is deliberately borrowed from the brilliant novel, *Things Fall Apart*, set in post-colonial Africa. See Chinua Achebe, *Things Fall Apart* (New York: Anchor, 1994).

25 Peter Kulchyski, *Like the Sound of a Drum: Aboriginal Cultural Politics in Denendeh and Nunavut* (Winnipeg: University of Manitoba Press, 2005), 17 and 66–68.

26 Spurr, *Rhetoric of Empire*, 2.

27 For more results of the survey see the association's website, http://www.nadbank.com/en/study/readership.

28 Ronald Graham Haycock, *The Canadian Indian as a subject and a concept in a sampling of the popular national magazines read in Canada, 1900–1970* (Waterloo, ON: Waterloo Lutheran University Press, 1971). Daniel Francis, *National Dreams: Myth, Memory, and Canadian History* (Vancouver: Arsenal Pulp Press, 1997). Sandra Lambertus, *Wartime Images, Peacetime Wounds: The Media and the Gustafsen Lake Standoff* (Toronto: University of Toronto Press, 2004). R. Scott Sheffield, *The Red Man's on the Warpath: The Image of the 'Indian' and the Second World War* (Vancouver: University of British Columbia Press, 2004). Furniss, *Burden of History*.

29 Francis, *National Dreams*.

30 Lambertus, *Wartime Images*, 10.

31 Philip Deloria puts it this way: "A stereotype is a simplified and generalized expectation...that comes to rest in an image, text, or utterance. It is a sound bite, a crudely descriptive connection between power, expectation, and representation." See Philip J. Deloria, *Indians in Unexpected Places* (Lawrence: University Press of Kansas, 2004), 9. Fleras and Elliott: "Stereotyping simplifies the process of representation. A pool of Aboriginal stereotypes provides a convenient shorthand that audiences can relate to because of shared cultural codes...Stereotypes are designed to keep Aboriginal peoples out of sight and out of mind." See Augie Fleras and Jean Leonard Elliott, *Unequal Relations: An Introduction to Race, Ethnic and Aboriginal Dynamics in Canada* (Toronto: Pearson, 2007), 318–319.

32 Sheffield, *Warpath*, 177.

33 Robert Harding, "Historical Representations of Aboriginal People in the Canadian News Media." *Discourse and Society* (2006): 231. Also see Robert Harding, "Media Discourse About Aboriginal Self-Government in 1990s British Columbia," First Nations, First Thoughts Conference, May 2005, University of Edinburgh, http://www.cst.ed.ac.uk/conferences.html (accessed 15 April 2010).

34 Also see Naila Clerici, "The Cree of James Bay and the Construction of their Identity for the Media," *Canadian Issues* 21 (1999): 143–159; Yale Belanger, "Journalistic Opinion as Free Speech or Promoting Racial Unrest? The Case of Ric Dolphin and the Calgary *Herald's* Editorial Presentation of Native Culture," *American Indian Quarterly* 26, 3 (2002): 393–417; Cora Voyageur, "They Think They Own the Land: A Media Account of the Government's Acquisition of Treaty Eight Lands," *Prairie Forum* 25, 2 (2000): 271–282.

35 Frances Henry and Carol Tator, *Discourses of Domination, Racial Bias in the Canadian English-Language Press* (Toronto: University of Toronto Press, 2002), 21.

36 Frances Henry and Carol Tator, *Racial Profiling in Canada* (Toronto: University of Toronto Press, 2006).

37 John M. Coward, *The Newspaper Indian, Native American Identity in the Press, 1820–90* (Urbana: Illinois University Press, 1999).

38 See Reginald Horsman, *Race and Manifest Destiny: Origins of American Racial Anglo-Saxonism* (Cambridge: Harvard University Press, 1981).

39 Coward, *Newspaper Indian*, 7. Also see Sharon Murphy, "American Indians and the Media: Neglect and Sterotype," *Journalism History* 6, 2 (Summer 1979): 39–46.

40 Mary Ann Weston, *Native Americans in the News: Images of Indians in the Twentieth Century Press* (Westport, CT: Greenwood, 1996).

41 Also see John Hartley, *The Indigenous Public Sphere: The Reporting and Reception of Aboriginal Issues in the Australian Media* (New York: Oxford University Press, 2001); Michael Meadows, *Voices in the Wilderness: Images of Aboriginal People in the Australian Media* (Westport, CT: Greenwood Press, 2000); Law, *Race in the News*, 13–15.

42 Elliott Parker, "'Securing the Affections of Those People at This Critical Juncture': Newspaper Portrayal of colonial-Native American Relations, 1754–1763," Association for Education in Journalism and Mass Communication Conference Papers, http://list.msu.edu/cgi-bin/wa?A2=ind9612b&L=aejmc&T=0&P=4775.

43 Elizabeth Bird, "Genderized Construction of the American Indian in Popular Media," *Journal of Communication* (Summer 1979): 61–83. Also see Bird's edited book, *Dressing in Feathers*.

44 See Vipond, *Mass Media*.

45 Wilfrid Kesterton, *A History of Journalism in Canada* (Ottawa: Carleton University Press, 1967). Also see Ross F. Collins and E.M. Palmegiano, eds., *The Rise of Western Journalism, 1815–1914: Essays on the Press in Australia, Canada, France, Germany, Great Britain and the United States* (Jefferson, NC: McFarland and Company, 2007).

46 Douglas Fetherling, *The Rise of the Canadian Newspaper* (Toronto: Oxford University Press, 1990).

47 Minko Sotiron, *From Politics to Profit* (Montreal: McGill-Queen's University Press, 1997).

48 Paul Rutherford, *A Victorian Authority: The Daily Press in Late Nineteenth-Century Canada* (Toronto: University of Toronto Press, 1982).

49 For example, William Randolph Hearst, famously fictionalized in what many film scholars consider the greatest movie ever made, *Citizen Kane*, has been the subject of several biographies and appears in countless studies. See also Robert C. Williams, *Horace Greeley: Champion of American Freedom* (New York: New York University Press, 2006); Coy F. Cross, *Go West Young Man!: Horace Greeley's Vision for America* (Albuquerque: University of New Mexico Press, 1995); William Harlan Hale, *Horace Greeley: Voice Of The People* (New York: Harper and Brothers, 1950); Roy Harris, *Pulitzer's Gold: Behind the Prize for Public Service Journalism* (University of Missouri Press, 2008); Denis Brian, *Pulitzer: A Life* (New York: Wiley, 2001).

50 From among many see, for example, William G. Bonelli, *Billion Dollar Blackjack : The Story of Corruption and the Los Angeles Times* (Washington: Civic Research Press, 1954); Robert Gottlieb, *Thinking Big: The Story of the Los Angeles Times, Its Publishers, and Their Influence on Southern California* (New York: Putnam, 1977); Digby Diehl, *Front Page: 100 years of the Los Angeles Times, 1881–1981* (New York: Harry N. Abrams, 1981); Dennis McDougal, *Privileged Son: Otis Chandler and the Rise and Fall of the L.A. Times Dynasty* (Cambridge, MA: Da Capo Press, 2002).

51 Mark Cronlund Anderson, *Pancho Villa's Revolution by Headlines* (Norman: University of Oklahoma Press, 2001). Also see Kenneth Whyte, *The Uncrowned King: The Sensational Rise of William Randolph Hearst* (Berkeley, CA: Counterpoint, 2009).

52 For a comprehensive discussion of this topic, see Carlos E. Cortés, *The Children Are Watching: How the Media Teach About Diversity* (New York: Teachers College Press, 2000). Also see James Winter, *Lies the Media Tell Us* (Montreal: Black Rose Books, 2007), xii.

53 Paul M. Kellstedt, *The Mass Media and the Dynamics of American Racial Attitudes* (New York: Cambridge University Press, 2003), 14.

54 See Shanto Iyengar and Donald R. Kinders, *News That Matters: Television and American Opinion* (Chicago: University of Chicago Press, 1989); Robert M. Entman, Jörg Matthes, and Lynn Pellicano, "Nature, Sources, and Effects of News Framing," in *Handbook of Journalism Studies*, ed. Wahl-Jorgensen and Hanitzsch, 175–190.

55 Autumn Miller and Susan Dente Ross, "They Are Not Us: Framing of American Indians by the *Boston Globe,*" *Howard Journal of Communication* 15 (2004): 245.

56 See Maxwell McCombs, *Setting the Agenda: The News Media and Public Opinion* (Cambridge, UK: Polity Press, 2004); Renita Coleman, Maxwell McCombs, Donald Shaw, and David Weaver, in *Handbook of Journalism Studies*, ed. Wahl-Jorgensen and Hanitzsch, 147–174.

57 Edward Said, *Covering Islam: How the Media and the Experts Determine How We See the Rest of the World* (New York: Vintage, 1997), 81.

58 Said, *Covering Islam*, 46. To put it more plainly, think about what you know about global warming or the political turmoil in the Middle East. How do you know it? How do you know about the 2008 housing crisis in the United States? What do you really know about Barack Obama? The answer for almost all of us is the same: the media told me. That is agenda-setting at work. It runs deeply. North Americans, for example, are collectively more fearful of violent crime today than they were forty years ago when the rates of violent crime were higher. What has happened in the meantime is that the mass media has played a role in nurturing what sociologist Barry Glassner has called a "culture of fear." See Barry Glassner, *The Culture of Fear: Why Americans Are Afraid of the Wrong Things* (New York: Basic Books, 2000). Also see Marc Siegel, *False Alarm: The Truth about the Epidemic of Fear* (New York: Wiley, 2006); Peter N. Stearns, *American Fear: The Causes and Consequences of High Anxiety* (New York: Routledge, 2006); David Altheide, *Creating Fear: News and the Construction of Crisis* (New York: Aldine Transaction, 2002)

59 McLuhan's work, penned decades ago, remains current and continually reissued. See Marshall McLuhan, *Understanding Media* (New York: Routledge, 2005). As with McLuhan's, Innis's work continues to cast a shadow in Canada, though he died in 1952. See Harold Innis, *Empire and Communications* (Toronto: Dundurn Press, 2007).

60 Andrew J. Perrin and Stephen Vaisey, "Parallel Public Spheres: Distance and Discourse in Letters to the Editor," *American Journal of Sociology* 114, 3 (November 2008): 785.

61 Warren H. Skea, "The Canadian Newspaper Industry's Portrayal of the Oka Crisis," *Native Studies Review* 9, 1 (1993–1994): 15.

62 Jeannette Marie Mageo, ed., "Introduction," *Power and Self* (London: Cambridge University Press, 2002), 5.

63 See Szuchewycz, "Re-Pressing Racism"; Elizabeth May, *Losing Confidence: Power, Politics and the Crisis in Canadian Democracy* (Toronto: McClelland and Stewart, 2009); John Ralston Saul, *A Fair Country: Telling Truth About Canada* (Toronto: Penguin, 2008).

64 As recorded in the Toronto *Globe*, 30 September 1873, 2. On another occasion, it is worth noting, Cameron claimed that Canada's press was the world's best. Toronto *Globe*, 30 September 1873, 2. Also see an editorial, "Newspapers in the States," Toronto *Globe*, 29 November 1873, 4

65 See Vipond, *Mass Media*, 6–11.

66 See Law, *Race in the News*, 35.

67 Noam Chomsky and Edward S. Herman, *Manufacturing Consent: The Political Economy of the Mass Media* (New York: Pantheon Books, 2002).

68 See Hall, *Representation*. Also see Paul Nesbitt-Larking, *Politics, Society and the Media*, 52; Said, *Covering Islam*; Edward Said. *Orientalism* (New York: Vintage, 1979); Edward Said, *Culture and Imperialism* (New York: Vintage, 1994).

69 Szuchewycz, "Re-Pressing Racism," 498. Also see Downing and Husband, *Representing 'Race'*, x.

70 See S. Elizabeth Bird and Robert W. Dardene, "Rethinking Myth and News as Storytelling," in *Handbook of Journalism Studies*, ed. Wahl-Jorgensen and Hanitzsch, 205–217.

71 Richard Slotkin, *Gunfighter Nation: The Myth of the Frontier in Twentieth-Century America* (Norman: University of Oklahoma Press, 1998), 7.

72 Lyle Dick, "Nationalism and Visual Media in Canada: The Case of Thomas Scott's Execution," *Manitoba History* 48 (Autumn/Winter, 2004–2005): 16.

CHAPTER ONE: This Land is Mine

1 For a comprehensive set of historical maps see the Government of Canada website, http://atlas.nrcan.gc.ca/site/english/maps/historical/territorialevolution/1870.

2 See Gramsci, *Antonio Gramsci Reader*.

3 Toronto *Globe*, 27 August 1869; Toronto *Globe*, 17 December 1869; Montreal *Gazette*, 25 August 1869.

4 So did John A. Macdonald, of course. See Richard Gwyn, *John A., The Man Who Made Us: The Life and Times of John A. Macdonald* (Toronto: Random House, 2007), 222–224.

5 See Toronto *Globe*, 16 June 1869; Toronto *Globe* 23 November 1869; Toronto *Globe*, 30 November 1869; Toronto *Globe*, 22 December 1869; Toronto *Globe*, 31 December 1869. Also see Montreal *Gazette*, 6 October 1869.

6 Toronto *Globe*, 16 March 1869.

7 Toronto *Globe*, 28 May 1869.

8 Montreal *Gazette*, 22 June 1869.

9 Toronto *Globe*, 16 February 1869.

10 Francis, *National Dreams*, 84.

11 See Rutherford, *Victorian Authority*, 212–227.

12 The Toronto *Globe* and the Toronto *Daily Mail* merged in 1936. See Kesterton, *History*, 85.

13 See Vipond, *Mass Media*, 14–15.

14 Rutherford provides a useful appendix in which he lists the various Canadian dailies of the late nineteenth century and their political affiliations. The list also identifies publishers and editors as selected circulation figures reaching into the early twentieth century. See Rutherford, *Victorian Authority*, 235–240.

15 Nesbitt-Larking, *Politics, Society, and the Media*, 39–44.

16 Sotiron, *From Politics to Profit*, 19.

17 Rutherford, *Victorian Authority*, 156–157. Also see Vipond, *Mass Media*, 2.

18 See Francis, *National Dreams*.

19   Anderson, *Imagined Communities*, 6.

20   Patricia Seed, *Ceremonies of Possession in Europe's Conquest of the New World, 1492-1640* (New York: Cambridge University Press, 1995), 69–99.

21   Seed, *Ceremonies*, 41–68.

22   Ibid., 33.

23   Ibid., 25.

24   Ibid., 16–40. Also see Anderson, *Imagined Communities*, 188. It is worth noting that American custom and law also surfaced from English antecedents. More than that, American core mythology, including what scholars have identified as America's creation story, embrace such notions about land ownership. See Richard Slotkin, *The Fatal Environment: The Myth of the Frontier in the Age of Industrialization, 1800-1890* (Norman: University of Oklahoma Press, 1998); Henry Nash-Smith, *Virgin Land: The American West as Symbol and Myth* (Cambridge: Harvard University Press, 2007).

25   Toronto *Globe*, 27 December 1869.

26   Toronto *Globe*, 29 December 1869; Toronto *Globe*, 08 March 1869.

27   Toronto *Globe*, 17 November 1869.

28   Toronto *Globe*, 20 March 1869; Montreal *Gazette*, 23 March 1869.

29   Toronto *Globe*, 16 June 1869.

30   Toronto *Globe*, 20 March 1869.

31   Toronto *Globe*, 9 July 1869. Also see Toronto *Globe*, 6 October 1869.

32   Toronto *Globe*, 28 May 1869. Also see Toronto *Globe*, 11 June 1869; Toronto *Globe*, 24 December 1869.

33   Toronto *Globe*, 16 July 1869. Also see Toronto *Globe*,16 January 1869.

34   Toronto *Globe*, 8 March 1869.

35   Toronto *Globe*, 16 June 1869.

36   Ibid.

37   Toronto *Globe*, 16 February 1869. Also see Toronto *Globe*, 1 January 1869.

38   Toronto *Globe*, 17 December 1869.

39   Toronto *Globe*, 21 July 1869.

40   Toronto *Globe*, 4 February 1869; Toronto *Globe*, 5 February 1869.

41   Toronto *Globe*, 16 January 1869. Also see Toronto *Globe*, 18 April 1869.

42   Toronto *Globe*, 21 May 1869. Also see Toronto *Globe*, 9 August 1869.

43   Toronto *Globe*, 2 April 1869; Toronto *Globe*, 17 August 1869. Also see Toronto *Globe*, 5 April 1869.

44   Toronto *Globe*, 17 April 1869. Also see Toronto *Globe*, 03 May 1869; Toronto *Globe*, 28 May 1869.

45   Toronto *Globe*, 28 May 1869. Toronto *Globe*, 12 July 1869.

46   Toronto *Globe*, 1 January 1869. Also see Toronto *Globe*, 23 March 1869; Toronto *Globe*, 20 April 1869.

47   Toronto *Globe*, 1 January 1869.

48   Toronto *Globe*, 19 April 1869.

49   Toronto *Globe*, 3 May 1869.

50   Toronto *Globe*, 4 January 1869.

51   Montreal *Gazette*, 5 January 1869.

52   Toronto *Globe*, 21 July 1869.

53   Montreal *Gazette*, 5 November 1869.

54   Toronto *Globe*, 13 December 1869.

55   Montreal *Gazette*, 10 June 1869.

56   Montreal *Gazette*, 14 August 1869.

57   Toronto *Globe*, 15 April 1869.

58   In fact, the daily invective, a story that goes beyond the pales of this book, increased markedly over the summer and fall as the short-lived insurgency under Louis Riel took flight. The Toronto *Globe* derived some satisfaction in claiming that had the government followed its advice and negotiated quickly for Rupert's Land as well as allowed for elections in Red River, the insurgency might never have occurred.

59   Gwyn, *John A.*, 222.

60   Montreal *Gazette*, 5 January 1869.

61   Montreal *Gazette*, 20 February 1869.

62   Montreal *Gazette*, 7 January 1869.

63   Montreal *Gazette*, 7 May 1869. Also see Montreal *Gazette*, 26 July 1869.

64   Montreal *Gazette*, 3 June 1869; Montreal *Gazette*, 11 August 1869. Also see Montreal *Gazette*, 2 November 1869.

65   Montreal *Gazette*, 23 June 1869.

66   Montreal *Gazette*, 15 February 1873. Also see Toronto *Globe*, 23 June 1873.

67   Montreal *Gazette*, 20 February 1869.

68   Montreal *Gazette*, 8 March 1869.

69   Montreal *Gazette*, 10 April 1869.

70   See, for example, Toronto *Globe*, 12 April 1869.

71   The term served as a ready signifier of Indian-ness. It was employed ubiquitously. See, for example: Toronto *Globe*, 1 January 1869.

72   Montreal *Gazette*, 5 November 1869.

73   Toronto *Globe*, 21 September 1869.

74   Toronto *Globe*, 2 August 1869.

75   Ibid.

76   See Carole Henderson Carpenter, "In Our Own Image: The Child, Canadian Culture, and Our Future." Ninth Annual Robarts Lecture, 29 March 1995: http://www.yorku.ca/robarts/projects/lectures/pdf/rl_carpenter.pdf (accessed 22 May 2010).

77   Montreal *Gazette*, 22 February 1869.

78   Toronto *Globe*, 23 March 1869.

79   Toronto *Globe*, 20 April 1869. "Self-preservation is the first law of national and individual life," it reported on another occasion. See Toronto *Globe*, 6 April 1869.

80   Any good survey text of Mexican history will explain this clearly. See, for example, Michael C. Meyer, William L. Sherman, and Susan M. Deeds, *The Course of Mexican History* (New York: Oxford University Press, 2007).

81   Toronto *Globe*, 2 August 1869.

82   Toronto *Globe*, 1 January 1869.

83   Montreal *Gazette*, 19 November 1869.

84   Montreal *Gazette*, 26 June 1869.

85   See Toronto *Globe*, 26 January 1869. Also see Toronto *Globe*, 13 May 1869; Toronto *Globe*, 7 July 1869; Toronto *Globe*, 9 July 1869; Toronto *Globe*, 4 September 1869; Toronto *Globe*, 6 September 1869; Toronto *Globe*, 5 October 1869. Also see Montreal *Gazette*, 29 June 1869; Montreal *Gazette*, 28 October 1869.

86   Toronto *Globe*, 13 February 1869.

87   Toronto *Globe*, 20 February 1869.

88   Toronto *Globe*, 26 March 1869. Also see Toronto *Globe*, 23 June 1869.

89   See Toronto *Globe*, 17 July 1869; Toronto *Globe*, 08 November 1869; Toronto *Globe*, 31 August 1869; Toronto *Globe*, 9 August 1869; Toronto *Globe*, 18 August 1869.

90   Montreal *Gazette*, 21 August 1869.

91   Toronto *Globe*, 4 March 1869.

92   Toronto *Globe*, 10 August 1869.

93   Toronto *Globe*, 8 July 1869.

94   Toronto *Globe*, 9 March 1869.

95   Toronto *Globe*, 16 July 1869. Also see Montreal *Gazette*, 28 October 1869.

96   Toronto *Globe*, 4 January 1869. Also see Toronto *Globe*, 26 February 1869; Toronto *Globe*, 8 May 1869; Toronto *Globe*, 30 June 1869.

97   Montreal *Gazette*, 16 April 1869.

98   See: Toronto *Globe*, 10 February 1869; Toronto *Globe*, 11 February 1869; Toronto *Globe*, 16 March 1869.

99   Toronto *Globe*, 19 January 1869. Also see Toronto *Globe*, 24 May 1869.

100 Toronto *Globe*, 8 June 1869.

101 Montreal *Gazette*, 8 November 1869.

102 Toronto *Globe*, 1 March 1869. Also see Toronto *Globe*, 7 April 1869; Toronto *Globe*, 26 June 1869.

103 Montreal *Gazette*, 1 July 1869.

104 Montreal *Gazette*, 2 October 1869.

105 Toronto *Globe*, 27 July 1869.

106 Montreal *Gazette*, 16 June 1869.

107 Toronto *Globe*, 27 July 1869.

108 Toronto *Globe*, 16 August 1869.

109 Toronto *Globe*, 23 March 1869. The same report was printed in the Montreal *Gazette*, on 10 April 1869. Also see Toronto *Globe*, 24 March 1869.

110 Toronto *Globe*, 11 January 1869.

111 See Horsman, *Race and Manifest Destiny*.

112 Toronto *Globe*, 9 January 1869. Also see Montreal *Gazette*, 27 January 1869; Montreal *Gazette*, 20 March 1869; Montreal *Gazette*, 7 April 1869; Toronto *Globe*, 11 January 1869; Toronto *Globe*, 27 February 1869; Toronto *Globe*, 3 March 1869; Toronto *Globe*, 9 March 1869; Toronto *Globe*, 22 March 1869; Toronto *Globe*, 31 March 1869; Toronto *Globe*, 10 April 1869; Toronto *Globe*, 14 May 1869; Toronto *Globe*, 21 September 1869; Toronto *Globe*, 21 October 1869; Toronto *Globe*, 17 December 1869; Toronto *Globe*, 18 December 1869.

113 See, for example, Larry McMurtry, *Oh What a Slaughter: Massacres in the American West: 1846–1890* (New York: Simon and Schuster, 2005); Dee Brown, *Bury My Heart at Wounded Knee, An Indian History of the American West* (New York: Holt Paperbacks, 2001).

114 Toronto *Globe*, 11 January 1869. Such stories flourished. See: Toronto *Globe*, 26 January 1869; Toronto *Globe*, 17 May 1869; Toronto *Globe*, 20 May 1869; Toronto *Globe*, 24 May 1869; Toronto *Globe*, 1 June 1869; Toronto *Globe*, 2 June 1869; Toronto *Globe*, 14 June 1869; Toronto *Globe*, 16 August 1869; Montreal *Gazette*, 10 February 1869; Montreal *Gazette*, 21 October 1869.

115 Montreal *Gazette*, 23 February 1869.

116 Toronto *Globe*, 11 January 1869. See Toronto *Globe*, 27 January 1869.

117 Toronto *Globe*, 1 July 1869.

118 Toronto *Globe*, 1 January 1869.

119 Toronto *Globe*, 31 March 1869. Mormons, too, were condemned for the practice. See Toronto *Globe*, 8 July 1869; Toronto *Globe*, 14 October 1869.

120 Toronto *Globe*, 10 November 1869.

121 Toronto *Globe*, 27 November 1869.

122 For a discussion on both American and Canadian captivity narratives see Sarah Carter, *Capturing Women: The Manipulation of Cultural Imagery in Canada's Prairie West* (Montreal: McGill-Queen's Press, 1997).

123 Toronto *Globe*, 27 July 1869.

124 Toronto *Globe*, 20 July 1869. This is an example of what Homi Bhabha has termed "splitting." Homi Bhabha, *The Location of Culture* (New York: Routledge, 2004).

125 Toronto *Globe*, 16 April 1869.

126 Toronto *Globe*, 6 January 1869.

127 Also see Toronto *Globe*, 16 February 1869; Toronto *Globe*, 17 February 1869.

128 Toronto *Globe*, 16 February 1869.

129 Toronto *Globe*, 16 February 1869.

130 Montreal *Gazette*, 7 January 1869.

131 Toronto *Globe*, 16 February 1869. Also see Toronto *Globe*, 15 March 1869.

132 Toronto *Globe*, 16 February 1869.

133 Toronto *Globe*, 16 February 1869.

134 Toronto *Globe*, 2 August 1869.

135 Sotiron avers that the struggle was disproportionately driven by political lust and economic greed. "In short, to the victor went the spoils." Sotiron, *From Politics to Profit*, 107.

136 Ibid., 135.

137 See Toronto *Globe*, 25 May 1869; Toronto *Globe*, 21 September 1869.

138 Toronto *Globe*, 1 September 1869.

139 Toronto *Globe*, 25 May 1869.

140 Ibid.

141 Toronto *Globe*, 17 August 1869.

142 Montreal *Gazette*, 10 April 1869. Also see Toronto *Globe*, 12 July 1869.

143 The term shows up several times in her work. See, for example, Arundhati Roy, *An Ordinary Person's Guide to Empire* (Cambridge, MA: South End Press, 2004).

144 Toronto *Globe*, 2 August 1869. Also see Toronto *Globe*, 19 October 1869.

145 Toronto *Globe*, 25 August 1869.

146 Toronto *Globe*, 24 November 1869. Also see Toronto *Globe*, 26 November 1869; Toronto *Globe*, 27 November 1869; Toronto *Globe*, 30 November 1869; Toronto *Globe*, 24 December 1869; Montreal *Gazette*, 27 December 1869.

147 Toronto *Globe*, 26 November 1869. Also see Toronto *Globe*, 30 November 1869; Toronto *Globe*, 13 December 1869.

148 Montreal *Gazette*, 7 December 1869; Toronto *Globe*, 7 December 1869.

149 Toronto *Globe*, 24 December 1869.

150 Toronto *Globe*, 1 December 1869.

151 Toronto *Globe*, 22 January 1869.

152 Toronto *Globe*, 31 December 1869.

153 Montreal *Gazette*, 7 January 1869. Also see Montreal *Gazette*, 22 February 1869; Montreal *Gazette*, 22 December 1869.

154 Toronto *Globe*, 2 August 1869. Also see Toronto *Globe*, 26 November 1869.

155 Toronto *Globe*, 30 October 1869.

156 Toronto *Globe*, 17 August 1869. Also see ibid.

157 Montreal *Gazette*, 7 January 1869.

158 Toronto *Globe*, 17 September 1869.

159 Toronto *Globe*, 20 December 1869.

160 Montreal *Gazette*, 29 June 1869.

161 Toronto *Globe*, 30 October 1869.

162 Toronto *Globe*, 25 August 1869. Also see Montreal *Gazette*, 18 December 1869.

163 See Hall, *Representation;* Roy, *Ordinary Person's Guide to Empire.*

164 Toronto *Globe*, 1 January 1869. Also see Toronto *Globe*, 15 July 1869.

165 Montreal *Gazette*, 14 August 1869. Also see Toronto *Globe*, 15 July 1869; Toronto *Globe*, 2 August 1869; Toronto *Globe*, 17 August 1869; Toronto *Globe*, 18 September 1869; Toronto *Globe*, 30 October 1869; Toronto *Globe*, 10 November 1869.

166 Toronto *Globe*, 1 January 1869. Also see Toronto *Globe*, January 22 1869; Montreal *Gazette*, 5 January 1869; Montreal *Gazette*, 7 January 1869; Toronto *Globe*, 21 September 1869.

167 Toronto *Globe*, 16 February 1869; Toronto *Globe*, 23 March 1869.

168 Toronto *Globe*, 6 January 1869.

169 Ibid.

170 Toronto *Globe*, 22 January 1869.

171 Toronto *Globe*, 9 February 1869.

172 Toronto *Globe*, 31 March 1869. Also see Toronto *Globe*, 25 August 1869.

173 Toronto *Globe*, 16 February 1869.

174 Ibid. Also see Toronto *Globe*, 27 February 1869.

175 Toronto *Globe*, 17 August 1869.

176 Toronto *Globe*, 23 March 1869.

177 Toronto *Globe*, 13 April 1869.

178 Toronto *Globe*, 28 April 1869.

179 Toronto *Globe*, 30 April 1869. Also see Toronto *Globe*, 17 August 1869.

180 Toronto *Globe*, 17 August 1869.

181 Toronto *Globe*, 20 May 1869. Also see Toronto *Globe*, 16 June 1869.

182 Toronto *Globe*, 2 August 1869.

183 Toronto *Globe*, 27 November 1869.

184 Toronto *Globe*, 2 August 1869.

185 Toronto *Globe*, 3 April 1869. Also see Toronto *Globe*, 18 September 1869.

186 Montreal *Gazette*, 4 September 1873. Also see Toronto *Globe*, 30 September 1873; Toronto *Globe*, 30 September 1873. On another occasion, it is worth noting, Cameron claimed that Canada's press was the world's best. Toronto *Globe*, 30 September 1873. Also see an editorial, "Newspapers in the States," Toronto *Globe*, 29 November 1873.

187 This is the gist of John R. Bone, Joseph T. Clark, A.H. Colquhoun, and John F. McKay, *A History of Canadian Journalism in the Several Portions of the Dominion, With a Sketch of the Canadian Press Association, 1859–1908* (New York: AMS Press, 1908).

188 Spurr, *Rhetoric of Empire*, 3.

189 Kulchyski, *Sound of a Drum*, 23–24.

190 Murphy, "American Indians and the Media," 40.

191 Coward, *Newspaper Indian*, 18.

192 Ibid., 44.

CHAPTER TWO: Fifty-Six Words

1 See Desmond Morton, "Reflecting on Gomery: Political Scandals and the Canadian Memory," *Policy Options*, June 2005, 14–21.

2 For a copy of the treaty document, see http://www.ainc-inac.gc.ca/pr/trts/trty3_e.html (accessed 9 September 2009).

3 See, for example, Toronto *Globe*, 31 July 1873.

4 See Toronto *Globe*, 6 October 1873; Montreal *Gazette*, 6 October 1873.

5 Toronto *Globe*, 31 July 1873.

6 Montreal *Gazette*, 4 June 1873. Also see Montreal *Gazette*, 18 June 1874.

7 As quoted in the Introduction. See Montreal *Gazette*, 4 June 1873.

8 Montreal *Gazette*, 2 July 1873.

9 Toronto *Globe*, 30 December 1873.

10 See Toronto *Globe*, 2 July 1873; Toronto *Globe*, 9 July 1873; Toronto *Globe*, 1 October 1873; Toronto *Globe*, 30 December 1873.

11 The Government of Canada provides a useful set of interactive maps as well as treaty documents. See the Indian and Northern Affairs (INAC) website and follow the links to Historic Treaty Information: http://www.ainc-inac.gc.ca/pr/trts/index-eng.asp (accessed 1 September 2009).

12 Toronto *Globe*, 2 July 1873.

13 Toronto *Globe*, 7 July 1873.

14 Toronto *Globe*, 2 July 1873. Also see Toronto *Globe*, 3 July 1873.

15   Toronto *Globe*, 3 July 1873. Also see Toronto *Globe*, 4 July 1873; Toronto *Globe*, 7 July 1873.

16   Indeed, the INAC website describes Treaty 3 this way: "With the Saulteaux surrendering title to an area of 14,245,000 hectares, Canada acquired land for agriculture, settlement and mineral discovery. More importantly, Canada secured communications with the Northwest Territories, including the route of the future Canadian Pacific Railway" http://www.ainc-inac.gc.ca/al/hts/tgu/tr3-eng.asp (accessed 13 September 2009).

17   While this issue was discussed at length in the previous chapter, the evidence to support it continued to fill news columns in 1873. See, for example, Toronto *Globe*, 3 July 1873; Montreal *Gazette*, 4 June 1873.

18   See Seed, *Ceremonies*, 16–40.

19   Montreal *Gazette*, 23 January 1873.

20   Toronto *Globe*, 8 October 1873.

21   Toronto *Globe*, 23 September 1873. Also see Toronto *Globe*, 30 September 1873. As discussed in Chapter 9, the spelling of the term Ojibwe remains open to interpretation. We have chosen to adopt the form used by the Ojibwe Cultural Foundation on Manitoulin Island, Ontario. See http://www.ojibweculture.ca (accessed 1 February 2010).

22   Toronto *Globe*, 13 October 1873.

23   Toronto *Globe*, 28 October 1873.

24   Clifford Geertz, "Thick Description: Toward an Interpretive Theory of Culture," in Geertz, *The Interpretation of Cultures* (New York: Basic Books, 2000), 3–30.

25   Toronto *Globe*, 31 July 1873.

26   Toronto *Globe*, 31 July 1873.

27   Montreal *Gazette*, 29 July 1873.

28   Toronto *Globe*, 7 July 1873. Also see Toronto *Globe*, 17 July 1873; Toronto *Globe*, 24 September 1873; Montreal *Gazette*, 14 February 1873; Montreal *Gazette*, 20 March 1869. See also Sarah Carter, *Aboriginal People and Colonizers of Western Canada to 1900* (Toronto: University of Toronto Press, 1999), 76.

29   Toronto *Globe*, 26 June 1873. Also see Toronto *Globe*, 23 September 1873. Yet it is worth noting that the federal government had also systematically failed in its efforts to socially engineer the disappearance of First Nations via policies of extinguishment and assimilation. See Haig-Brown, *Resistance and Renewal*. Also see Ward Churchill, *Kill the Indian, Save the Man: The Genocidal Impact of American Indian Residential Schools* (San Francisco: City Light Publishers, 2004).

30   Montreal *Gazette*, 23 January 1873.

31   Examples abound. See Montreal *Gazette*, 3 February 1873; Montreal *Gazette*, 11 February 1873; Montreal *Gazette*, 11 June 1873; Montreal *Gazette*, 17 June 1873; Montreal *Gazette*, 19 June 1873; Toronto *Globe*, 29 August 1873; Toronto *Globe*, 3 July 1873; Toronto *Globe*, 15 September 1873; Toronto *Globe*, 24 September 1873; Toronto *Globe*, 6 October 1873.

32   See, for example, Toronto *Globe*, 10 June 1873; Toronto *Globe*, 11 June 1873; Montreal *Gazette*, 13 January 1873.

33   Toronto *Globe*, 9 October 1873. Also see Toronto *Globe*, 22 October 1873.

34   Montreal *Gazette*, 10 January 1873. Also see Montreal *Gazette*, 23 January 1873.

35   Montreal *Gazette*, 10 January 1873.

36 Montreal *Gazette* 23 January 1873.

37 Toronto *Globe*, 3 July 1873.

38 Montreal *Gazette*, 15 February 1873. Also see Toronto *Globe*, 23 June 1873.

39 Toronto *Globe*, 23 June 1873. Also see Toronto *Globe*, 3 July 1873; Montreal *Gazette*, 10 January 1873.

40 Toronto *Globe*, 17 July 1873. See Dickason, *Canada's First Nations*.

41 Montreal *Gazette*, 4 June 1873; Toronto *Globe*, 23 June 1873; Toronto *Globe*, 3 July 1873. Also see Toronto *Globe*, 4 August 1873.

42 Toronto *Globe*, 25 May 1869.

43 Toronto *Globe*, 7 July 1873.

44 Ibid. Also see Raymond A. Bucko, *The Lakota Ritual of the Sweat Lodge: History and Contemporary Practice* (Lincoln: Bison Books, 1999).

45 Toronto *Globe*, 6 October 1873.

46 Toronto *Globe*, 7 July 1873.

47 Montreal *Gazette*, 13 October 1973; Toronto *Globe*, 13 October 1873; Toronto *Globe*, 31 July 1873.

48 Toronto *Globe*, 7 July 1873; Toronto *Globe*, 17 July 1873.

49 Toronto *Globe*, 5 February 1873; Toronto *Globe*, 4 July 1873; also see Toronto *Globe*, 30 July 1873; Toronto *Globe*, 6 June 1873.

50 Toronto *Globe*, 4 July 1973; Toronto *Globe*, 4 July 1873; Toronto *Globe*, 21 July 1873; Toronto *Globe*, 12 February 1873.

51 Toronto *Globe*, 4 July 1873; Montreal *Gazette*, 18 December 1873. Also see Toronto *Globe*, 16 October 1873.

52 Montreal *Gazette*, 22 December 1873. Also see Montreal *Gazette*, 29 July 1873; Toronto *Globe*, 16 October 1873; Montreal *Gazette*, 4 October 1873; Toronto *Globe*, 2 June 1973.

53 Toronto *Globe*, 5 February 1873.

54 Toronto *Globe*, 3 July 1873.

55 Toronto *Globe*, 9 August 1873.

56 Montreal *Gazette*, 28 August 1873.

57 See Toronto *Globe*, 2 July 1873; Toronto *Globe*, 3 July 1873; Toronto *Globe*, 4 July 1873; Toronto *Globe*, 3 July 1873. Also see Toronto *Globe*, 8 July 1873.

58 Montreal *Gazette*, 14 August 1873. Also see Toronto *Globe*, 2 June 1873; Toronto *Globe*, 5 November 1873.

59 Montreal *Gazette*, 8 October 1873; Toronto *Globe*, 12 August 1873.

60 Toronto *Globe*, 8 July 1873; Toronto *Globe*, 2 June 1873.

61 See Henry and Tator, *Discourse*.

62 Toronto *Globe*, 21 July 1873.

63 Toronto *Globe*, 5 February 1873; Toronto *Globe*, 7 July 1873; Toronto *Globe*, 17 July 1873. Also see Toronto *Globe*, 4 July 1873; Toronto *Globe*, 27 July 1873; Montreal *Gazette*, 18 July 1873; Toronto *Globe*, 4 July 1873; Toronto *Globe*, 5 February 1873.

64 Toronto *Globe*, 2 July 1873.

65 Toronto *Globe*, 4 July 1873. Also see Toronto *Globe*, 8 July 1873.

66 See: Toronto *Globe*, 8 February 1873; Toronto *Globe*, 5 July 1873; Montreal *Gazette*, 15 October 1873; Toronto *Globe*, 15 November 1873.

67 Toronto *Globe*, 17 July 1873.

68 Toronto *Globe*, 9 October 1873.

69 Toronto *Globe*, 19 June 1873.

70 Montreal *Gazette*, 30 January 1873. Also see Montreal *Gazette*, 3 June 1973; Montreal *Gazette*, 4 June 1873; Toronto *Globe*, 3 July 1873; Toronto *Globe*, 24 July 1873.

71 Toronto *Globe*, 14 August 1873; Montreal *Gazette*, 3 June 1873; Toronto *Globe*, 4 June 1873.

72 Montreal *Gazette*, 1 July 1873.

73 Toronto *Globe*, 22 July 1873.

74 Toronto *Globe*, 18 June 1873.

75 Montreal *Gazette*, 8 June 1874. Also see Toronto *Globe*, 11 June 1873.

76 Toronto *Globe*, 4 July 1873. The *leyenda negra* (black legend), in which Spaniards and Spanish culture are portrayed as inferior to the Anglo-Saxon world, had a long history well before it was expressed in the Toronto *Globe*. In part, this vision of things Iberian contributed to the pejorative portrayals of Mexicans because they were seen as half Native and half Spanish. See Margaret R. Greer, Maureen Quilligan, and Walter D. Mignolo, eds., *Rereading the Black Legend: The Discourses of Religious and Racial Difference in the Renaissance Empires* (Chicago: University of Chicago Press, 2008); Maria DeGuzman, *Spain's Long Shadow: The Black Legend, Off-Whiteness, and Anglo-American Empire* (Minneapolis: University of Minnesota Press, 2005).

77 Montreal *Gazette*, 4 June 1874.

78 Montreal *Gazette*, 13 February 1873.

79 Toronto *Globe*, 29 December 1873.

80 Toronto *Globe*, 27 November 1873; Montreal *Gazette*, 13 February 1873.

81 Montreal *Gazette*, 1 July 1873.

82 Montreal *Gazette*, 17 June 1873. Also see Montreal *Gazette*, 19 June 1873.

83 Montreal *Gazette*, 7 July 1973.

84 Toronto *Globe*, 29 July 1873.

85 Toronto *Globe*, 6 June 1873.

86 Montreal *Gazette*, 31 July 1873.

87 Toronto *Globe*, 13 January 1873.

88 Toronto *Globe*, 7 July 1873.

89 Montreal *Gazette*, 19 June 1873.

90 Toronto *Globe*, 18 June 1873.

91 Toronto *Globe*, 12 February 1873. Also see Toronto *Globe*, 4 June 1873; Toronto *Globe*, 31 July 1873; Montreal *Gazette*, 15 February 1873; Montreal *Gazette*, 3 June 1873; Montreal *Gazette*, 4 June 1873; Montreal *Gazette*, 5 June 1873; Montreal *Gazette*, 31 June 1873.

92 Montreal *Gazette*, 4 June 1873.

93 Toronto *Globe*, 16 June 1873.

94 Montreal *Gazette*, 14 February 1873.

95 Montreal *Gazette*, 4 June 1873.

96 Montreal *Gazette*, 10 January 1873. Also see Montreal *Gazette*, 2 July 1873.

97 Toronto *Globe*, 17 July 1873.

98   Toronto *Globe*, 27 January 1873.

99   Montreal *Gazette*, 2 August 1873. Also see Toronto *Globe*, 4 August 1873; Toronto *Globe*, 17 July 1873. Paupers, according to the Toronto *Globe*, were poor because they deserved to be poor. Toronto *Globe*, 14 November 1873. Also see Toronto *Globe*, 23 June 1873; Toronto *Globe*, 5 September 1873.

100   Toronto *Globe*, 2 June 1873.

101   Toronto *Globe*, 4 August 1873.

102   Toronto *Globe*, 21 July 1873.

103   Toronto *Globe*, 4 July 1873. Also see Toronto *Globe*, 17 October 1873.

104   Toronto *Globe*, 14 July 1873. Also see Toronto *Globe*, 17 July 1873.

105   Toronto *Globe*, 2 July 1873.

106   Montreal *Gazette*, 5 June 1873. Also see Toronto *Globe*, 7 July 1873.

107   Montreal *Gazette*, 4 June 1873.

108   Toronto *Globe*, 9 August 1873.

109   Toronto *Globe*, 13 October 1873.

110   This native-nature blending appeared on scores of occasions, in nearly every report that discussed Canada's Natives. See, for example, Toronto *Globe*, 8 July 1873; Toronto *Globe*, 17 July 1873; Toronto *Globe*, 4 July 1873; Toronto *Globe*, 10 July 1873.

111   Montreal *Gazette*, 15 February 1873.

112   Toronto *Globe*, 30 September 1873.

113   William A. Stahl, *God and the Chip, Religion and the Culture of Technology* (Waterloo: Wilfrid Laurier University Press, 2002), 33. Also see Nesbitt-Larking, *Politics, Society, and the Media*, 335–370.

114   Toronto *Globe*, 29 November 1873.

115   Toronto *Globe*, 9 August 1873. Also see Montreal *Gazette*, 10 January 1873.

116   See Miller, *Shingwauk's Vision*; Milloy, *National Crime*; and Haig-Brown, *Resistance and Renewal*.

117   Toronto *Globe*, 22 October 1873.

118   Toronto *Globe*, 9 July 1873. The paper provided no number five, but simply skipped, in error, from four to six.

119   Toronto *Globe*, 15 July 1873.

120   Montreal *Gazette*, 15 February 1873.

121   Montreal *Gazette*, 4 June 1873.

122   Toronto *Globe*, 22 July 1873.

123   Toronto *Globe*, 17 June 1873.

CHAPTER THREE: "Our Little War"

1   Montreal *Gazette*, 16 May 1885.

2   Maggie Siggins and Tom Flanagan, the first a popular writer and the second an academic, probably serve as the best examples of the polar positions taken on Riel. Both write well, both engage critically with the primary and secondary literature, and both arrive at starkly different conclusions. Siggins paints Riel in a sympathetic light, whereas Flanagan, a right-wing ideologue who portrays himself as one interested in the past "as it really was," takes few prisoners in a relentless and generally clever defence of the status quo. More interestingly but less successfully Albert Braz has argued that Riel is a social construction who changes in lockstep with prevailing ideological currents. Miller presents probably the most nuanced interpretation of 1885, Riel, and the literature thereof. See Maggie Siggins, *Riel, A Life of Revolution* (Toronto: Harper Collins, 1994); Thomas Flanagan, *Riel and Rebellion, 1885 Reconsidered* (Toronto: University of Toronto Press, 2000); Thomas Flanagan, *Louis 'David' Riel, 'Prophet of the New World'* (Toronto: University of Toronto Press, 1996); Albert Braz, *The False Traitor, Louis Riel in Canadian Culture* (Toronto: University of Toronto Press, 2003); Miller, "The Northwest Rebellion of 1885," in Miller, *Sweet Promises*, 243–258.

3   This was a term favoured by the Tory press. See, for example, Montreal *Gazette*, 3 October 1885.

4   Spurr, *Rhetoric of Empire*, 4.

5   See Steven C. Topik and Allen Wells, eds., *The Second Conquest of Latin America: Coffee, Henequen and Oil During the Export Boom, 1850–1930* (Austin: University of Texas Press, 1998).

6   Roger Nichols, *Indians in the United States and Canada: A Comparative History* (Lincoln: University of Nebraska Press, 1999).

7   This pervaded reports of the fighting. See, for example, Ottawa *Citizen*, 1 June 1885.

8   Manitoba *Free Press*, 15 April 1885; Charlottetown *Daily Examiner*, 28 May 1885. See also Vine Deloria Jr., *Custer Died for Your Sins, An Indian Manifesto* (Norman: University of Oklahoma Press, 1988); Dee Brown, *Bury My Heart*; Patricia Nelson Limerick, *Legacy of Conquest, The Unbroken Past of the American West* (New York: W.W. Norton, 1987).

9   Deloria, *Indians in Unexpected Places*, 20, 50.

10 See Coward, *Newspaper Indian*.

11 See Alan Knight, *The Mexican Revolution*, 2 vols. (Lincoln: University of Nebraska Press, 1990). For an overview of these issues, see Meyer, Sherman, and Deeds, *Mexican History*.

12 See Greg Grandin, *The Blood of Guatemala: A History of Race and Nation* (Durham: Duke University Press, 2000). See also Ralph Lee Woodward, *A Short History of Guatemala* (Antigua, Guatemala: Editorial Laura Lee, 2005).

13 See E. Bradford Burns, *The Poverty of Progress: Latin America in the Nineteenth Century* (Los Angeles: University of California Press, 1983); Walter Lafeber, *Inevitable Revolutions: The United States in Central America* (New York: W.W. Norton, 1993); Grandin, *The Blood of Guatemala*; Topik and Wells, *Second Conquest*.

14 One collective political expression of white cultural dominance is that historically the United States has tended to see and treat Mexico and Guatemala as at best "half-breed" nations. See John J. Johnson, *Latin America in Caricature* (Austin: University of Texas Press, 1993); Lars Schoultz, *Beneath the United States: A History of U.S. Policy Toward Latin America* (Cambridge: Harvard University Press, 1998).

15 Diego Sarmiento, the Argentine minister of education, summed it up pithily in his famous 1868 study, *Civilization versus Barbarism*. See Domingo F. Sarmiento, *Life in the Argentine Republic in the Days of the Tyrants; Or, Civilization and Barbarism* (New York: Hafner, [1868] 1974).

16 Richard Slatta, *Gauchos and the Vanishing Frontier* (Lincoln: University of Nebraska Press, 1992).

17 Also see Rutherford, *Victorian Authority*, 235–240.

18 In 1859 twenty-one Canadian newspapers, based on the American model of the Associated Press (AP) in 1848, established the consortium Canadian Press (CP) wire service. Throughout the nineteenth century, the AP and CP cooperated in sharing and delivering world and North American news. See Collins and Palmegiano, *Rise of Western Journalism*, 50. Also see Kesterton, *History*, 158–159, Rutherford *Victorian Authority*, 94.

19 Halifax *Citizen and Evening Chronicle*, 25 April 1885.

20 Ottawa *Citizen*, 18 May 1885.

21 Halifax *Citizen and Evening Chronicle*, 25 April 1885. Also see Ottawa *Citizen*, 21 April 1885; Ottawa *Citizen*, 22 April 1885; Halifax *Citizen and Evening Chronicle*, 26 May 1885; Halifax *Citizen and Evening Chronicle*, 3 June 1885; Halifax *Citizen and Evening Chronicle*, 11 July 1885; Halifax *Citizen and Evening Chronicle*, 14 July 1885; Halifax *Citizen and Evening Chronicle*, 17 August 1885; Halifax *Citizen and Evening Chronicle*, 19 August 1885; Halifax *Citizen and Evening Chronicle*, 24 August 1885; Halifax *Citizen and Evening Chronicle*, 25 August 1885; Halifax *Citizen and Evening Chronicle*, 6 September 1885; Halifax *Citizen and Evening Chronicle*, 21 November 1885.

22 Halifax *Citizen and Evening Chronicle*, 25 April 1885.

23 Halifax *Citizen and Evening Chronicle*, 29 April 1885.

24 See E. Brian Titley, *The Frontier World of Edgar Dewdney* (Vancouver: University of British Columbia Press, 1999). Also see Halifax *Citizen and Evening Chronicle*, 29 April 1885; Halifax *Citizen and Evening Chronicle*, 3 June 1885.

25 Halifax *Citizen and Evening Chronicle*, 16 May 1885.

26 Calgary *Herald*, 2 April 1885.

27 Calgary *Herald*, 7 May 1885; Calgary *Herald*, 11 June 1885. Also see Calgary *Herald*, 11 November 1885; Calgary *Herald*, 22 July 1885.

28 Calgary *Herald*, 16 April 1885; Calgary *Herald*, 7 May 1885.

29 Calgary *Herald*, 15 July 1885; Calgary *Herald*, 2 December 1885.

30 Manitoba *Free Press*, 28 March 1885.

31 Manitoba *Free Press*, 18 June 1885. Also see Manitoba *Free Press*, 25 June 1885; Manitoba *Free Press*, 7 1885; Manitoba *Free Press*, 23 November 1885.

32 Manitoba *Free Press*, 28 March 1885. Also see Manitoba *Free Press*, 14 July 1885.

33 Manitoba *Free Press*, 20 May 1885. Also see Manitoba *Free Press*, 23 May 1885; Manitoba *Free Press*, 2 June 1885; Manitoba *Free Press*, 18 August 1885.

34 Manitoba *Free Press*, 6 June 1885.

35 Manitoba *Free Press*, 9 June 1885.

36 Manitoba *Free Press*, 13 April 1885.

37 Manitoba *Free Press*, 29 April 1885; Manitoba *Free Press*, 23 May 1885; Manitoba *Free Press*, 1 July 1885; Calgary *Herald*, 2 December 1885.

38 Victoria *Daily Colonist*, 31 March 1885.

39   Manitoba *Free Press*, 1 May 1885.

40   See, for example, Toronto *Globe*, 27 March 1885; Toronto *Globe*, 30 March 1885; Toronto *Globe*, 10 April 1885; Toronto *Globe*, 15 April 1885.

41   Toronto *Globe*, 30 March 1885.

42   Toronto *Globe*, 21 April 1885. Also see Toronto *Globe*, 1 May 1885; Toronto *Globe*, 15 May 1885.

43   Toronto *Globe*, 13 August 1885.

44   Montreal *Gazette*, 8 April 1885.

45   Montreal *Gazette*, 19 May 1885. Also see Montreal *Gazette*, 1 September 1885; Montreal *Gazette*, 19 December 1885.

46   Ottawa *Citizen*, 28 May 1885. Also see Charlottetown *Daily Examiner*, 19 June 1885.

47   See, for example, Montreal *Gazette*, 22 April 1885.

48   See Montreal *Gazette*, 18 March 1885; Montreal *Gazette*, 8 June 1885. Also see Montreal *Gazette*, 19 December 1885.

49   See, for example, Ottawa *Citizen*, 16 April 1885; Ottawa *Citizen*, 3 June 1885; Montreal *Gazette*, 30 November 1885.

50   See, for example, Montreal *Gazette*, 13 August 1885; Montreal *Gazette*, 12 November 1885; Montreal *Gazette*, 19 December 1885; Montreal *Gazette*, 24 December 1885.

51   Victoria *Daily Colonist*, 10 May 1885. Virtually any issue of the paper in January or February contains news stories exploring ongoing land claims issues in British Columbia. One result is that the paper evinced an unusual Tory sympathy for the Métis land gripes yet remained consistent with other Conservative papers in still laying the blame squarely upon Riel.

52   Montreal *Gazette*, 30 November 1885. Also see Ottawa *Citizen*, 1 May 1885; Montreal *Gazette*, 29 December 1885.

53   Victoria *Daily Colonist*, 15 May 1885.

54   Manitoba *Free Press*, 20 July 1885.

55   See, for example, Montreal *Gazette*, 31 October 1885; Montreal *Gazette*, 19 December 1885. The *Citizen* employed the headline, "RIEL AND HIS GRIT ALLIES." Ottawa *Citizen*, 16 May 1885; Ottawa *Citizen*, 26 June 1885.

56   Montreal *Gazette*, 16 May 1885. Also see Montreal *Gazette*, 19 May 1885; Montreal *Gazette*, 20 June 1885; Montreal *Gazette*, 10 December 1885; Ottawa *Citizen*, 30 April 1885; St. John's *Evening Mercury*, 7 May 1885; Charlottetown *Daily Examiner*, 9 May 1885; Victoria *Daily Colonist*, 31 March 1885; Victoria *Daily Colonist*, 1 April 1885.

57   Manitoba *Free Press*, 20 May 1885.

58   Montreal *Gazette*, 13 April 1885; Ottawa *Citizen*, 13 June 1885. See also Manitoba *Free Press*, 11 April 1885

59   Bill Kovach and Tom Rosenstiel, *The Elements of Journalism, What Newspeople Should Know and the Public Should Expect* (New York: Three Rivers Press, 2007).

60   St. John's *Evening Mercury*, 28 April 1885.

61   Montreal *Gazette*, 20 August 1885.

62   See, for example, Charlottetown *Daily Examiner*, 30 May 1885; Victoria *Daily Colonist*, 24 May 1885.

63   Ottawa *Citizen*, 31 January 1885. Also see Calgary *Herald*, 19 February 1885.

64   Ottawa *Citizen*, 9 February 1885.

65   Ottawa *Citizen*, 19 February 1885. Also see Manitoba *Free Press*, 5 May 1885.

66   Toronto *Globe*, 2 January 1885.

67   Charlottetown *Daily Examiner*, 8 May 1885.

68   Ottawa *Citizen*, 24 March 1885.

69   Ottawa *Citizen*, 25 March 1885.

70   Ottawa *Citizen*, 26 March 1885.

71   Ottawa *Citizen*, 27 March 1885.

72   Ottawa *Citizen*, 28 March 1885.

73   Ibid.

74   Ottawa *Citizen*, 26 March 1885.

75   Ibid.

76   Ottawa *Citizen*, 28 March 1885.

77   Ottawa *Citizen*, 27 March 1885.

78   Ottawa *Citizen*, 30 March 1885. Also see Ottawa *Citizen*, 20 April 1885.

79   Ottawa *Citizen*, 28 March 1885.

80   Toronto *Globe*, 28 March 1885.

81   Victoria *Daily Colonist*, 31 May 1885.

82   Ottawa *Citizen*, 31 March 1885.

83   Ottawa *Citizen*, 30 March 1885; Toronto *Globe*, 1 May 1885.

84   Ottawa *Citizen*, 16 May 1885. Also see Victoria *Daily Colonist*, 11 December 1885.

85   Manitoba *Free Press*, 16 May 1885.

86   Calgary *Herald*, 12 March 1885.

87   Montreal *Gazette*, 4, 8, 13 April 1885; Montreal *Gazette*, 30 May 1885. Also see Calgary *Herald*, 12 February 1885; Calgary *Herald*, 19 February 1885; Victoria *Daily Colonist*, 1 April 1885; Toronto *Globe*, 11 April 1885; Manitoba *Free Press*, 15 April 1885; Victoria *Daily Colonist*, 22 April 1885; Manitoba *Free Press*, 20 May 1885; Toronto *Globe*, 6 July 1885.

88   See, for example, Manitoba *Free Press*, 13 March 1885; Montreal *Gazette*, 8 June 1885; Calgary *Herald*, 16 April 1885; Halifax *Citizen and Evening Chronicle*, 10 April 1885; Charlottetown *Daily Examiner*, 30 October 1885. Also see Halifax *Citizen and Evening Chronicle*, 2 January 1885; Manitoba *Free Press*, 16 January 1885; Calgary *Herald*, 5 February 1885; Manitoba *Free Press*, 11 August 1885.

89   Montreal *Gazette*, 9 December 1885. Also see Calgary *Herald*, 15 January 1885; St. John's *Evening Mercury*, 8 May 1885; Manitoba *Free Press*, 29 May 1885.

90   S. Elizabeth Bird, "Savage Desires, The Gendered Construction of the American Indian in Popular Media," in Carter Jones Meyer and Diana Royer, eds., *Selling the Indian, Commercializing and Appropriating American Indian Cultures* (Tucson: University of Arizona Press, 2001), 80.

91   Charlottetown *Daily Examiner*, 22 June 1885. Also see Victoria *Daily Colonist*, 1 April 1885.

92   Manitoba *Free Press*, 23 May 1885.

93   Manitoba *Free Press*, 30 January 1885.

94   Montreal *Gazette*, 18 September 1885.

95   Victoria *Daily Colonist*, 3 March 1885; Charlottetown *Daily Examiner*, 10 April 1885; Toronto *Globe*, 10 April 1885; Ottawa *Citizen*, 11 April 1885; Toronto *Globe* 11 April 1885; St. John's *Evening Mercury*, 11 April 1885; Ottawa *Citizen*, 23 April 1885; Victoria *Daily Colonist*, 1 May 1885; St. John's *Evening Mercury*, 4 May 1885; St. John's *Evening Mercury*, 15 May 1885; Ottawa *Citizen*, 5 June 1885; Ottawa *Citizen*, 6 June 1885; Charlottetown *Daily Examiner*, 10 June 1885; Ottawa *Citizen*, 11 June 1885; Manitoba *Free Press*, 16 June 1885. See, for example, Manitoba *Free Press*, 6 June 1885; Ottawa *Citizen*, 20 May 1885; Victoria *Daily Colonist*, 8 May 1885; Ottawa *Citizen*, 26 May 1885; Charlottetown *Daily Examiner*, 11 May 1885; Victoria *Daily Colonist*, 21 May 1885; Ottawa *Citizen*, 4 July 1885; Victoria *Daily Colonist*, 31 January 1885; Halifax *Citizen and Evening Chronicle*, 3 June 1885. Montreal *Gazette*, 3 May 1885; Toronto *Globe*, 28 March 1885; Ottawa *Citizen*, 30 May 1885.

96   Ottawa *Citizen*, 6 July 1885. Also see Toronto *Globe*, 17 April 1885; Manitoba *Free Press*, 18 June 1885; Manitoba *Free Press*, 25 July 1885; Halifax *Citizen and Evening Chronicle*, 22 April 1885; St. John's *Evening Mercury*, 5 May 1885; Ottawa *Citizen*, 27 April 1885; Ottawa *Citizen*, 1 June 1885; Ottawa *Citizen*, 11 June 1885; Victoria *Daily Colonist*, 1 April 1885; Ottawa *Citizen*, 9 May 1885; Montreal *Gazette*, 6 June 1885; Ottawa *Citizen*, 11 April 1885; Montreal *Gazette*, 6 June 1885. Also see Ottawa *Citizen*, 18 April 1885; Ottawa *Citizen*, 9 May 1885; Ottawa *Citizen*, 15 June 1885; Montreal *Gazette*, 4 December 1885; Toronto *Globe*, 30 March 1885; Calgary *Herald*, 2 April 1885; Manitoba *Free Press*, 23 June 1885; Halifax *Citizen and Evening Chronicle*, 25 August 1885.

97   See, for example, Toronto *Globe*, 17 April 1885; Victoria *Daily Colonist*, 22 April 1885; Ottawa *Citizen*, 4 May 1885; Victoria *Daily Colonist*, 8 May 1885; Ottawa *Citizen*, 9 May 1885; Montreal *Gazette*, 28 July 1885; Montreal *Gazette*, 3 August 1885.

98   Ottawa *Citizen*, 21 May 1885. Also see Ottawa *Citizen*, 23 May 1885.

99   Ottawa *Citizen*, 30 May 1885.

100   Montreal *Gazette*, 30 May 1885.

101   St. John's *Evening Mercury*, 15 May 1885.

102   Toronto *Globe*, 10 April 1885.

103   St. John's *Evening Mercury*, 17 June 1885; Victoria *Daily Colonist*, 13 June 1885. Also see Victoria *Daily Colonist*, 1 June 1885; Manitoba *Free Press*, 8 June 1885; Montreal *Gazette*, 8 June 1885.

104   Historian Sarah Carter has written a nuanced study of the affair. See Sarah Carter, *The Importance of Being Monogamous: Marriage and Nation Building in Western Canada to 1915* (Edmonton: University of Alberta Press, 2008); Carter, *Capturing Women*. Also see Montreal *Gazette*, 8 June 1885; Manitoba *Free Press*, 13 June 1885; Montreal *Gazette*, 13 June 1885; Victoria *Daily Colonist*, 19 June 1885.

105   Montreal *Gazette*, 25 June 1885.

106   Calgary *Herald* 17 June 1885. Also see Halifax *Citizen and Evening Chronicle*, 29 May 1885; Manitoba *Free Press*, 25 July 1885.

107   Halifax *Citizen and Evening Chronicle*, 8 June 1885.

108   Halifax *Citizen and Evening Chronicle*, 13 June 1885.

109   Toronto *Globe*, 7 April 1885.

110   Toronto *Globe*, 10 April 1885.

111   Montreal *Gazette*, 11 August 1885. Also see Charlottetown *Daily Examiner*, 10 April 1885; Manitoba *Free Press*, 29 June 1885.

112   Manitoba *Free Press*, 13 April 1885.

113 Calgary *Herald*, 5 March 1885. Also see Calgary *Herald*, 7 May 1885.

114 Halifax *Citizen and Evening Chronicle*, 27 June 1885.

115 Nichols writes: "While the United States and its tribal peoples fought bloody wars in the decades after 1860, Canada usually avoided major confrontation and bloodshed. More often than not, this resulted from the vast area and small populations north of the border rather than to any superior policy or more careful handling of Indian-related issues by Canadian officials. In fact, in many ways leaders in Ottawa knew less about their western regions and peoples than did their counterparts in the United States." See Nichols, *Indians*, 220.

116 Charlottetown *Daily Examiner*, 3 August 1885.

117 See Lauren L. Basson, "Savage Half-Breed, French Canadian of White U.S. Citizen? Louis Riel and U.S. Perceptions of Nation and Civilisation," *National Identities* 7, 4 (December 2005): 370–371.

118 Manitoba *Free Press*, 15 June 1885.

119 See two books by literary historian Richard Slotkin: *The Fatal Environment*; *Gunfighter Nation*.

120 Basson, "Savage Half-Breed," 384–385.

121 Montreal *Gazette*, 25 February 1885. Also see Victoria *Daily Colonist*, 31 March 1885; Ottawa *Citizen*, 21 April 1885; Toronto *Globe*, 15 May 1885; Halifax *Citizen and Evening Chronicle*, 16 May 1885; Montreal *Gazette*, 31 July 185.

122 Ibid.

123 Ottawa *Citizen*, 11 April 1885.

124 Montreal *Gazette*, 18 April 1885. Also see Montreal *Gazette*, 21 April 1885;

125 Charlottetown *Daily Examiner*, 17 February 1885. Also see Manitoba *Free Press*, 14 April 1885; Calgary *Herald*, 7 May 1885; Toronto *Globe*, 15 May 1885; Toronto *Globe*, 29 June 1885.

126 Montreal *Gazette*, 16 May 1885. Also see Victoria *Daily Colonist*, 29 April 1885.

127 See, for example, *Citizen*, 14 April 1885; Charlottetown *Daily Examiner*, 7 April 1885; Victoria *Daily Colonist*, 22 April 1885; Halifax *Citizen and Evening Chronicle*, 26 May 1885.

128 Montreal *Gazette*, 25 May 1885; Montreal *Gazette*, 29 May 1885; Montreal *Gazette*, 12 June 1885; Montreal *Gazette*, 25 June 1885; Montreal *Gazette*, 9 July 1885; Montreal *Gazette*, 16 July 1885; Montreal *Gazette*, 15 August 1885; Montreal *Gazette*, 28 September 1885; Montreal *Gazette*, 5 October 1885; Montreal *Gazette*, 17 November 1885; Montreal *Gazette*, 24 December 1885; Montreal *Gazette*, 4 December 1885. See also Montreal *Gazette*, 30 May 1885. Also see Montreal *Gazette*, 8 June 1885; St. John's *Evening Mercury*, 17 June 1885; Fredericton *Maritime Farmer*, 14 January 1885; Fredericton *Maritime Farmer*, 30 December 1885.

129 Ottawa *Citizen*, 11 May 1885. Also see St. John's *Evening Mercury*, 14 May 1885.

130 Ottawa *Citizen*, 16 May 1885.

131 Montreal *Gazette*, 8 April 1885. Also see Calgary *Herald*, 22 January 1885; Calgary *Herald*, 5 February 1885; Victoria *Daily Colonist*, 4 August 1885.

132 Charlottetown *Daily Examiner*, 11 April 1885.

133 Toronto *Globe*, 10 April 1885. Also see Manitoba *Free Press*, 30 April 1885.

134 Toronto *Globe*, 15 May 1885.

135 Stonechild and Waiser note that "the United States spent more money fighting Indian wars in 1870 than the entire Canadian budget for that year." See Blair Stonechild and Bill Waiser, *Loyal till Death, Indians and the North-West Rebellion* (Markham, ON: Fifth House, 1997), 7, 32. Also see Carter, *Aboriginal People*, 119.

136 Charlottetown *Daily Examiner*, 28 May 1885. Also see Calgary *Herald*, 16 April 1885; *Citizen and Evening Chronicle*, 27 April 1885; Charlottetown *Daily Examiner*, 10 June 1885; Charlottetown *Daily Examiner*, 19 June 1885; Calgary *Herald* 19 August 1885.

137 Manitoba *Free Press*, 13 April 1885.

138 Manitoba *Free Press*, 20 May 1885.

139 Montreal *Gazette*, 18 March 1885.

140 Toronto *Globe*, 29 June 1885.

141 Montreal *Gazette*, 16 March 1885. Also see Charlottetown *Daily Examiner*, 17 February 1885.

142 See, for example, Montreal *Gazette*, 8 April 1885.

143 Toronto *Globe*, 29 June 1885.

144 Calgary *Herald*, 23 April 1885.

145 See Alfred W. Crosby, *The Columbian Exchange: Biological and Cultural Consequences of 1492* (New York: Praeger, 2002).

146 Calgary *Herald*, 23 April 1885.

147 Ibid.

148 Manitoba *Free Press*, 20 July 1885.

149 Manitoba *Free Press*, 30 January 1885. Also see Manitoba *Free Press*, 13 April 1885; Manitoba *Free Press*, 14 September 1885.

150 Montreal *Gazette*, 5 May 1885. Also see St. John's *Evening Mercury*, 4 May 1885; Montreal *Gazette*, 25 May 1885.

151 Charlottetown *Daily Examiner*, 19 June 1885.

152 St. John's *Evening Mercury*, 7 May 1885.

153 Montreal *Gazette*, 8 June 1885.

154 Charlottetown *Daily Examiner*, 10 August 1885.

155 Calgary *Herald*, 9 April 1885.

156 Montreal *Gazette*, 18 September 1885.

157 Ottawa *Citizen*, 12 June 1885.

158 Charlottetown *Daily Examiner*, 22 July 1885. Also see Victoria *Daily Colonist*, 27 January 1885; Manitoba *Free Press*, 1 May 1885; Charlottetown *Daily Examiner*, 9 November 1885.

159 Montreal *Gazette*, 3 February 1885. Also see Montreal *Gazette*, 5 May 1885; Montreal *Gazette*, 5 May 1885; Montreal *Gazette*, 8 December 1885.

160 Toronto *Globe*, 28 March 1885.

161 Montreal *Gazette*, 5 May 1885.

162 Montreal *Gazette*, 16 December 1885. Also see Charlottetown *Daily Examiner*, 10 June 1885.

163 Charlottetown *Daily Examiner*, 17 June 1885.

164 Victoria *Daily Colonist*, 23 April 1885.

165 Halifax *Citizen and Evening Chronicle*, 3 April 1885.

166   Montreal *Gazette*, 8 April 1885.

167   Ottawa *Citizen*, 16 April 1885.

168   Toronto *Globe*, 6 July 1885; Ottawa *Citizen*, 23 July 1885. Also see Ottawa *Citizen*, 20 April 1885; St. John's *Evening Mercury*, 8 May 1885; Ottawa *Citizen*, 20 May 1885; Ottawa *Citizen*, 8 June 1885; Manitoba *Free Press*, 9 June 1885.

169   Ottawa *Citizen*, 18 April 1885. Also see Ottawa *Citizen*, 5 May 1885; Halifax *Citizen and Evening Chronicle*, 3 June 1885.

170   Ottawa *Citizen*, 29 May 1885; Toronto *Globe*, 30 March 1885.

171   Ottawa *Citizen*, 20 April 1885. Also see Ottawa *Citizen*, 4 May 1885

172   Ottawa *Citizen*, 4 May 1885. Also see Ottawa *Citizen*, 27 June 1885; Ottawa *Citizen*, 22 July 1885. Also see Victoria *Daily Colonist*, 8 April 1885.

173   Calgary *Herald*, 12 April 1885.

174   Ottawa *Citizen*, 27 May 1885; Ottawa *Citizen*, 4 August 1885.

175   Charlottetown *Daily Examiner*, 19 June 1885.

176   Montreal *Gazette*, 4 May 1885.

177   Toronto *Globe*, 21 April 1885; Halifax *Citizen and Evening Chronicle*, 23 April 1885; St. John's *Evening Mercury*, 8 May 1885; Ottawa *Citizen*, 27 June 1885; Ottawa *Citizen*, 4 August 1885; Charlottetown *Daily Examiner*, 20 June 1885.

178   Montreal *Gazette*, 6 April 1885. Also see Manitoba *Free Press*, 13 April 1885.

179   Ottawa *Citizen*, 20 April 1885. Also see St. John's *Evening Mercury*, 28 April 1885; Ottawa *Citizen*, 4 May 1885; Manitoba *Free Press*, 26 June 1885; Ottawa *Citizen*, 3 July 1885. See also Ottawa *Citizen*, 22 April 1885; Manitoba *Free Press*, 15 April 1885; Ottawa *Citizen*, 7 May 1885; Ottawa *Citizen*, 5 June 1885.

180   Ottawa *Citizen*, 4 May 1885. Also see Toronto *Globe*, 1 May 1885; Ottawa *Citizen*, 26 May 1885.

181   Ottawa *Citizen*, 9 June 1885. Also see Charlottetown *Daily Examiner*, 22 July 1885; Charlottetown Victoria *Daily Colonist*, 11 December 1885.

182   Ottawa *Citizen*, 4 August 1885.

183   Charlottetown *Daily Examiner*, 11 April 1885.

184   Montreal *Gazette*, 18 March 1885; Charlottetown *Daily Examiner*, 28 May 1885.

185   Calgary *Herald*, 7 May 1885.

186   Toronto *Globe*, 15 May 1885.

187   Manitoba *Free Press*, 18 February 1885.

188   See Churchill, *Kill the Indian*. Also see Milloy, *National Crime*; Miller, *Shingwauk's Vision*; and Haig-Brown, *Resistance and Renewal*.

189   Montreal *Gazette*, 27 July 1885.

190   Montreal *Gazette*, 20 August 1885.

191   St. John's *Evening Mercury*, 27 April 1885.

CHAPTER FOUR: The Golden Rule

1 Kenneth Coates, *Canada's Colonies: A History of the Yukon and Northwest Territories* (Toronto: Lorimer, 1985), 67–99; William R. Morrison, *True North: The Yukon and Northwest Territories* (New York: Oxford University Press, 1998), 78–104.

2 Coates, *Canada's Colonies*, 79.

3 Ibid., 83.

4 *Shane* (1953), dir. George Stevens.

5 *Dances With Wolves* (1990), dir. Kevin Costner.

6 See *Red River* (1948), dir. John Ford, or *Hondo* (1953), dir. John Farrow.

7 Dawson City *Yukon Sun*, 18 December 1902.

8 See Richard Slotkin, *Regeneration Through Violence: The Mythology of the American Frontier, 1600-1860* (Norman: Unversity of Oklahoma Press, 2001).

9 Gold was struck in August 1896. Word did not reach Seattle till the following summer, hence the rush in 1898. Turner presented a paper, "The Significance of the Frontier in American History," in 1893 in Chicago at the annual conference of the American Historical Association, which was subsequently published in the *American Historical Review*. The essay has been anthologized many times since. The essay was so profoundly influential that Turner was never able to escape it. See Patricia Nelson Limerick, "Turnerians All: The Dream of a Helpful History in an Intelligible World," *The American Historical Review* 100, 3 (June 1995): 697–715. Also see Frederick Jackson Turner, "The Significance of the Frontier in American History," in Frederick Jackson Turner, *Frontier and Section, Selected Essays of Frederick Jackson Turner* (Englewood Cliffs, NJ: Prentice-Hall, [1893] 1961), 37–62.

10 Turner, "Significance of the Frontier," 43.

11 See, for example, *The Last of the Mohicans* (New York: Signet Classics, [1826] 2005); *Deerslayer, or The First Warpath* (New York: Barnes and Noble Classics, [1841] 2005).

12 Wister's *The Virginian* is often considered the class of the field. Yet the genre has made household names of many of its authors—Zane Grey, Louis L'Amour, Elmore Leonard, and Cormac McCarthy come to mind.

13 See the Introduction to Slotkin, *Gunfighter Nation*.

14 Wayne starred in dozens of Western over several decades. See Garry Wills, *John Wayne's America: The Politics of Celebrity* (New York: Simon and Schuster, 1997).

15 Stewart starred in several Westerns, not least of which was directed by John Ford, *The Man Who Shot Liberty Valance* (1962), a powerful meditation on masculinity and violence and nation-building on the mythical frontier. Also see *Winchester '73* (1950), dir. Anthony Man.

16 See director Ron Howard's *Far and Away* (1992).

17 See director Steven Spielberg's *Raiders of the Lost Ark* (1982), a film that affords the Indian treatment to Arabs and South American Natives. For more on the former, see Edward Said, *Orientalism*, and Said, *Culture and Imperialism*.

18 *A Man Named Horse* (1970), dir. Elliot Silverstein; and *Man in the Wilderness* (1971), dir. Richard C. Sarafian.

19 Turner, "Significance of the Frontier," 38.

20 Ibid., 61. Also see ibid., 46, 57.

21 Ibid., 39.

22 See Garry Wills, "John Wayne's Body," *New Yorker*, 19 August 1996, 38.

23 Dawson City *Dawson News*, 9 April 1900.

24   Furniss, *Burden of History*.

25   Ibid., 23.

26   Nichols, *Indians in the United States and Canada*.

27   Furniss, *Burden of History*, 18–19.

28   See Churchill, *Kill the Indian*; David Wallace Adams, *Education for Extinction: American Indians and the Boarding School Experience 1875–1928* (Lawrence: University Press of Kansas, 1997).

29   Dawson City *Dawson Record*, 16 June 1905.

30   Dawson City *Dawson News*, 25 August 1903. Also see Dawson City *Dawson News*, 10 December 1903; Dawson City *Klondike Nugget*, 2 August 1902; *Whitehorse Star*, 9 August 1902.

31   Dawson City *Dawson News*, 28 December 1899.

32   Dawson City *Dawson News*, 29 November 1899; Dawson City *Dawson News*, 1 December 1900.

33   See Dawson City *Dawson Record*, 23 July 1903; Dawson City *Dawson Record*, 13 August 1903; Dawson City *Dawson Record*, 16 August 1903; Dawson City *Dawson Record*, 18 September 1903; Dawson City *Dawson Record*, 4 October 1903; Dawson City *Dawson Record*, 15 October 1903. See Dawson City *Klondike Nugget*, 18 February 1899; Dawson City *Klondike Nugget*, 5 April 1899; Dawson City *Klondike Nugget*, 7 November 1902. See *Whitehorse Star*, 10 January 1903; *Whitehorse Star*, 23 September 1905; *Whitehorse Star*, 16 December 1905.

34   For accounts of the gold rush based on oral history see Julie Cruikshank, "Images of Society in Klondike Goldrush Narratives: Skookum Jim and the Discovery of Gold," *Ethnohistory* 39, 1 (1992): 20–41.

35   Dawson City *Klondike Nugget*, 17 September 1902.

36   Dawson City *Klondike Nugget*, 18 February 1899; Dawson City *Klondike Nugget*, 8 April 1899; Dawson City *Dawson News*, 12 January 1900; Dawson City *Dawson News*, 22 August 1902; Dawson City *Yukon Sun*, 31 August 1902; Dawson City *Dawson News*, 20 November 1902; Dawson City *Klondike Nugget*, 7 November 1902; Dawson City *Dawson News*, 15 December 1902; Dawson City *Yukon Daily Morning World*, 15 March 1904; Dawson City *Dawson News*, 25 July 1903; Dawson City *Dawson News*, 25 July 1903; Dawson City *Dawson Record*, 18 September 1903; Dawson City *Dawson Record*, 15 October 1903; Dawson City *Dawson News*, 2 December 1903; Dawson City *Yukon Daily Morning World*, 25 May 1904; *Whitehorse Star*, 30 June 1904; Dawson City *Yukon Daily Morning World*, 5 May 1905; Dawson City *Dawson News*, 6 April 1905; *Whitehorse Star*, 7 April 1905; Dawson City *Yukon Daily Morning World*, 9 July 1905; Dawson City *Yukon Daily Morning World*, 3 September 1905.

37   For example, see Dawson City *Klondike Nugget*, 29 March 1899; Dawson City *Dawson News*, 12 January 1900; *Whitehorse Star*, 30 June 1904; Dawson City *Yukon Daily Morning World*, 19 May 1905.

38   Dawson City *Yukon Sun*, 14 January 1903.

39   Dawson City *Klondike Nugget*, 20 April 1902.

40   Dawson City *Dawson News*, 11 November 1899.

41   Dawson City *Yukon Daily Morning World*, 28 May 1904.

42   Dawson City *Dawson News*, 2 December 1903.

43   Dawson City *Dawson Record*, 13 August 1903.

44   Ibid.

45   Dawson City *Dawson Record*, 23 August 1903; Dawson City *Dawson News*, 2 January 1904.

46   Dawson City *Dawson News*, 1 August 1903; Dawson City *Dawson News*, 24 October 1903.

47   Dawson City *Yukon Sun*, 18 December 1902. Also see Dawson City *Klondike Nugget*, 19 April 1899; Dawson City *Dawson News*, 11 November 1899; Dawson City *Dawson News*, 25 October 1902. The charge of insanity surfaced elsewhere. See *Whitehorse Star*, 23 September 1904; *Whitehorse Star*, 27 September 1904; *Whitehorse Star*, 28 September 1904.

48   Dawson City *Yukon Sun*, 15 July 1903.

49   Dawson City *Yukon Sun*, 29 January 1903. Also see Dawson City *Dawson Record*, 16 September 1903; Dawson City *Yukon Daily Morning World*, 2 May 1905.

50   Dawson City *Yukon Sun*, 15 July 1905.

51   Dawson City *Yukon Sun*, 23 August 1903. Also see Dawson City *Klondike Nugget*, 19 April 1899.

52   Dawson City *Dawson News*, 19 June 1903. Also see *Whitehorse Star*, 10 June 1904.

53   Dawson City *Dawson News*, 2 January 1904.

54   *Whitehorse Star*, 18 October 1905.

55   Dawson City *Yukon Sun*, 25 May 1902.

56   *Whitehorse Star*, 11 June 1903.

57   Dawson City *Yukon Sun*, 22 September 1904.

58   Dawson City *Yukon Sun*, 11 November 1899.

59   Dawson City *Klondike Nugget*, 8 October 1898.

60   Dawson City *Klondike Nugget*, 30 August 1899.

61   Dawson City *Dawson News*, 7 June 1902.

62   *Whitehorse Star*, 6 September 1902.

63   *Whitehorse Star*, 7 June 1904.

64   Dawson City *Yukon Sun*, 10 July 1902.

65   Dawson City *Klondike Nugget*, 18 February 1899.

66   Dawson City *Dawson News*, 13 April 1900.

67   Dawson City *Dawson News*, 22 August 1902.

68   Dawson City *Dawson News*, 7 June 1902.

69   Dawson City *Dawson News*, 25 June 1904.

70   Dawson City *Dawson News*, 29 December 1899.

71   Dawson City *Dawson News*, 9 April 1900. Also see Dawson City *Dawson News*, 10 April 1900.

72   *Whitehorse Star*, 14 February 1903.

73   Dawson City *Yukon Sun*, 31 August 1902.

74   Dawson City *Yukon Sun*, 31 August 1902.

75   Dawson City *Dawson News*, 12 January 1900.

76   See John Mack Faragher, *Daniel Boone: The Life and Legend of an American Pioneer* (New York: Holt Paperbacks, 1993).

77   Dawson City *Dawson Record*, 4 October 1903.

78   Dawson City *Dawson News*, 29 November 1899. Also see *Whitehorse Star*, 10 January 1903.

79   *Whitehorse Star*, 16 December 1905.

80   Dawson City *Dawson News*, 11 November 1899.

81   Dawson City *Dawson News*, 7 May 1900.

82   Also see Dawson City *Dawson News*, 10 April 1902.

83   Dawson City *Dawson News*, 8 May 1903.

84   Dawson City *Yukon Daily Morning World*, 22 October 1904.

85   Dawson City *Yukon Daily Morning World*, 3 April 1904.

86   Dawson City *Yukon Daily Morning World*, 26 July 1905.

87   See Dawson City *Yukon Sun*, 15 July 1902; Dawson City *Dawson Record*, 3 September 1903; Dawson City *Dawson Record*, 20 October 1903; Dawson City *Dawson News*, 11 November 1899; Dawson City *Dawson News*, 30 July 1903; *Whitehorse Star*, 15 November 1902; Dawson City *Yukon Daily Morning World*, 15 March 1904; Dawson City *Yukon Daily Morning World*, 18 March 1905.

88   Dawson City *Dawson News*, 12 January 1900; *Whitehorse Star*, 6 September 1902; Dawson City *Yukon Daily Morning World*, 25 May 1904; Dawson City *Yukon Daily Morning World*, 27 October 1905.

89   Dawson City *Klondike Nugget*, 26 October 1898.

90   Dawson City *Dawson News*, 7 June 1902.

91   Bird, "Savage Desires," 81.

92   Dawson City *Klondike Nugget*, 8 April 1899.

93   See *Klondike Sun*, 19 April 1899; Dawson City *Dawson News*, 18 April 1904.

94   Dawson City *Dawson News*, 25 August 1903, 2.

95   *Whitehorse Star*, 6 September 1902.

96   Dawson City *Dawson News*, 7 June 1902.

97   Dawson City *Yukon Daily Morning World*, 26 July 1905.

98   Dawson City *Dawson News*, 7 June 1902.

99   Dawson City *Yukon Sun*, 31 August 1902. Also see Dawson City *Dawson News*, 29 November 1899.

100   Dawson City *Klondike Nugget*, 30 August 1899.

101   Dawson City *Yukon Daily Morning World*, 9 July 1905.

CHAPTER FIVE: *Poet, Princess, Possession*

1   Vancouver (*Daily*) *Province*, 7 March 1913.

2   Ibid. Hiawatha, a figure wrapped in fact and fiction, was claimed as a leader of the Onondaga and Mohawk nations and was a follower of the Great Peacemaker who founded the Iroquois Confederacy. Hiawatha lived, depending on the source, in the 1100s, 1400s, or 1500s. Henry Wadsworth Longfellow's epic poem *The Song of Hiawatha* (1855) offered a romantic construction of a fictional character named Hiawatha, making the name well-known.

3   Vancouver (*Daily*) *Province*, 7 March 1913.

4   Ibid.

5   Mikhail Bakhtin, "Discourse in the Novel," in Michael Holquist and Caryl Emerson, eds., *The Dialogic Imagination: Four Essays* (Austin: University of Texas Press, 1981), 366.

6   Spurr, *Rhetoric of Empire*, 157.

7   Excerpts reprinted in Edmonton *Journal*, 8 March 1913, and Toronto *Star*, 8 March 1913.

8   Reprinted in Regina *Leader*, 8 March 1913.

9   Excerpts published in Toronto *Star*, 8 March 1913, and Toronto *Globe*, 7 March 1913.

10 W. Garland Foster, *The Mohawk Princess: Being Some Account of the Life of Teka-hion-wake (E. Pauline Johnson)* (Vancouver: Lion's Gate Publishing, 1931); Betty Keller, *Pauline: A Biography of Pauline Johnson* (Toronto: Douglas and McIntyre, 1981).

11 Keller, *Pauline*, 1.

12 Charlotte Gray, *Flint and Feather: The Life and Times of E. Pauline Johnson* (Toronto: Harper Collins, 2002); Veronica Strong-Boag and Carole Gerson, *Paddling Her Own Canoe: The Times and Texts of E. Pauline Johnson, Tekahionwake* (Toronto: University of Toronto Press, 2000).

13 Strong-Boag and Gerson, *Paddling*, 3-15.

14 Ibid., 3.

15 Gray, *Flint and Feather*, 399.

16 Daniel Francis, *The Imaginary Indian: The Image of the Indian in Canadian Culture* (Vancouver: Arsenal Pulp Press, 1992), 117; see 111-117 for his full account of E. Pauline Johnson.

17 Janice Fiamengo, "'This Graceful Olive Branch of the Iroquois': Pauline Johnson's Rhetoric of Reconciliation," in *The Woman's Page: Journalism and Rhetoric in Early Canada* (Toronto: University of Toronto Press, 2008), 89–120.

18 Keller, *Pauline*, 17–18.

19 Strong-Boag and Gerson, *Paddling*, 30–31.

20 For a detailed account of Johnson's national audience, often reached by Canada's national rail lines, see Gray, *Flint and Feather*; Keller, *Pauline*, Strong-Boag and Gerson, *Paddling*.

21 Obituaries made much of the influence of the English governess in preparing Johnson's literary skills.

22 Keller, *Pauline*, 30–31.

23 Gray, *Flint and Feather*, 47.

24 Julie Rak investigates the problematic role assigned her by Schoolnet, an educational Internet source, to provide information about Johnson that presented the poet as spectacle. See Julie Rak, "Double Wampum, Double Life, Double Click: E. Pauline Johnson by and for the World Wide Web," *Textual Studies in Canada* 13/14 (1996): 153–170.

25 Francis, *Imaginary Indian*, 116.

26 Ibid., 111.

27 Toronto *Globe*, 18 January 1892, reprinted in Francis, *Imaginary Indian*, 113.

28 Gray, *Flint and Feather*, 91.

29 Margaret Atwood, *Strange Things: The Malevolent North in Canadian Literature* (Toronto: Oxford University Press, 1995), 90–91; Strong-Boag and Gerson, *Paddling*, 105.

30 Fiamengo, *Woman's Page*, 97.

31 Francis, *Imaginary Indian*, 115. Fiamengo describes the scalp as Sioux. Fiamengo, *Woman's Page*, 94.

32 Fiamengo, *Woman's Page*, 97; Rick Monture, "'Beneath the British Flag': Iroquois and Canadian Nationalism in the work of E. Pauline Johnson and Duncan Campbell Scott," *Essays on Canadian Writing* 75 (Winter 2002): 129.

33 E. Pauline Johnson, "A Cry From An Indian Wife," *White Wampum* (London: John Lane, 1895), rpt. in *Flint and Feather* (Toronto: The Musson Book Co., 1931): 17-19.

34 Johnson, "Canada," *Flint and Feather*, 148.

35 While they speculate this might have caused the audience to later read or reread her poetry with attention to questions or race, sympathy, or national justice, little evidence supports this claim. Strong-Boag and Gerson, *Paddling*, 115.

36 Undated review from the Michigan *Newsreporter* documented by Fiamengo, *Woman's Page*, 98; Monture, "Beneath the British Flag,"129.

37 Keller, *Pauline*, 260.

38 Newspapers included: Calgary *Herald*; Charlottetown *Guardian*; Fredericton *Daily Gleaner*; Edmonton *Journal*; Halifax *Herald*; Hamilton *Spectator*; Winnipeg *Free Press*; Montreal *Gazette*; Sudbury *Star*; St. John's *Evening Telegram*; Toronto *Globe*; Toronto Daily *Star*; Vancouver *(Daily) Province*; Victoria *Daily Colonist*; Windsor *Evening Record*.

39 Vancouver *(Daily) Province*, 7 March 1913.

40 For a detailed account of the events surrounding the funeral, see Gray, *Flint and Feather*, 389–391; Keller, *Pauline*, 268–271.

41 Keller describes the Women's Canadian Club as a recently formed group of "570 enthusiastic patriotic ladies in the fold—Vancouver's social elite." Keller, *Pauline*, 268.

42 Vancouver *(Daily) Province*, 7 March 1913. The story refers to Chip three times. No other report mentions the importance of the dog in her educational process.

43 Victoria *Daily Colonist*, 7 March 1913.

44 Edmonton *Journal*, 7 March 1913.

45 Ibid.

46 Toronto *Star*, 8 March 1913.

47 Toronto *Globe*, 8 March 1913.

48 Toronto *Globe*, 7 March 1913.

49 Toronto *Globe*, 8 March 1913.

50 Ibid.

51 Letter to the Editor, Evelyn Johnson, Toronto *Globe*, 18 April 1913.

52 Vancouver *Province*, 9 March 1913.

53 Toronto *Star*, 8 March 1913.

54 Johnson, *Flint and Feather*, 71-72. In 1889 Johnson wrote her poem titled "The Happy Hunting Grounds" that equated the demise of the buffalo to that of "the brave."

55 See 8 March 1913 reports in the following newspapers: Edmonton *Journal*; Hamilton *Spectator*; Regina *Leader*; Toronto *Globe*; Toronto *Star*; Vancouver *(Daily) Province*; Victoria *Daily Colonist*; and the Windsor *Evening Record*.

56 Regina *Leader*, 8 March 1913.

57 See Toronto *Star*, 8 March, 1913; Toronto *Globe*, 11 March 1913 and 13 March 1913.

58 Regina *Leader*, 8 March 1913.

59 Biographers, however, say Johnson's mother was an American Quaker and she benefited from the governess for only two years.

60 Regina *Leader*, 8 March 1913.

61 Ibid.

62 Ibid.

63 Edmonton *Journal*, 8 March 1913.

64 Windsor *Evening Record*, 10 March 1913.

65 Ibid.

66 Hamilton *Spectator*, 8 March 1913.

67 Ibid.

68 Seed, *Ceremonies*, 179.

69 Vancouver *(Daily) Province*, 10 March 1913.

70 Ibid.

71 Ibid.

72 Fredericton *Daily Gleaner*, 10 March 1913.

73 Fredericton *Daily Gleaner*, 11 March 1913.

74 Calgary *Herald*, 11 March 1913.

75 Ibid.

76 Gray, *Flint and Feather*, 390.

77 Windsor *Evening Record*, 10 March 1913.

78 Windsor *Evening Record*, 11 March 1913.

79 Toronto *Globe*, 11 March 1913.

80 Toronto *Globe*, 13 March 1913.

81 Sudbury *Star*, 12 March 1913.

CHAPTER SIX: Disrobing Grey Owl

1 The 1999 film *Grey Owl* was directed by Richard Attenborough and starred Pierce Brosnan, of James Bond fame, in the title role. David Collier features Grey Owl in his comic book compilation *Portraits From Life*. David Collier, *Portraits from Life* (Montreal: Drawn and Quarterly, 2001).

2 See, for example, Anahareo, *Devil in Deerskins* (Oshawa: Alger Press, 1972); Jane Billinghurst, *The Many Faces of Archie Belaney: Grey Owl* (Vancouver: Greystone Books, 1999); Irene Trenier-Gordon, *Grey Owl, Junior Edition* (Toronto: Altitude Publishing, 2007); Allison Mitchum, *Grey Owl: Favorite Wilderness* (Manotick, ON: Penumbra Press, 1981); Gary McGuffin, Joanie McGuffin, *In The Footsteps of Grey Owl: Journey into The Ancient Forest* (Toronto: McClelland and Stewart, 2002); Vicky Shipton, *Grey Owl* (London: Penguin, 2008).

3 Saskatoon *Star Phoenix*, 5 August 1988.

4 See Jean Baudrillard, *Simulacra and Simulations*, P. Foss, P. Patton and P. Beitchman, trans. (New York: Semiotexte, 1981).

5 See Roland Barthes, *Mythologies* (New York: Hill and Wang, 1972).

6 Elizabeth Bird, *The Audience in Everyday Life: Living in a Media World* (New York: Routledge, 2003), 117.

7   Deborah Root, *Cannibal Culture: Art, Appropriation, and the Commodification of Difference* (Boulder, CO: Westview Press, 1996), 105–106.

8   New York *Times*, 24 June 1934.

9   London *Times*, 14 April 1938.

10 London *Daily Express*, 20 April 1938.

11 Albert Braz, "The Modern Hiawatha: Grey Owl's Construction of His Aboriginal Self," in *Auto/biography in Canada*, ed. Julie Rak (Waterloo, ON: Wilfrid Laurier University Press, 2005), 53–68; Armand G. Ruffo, *Grey Owl: The Mystery of Archie Belaney* (Regina: Coteau, 1996).

12 David Chapin, "Gender and Indian Masquerade in the Life of Grey Owl," *American Indian Quarterly* 24, 1 (Winter 2000): 91–109.

13 Marjorie Garber, *Vested Interests: Cross-Dressing and Cultural Anxiety* (New York: Routledge, 1992), 10–11.

14 Deloria, *Indians in Unexpected Places*, 3–14.

15 Biographies of Grey Owl include: Lovat Dickson, *Half-Breed: The Story of Grey Owl* (London: Macmillan, 1939); Anahareo, *My Life with Grey Owl* (London: Peter Davies, 1940); Anahareo, *Grey Owl and I: A New Autobiography* (Toronto: New Press, 1972); Donald B. Smith, *From the Land of Shadows: the Making of Grey Owl* (Saskatoon: Western Producer Prairie Books, 1990); Ruffo, *Grey Owl*.

16 Bird, "Savage Desires," 76.

17 For further discussion of Indigenous stereotypes in popular culture see: Francis, *Imaginary Indian*; Scott Vickers, *Native American Identities: From Stereotype to Archetype in Art and Literature* (Albuquerque: University of New Mexico Press, 1998).

18 Shari Huhndorf, *Going Native: Indians in the American Cultural Imagination*. (Ithaca, NY: Cornell University Press, 2001).

19 Francis, *Imaginary Indian*, 123–131.

20 Ibid.

21 The story played out over many days in the Regina *Leader-Post* but also made national news on the CTV and CBC television networks.

22 Huhndorf, *Going Native*, 19

23 Ibid., 20.

24 Regina *Leader-Post*, 16 April 1938.

25 Saskatoon *Star Phoenix*, 14 April 1938.

26 For a biography of Tootoosis, see Jean Cuthand Goodwill and Norma Sluman, *John Tootoosis: Biography of a Cree Leader* (Ottawa: Golden Dog Press, 1982).

27 Historian Donald Smith's biography provides a good account of Grey Owl's youth. See Donald Smith, *From the Land of Shadows: the Making of Grey Owl* (Saskatoon: Western Producer Prairie Books, 1990).

28 Smith, *Land of Shadows*, 89.

29 Ibid., 89–91.

30 Ibid., 89.

31 Ibid.

32 Ruffo, *Grey Owl*, 77–78.

33 Smith, *Land of Shadows*, 91.

34 Anahareo, *Devil in Deerskins*, 143–145.

35 Smith, *Land of Shadows*, 110–113.

36 For a discussion of the period and geographic location surrounding the North-West Rebellion, see Stonechild and Waiser, *Loyal till Death*.

37 See Chapter 3 for a discussion of the press coverage of the 1885 North-West Rebellion. See also Dickason, *Canada's First Nations*, 285–298.

38 For a case study of a northern Saskatchewan Cree community near Prince Albert, Saskatchewan, see Maggie Siggins, *Bitter Embrace: White Society's Assault on the Woodland Cree* (Toronto: McClelland and Steward, 2005).

39 Goodwill and Sluman, *John Tootoosis*, 153–232.

40 Regina *Leader-Post*, 2 November 1936.

41 Ibid.

42 Throughout his life John Tootoosis was more likely to sport a cowboy hat than braids and an eagle feather (see photos of Tootoosis in the biography by Goodwill and Sluman), although a 1948 photograph of him in the Regina *Leader-Post* where he was dressed in a beaded buckskin outfit and feather headdress to commemorate his re-election as Grand Chief of the Federation of Saskatchewan Indian Nations reads more like the Grey Owl images. Regina *Leader-Post*, 11 August 1948.

43 Goodwill and Sluman, *John Tootoosis*, 167.

44 Ibid., 168.

45 Ibid.

46 Ibid., 153–232.

47 Regina *Leader-Post*, 2 November 1936.

48 Examples include: Fredericton *Daily Gleaner* 14 April 1938; Lethbridge *Herald*, 13 April 1938; Ottawa *Citizen*, 13 April 1938; Saskatoon *Star Phoenix*, April 13, 1938; St. John *Telegraph-Journal*, 14 April 1938; Sudbury *Star*, 13 April 1938; Windsor *Daily Star*, 13 April 1938.

49 Lethbridge *Herald*, 13 April 1938.

50 Fredericton *Daily Gleaner*, 14 April 1938; Lethbridge *Herald*, 13 April 1938.

51 Ottawa *Citizen*, 13 April 1938.

52 Ibid.

53 Windsor *Daily Star*, 13 April 1938; Sudbury *Star*, 13 April 1938; Hamilton *Spectator*, 13 April 1938.

54 Ottawa *Citizen*, 14 April 1938.

55 Hamilton *Spectator*, 14 April 1938.

56 Windsor *Daily Star*, 14 April 1938.

57 Winnipeg *Free Press*, 15 April 1938.

58 Edmonton *Journal*, 14 April 1938.

59 Ibid.

60 Vancouver *Province*, 14 April 1938.

61 For discussions of Disney's Pocahontas and stereotypes, see Lauren Dundes, "Disney's modern heroine Pocahontas: revealing age-old gender stereotypes and role discontinuity under a façade of liberation," *Social Science Journal* 38, 3 (2001): 353–365; G. Edgerton and K. Jackson, "Redesigning Pocahontas: Disney, the 'Whiteman's Indian,' and the Marketing of Dreams," *Journal of Popular Film and Television* 24, 2 (1996): 90–98; Celeste Lacroix, "Images of Animated Others: The Orientalization of Disney's Cartoon Heroines From The Little Mermaid to The Hunchback of Notre Dame," *Popular Communication* 2, 4 (2004): 213–229; Ziauddin Sadar, "Walt Disney and the Double Victimization of Pocahontas," *Third Text* 10, 37 (1996): 17–26.

62 Prince Albert *Daily Herald*, 13 April 1938.

63 Saskatoon *Star Phoenix*, 13 April 1938.

64 Ibid.

65 Ibid.

66 Ibid.

67 Ibid.

68 Ibid.

69 Saskatoon *Star Phoenix*, 14 April 1938.

70 Prince Albert *Daily Herald*, 14 April 1938.

71 No further connection with Grey Owl beyond the meeting in Ottawa is mentioned in Tootoosis's biography. Papers outside of Saskatchewan made no mention of any concrete Indigenous leadership role assumed by Grey Owl, though a number of references to him being a "warrior" and a "protector" were stressed in news reports.

72 Saskatoon *Star Phoenix*, 14 April 1938.

73 Ibid.

74 Regina *Leader-Post*, 16 April 1938.

75 Ibid.

76 North Bay *Nugget*, 13 April 1938.

77 Windsor *Daily Star*, 19 April 1938; Toronto *Star*, 14 April 1938; Sudbury *Star*, 18 April 1938; Toronto *Star*, 18 April 1938; Toronto *Star*, 20 April 1938; Windsor *Daily Star*, 25 April 1938; Sudbury *Star*, 20 April 1938.

78 Prince Albert *Daily Herald*, 14 April 1938.

79 Saskatoon *Star Phoenix*, 16 April 1938.

80 Ibid.

81 Ibid.

82 Saskatoon *Star Phoenix*, 18 April 1938.

83 Braz refers to Grey Owl as the modern Hiawatha because he modeled himself on Longfellow's poetic character from his epic poem, "The Song of Hiawatha," Braz, "Hiawatha," 54.

84 Toronto *Star*, 19 April 1938.

85 Ibid.

86 Regina *Leader-Post*, 20 April 1938.

87 Ibid.

88 Regina *Leader-Post*, 30 July 1938.

89 Prince Albert *Daily Herald*, 20 April 1938.

90 Ibid.

91 Ibid.

92 See, for example, Saskatoon *Star Phoenix*, 20 April 1938; Saskatoon *Star Phoenix*, 21 April 1938; Saskatoon *Star Phoenix*, 22 April 1938.

93 Saskatoon *Star Phoenix*, 23 April 1938.

94 Regina *Leader-Post*, 25 April 1938.

95 Ibid.

96 Calgary *Herald*, 21 April 1938.

97 Ibid.

98 St. John *Telegraph-Journal*, 26 April 1938.

99 Ibid.

100 Smith, *Land of Shadows*, 214.

101 Regina *Leader-Post*, 9 May 1938.

102 See Parks Canada website for information and a history of Grey Owl's contributions at Prince Albert National Park, http://www.pc.gc.ca/pn-np/sk/princealbert/natcul/natcul1_c_e.asp (accessed 1 May 2009).

103 Pratt made the claim at an 1892 convention. See Pratt, *Advantages*, 260.

CHAPTER SEVEN: *"Potential Indian Citizens?"*

1 We use the term First Nations in this context to identify the status Indians who fought in the war. No records were kept of other Aboriginal enlistments.

2 There is no complete extant account of First Nations experiences in wars and as veterans. See Dickason, *Canada's First Nations*; Miller, *Skyscrapers*.

3 Sheffield, *Warpath*.

4 Ibid., 180.

5 Miller, *Skyscrapers*, 324.

6 Dickason, *Canada's First Nations*, 310–312.

7 Sheffield, *Warpath*, 128–148.

8 Dickason, *Canada's First Nations*, 310–312.

9 Montreal *Gazette*, 16 August 1948.

10 Regina *Leader-Post*, 30 September 1948.

11 Sheffield, *Warpath*, 30–33.

12 Regina *Leader-Post*, 14 August 1948.

13 Sheffield, *Warpath*, 178.

14 Regina *Leader-Post*, 23 September 1948.

15 See Doug Cuthand, "Aboriginal Veterans Were Left On Their Own," Regina *Leader-Post*, 12 November 2002; "Fewer and Fewer Veterans Still Around," Regina *Leader-Post*, 22 November 2004; "First Nations Veterans Made Huge Contributions," Saskatoon *Star Phoenix*, 11 November 2005.

16 See Haycock, *Canadian Indian*.

17 Goodwill and Sluman, *John Tootoosis*, 192.

18 Laurie Meijer Drees, *The Indian Association of Alberta: A History of Political Action* (Vancouver: University of British Columbia Press, 2002), 6–7.

19   Robert Innes, "Socio-political Influence of the Second World War: Saskatchewan Aboriginal Veterans, 1945–1960," MA thesis, University of Saskatchewan, 2002.

20   Robert Innes, "'I'm on Home Ground Now. I'm Safe.' Saskatchewan Aboriginal Veterans in the Immediate Postwar Years, 1945–1946," *American Indian Quarterly* 28, 3–4 (2004): 645–718.

21   Innes, "I'm on Home Ground," 706.

22   Ibid.

23   Alison Bernstein, *Toward a New Era in Indian Affairs: American Indians and World War II* (Norman: University of Oklahoma Press, 1991).

24   Ibid., 175.

25   Guy Debord, *Society of the Spectacle*, trans. Ken Knabb (Oakland: AK Press, 2006), 8.

26   Sudbury *Star*, 30 July 1948.

27   Toronto *Globe and Mail*, 6 July 1948.

28   Montreal *Gazette*, 23 August 1948.

29   Winnipeg *Free Press*, 21 September 1948.

30   Vancouver *Province*, 30 September 1948.

31   Toronto *Globe and Mail*, 4 August 1948.

32   Ibid.

33   See, for example, Toronto *Globe and Mail*, 2 August 1948; Montreal *Gazette*, 18 August 1948; Montreal *Gazette*, 25 September 1948.

34   See Peter C. Rollins and John E. O'Connor, eds. *Hollywood's Indians: The Portrayal of the Native American in Film* (Lexingtion: University of Kentucky Press, 2003).

35   St. John's *Evening Telegram*, 29 September 1948; Montreal *Gazette*, 21 August 1948; Calgary *Herald*, 20 August 1948.

36   Calgary *Herald*, 20 August 1948.

37   Winnipeg *Free Press*, 16 September 1948; Regina *Leader-Post*, 21 September 1948; Halifax *Herald*, 22 September 1948.

38   Innes, "I'm on Home Ground," 703.

39   Halifax *Herald*, 22 September 1948.

40   Calgary *Herald*, 2 September 1948; Montreal *Gazette*, 21 September 1948; Sudbury *Star*, 24 September 1948; St. John's *Evening Telegram*, 27 September 1948.

41   See Seed, *Ceremonies*.

42   Calgary *Herald*, 2 September 1948.

43   Calgary *Herald*, 2 September 1948.

44   Vancouver *Province*, 20 August 1948.

45   Ibid.

46   Calgary *Herald*, 23 August 1948. Five days later, the Sudbury *Star* printed the CP wire service story on their editorial page. See the Sudbury *Star*, 28 August 1948.

47   For an overview of the formation of Aboriginal leadership groups see Dickason, *Canada's First Nations*, 309–310; Harold Cardinal, "Hat in Hand: The Long Fight to Organize," in Miller, ed. *Sweet Promises*, 393–401.

48   Sheffield, *Warpath*, 163.

49   Miller, *Skyscrapers*, 301–304.

50   Dickason, *Canada's First Nations*, 414–415.

51   Montreal *Gazette*, 4 February 1993; Toronto *Globe and Mail*, 6 February 1996. Also see Regina *Leader-Post*, 19 November 2002; Charlottetown *Guardian*, 12 December 2002.

52   St. John's *Evening Telegram*, 10 September 1948.

53   Calgary *Herald*, 31 August 1948; Winnipeg *Free Press*, 16 September 1948. A Sudbury *Star*'s editorial argued that it is not the food but the lack of food provided to James Bay Indians that was to blame for the poor health levels. Sudbury *Star*, 31 July 1948.

54   Sudbury *Star*, 30 July 1948; Edmonton *Journal*, 14 September 1948.

55   Victoria *Times Colonist*, 29 September 1948.

56   Ibid.

57   Toronto *Globe and Mail*, 17 August 1948; Montreal *Gazette*, 18 August 1948; Fredericton *Daily Gleaner*, 30 September 1948.

58   Miller, *Skyscrapers*, 302.

59   Montreal *Gazette*, 18 August 1948.

60   Sheffield, *Warpath*, 62–64.

61   Toronto *Star*, 27 August 1948.

62   Sudbury *Star*, 25 August 1948.

63   Sudbury *Star*, 13 August 1948. Sheffield notes that Indian lists were also common in Alberta. See Sheffield, *Warpath*, 64.

64   Regina *Leader-Post*, 14 August 1948.

65   Toronto *Globe and Mail*, 27 September 1948; Montreal *Gazette*, 28 September 1948; Sudbury *Star*, 27 September 1948.

66   Toronto *Globe and Mail*, 27 September 1948.

67   Sudbury *Star*, 3 August 1948.

68   Toronto *Globe and Mail*, 27 September 1948.

69   Ibid.

70   The Sudbury *Star*'s proximity to the trial and murder scene suggests that readers had a stronger interest in this case. As a result the Sudbury *Star* printed five reports on this case between 30 July and 30 September 1948. "Rivers Verdict Due Today, Ojibway Indian, 20, Denies Slaying Sister-in-Law After Drinking Bout in Blind River Hotel," Sudbury *Star*, 29 September 1948.

71   Toronto *Globe and Mail*, 30 September 1948.

72   Toronto *Globe and Mail*, 24 September 1948.

73   Toronto *Star*, 7 August 1948; Sudbury *Star*, 9 August 1948. A follow-up story regarding a trial date for Hill was published in the Sudbury *Star*, 17 August 1948.

74   Toronto *Star*, 7 August 1948.

75   Toronto *Globe and Mail*, 31 July 1948.

76   Fredericton *Daily Gleaner*, 3 August 1948.

77   Toronto *Globe and Mail*, 31 July 1948.

78   Ibid.

79   Ibid.

80   Edmonton *Journal*, 9 August 1948.

81   The headline straddles two columns of page ten but the other story encapsulated by the headline was a lighthearted report where youngsters at a park in Edmonton dressed up in costumes and played Indian for the day. Edmonton *Journal*, 9 August 1948.

82   Sudbury *Star*, 18 September 1948; Vancouver *Province*, 17 September 1948.

83   Sudbury *Star*, 18 September 1948.

84   SJC Minutes and Proceedings no. 5, 13 April to 21 June 1948, p. 187; rpt. in Sheffield, *Warpath*, 172.

85   Edmonton *Journal*, 16 September 1948.

86   Ottawa *Citizen*, 24 September 1948.

CHAPTER EIGHT: Cardboard Characters

1   Adrienne Clarkson, 7 October 1999; rpt. in Fleras and Elliott, *Unequal Relations*, 348.

2   Though beyond the scope of this study, a recent text by Mohawk scholar Taiaiake Alfred outlines Indigenous paths of action for self-governance, a process that requires close consideration of the complexities inherent in notions of citizenship for Aboriginals in Canada. See Taiaiake Alfred, *Wasáse: Indigenous Pathways of Action and Freedom* (Peterborough: Broadview Press, 2005).

3   Aboriginal peoples, made up of Indian, Inuit, and Métis people, are recognized officially in section 35 of the Constitution Act of 1982.

4   Joyce Green, "Canaries in the Mines of Citizenship: Indian Women in Canada," *Canadian Journal of Political Science* 34, 4 (2001): 719.

5   Miller, *Skyscrapers*, 333. Also see Dickason, *Canada's First Nations*, 377–179. The White Paper document is available at http://ainc-inac.net/ai/arp/ls/pubs/cp1969/cp1969-eng. pdf (accessed 30 May 2009).

6   See Carmen Robertson, "Trickster in the Press," *Media History* 14, 1 (2008): 72–93.

7   The Halifax *Chronicle* and Halifax *Herald* merged in 1949. See Kesterton, *History*, 109.

8   Karen Froman discusses the role of Indigenous humour in an academic context. See Karen Froman, "Buffalo Tales and Academic Trails," in Drew Hayden Taylor, ed., *Me Funny* (Vancouver: Douglas and McIntyre, 2005): 133–144.

9   See Miller, *Skyscrapers*.

10   Dickason, *Canada's First Nations*, 376–377.

11   Sally Weaver's comprehensive study of the historical events about the ways the White Paper was developed provides an excellent analysis of this contentious period. Sally Weaver, *Making Canadian Indian Policy: The Hidden Agenda, 1968–70* (Toronto: University of Toronto Press, 1981).

12   See Thomas Axworthy and Pierre Trudeau, *Towards a Just Society* (Markham, ON: Viking, 1990); Kevin J. Christiano, "Federalism as a Canadian National Ideal: The Civic Rationalism of Pierre Elliott Trudeau," *Dalhousie Review* 69, 2 (Summer 1989): 248–52.

13   Printed in Harold Cardinal, *The Unjust Society* (Edmonton: Hurtig Publishers, 1969), 28.

14   Weaver, *Making*, 54.

15   Joanne Barker, "Gender, Sovereignty, and the Discourse of Rights," *Meridians: Feminism, Race, Transnationalism* 7, 1 (2006): 134.

16   The American Indian Movement (AIM) was co-founded by Anishinaabe activists Mary Jane Wilson, Clyde Bellecourt, and Dennis Banks in Minneapolis and advocated "Red Power" as other groups pushed "Black Power" and feminism. See Timothy Baylor, "Modern Warriors: Mobilization and Decline of the American Indian Movement (AIM) 1969–1979," PhD diss., University of North Carolina, Chapel Hill, 1994.

17   See Cardinal, *Unjust Society*.

18   Donald Purich, "The Future of Native Rights," in Miller, ed., *Sweet Promises* 424.

19   Peter McFarlane, *Brotherhood to Nationhood* (Toronto: Between The Lines, 1993), 102.

20   An address by Jean Chrétien to the Indian-Eskimo Association, 20 September 1968, rpt. in McFarlane, *Brotherhood to Nationhood*, 108.

21   McFarlane, *Brotherhood to Nationhood*, 103.

22   Toronto *Star*, 26 June 1969; Toronto *Star*, 26 June 1969; Ottawa *Citizen*, 26 June 1969; Toronto *Daily Star*, 26 June 1969; Toronto *Globe and Mail*, 26 June 1969; Calgary *Herald*, 25 June 1969; Halifax *Chronicle-Herald*, 26 June 1969.

23   Ottawa *Citizen*, 26 June 1969; Winnipeg *Free Press*, 26 June 1969. See also Calgary *Herald*, 26 June 1969; Calgary *Herald*, 25 June 1969; Toronto *Globe and Mail*, 26 June 1969; Toronto *Daily Star*; Edmonton *Journal*, 26 June 1969; Edmonton *Journal*, 26 June 1969; Halifax *Chronicle Herald*, 26 June 1969; *Telegraph-Journal*, 26 June 1969; Montreal *Gazette*, 26 June 1969; Regina *Leader-Post*, 26 June 1969; Vancouver *Province*, 27 June 1969; Victoria *Daily Colonist*, 26 June 1969; Fredericton *Daily Gleaner*, 27 June 1969; Sudbury *Star*, 27 June 1969.

24   See St. John *Telegraph-Journal*, 26 June 1969; Toronto *Star*, 26 June 1969; Sudbury *Star*, 26 June 1969.

25   Kahn Tineta-Horn is described as a former Indian model who has become an outspoken champion of traditional Indian rights. Toronto *Globe and Mail*, 26 June 1969.

26   A common spelling for Mohawk community of Kanesatake near Montreal, Quebec, was not in place in 1969 in the press. We have preserved press usage within all quotations.

27   Montreal *Gazette*, 26 June 1969.

28   Toronto *Globe and Mail*, 26 June 1969.

29   Winnipeg *Free Press*, 26 June 1969.

30   The Toronto *Globe and Mail* reported that the federal Opposition spokesman Progressive Conservative G.W. Baldwin welcomed this new policy, though he noted there was bound to be some apprehension about it. Toronto *Globe and Mail*, 26 June 1969.

31   Toronto *Star*, 25 June 1969.

32   Sudbury *Star*, 27 June 1969.

33   Toronto *Star*, 26 June 1969.

34   Ibid.

35   Toronto *Globe and Mail*, 5 July 1969.

36   Montreal *Gazette*, 8 July 1969.

37   Calgary *Herald*, 7 July 1969.

38   Charlottetown *Guardian*, 5 July 1969. See also Vancouver *Province*, 27 June 1969; Calgary *Herald*, 26 June 1969; Vancouver *Province*, 9 July 1969.

39   Halifax *Chronicle-Herald*, 8 July 1969.

40   See Fredericton *Daily Gleaner*, 12 July 1969; Halifax *Chronicle-Herald*, 15 July 1969; Fredericton *Daily Gleaner*, 8 August 1969.

41   Fredericton *Daily Gleaner*, 30 July 1969.

42   Winnipeg *Free Press*, 17 July 1969.

43 Montreal *Gazette*, 16 July 1969. A letter expressing similar sentiments was published in the Edmonton *Journal* on 8 July 1969.

44 Toronto *Globe and Mail*, 4 July 1969.

45 Ibid.

46 Letter to the editor, "Indians Protest," Chief Harold Sappier, Fredericton *Daily-Gleaner*, 10 July 1969. Sappier wrote another letter to the editor on 16 July 1969 that also received the headline, "Indians Protest." In it he took exception to a local store's advertisement that read, "Come Barter With The Indians," arguing, "Indians do not like to have our customs and culture exploited."

47 Edmonton *Journal*, 4 July 1969.

48 Edmonton *Journal*, 9 July 1969.

49 Victoria *Daily Colonist*, 15 July 1969.

50 Victoria *Daily Colonist*, 25 July 1969.

51 Sudbury *Star*, 2 July 1969.

52 Montreal *Gazette*, 7 July 1969.

53 Toronto *Star*, 13 August 1969.

54 Fredericton *Daily Gleaner*, 30 July 1969.

55 The NIB embraced and adopted the Red Paper, written by Harold Cardinal, on 3 June 1970.

56 Regina *Leader-Post*, 9 June 1970.

57 Edmonton *Journal*, 5 June 1970.

58 Calgary *Herald*, 8 June 1970; Vancouver *Province*, 8 June 1970.

59 St. John's *Evening Telegram*, 5 June 1970.

60 Regina *Leader-Post*, 9 June 1970. Also see an editorial in the Toronto *Star*, 6 June 1970.

61 Regina *Leader-Post*, 4 June 1970.

62 Toronto *Star*, 27 November 1971.

63 William Wuttunee, *Ruffled Feathers, Indians in Canadian Society* (Calgary: Bell Books, 1971).

64 Toronto *Star*, 27 November 1971.

65 "Indians Create, Perpetuate Their Own Problems, Cree Lawyer-Author Charges," Halifax *Chronicle-Herald*, 27 November 1971.

66 St. John *Telegraph-Journal*, 13 December 1971.

67 Ibid.

68 Halifax *Chronicle-Herald*, 26 October 1971.

69 Ibid.

70 Octavio Paz, *The Labyrinth of Solitude: The Other Mexico, Return to the Labyrinth of Solitude, Mexico and the United States, the Philanthropic Ogre* (New York: Grove Press, 1994).

71 Peter Desbarats, *Guide to Canadian News Media* (Toronto: Harcourt Brace, 1996), 9; Kevin G. Barnhurst and John Nerone, "Journalism History," *Handbook of Journalism Studies*, ed. Wahl-Jorgensen and Hanitzsch, 24.

72 Regina *Leader-Post*, 27 June 1970.

73 Regina *Leader-Post*, 27 June 1970.

74 Toronto *Star*, 5 November 1971.

75 Toronto *Star*, 30 December 1971.

76 St. John *Telegraph-Journal*, 15 October 1971; Charlottetown *Guardian*, 8 October 1971; Charlottetown *Guardian*, 18 October 1971; Victoria *Daily Colonist*, 10 November 1971; Charlottetown *Guardian*, 11 November 1971; Vancouver *Province*, 29 November 1971; Vancouver *Province*, 13 December 1971; St. John *Telegraph-Journal*, 18 December 1971; Victoria *Daily Colonist*, 18 December 1971.

77 Toronto *Globe and Mail*, 24 February 2009. In 2002 then Pime Minister Jean Chrétien attempted to push through the First Nations Governance Act despite vocal opposition from the Assembly of First Nations (AFN). Then-AFN president Matthew Coon Come characterized it as another attempt to 'solve' the Indian Act. The bill failed. For a more complete account of ongoing federal negotiations concerning the Indian Act, see Julian Beltrame, 'Chrétien Promises to Help Aboriginals,' *Maclean's*, 14 October 2002 (115): 17–18.

CHAPTER NINE: Bended Elbow News

1 The Ojibway Warrior Society, alternatively known as the Ojibwa Warrior/Warriors Society, was led by Louis Cameron. According to Cameron, the organization had its roots in traditional culture. The group acted independently from the area chiefs of Ground Council Treaty Three, which encompasses much of northwestern Ontario. Cameron explained the Warrior Society did not want to compete with the efforts of the Grand Council but rather its mandate was to "bring unity to the Indians." *Canadian Dimension* 10, 5 (November 1974): 34.

2 See Mark Cronlund Anderson and Carmen L. Robertson. "The 'Bended Elbow' News, Kenora, 1974, How a Small-Town Newspaper Promoted Colonialism," *American Indian Quarterly* 31, 3 (2007): 1–29.

3 The original peoples of northwestern Ontario have been accorded many labels. For example, in the Kenora *Miner and News* they are referred to as Indians, Natives, Ojibway, Ojibwe, and/or Ojibwa. Ojibwe has been adopted as the correct form of spelling by the Ojibwe Cultural Foundation of Manitoulin Island. See http://www.ojibweculture.ca/ (accessed 19 May 2010). Those who encountered the Ojibwe at the time of contact found their dialect impenetrable and could not agree on the name or spelling. Some said Ojibway, others Chippewa. In their first language the original people translates as Anishinaabe. The spelling of this term takes on many forms also, including Anicinabe, Anishnabe, and Anishinabe. See E. Benton-Banai, *The Mishomis Book: The Voice of the Ojibway* (Hayward WI: Indian Country Communications, 1988).

4 Dickason, *Canada's First Nations*, 383.

5 See Rollins and O'Connor, *Hollywood's Indian*.

6 A policy was established in early November 1973 that kept the *Miner and News* at a minimum of eight daily pages. See the Kenora *Miner and News*, 3 November 1973.

7 While Kenora is located in Ontario roughly forty miles east of the Manitoba border, it devoted heavy coverage to the West, especially Winnipeg, the nearest large urban center, located 140 miles away (by contrast, Thunder Bay lies 350 miles to the east of Kenora).

8 Bowes Publishers Ltd. owned the *Miner and News*. However, the avowed policy of the paper championed local editorial autonomy. See Kenora *Miner and News*, 3 November 1973.

9   Anastasia M. Shkilnyk, *A Poison Stronger than Love* (New Haven: Yale University Press, 1985).

10   The centripetal cultural imperative to naturalize cultural constructions may be identified as basic Gramscian hegemony at work, where the imperial agent embodies the normative and assumes the right to impugn and punish the Other. See Said, *Covering Islam*; and Hall, *Representation*. Also see Said, *Orientalism*; Said, *Culture and Imperialism*.

11   See Devon Mihesuah, *American Indians: Stereotypes and Realities* (Atlanta: Clarity Press, 2001). Also see Johnson, *Latin America*; Fredrick Pike, *The United States and Latin America, Myths and Stereotypes of Civilization and Nature* (Austin: University of Texas Press, 1991).

12   See Coward, *Newspaper Indian*; Weston, *Native Americans in the News*.

13   See, for example, Mihesuah, *American Indians*.

14   Fourteen issues of the Kenora *Miner and News* from the summer of 1974 (i.e., covering May-September) are not available on microfilm or in the newspaper's bound collection that otherwise dates back without interruption for nearly a century. Many of these missing issues date from the height of the standoff (e.g., 9-12 and 14-18 July). The authors received two versions of what happened to the missing issues. When we visited the newspaper's Kenora office we were told that the missing bound volume had been stolen. Yet, later by phone, officials at the Kenora *Miner and News* claimed that, because of a change in ownership at the paper during the summer of 1974, a cost-cutting decision had been taken to not bind the daily publication for a period of three months. Yet this latter claim makes little sense because the paper did not, in fact, change hands at that time (the sale had taken place the year before). Meanwhile, while the Kenora Public Library maintains a file on the seizure and standoff at the park it is neither lengthy nor comprehensive. The Kenora Public Museum keeps no copies from that period. In an effort to obtain samples of the missing copies the authors ran an advertisement in the classified section of the newspaper for two months, which turned up nothing.

15   See Carlos E. Cortes, *The Children Are Watching*, 146–151.

16   Kenora *Miner and News*, 25 March 1974.

17   Kenora *Miner and News*, 13 June 1974.

18   Kenora *Miner and News* insert, "Visitors Guide," 8 July 1974.

19   To cite one of many occasions, in early July in a discussion of Treaty 3, which had been signed in 1873, the paper recorded: "The Indians, always noted for their eloquence, clearly loved the country. See Kenora *Miner and News*, 8 July 1974.

20   See Kenora *Miner and News*, 3 January 1974.

21   Kenora *Miner and News*, 7 January 1974.

22   Kenora *Miner and News*, 14 June 1974.

23   Kenora *Miner and News*, "Court docket." 19 March 1974.

24   See, for example, "Happenings in provincial court," Kenora *Miner and News*, 31 July 1974; "Man found guilty of rape," Kenora *Miner and News*, 1 August 1974; "Man gets five years on rape conviction," Kenora *Miner and News*, 26 August 1974; "Two Whitedog Indians found guilty," Kenora *Miner and News*, 27 August 1974; "Kenora provincial court, Teenager gets nine months," Kenora *Miner and News*, 12 September 1974; "Court docket," Kenora *Miner and News*, 16 September 1974; "Man sentenced to 18 months," Kenora *Miner and News*, 17 October 1974.

25   Kenora *Miner and News*, 10 May 1974.

26   Kenora *Miner and News*, 7 January 1974.

27   Kenora *Miner and News*, 10 January 1974.

28   Kenora *Miner and News*, 15 March 1974.

29   Kenora *Miner and News*, 23 April 1974. For other examples of the local press alleging inveterate Indigenous alcoholism, see Kenora *Miner and News*, 14 February 1974; Kenora *Miner and News*, 4 March 1974.

30   Ibid.

31   Relatedly, Vickers identifies the noble savage this way: "Childlike race in need of paternalistic guidance, self-improvement, education, civilization, conversion and/or patronization." See Vickers, *Native American Identities*, 4.

32   "Children and adults of all ages quietly nodded to one another in astonishment and approval as they watched the dancers and drummers really become involved in the magic reality that is the pow wow." Kenora *Miner and News*, 19 February 1974.

33   See, for example, Kenora *Miner and News*, 4 March 1974; Kenora *Miner and News*, 18 February 1974; Kenora *Miner and News*, 19 February 1974.

34   See Kenora *Miner and News*, 4 January 1974.

35   Kenora *Miner and News*, 5 March 1974.

36   See, for example, Kenora *Miner and News*, 19 February 1974; Kenora *Miner and News*, 25 July 1974; Kenora *Miner and News*, 9 August 1974.

37   See, for example, Kenora *Miner and News*, 7 January 1974; Kenora *Miner and News*, 11 February 1974; Kenora *Miner and News*, 2 April 1974; Kenora *Miner and News*, 21 May 1974.

38   Kenora *Miner and News*, 15 March 1974.

39   Kenora *Miner and News* 1 April 1974

40   Kenora *Miner and News*, 8 May 1974.

41   Kenora *Miner and News*, 3 June 1974.

42   Letter to the editor, Kenora *Miner and News*, 27 June 1974.

43   Jacobson's vituperative and hate-filled manifesto was published in 1975 and written as a direct response to the temporary park seizure in 1974. It employs nearly every negative stereotype of Aboriginals imaginable. Central to its claims are that, first, whites (and not Aboriginals) have long suffered racial discrimination; second, that Indigenous peoples are lazy, no-good drunkards by nature; and third, that they wallow in filth. While she provides no rational evidence to substantiate her claims, the book recapitulates and stresses the most pejorative of the many characteristics of the Native *qua* colonial Other and closely resonates with colonialized press imagery of Indigenous peoples elsewhere. See Eleanor Jacobson, *Bended Elbow, Kenora Talks Back* (Kenora: Central Publications, 1975).

44   Shkilnyk, *Poison*, 125.

45   Letter to the editor, Kenora *Miner and News*, 2 July 1974.

46   "Visitors Guide," Kenora *Miner and News*, 8 July 1974.

47   See Seed, *Ceremonies*.

48   "Visitors Guide," Kenora *Miner and News*, 8 July 1974.

49   Ibid.

50   Ibid.

51   "Guest Editorial," by William Laffin," Kenora *Miner and News*, 19 July 1974.

52 Ibid.

53 Kenora *Miner and News*, 19 July 1974.

54 Kenora *Miner and News*, 22 July 1974.

55 Kenora *Miner and News*, 23 July 1974.

56 Ibid.

57 Kenora *Miner and News*, 9 January 1974. Also see Kenora *Miner and News*, 14 February 1974; Kenora *Miner and News*, 4 March 1974.

58 For example, see "150 Indians occupy Anicinabe park," Kenora *Miner and News*, 23 July 1974; Kenora *Miner and News*, 24 July 1974; "Sessions held over protest," Kenora *Miner and News*, 24 July 1974; "Indian issue talks underway," Kenora *Miner and News*, 25 July 1974; "Warriors prepare for lengthy siege," Kenora *Miner and News*, 29 July 1974.

59 Kenora *Miner and News*, 23 July 1974.

60 Kenora *Miner and News*, 30 July 1974.

61 Kenora *Miner and News*, 23 July 1974.

62 Kenora *Miner and News*, 22 July 1974.

63 See Kenora *Miner and News*, 24 July 1974. See also the photographic essay in Kenora *Miner and News*, 24 July 1974.

64 Kenora *Miner and News*, 24 July 1974.

65 Indian activism in North America in the early 1970s had important roots in AIM, organized in Minneapolis in 1968. Originally the group comprised mostly Chippewa or Ojibwe, though it quickly became a national voice for Native people. AIM achieved notoriety with its 1972 march on the Bureau of Indian Affairs offices in Washington, D.C. The bloody 1973 events at Wounded Knee on the Pine Ridge in South Dakota gave AIM the reputation of being a volatile force in Indian country. See Paul Chaat Smith and Robert Allen Warrior, *Like a Hurricane: The Indian Movement from Alcatraz to Wounded Knee* (New York: New Press, 1996).

66 Kenora *Miner and News*, 26 July 1974.

67 Kenora *Miner and News*, 24 July 1974.

68 Letter to the editor, Kenora *Miner and News*, 26 July 1974.

69 Ibid.

70 Ibid.

71 Ken Nelson, "Leader vows he won't leave park," Kenora *Miner and News*, 25 July 1974.

72 Ibid.

73 Ken Nelson, "Indian talks resume," Kenora *Miner and News*, 26 July 1974.

74 An editorial in the Toronto *Globe and Mail* began: "We have had more than time enough in Canada to learn how grossly we have failed to deal decently and honorably with the Indian people." See the Toronto *Globe and Mail*, 7 July 1974; Winnipeg *Free Press*, 25 July 1974. Also see Kenora *Miner and News*, 25 July 1974; Kenora *Miner and News*, 21 July 1974; Kenora *Miner and News*, 12 August 1974; Kenora *Miner and News*, 16 August 1974; Kenora *Miner and News*, 13 September 1974.

75 Kenora *Miner and News*, 31 July 1974.

76 Kenora *Miner and News*, 12 August 1974.

77 Letter to the editor, 26 August 1974. In the "Letters to the editor" section also see, for example, "Time to end hand-outs to Indians, Kenora *Miner and News*, 31 July 1974; "We don't owe Indians anything," Kenora *Miner and News*, 1 August 1974; Letter to the editor, Kenora *Miner and News*, 15 August 1974; "Where's all the law and order?" Kenora *Miner and News*, 16 August 1974; Letter to the editor, Kenora *Miner and News*, 22 August 1974; "Poem: Heap Big Smoke, with fire," Kenora *Miner and News*, 27 August 1974; "Taxpayers shouldn't support Indians," Kenora *Miner and News*, 29 August 1974; Letter to the editor, Kenora *Miner and News*, 6 September 1974, "Reader wants truth from Cameron," Kenora *Miner and News*, 10 September 1974; Letter to the editor, Kenora *Miner and News*, 12 September 1974.

78 Kenora *Miner and News*, 18 September 1974.

79 Kenora *Miner and News*, 24 September 1974. Also see Kenora *Miner and News*, 2 October 1974.

80 Kenora *Miner and News*, 22 August 1974.

81 Kenora *Miner and News*, 4 September 1974.

82 Letter to the editor, Kenora *Miner and News*, 6 September 1974.

83 Kenora *Miner and News*, 1 August 1974.

84 Kenora *Miner and News*, 3 December 1974. Also see Kenora *Miner and News*, 4 December 1974.

85 Kenora *Miner and News*, 25 September 1974.

86 Kenora *Miner and News*, 2 August 1974.

87 Ibid.

88 Ibid.

CHAPTER TEN: *Indian Princess/Indian "Squaw"*

1 Green, "Canaries in the Mines of Citizenship," 715–738.

2 For a comprehensive bibliography related to Bill C-31 analysis, see *A Select and Annotated Bibliography Regarding Bill C-31, Indian Registration, and Band Membership, Aboriginal Identity, Women and Gender Issues* (Ottawa: AINC/INAC, 2004).

3 B.C. resident Sharon McIvor challenged Bill C-31 as sexist in 1989. In 2009 the case was heard in the B.C. Supreme Court. The court supported McIvor and in August 2009 Indian and Northern Affairs Canada proposed changes to the 1985 Indian Act to reconfigure the inequities. The literature surrounding the issue reflects the interest in it. See Joanne Barker, "Gender, Sovereignty, and the Discourse of Rights" in *Native Women's Activism, Meridians: Feminism, Race, Transnationalism* 7, 1 (2006): 127–161; Joyce Green, "Sexual Equality and Indian Government: An Analysis of Bill C-31 Amendments to the Indian Act," *Native Studies Review* 1, 1 (1985): 81–95; Joan Holmes, *Bill C-31, Equality or Disparity? The Effects of the New Indian Act on Native Women* (Ottawa: Canadian Advisory Council on the Status of Women, 1987); Lilianne E. Krosenbrink-Gelissen, "Caring Is Indian Women's Business, But Who Takes Care of Them? Canada's Indian Women, The Renewed Indian Act, and Its Implications for Women's Family Responsibilities, Roles, and Rights," *Law and Anthropology* 7 (1994): 107–130; Patricia Monture-Okanee, "The Rights of Indian Inclusion: Aboriginal Rights and/or Aboriginal Women," in *Advancing Aboriginal Claims: Visions/Strategies/Directions*, ed. Kerry Wilkins (Edmonton: Purich Publishers, 2004), 39–66; Mary Ellen Turpel, "Aboriginal Peoples and the Canadian Charter of Rights and Freedoms," *Canadian Women Studies* 10, 2–3 (1989): 149–157.

4   Bird, ed., *Dressing in Feathers*. Also see Bird, "Gendered Construction."

5   Bird, "Gendered Construction," 78.

6   For nineteenth-century examples, see Carter, *Capturing Women*.

7   For examples, see Bird, "Gendered Construction"; Bridget Keating, "Raping Pocahontas: History, Territory and Ekphrasis in the Representation of an Indigenous Girl," MA thesis, University of Regina, 2008.

8   Calgary *Herald*, 25 May 1939; Calgary *Herald*, 27 May 1939.

9   While on-line shopping sites such as Amazon will confirm the ready availability of these toys for purchase, anthropologist Cheryl Mattingly's essay about the use of cultural icons such as Disney's *Pocahontas* argues that they serve as a form of *lingua franca* for health care providers to engender easier communication with children and families in clinics and hospitals, which in turn supports the pervasive use of the imagery. See Cheryl Mattingly, "Pocahontas Goes to the Clinic: Popular Culture as Lingua Franca in a Cultural Borderland," *American Anthropologist* 108, 3 (2006): 494–501. Giroux's critique of Disney draws attention to the power of this cultural icon. See: Henry Giroux, *The Mouse that Roared: Disney and the End of Innocence* (Lanham, MD: Rowman and Littlefield, 1999).

10   See Rayna Green, "The Pocahontas Perplex: The Image of Indian Women in American Culture," *The Massachusetts Review* 16, 4 (1975): 698–714; Robert Tilton, *Pocahontas: The Evolution of an American Narrative* (Cambridge: Cambridge University Press, 1994).

11   "Claims Descent from Renowned Indian Princess," Montreal *Gazette*, 21 August 1948.

12   See Toronto *Globe and Mail*, 29 June 1970; Hamilton *Spectator*, 1 November 1971.

13   Edmonton *Journal*, 17 July 1969.

14   According to Aboriginal artist and pow wow dancer Bob Boyer, pow wow has long served as a positive form of empowerment and self-identity. Alexandra Harmon argues that after WW II pow wow served as nourishment for Indigenous identity in western Washington. Devon Mihesuah examines varying ways identity and empowerment are linked for Indigenous women. See Lee-Ann Martin and Bob Boyer, eds., *pow wow: An Art History* (Regina: MacKenzie Art Gallery, 2000); Alexandra Harmon, *Indians in the Making: Ethnic Relations and Indian Identities around Puget Sound* (Berkeley: University of California Press, 1998); Devon Mihesuah, *Indigenous American Women: Decolonization, Empowerment, Activism* (Lincoln: University of Nebraska Press, 2003).

15   Calgary *Herald*, 30 June 1969.

16   Reports in the Calgary *Herald*, Edmonton *Journal*, Fredericton *Daily Gleaner*, Toronto *Star*, Victoria *Daily Colonist*, Vancouver *Province*, and the Winnipeg *Free Press* all covered the national Indian Princess pageants. The Fredericton *Daily Gleaner*, however, included the most coverage focusing on the national competition held in Maliseet, New Brunswick, in July 1969, marking the first time the competition had been held in eastern Canada. It contained seven reports between 16 and 22 July 1969.

17   Fredericton *Daily Gleaner*, 23 July 1969.

18   See Toronto *Globe and Mail*, 25 July 1969; Victoria *Daily Colonist*, 14 July 1970.

19   Winnipeg *Free Press*, 5 July 1969.

20   Edmonton *Journal*, 17 July 1969.

21   Ibid.

22   Ibid.

23 Fredericton *Daily Gleaner*, 23 July 1969. The Toronto *Star* reported in the Lifestyles section of the paper that Evelyn Joseph had been named "Indian Princess of Canada 1969" at a competition in Maliseet, New Brunswick. A large photo of the woman in traditional regalia offers Canadians a reinforced image of the frozen-in-time construction. See Toronto *Star*, 23 July 1969.

24 Coverage in the *Daily Gleaner* ran from 16 to 23 July 1969. The same paper largely ignored the following year's events.

25 Toronto *Globe and Mail*, 25 July 1969.

26 Calgary *Herald*, 27 June 1970.

27 Vancouver *Province*, 6 July 1970.

28 The photograph in the Vancouver *Province* was edited so that the large space between the prince and princess was reduced and thus gave the impression the British prince was inspecting the Indian Princess's tongue. See Vancouver *Province*, 10 July 1970, and Victoria *Daily Colonist*, 10 July 1970. The Victoria *Daily Times* and the Victoria *Daily Colonist* merged in 1980.

29 Vancouver *Province*, 10 July 1970.

30 While the national Indian Princess pageant has not been the subject of study, feminist labour historian Joan Sangster argues that beauty contests were popularized after World War II and that by the 1970s their popularity dwindled and a number of contests were abandoned. See Joan Sangster, " 'Queen of the Picket Line': Beauty Contests in the Post-World War II Canadian Labour Movement, 1945–1970," *Labor* 5, 4 (2008): 83–106.

31 Toronto *Globe and Mail*, 19 July 1971.

32 Hamilton *Spectator*, 1 November 1971.

33 Robert Pickton was sentenced to twenty-five years in prison in 2007 for a number of the murders connected to his pig farm. The shocking evidence related to the case and trial brought attention to the high numbers of missing women and violence against women in Canada. See Toronto *Globe and Mail*, 10 December 2007.

34 Amnesty International, 2004, "Stolen Sisters: Discrimination and Violence against Indigenous Women in Canada: A Summary of Amnesty International's Concerns," 4 October 2004, AMR 20/001/2004, http://web.amnesty.org/library/ (accessed 3 March 2009).

35 Saskatoon *Star Pheonix*, 8 October 2004.

36 Victoria *Times-Colonist*, 8 March 2009.

37 Carter, *Capturing Women*, 179–82.

38 See *Report of the Royal Commission on Aboriginal Peoples: Looking Forward, Looking Back*, vol. 1 (Ottawa: Supply and Services Canada, 1996), 289; Carter, *Capturing Women*, 158–193.

39 Carter, *Capturing Women*, 189.

40 Ibid., 189–190.

41 Calgary *Herald*, 6 March 1889.

42 Geographer Margath Walker, in a media study related to the violence against maquiladora workers in Mexican border towns, contends that the identity of Indigenous and mixed blood women in the press is constructed as disposable and anonymous and thus not worthy of extensive investigation. See Margath Walker, "Guada-narco-lupe, Maquilarañas and the Discursive Construction of Gender and Difference on the US-Mexico Border in Mexican Media Re-presentations," *Gender, Place, and Culture* 12,1 (2005): 95-111.

43 Henry and Tator, *Discourse*, 163-205.

44 Lisa Priest, *Conspiracy of Silence* (Toronto: McClelland and Stewart, 1989).

45 Sherene Razack, ed., *Race, Space, and the Law: Unmapping a White Settler Society* (Toronto: Between the Lines, 2002).

46 Winnipeg *Free Press*, 17 November 1971.

47 Ibid.

48 Winnipeg *Free Press*, 16 November 1987.

49 Another November 1987 story that made the Winnipeg *Free Press* front page explained that giving priority to Aboriginal wild rice harvesters was found to be discriminatory against non-Indians. See "Native Priority Discriminates, Judge Rules," Winnipeg *Free Press* 18 November 1987.

50 Montreal *Gazette*, 2 December 1987; Charlottetown *Guardian*, 1 December 1987. Henry and Tator argue that newspapers in eastern Canada present stories differently from western Canadian papers. Proximity to events appears to change the way papers cover issues though their thesis does not satisfactorily explain the differences. See Henry and Tator, *Discourse*, 215.

51 Montreal *Gazette*, 2 December 1987.

52 The order was confirmed subsequently by an act of the Legislature, entitled An Act to Establish and Validate the Public Inquiry into the Administration of Justice and Aboriginal People.

53 Aboriginal Justice Implementation Commission Report, http://www.ajic.mb.ca/volumell/toc.html (accessed 25 March 2009).

54 Ibid.

55 Regina *Leader-Post*, 11 December 1996. For a deeper analysis of the court record versus print media coverage of the trail see Keating, "Raping Pocahontas," 77–85.

56 Razack, *Race*, 135.

57 Henry and Tator, *Discourse*, 215.

58 Ibid.

59 See Keating, "Raping Pocahontas."

60 Walker, "Guada-narco-lupe," 95–111.

61 Holmes, *Bill C-31*, 8. 14

62 Bonita Lawrence, "Gender, Race, and the Regulation of Native Identity in Canada and the United States: An Overview," *Hypatin* 18, 2 (2003): 3–31. See also Lawrence, *"Real" Indians and Others: Mixed-Blood Urban Native Peoples and Indigenous Nationhood* (Vancouver: University of British Columbia Press, 2004).

63 Coverage of the issues between 5 October and 16 December 1971 were found in the Charlottetown *Guardian*; Edmonton *Journal*; Fredericton *Daily Gleaner*; Hamilton *Spectator*; Regina *Leader-Post*; Saskatoon *Star Phoenix*; Toronto *Star*; Vancouver *Province*; Victoria *Daily Colonist*. Front-page stories with photos relating to the Lavell ruling ran in the Vancouver *Province*, 2 December 1971; Victoria *Daily Colonist*, 2 December 1971; and the Toronto *Star*, 8 October 1971. A photo of Bédard with her children ran in the Hamilton *Spectator* on 16 December 1971.

64 *Indian Act* (1970).

65 Saskatoon *Star Phoenix*, 2 December 1971.

66 The council later adopted two additional resolutions allowing Bédard to live in the house for another six months, and then another two months, but no longer than that. In order to act in accordance with the council's resolutions, Bédard eventually transferred ownership of the property to her brother (a registered member of the band) who was granted a Certificate of Possession of the property on 15 March 1971, by the Minister of Indian Affairs as required by the *Indian Act*. On 15 September 1971, the Six Nations Band Council passed Resolution 15, requesting the Brantford District Supervisor to serve notice to Bédard that she shall quit the reserve.

67 Bédard v. Isaac (1971), 25 D.L.R. (3d) 551 (also reported: [1972] 2 O.R. 391) Ontario High Court, Osler J., 15 December 1971 (appealed to Supreme Court of Canada, reported sub nom. Attorney-General of Canada v. Lavell; Isaac v. Bedard, infra., p. 236).

68 Victoria *Daily Colonist,* 9 October 1971.

69 Saskatoon *Star Phoenix,* 2 December 1971.

70 Ibid.

71 Victoria *Daily Colonist,* 2 December 1971.

72 Ibid.

73 Hamilton *Spectator,* 16 December 1971.

74 Victoria *Times-Colonist,* 2 December 1971.

75 Victoria *Daily Colonist,* 2 December 1971.

76 Ibid. The Nisga'a Land Claim was finally settled in 1998.

77 Barker, "Gender," 136–137.

78 Victoria *Daily Colonist,* 2 December 1971. See also Fredericton *Daily Gleaner,* 2 December 1971.

79 Fredericton *Daily Gleaner,* 5 October 1971.

80 Victoria *Daily Colonist,* 2 December 1971.

81 Fredericton *Daily Gleaner,* 2 December 1971.

82 Hamilton *Spectator,* 16 December 1971.

83 Fredericton *Daily Gleaner,* 5 October 1971.

84 Edmonton *Journal,* 13 December 1971.

85 Hamilton *Spectator,* 9 October 1971.

86 Vancouver *Province,* 11 December 1971.

87 Barker, "Gender," 137.

88 Joyce Green, ed., *Making Space for Indigenous Feminism* (New York: Zed Books, 2007), 140.

89 Constance Backhouse, *Colour-Coded: A Legal History of Racism in Canada, 1900–1950* (Toronto: University of Toronto Press, 1999).

90 Toronto *Globe and Mail,* 3 July 1973.

91 Lynda Hurst, "We've Set the Pace For Our Sisters to the South," Toronto *Star,* 18 April 1985.

92 For example, see St. John's *Evening Telegram,* 17 April 1985; Winnipeg *Free Press,* 18 April 1985; Toronto *Star,* 18 April 1985.

93 While news items related to other Aboriginal issues arose in April 1985, papers were silent on efforts to change the Indian Act.

94 Toronto *Star,* 20 April 1985. Also see Toronto *Star,* 19 April 1985.

95 St. John's *Evening Telegram,* 17 April 1985.

96   Regina *Leader-Post*, 18 April 1985.

97   Barker, "Gender," 45.

98   For a discussion of the problems related to the passage of Bill C-31 see Holmes *Bill C-31*; Green, "Canaries in the Coal Mine"; Green, "Sexual Equality and Indian Government."

99   Edmonton *Journal*, 30 June 1985.

100 "Indian Act Amendment 'Catastrophic,' Warns Band," Calgary *Herald*, 30 June 1985.

101 "Treaty Women to Fight Change to Indian Act," Regina *Leader-Post*, 9 July 1985.

102 "Indians Fear Effects of Law," Toronto *Globe and Mail*, 9 July 1985.

103 Toronto *Globe and Mail*, 6 February 1986.

104 Toronto *Globe and Mail*, 16 October 1987.

105 Ibid.

106 See Green, ed., *Making Space*, 27.

107 Lawrence, "Gender, Race," 3.

108 Toronto *Globe and Mail*, 14 April 2009.

109 Ibid.

110 For a discussion of McIvor's Aboriginal feminist ideas, see Sharon McIvor with Rauna Kuokkanen, "Sharon McIvor, Woman of Action," in Green, ed., *Making Space*, 241–254.

111 News release, FAFIA, 28 January 2011, http://www.nationtalk.ca/modules/news/articlephp?storyid=4888 (accessed 5 Feburary 2011).

112 For a discussion of the creation of ethnic or racial diversity in beauty culture from an African American perspective, see bell hooks, *Black Looks: Race and Representation* (Toronto: Between the Lines, 1992), 71–73.

113 Donna Barbie Kessler, "Sacagawea: The Making of a Myth," *Sifters: Native American Women's Lives* (New York: Oxford University Press, 2001), 63.

114 Monture-Okanee, "The Right of Indian Inclusion," 39–66.

115 Barker, "Gender," 150.

116 See Eagleton, *Holy Terror*, 65.

117 Stephen Bertman, *Cultural Amnesia America's Future and the Crisis of Memory* (Santa Barbara: Greenwood Press, 2000).

CHAPTER ELEVEN: Letters from the Edges

1   See Thomas S. Kuhn, *The Structure of Scientific Revolutions* (Chicago: University of Chicago Press, [1970] 1996).

2   Amelia Kalant, *National Identity and the Conflict at Oka: Native Belonging and Myths of Postcolonial Nationhood in Canada* (New York: Routledge, 2004), 1.

3   Wente's columns are considered more fully in the conclusions. From among many see, for example, 3 September 1994; Toronto *Globe and Mail*, 2 December 1994; Toronto *Globe and Mail*, 20 May 1999; Toronto *Globe and Mail*, 23 September 1999; Toronto *Globe and Mail*, 22 January 2000; Toronto *Globe and Mail*, 11 July 2000; Toronto *Globe and Mail*, 7 October 2000; Toronto *Globe and Mail*, 28 November 2000; Toronto *Globe and Mail*, 1 February 2001; Toronto *Globe and Mail*, 12 April 2001; Toronto *Globe and Mail*, 23 June 2001.

4   Szuchewycz, "Re-Pressing Racism," 501.

5 Cited in Geoffrey York and Loreen Pindera, *People of the Pines: The Warriors and the Legacy of Oka* (Toronto: McArthur and Company, 1999), 417.

6 Heather Smyth, "The Mohawk Warrior: Reappropriating the Colonial Stereotype," *Topia* 3 (Spring 2000): 60. York and Pindera, *People*, 413.

7 Dickason, *Canada's First Nations*, 329.

8 Miller, *Skyscrapers*, 384.

9 Francis, *Imaginary Indian*, 220.

10 Nichols, *Indians in the United States and Canada*, 318.

11 See Nesbitt-Larking, *Politics, Society, and the Media*, 272–274.

12 To get a first-hand sense of this, visit Amazon.com and search the term "Oka crisis."

13 This includes, for example, Quebec's heavily criticized then-Indian Affairs minister John Ciaccia, *The Oka Crisis: A Mirror of the Soul* (Dorval: Maren Publishers, 2000). See, for example, York and Pindera, *People*. Also see Craig MacLaine, *This Land is Our Land: The Mohawk Revolt at Oka* (Maxville, Ontario: Optimum Publishers, 1990).

14 See, for example, Gerald Alfred, *Heeding the Voices of Our Ancestors: Kahnawake Mohawk Politics and the Rise of Native Nationalism* (New York: Oxford University Press, 1995); Alfred, *Wasáse*; Taiaiake Alfred, *Peace, Power, Righteousness: An Indigenous Manifesto* (New York: Oxford University Press, 2009).

15 See, for example, Miller, *Skyscrapers*, 380–384; Dickason's *Canada's First Nations*, 328–329; and Ronald Wright, *Stolen Continents: The "New World" Through Indian Eyes* (Toronto: Mariner Books, 1993), 313.

16 The list is too long to provide here in full. See, for example, Paul R. Carr and Darren E. Lund, *The Great White North? Exploring Whiteness, Privilege and Identity in Education* (Rotterdam: Sense Publishers, 2007), 80; Henry Giroux, *Education and Cultural Studies: Toward a Performative Practice* (New York: Routledge, 1997), 67; see the "First People" section of Jim Hynes, *Montreal Book of Everything* (MacIntyre Purcell Publishing, 2007), 185–196; Allan J. Ryan, *The Trickster Shift: Humour and Irony in Contemporary Native Art* (Seattle: University of Washington Press, 1999).

17 You can watch much of this on your computer screen. A good deal of it is available on YouTube or Google. Simply search the words "Oka crisis."

18 Nichols, *Indians in the United States and Canada*, 318. Also see Gail Guthrie Valaskakis, "Right and Warriors: First Nations, Media, and Identity," in Nancoo and Nancoo, *Mass Media and Canadian Diversity*, 110–123. Valaskakis's essay was reprinted in Gail Guthrie Valaskakis, *Indian Country, Essays on Contemporary Native Culture* (Waterloo, ON: Wilfrid Laurier University Press, 2005), 35–65.

19 Rick Ponting, "Internationalization: Perspectives on an Emerging Direction in Aboriginal Affairs," *Canadian Ethnic Studies* 22, 3 (1990): 85–109.

20 Marc Grenier, "Native Indians in the English-Canadian Press: The case of the 'Oka Crisis,'" *Media, Culture, and Society* 16, 2 (1994): 313–336.

21 Skea, "The Canadian Newspaper Industry's Portrayal of the Oka Crisis," 15–31.

22 Ibid., 29.

23 Martin J. Morris, "Overcoming the Barricades: The Crisis at Oka as a Case Study in Political Communication," *Journal of Canadian Studies* 30, 2 (1995): 74–92. Also see Fleras and Kunz, *Media and Minorities*, 81.

24 Morris, "Overcoming," 81.

25 Charles Stuart, "The Mohawk Crisis: A Crisis of Hegemony, An Analysis of Media Discourse," MA thesis, University of Ottawa, 1993, 106. Also see Nesbitt-Larking, *Politics, Society, and the Media*, 273.

26 Smyth, "The Mohawk Warrior," 2.

27 James Winter, *Common Cents: Media Portrayal of the Gulf War and Other Events* (Montreal: Black Rose Books, 1995). Morris simply claims that the federal government negotiated in "bad faith." See Morris, "Overcoming the Barricades," 85. Also see Nesbitt-Larking, *Politics, Society, and the Media*, 301.

28 P. Whitney Lackenbauer, "Carrying the Burden of Peace: The Mohawks, the Canadian Forces, and the Oka Crisis," *Journal of Military and Strategic Studies* 10, 2 (2008): 2–71.

29 Skea, "The Canadian Newspaper Industry's Portrayal of the Oka Crisis," 15.

30 Mageo, "Introduction," *Power and Self*, 5.

31 Stuart, "The Mohawk Crisis: A Crisis of Hegemony, An Analysis of Media Discourse," 5.

32 Claude Beauregard, "The Military Intervention in Oka," *Canadian Military History* 2, 1 (1993): 23–47.

33 The *Times* and *Transcript* merged in 1983. The former dates to 1868 and the latter to 1882.

34 The Prince George *Citizen* was founded in 1916 in the wake of the area's emergence as a centre of British Columbia's lumber industry.

35 Curtis D. McDougall, *Principles of Editorial Writing* (Dubuque, IA: William C. Brown, 1973), 141.

36 Kim Fletcher, *The Journalist's Handbook* (London: Pan Macmillan, 2005), 186.

37 Perrin and Vaisey, "Parallel Public Spheres," 786.

38 Ibid., 782.

39 Bill Reader, "An Ethical 'Blind Spot': Problems of Anonymous Letters the Editor," *Journal of Mass Media Ethics* 20, 1 (2005): 66.

40 Reader, "Blind Spot," 68.

41 Ronald N. Jacobs makes a similar case about coverage of African-Americans in American newspapers, referring to the phenomenon as the "political economy of space." Ronald N. Jacobs, *Race, Media and the Crisis of Civil Society, From Watts to Rodney King* (New York: Cambridge University Press, 2000), 141.

42 Reader, "Blind Spot," 63.

43 Perrin and Vaisey, "Parallel Public Spheres," 787. The authors here offer no particular argument, just a conclusion that gatekeeping is not a significant factor.

44 Reader, "Blind Spot," 63. Reader's conclusion derives from those instances where unsigned letters are automatically rejected, thereby eliminating the range of voices on a given issue.

45 Szuchewycz, "Re-Pressing Racism," 498.

46 This conclusion is somewhat ironic, since the authors also note that the idea of a public sphere, at least for the United States, is "contested." See Perrin and Vaisey, "Parallel Public Spheres," 781.

47 See Reader, "An Ethical 'Blind Spot.'"

48 See Prince George *Citizen*, 17 August 1990.

49 See Prince George *Citizen*, 1 September 1990.

50 Moncton *Times-Transcript*, 1 August 1990.

51 Prince George *Citizen*, 2 August 1990.

52 Ibid.

53 Prince George *Citizen*, 10 August 1990.

54 Prince George *Citizen*, 17 August 1990.

55 Prince George *Citizen*, 29 August 1990.

56 Ibid. Without explanation, the paper reprinted this letter on 1 September 1990.

57 Prince George *Citizen*, 1 September 1990.

58 Prince George *Citizen*, 20 September 1990.

59 Prince George *Citizen*, 26 September 1990.

60 Prince George *Citizen*, 12 October 1990.

61 Prince George *Citizen*, 22 October 1990.

62 Prince George *Citizen*, 16 August 1990.

63 Ibid.

64 Prince George *Citizen*, 29 September 1990.

65 Ibid.

66 Moncton *Times-Transcript*, 17 August 1990.

67 Moncton *Times-Transcript*, 1 August 1990.

68 Moncton *Times-Transcript*, 20 July 1990. The anti-Quebec content of this letter drew a vociferous rebuke on 14 August.

69 Moncton *Times-Transcript*, 20 July 1990.

70 Moncton *Times-Transcript*, 1 August 1990.

71 Moncton *Times-Transcript*, 4 September 1990.

72 Moncton *Times-Transcript*, 11 August 1990.

73 Moncton *Times-Transcript*, 16 August 1990.

74 Moncton *Times-Transcript*, 10 August 1990.

75 Moncton *Times-Transcript*, 24 August 1990. An irony here is that many Mohawks also argue that they are not Canadian. The line of reasoning is starkly different, however. These Mohawks argue that they never surrendered to Canada and thus are not part of it. See Alfred, *Heeding the Voices*; *Peace, Power, Righteousness*; *Wasáse*.

76 Moncton *Times-Transcript*, 12 September 1990.

77 Moncton *Times-Transcript*, 30 August 1990.

78 Moncton *Times-Transcript*, 13 August 1990.

79 Also see Smyth, "Mohawk Warrior," 63.

80 Moncton *Times-Transcript*, 13 August 1990.

81 Moncton *Times-Transcript*, 28 August 1990.

82 Moncton *Times-Transcript*, 29 August 1990.

83 Also see Moncton *Times-Transcript*, 17 October 1990.

84 Moncton *Times-Transcript*, 11 September 1990.

85 Moncton *Times-Transcript*, 14 September 1990.

86 Moncton *Times-Transcript*, 21 September 1990.

87 Moncton *Times-Transcript*, 1 October 1990.

88 Moncton *Times-Transcript*, 2 October 1990.

89 This tactic was also widely employed at the Gustafsen Lake Standoff in British Columbia in 1995. See Lambertus, *Wartime Images*.

90 Law, *Race in the News*, 25.

91 Kalant, *National Identity*, 240.

92 Szuchewycz, "Re-Pressing Racism," 500.

93 Kalant, *National Identity*, 240.

CHAPTER TWELVE: Back to the Future

1 In recognition of the anniversary in 1992 the National Gallery of Canada mounted "Land, Spirit, Power," curated by Diana Nemiroff, Charlotte Townsend-Gault, and Robert Houle. The National Gallery declined to call it an exhibition that recognized the quincentennial. In response, curators Lee-Ann Martin and Gerald McMaster challenged the privileged position of the National Gallery with a national touring exhibition, "Indigena," that confronted some of the related problematic issues. It was mounted by the Canadian Museum of Civilization. See Diana Nemiroff, Charlotte Townsend-Gault, and Robert Houle, *Land, Spirit, Power: First Nations at the National Gallery of Canada* (Ottawa: National Gallery of Canada, 1992); Lee-Ann Martin and Gerald McMaster, *Indigena: Contemporary Native Perspectives on Contemporary Art* (Vancouver: Craftsman House, 1992).

2 Edmonton *Journal*, 29 July 1905.

3 Fleras and Kunz, *Media and Minorities*, 32.

4 Red Deer *Alberta Advocate*, 21 June 1905.

5 Saskatoon *Phenix*, 27 January 1905.

6 Saskatoon *Phenix*, 30 June 1905. Also see Saskatoon *Phenix*, 27 January 1905; Saskatoon *Phenix*, 27 January 1905.

7 Calgary *Herald*, 25 January 1905.

8 Saskatoon *Phenix*, 4 August 1905; Red Deer *Alberta Advocate*, 1 September 1905.

9 Red Deer *Alberta Advocate*, 8 September 1905. Also see Red Deer *Alberta Advocate*, 6 October 1905; Edmonton *Journal*, 1 July 1905.

10 Saskatoon *Phenix*, 27 January 1905.

11 The Regina *Leader*, like most of the papers in western Canada, ran a series of backgrounder stories feting the heroic exploits of key journalists in the region. This included pieces on Walter Scott (see Regina *Leader*, 26 October 1905) and the Regina *Leader*'s managing editor W.F. Kerr (see Regina *Leader*, 5 July 1905). The Regina *Leader* was founded in 1883 by Nicholas Flood Davin, whose *Report on Industrial Schools for Indians and Half-Breeds*, otherwise known as *The Davin Report* (1879), advised John A. Macdonald's federal government to institute residential schools for Indigenous youth.

12 Regina *Leader*, 4 January 1905. Also see Calgary *Herald*, 12 January 1905.

13 Red Deer *Alberta Advocate*, 2 June 1905. Also see Edmonton *Journal*, 15 April 1905.

14 Battleford *Saskatchewan Herald*, 20 December 1905. Also see Red Deer *Alberta Advocate*, 22 December 1905.

15 Edmonton *Journal*, 1 July 1905. Also see Edmonton *Journal*, 22 February 1905.

16 Edmonton *Journal*, 16 March 1905.

17 Saskatoon *Phenix*, 16 June 1905.

18 Battleford *Saskatchewan Herald*, 22 February 1905; Battleford *Saskatchewan Herald*, 5 July 1905.

19 Saskatoon *Phenix*, 10 March 1905.

20 Battleford *Saskatchewan Herald*, 8 February 1905.

21 Regina *Leader*, 4 January 1905.

22 Ibid.

23 Calgary *Herald*, 13 January 1905.

24 Edmonton *Journal*, 10 June 1905.

25 Calgary *Herald*, 23 January 1905.

26 Red Deer *Alberta Advocate*, 1 December 1905.

27 Edmonton *Journal*, 22 June 1905.

28 Edmonton *Journal*, 23 June 1905. Also see Edmonton *Journal*, 26 June 1905. Also see Calgary *Herald*, 28 January 1905.

29 See, for example, Battleford *Saskatchewan Herald*, 18 January 1905; Battleford *Saskatchewan Herald*, 8 February 1905; Battleford *Saskatchewan Herald*, 8 March 1905; Battleford *Saskatchewan Herald*, 15 March 1905; Battleford *Saskatchewan Herald*, 28 April 1905; Battleford *Saskatchewan Herald*, 12 July 1905; Battleford *Saskatchewan Herald*, 15 November 1905; Battleford *Saskatchewan Herald*, 20 December 1905; Regina *Leader*, 4 January 1905; Regina *Leader*, 26 April 1905.

30 Battleford *Saskatchewan Herald*, 4 January 1905. The paper did not reserve its attempted humor solely to belittle Aboriginals. A brief item in January noted that Adam and Eve were likely Ethiopian (read: Black) and, thus, it followed "that the forbidden fruit was a watermelon." See Battleford *Saskatchewan Herald*, 11 January 1905. Also see Battleford *Saskatchewan Herald*, 6 September 1905

31 Saskatoon *Phenix*, 4 August 1905.

32 Framing non-Aboriginals as Others, including white women, in allegations of physical inferiority were extremely common in 1905, but fall outside the parameters of this chapter. See, for example, Battleford *Saskatchewan Herald*, 11 January 1905. Also see Saskatoon *Phenix*, 6 January 1905.

33 Battleford *Saskatchewan Herald*, 8 February 1905.

34 Battleford *Saskatchewan Herald*, 3 May 1905. Also see Battleford *Saskatchewan Herald*, 10 May 1905; Battleford *Saskatchewan Herald*, 31 May 1905; Battleford *Saskatchewan Herald*, 8 November 1905; Moose Jaw *Times*, 4 August 1905; Saskatoon *Phenix*, 28 July 1905; Battleford *Saskatchewan Herald*, 23 August 1905; Red Deer *Alberta Advocate*, 2 June 1905; Red Deer *Alberta Advocate*, 29 December 1905.

35 Battleford *Saskatchewan Herald*, 10 May 1905.

36 Battleford *Saskatchewan Herald*, 22 February 1905.

37 Moose Jaw *Times*, 12 January 1905. Also see Moose Jaw *Times*, 12 May 1905; Moose Jaw *Times*, 4 August 1905; Moose Jaw *Times*, 28 July 1905; Moose Jaw *Times*, 4 August 1905. Also see Regina *Leader*, 18 January 1905; Saskatoon *Phenix*, 6 January 1905; Saskatoon *Phenix*, 7 January 1905; Saskatoon *Phenix*, 10 March 1905; Macleod *Gazette*, 26 October 1905; Macleod *Gazette*, 16 November 1905; Macleod *Gazette*, 22 November 1905.

38 Edmonton *Journal*, 3 August 1905; Edmonton *Journal*, 6 January 1905.

39 Moose Jaw *Times*, 22 December 1905. Also see Regina *Leader*, 1 February 1905; Saskatoon *Phenix*, 4 August 1905; Saskatoon *Phenix*, 17 February 1905.

40 Red Deer *Alberta Advocate*, 11 August 1905.

41 Moose Jaw *Times*, 28 July 1905.

42   Moose Jaw *Times*, 14 June 1905. Also see Calgary *Herald*, 16 February 1905.

43   See Saskatoon *Phenix*, 27 January 1905; Macleod *Gazette*, 31 August 1905; Macleod *Gazette*, 14 September 1905; Edmonton *Journal*, 3 August 1905; Regina *Leader*, 14 June 1905; Regina *Leader*, 30 May 1905; Regina *Leader*, 2 August 1905; Regina *Leader*, 27 December 1905; Saskatoon *Phenix*, 26 May 1905; Saskatoon *Phenix*, 6 January 1905; Saskatoon *Phenix* 17 February 1905; Battleford *Saskatchewan Herald*, 9 August 1905.

44   Saskatoon *Phenix*, 28 July 1905.

45   The Toronto *Globe and Mail*, for example, continues this practice in 2009.

46   See, for example, Macleod *Gazette*, 14 September 1905; Edmonton *Journal*, 1 July 1905.

47   Red Deer *Alberta Advocate*, 3 February 1905.

48   Red Deer *Alberta Advocate*, 12 May 1905. Also see Edmonton *Journal*, 1 July 1905.

49   Red Deer *Alberta Advocate*, 3 November 1905.

50   Macleod *Gazette*, 12 October 1905.

51   Macleod *Gazette*, 22 November 1905. Also see Edmonton *Journal*, 3 August 1905.

52   Edmonton *Journal*, 4 August 1905.

53   Edmonton *Journal*, 1 July 1905. Also see *Phenix*, 27 January 1905.

54   This is generic textbook material. See Fleras and Elliott, *Unequal Relations*, 238–242. Also see Richard J.F. Day, *Multiculturalism and the History of Canadian Diversity* (Toronto: University of Toronto Press, 2000).

55   See http://www.merriam-webster.com/dictionary/hatred (accessed 13 May 2010).

56   Regina *Leader-Post*, 2 July 2005; Saskatoon Saskatoon *Star Pheonix*, 2 July 2005. Also see Calgary *Herald*, 2 July 2005; Edmonton *Journal*, 2 July 2005; Regina *Leader-Post*, 7 July 2005; Saskatoon *Star Pheonix*, 7 July 2005; Calgary *Herald*, 8 July 2005; Regina *Leader-Post*, 8 July 2005; Saskatoon *Star Pheonix*, 8 July 2005.

57   Regina *Leader-Post*, 8 July 2005.

58   Regina *Leader-Post*, 9 July 2005.

59   Saskatoon *Star Pheonix*, 9 July 2005.

60   A column by Paula Simmons in the Edmonton *Journal* reached a similar conclusion—that Ahenakew's comments were vile but that the real problem lay with a faulty law and not with Ahenakew's ignorance of history. See Edmonton *Journal*, 9 July 2005. The piece also draws attention to what Natives and Jews share—common history on the receiving end of discriminatory behaviour.

61   The same article was printed in the Edmonton *Journal*, 9 July 2005.

62   Saskatoon *Star Pheonix*, 9 July 2005. Also see a similar story printed in the Calgary *Herald*, 9 July 2005.

63   Battleford *Saskatchewan Herald*, 12 July 1905.

64   Also see Edmonton *Journal*, 8 July 2005.

65   Calgary *Herald*, 2 July 2005.

66   Regina *Leader-Post*, 2 July 2005. A shorter version of a similar article, *sans* ministerial comments and background context, was published in Saskatoon Saskatoon *Star Pheonix*, 2 July 2005.

67   Constitutionally education is a provincial responsibility. However, this distinction clashes with the treaty obligations, which were made between First Nations and the federal government.

68   Regina *Leader-Post*, 2 July 2005. Also see Regina *Leader-Post*, 7 July 2005.

69   Edmonton *Journal*, 2 July 2005.

70   Edmonton *Journal*, 7 July 2005.

71   Also see Edmonton *Journal*, 6 July 2005.

72   Regina *Leader-Post*, 4 July 2005. Also see Regina *Leader-Post*, 5 July 2005. For a similar listing of allegations see the article about suicide in a Native Vancouver Island community. Edmonton *Journal*, 7 July 2005. For an article associating Natives with violence and crime see, Edmonton *Journal*, 9 July 2005.

73   Regina *Leader-Post*, 4 July 2005; Saskatoon *Star Pheonix*, 4 July 2005.

74   Saskatoon *Star Pheonix*, 7 July 2005; Regina *Leader-Post*, 7 July 2005.

75   See Regina *Leader-Post*, 2 July 2005; Regina *Leader-Post*, 6 Jul 2005; Regina *Leader-Post*, 7 July 2005.

76   Regina *Leader-Post*, 8 July 2005.

77   Saskatoon *Star Pheonix*, 6 July 2005; Regina *Leader-Post*, 6 July 2005.

78   Edmonton *Journal*, 1 July 2005.

79   Saskatoon *Star Pheonix*, 4 July 2005; Regina *Leader-Post*, 4 July 2005. Also see a news item about an attack in which a teenager was beaten with a baseball bat on a reservation outside Edmonton. Edmonton *Journal*, 2 July 2005. A similar story ran of a stabbing "on a reserve north of Edmonton." Edmonton *Journal*, 4 July 2005.

80   Edmonton *Journal*, 2 July 2005.

81   Ibid.

82   Edmonton *Journal*, 6 July 2005.

83   Calgary *Herald*, 1 July 2005.

84   Regina *Leader-Post*, 2 July 2005.

85   Also see a Calgary *Herald* article about the "authentic as it gets...Indian Village" at the Calgary Stampede. See Calgary *Herald*, 8 July 2005. Also see Calgary *Herald*, 9 July 2005.

86   Regina *Leader-Post*, 2 July 2005. Also see Calgary *Herald*, 2 July 2005. On the topic of nostalgia also see Regina *Leader-Post*, 7 July 2005.

87   Calgary *Herald*, 1 July 2005.

88   Ibid.

89   Calgary *Herald*, 2 July 2005.

90   Saskatoon *Star Pheonix*, 7 July 2005.

91   See, for example, Cuthand's column in the Saskatoon *Star Pheonix*, 8 July 2005. For additional examples see Doug Cuthand, *Tapwe: Selected Columns of Doug Cuthand* (Penticton: Theytus Books, 2005).

92   Saskatoon *Star Pheonix*, 7 July 2005. Also see a column written by Delbert P. Wapass, published in the Saskatoon *Star Pheonix*, 8 July 2005.

CONCLUSION: *Return of the Native*

1   John Raulston Saul, *A Fair Country* (Toronto: Penguin, 2008), 243.

2   Michael Ignatieff, *True Patriot Love* (Toronto: Viking Canada, 2009), 1.

3   Benedict Anderson, *Imagined Communities*, 7.

4   Vipond, *Mass Media*, 133.

5   See, for example, Sotiron, *From Politics to Profit*. Also see Winter, *Common Cents*, 9; Vipond, *Mass Media*, 73–74; Nesbitt-Larking, *Politics, Society, and the Media*, 110–113, 119–126.

6   Teun Van Dijk, *Racism in the Press* (London: Routledge, 1991), 245. Also see Weston, *Native Americans in the News*; Sheffield, *Warpath*; Haycock, *Canadian Indian*.

7   Miller and Ross, "They Are Not Us," passim.

8   Harding, "Historical Representations," 224.

9   Ibid.

10 Richard White, *The Middle Ground: Indians, Empires, and Republics in the Great Lakes Region, 1650–1815* (New York: Cambridge University Press, 1991).

11 See Van Dijk, *Elite Discourse*, 182–185.

12 Miller and Ross, "They Are Not Us," 256.

13 Wente, whose column runs front and centre in Canada's most respected newspaper, is certainly not alone. For example, a recent book published by one of Canada's leading academic presses, McGill-Queen's University Press, *Disrobing the Aboriginal Industry*, by Frances Widdowson and Albert Howard, angrily claims that the basic problem with Natives is they remain wedded to Neolithic cultural traditions. See Frances Widdowson and Albert Howard, *Disrobing the Aboriginal Industry: The Deception Behind Indigenous Cultural Preservation* (Montreal: McGill-Queen's University Press, 2008).

14 Miller and Ross argue that the rules of evidence governing contemporary journalistic practice are sharply reduced as one moves away from hard news to feature stories and then again to editorial comment.

15 Toronto *Globe and Mail*, 30 June 2007.

16 Toronto *Globe and Mail*, 20 May 1999.

17 Toronto *Globe and Mail*, 12 August 1995.

18 Toronto *Globe and Mail*, 23 September 1999. Also see Toronto *Globe and Mail*, 28 November 2000.

19 Toronto *Globe and Mail*, 28 September 1999. Also see Toronto *Globe and Mail*, 11 July 2000.

20 Toronto *Globe and Mail*, 22 January 2000.

21 Toronto *Globe and Mail*, 28 March 2000.

22 Toronto *Globe and Mail*, 6 May 2000.

23 Toronto *Globe and Mail*, 7 October 2000.

24 Toronto *Globe and Mail*, 28 November 2000.

25 Toronto *Globe and Mail*, 25 April 2006.

26 Toronto *Globe and Mail*, 23 June 2001; Toronto *Globe and Mail*, 2 April 2002; Toronto *Globe and Mail*, 28 September 2002; Toronto *Globe and Mail*, 22 February 2003.

27 Toronto *Globe and Mail*, 23 June 2001; Toronto *Globe and Mail*, 18 June 2002; Toronto *Globe and Mail*, 21 June 2008.

28 See Toronto *Globe and Mail*, 1 February 2001; Toronto *Globe and Mail*, 23 June 2001; Toronto *Globe and Mail*, 30 July 2002; Toronto *Globe and Mail*, 28 September 2002; Toronto *Globe and Mail*, 22 February 2003; Toronto *Globe and Mail*, 14 August 2003; Toronto *Globe and Mail*, 25 November 2003.

29   Toronto *Globe and Mail*, 12 April 2001; Toronto *Globe and Mail*, 23 June 2001; Toronto *Globe and Mail*, 18 June 2002; Toronto *Globe and Mail*, 28 September 2002; Toronto *Globe and Mail*, 22 February 2003; Toronto *Globe and Mail*, 22 February 2003; Toronto *Globe and Mail*, 14 August 2003; Toronto *Globe and Mail*, 25 November 2003; Toronto *Globe and Mail*, 05 June 2004; Toronto *Globe and Mail*, 1 November 2005; Toronto *Globe and Mail*, 5 June 2004; Toronto *Globe and Mail*, 24 December 2004.

30   Toronto *Globe and Mail*, 12 April 2001; Toronto *Globe and Mail*, 11 April 2002; Toronto *Globe and Mail*, 30 June 2007.

31   Toronto *Globe and Mail*, 22 February 2003; Toronto *Globe and Mail*, 22 February 2003; Toronto *Globe and Mail*, 2 August 2003; Toronto *Globe and Mail*, 6 March 2008; Toronto *Globe and Mail*, 12 June 2008.

32   Toronto *Globe and Mail*, 8 November 2001; Toronto *Globe and Mail*, 28 September 2002; Toronto *Globe and Mail*, 17 December 2002; Toronto *Globe and Mail*, 15 July 2003; Toronto *Globe and Mail*, 2 August 2003; Toronto *Globe and Mail*, 13 September 2003; Toronto *Globe and Mail*, 15 July 2006.

33   Toronto *Globe and Mail*, 1 February 2001; Toronto *Globe and Mail*, 23 June 2001; Toronto *Globe and Mail*, 28 September 2002; Toronto *Globe and Mail*, 5 June 2004; Toronto *Globe and Mail*, 25 April 2006; Toronto *Globe and Mail*, 15 July 2006.

34   Toronto *Globe and Mail*, 1 February 2001; Toronto *Globe and Mail*, 5 June 2004; Toronto *Globe and Mail*, 20 November 2004; Toronto *Globe and Mail*, 15 July 2006; Toronto *Globe and Mail*, 28 June 2007 Toronto *Globe and Mail*, 1 May 2008.

35   Toronto *Globe and Mail*, 23 June 2001; Toronto *Globe and Mail*, 15 November 2005; Toronto *Globe and Mail*, 25 April 2006; Toronto *Globe and Mail*, 15 July 2006; Toronto *Globe and Mail*, 28 June 2007.

36   See, for example, Toronto *Globe and Mail*, 7 February 2009; Toronto *Globe and Mail*, 23 April 2009.

37   See Geertz, *Interpretation of Cultures*.

38   Frank Sulloway, *Born to Rebel: Birth Order, Family Dynamics, and Creative Lives* (New York: Vintage, 1997).

39   See William Appleman Williams, *Empire As A Way of Life* (New York: Ig Publishing, 2006).

40   Kellstedt, *Mass Media*, 53.

41   Bonita Lawrence, "Rewriting Histories of the Land: Colonization and Indigenous Resistance in Eastern Canada," in *Race, Space, and the Law: Unmapping a White Settler Society*, ed. Sherene Razack (Toronto: Between the Lines, 2002), 23.

BIBLIOGRAPHY

NEWSPAPERS

Battleford *Saskatchewan Herald*
Brantford *Expositor*
Calgary *Herald*
Charlottetown *Guardian*
Dawson City *Daily News*
Dawson City *Klondike Nugget*
Dawson City *Record*
Dawson City *Yukon Daily Morning World*
Dawson City *Yukon Sun*
Edmonton *Journal*
Fort Macleod *Gazette*
Fredericton *Daily Gleaner*
Fredericton *Maritime Farmer*
Halifax *Chronicle-Herald* (nee *Citizen and Evening Chronicle*)
Hamilton *Spectator*
Kenora *Miner and News*
Lethbridge *Herald*
London *Advertiser*
London *Daily Express* (England)
Moose Jaw *Times*
Moncton *Times-Transcript*
Montreal *Gazette*
North Bay *Nugget*
Ottawa *Citizen*
Prince Albert *Daily Herald*
Prince George *Citizen*
Red Deer *Alberta Advocate*
Regina *Leader-Post* (nee *Leader*)
Saskatoon *Star Phoenix* (nee *Phenix*)
St. John *Telegraph-Journal*
St. John's *Evening Mercury*
St. John's *Evening Telegram*

Sudbury *Star*

Toronto *Globe and Mail* (nee *Globe*)

Toronto *National Post*

Toronto *Star*

Vancouver (*Daily*) *Province*

Victoria *Times Colonist* (nee *Daily Colonist*)

Whitehorse Star

Windsor *Evening Record*

Winnipeg *Free Press* (nee Manitoba *Free Press*)

Winnipeg *Tribune*

GOVERNMENT DOCUMENTS

Aboriginal Justice Implementation Commission Report. http://www.ajic.mb.ca/volumeII/toc. html (accessed 25 March 2009).

Indian Act. Government of Canada, 1868.

Province of Ontario v. Bedard [1971], 25 D.L.R. (3d) 551 (also reported: [1972] 2 O.R. 391) Ontario High Court, Osler J., 15 December 1971 (Appealed to Supreme Court of Canada, reported sub nom. ATTORNEY-GENERAL OF CANADA v. LAVELL; ISAAC v. BEDARD, infra p. 236).

Royal Commission on Aboriginal Peoples. *Report of the Royal Commission on Aboriginal Peoples: Looking Forward, Looking Back.* (RCAP). Volume 1. Ottawa: Ministry of Supply and Services, 1996.

Select and Annotated Bibliography Regarding Bill C-31, Indian Registration, and Band *Membership, Aboriginal Identity, Women and Gender Issues.* Ottawa: Indain and Northern Affairs Canada, 2004.

SECONDARY SOURCES

Achebe, Chinua. *Things Fall Apart.* New York: Anchor, 1994.

Adams, David Wallace. *Education for Extinction: American Indians and the Boarding School Experience 1875–1928.* Lawrence: University Press of Kansas, 1997.

Aleiss, Angela. *Making the White Man's Indian: Native Americans and Hollywood Movies.* New York: Praeger, 2005.

Alfred, Gerald Taiaiake. *Heeding the Voices of Our Ancestors: Kahnawake Mohawk Politics and the Rise of Native Nationalism.* New York: Oxford University Press, 1995.

—. *Peace, Power, Righteousness: An Indigenous Manifesto.* New York: Oxford University Press, 2009.

—. *Wasáse, Indigenous Pathways of Action and Freedom.* Peterborough: Broadview Press, 2005.

Alia, Valerie. *Un/Covering the North: News, Media, and Aboriginal People.* Vancouver: University of British Columbia Press, 2000.

Altheide, David. *Creating Fear: News and the Construction of Crisis.* New York: Aldine Transaction, 2002.

Amnesty International, 2004, "Stolen Sisters: Discrimination and Violence Against Indigenous Women in Canada: A Summary of Amnesty International's Concerns." 4 October 2004. http://www.amnesty.org/en/library/info/AMR20/001/2004/en (accessed 3 March 2009).

Anahareo. *Devil in Deerskins*. Oshawa: Alger Press, 1972.

—. *Grey Owl and I: A New Autobiography*. Toronto: New Press, 1972.

—. *My Life with Grey Owl*. London: Peter Davies, 1940.

Anderson, Benedict. *Imagined Communities: Reflections on the Origin and Spread of Nationalism*. London: Verso, 1991.

Anderson, Mark Cronlund. *Pancho Villa's Revolution by Headlines*. Norman: University of Oklahoma Press, 2001.

Anderson, Mark Cronlund, and Carmen L. Robertson. "The 'Bended Elbow' News, Kenora, 1974, How a Small-Town Newspaper Promoted Colonialism." *American Indian Quarterly* 31, 3 (2007): 1–29.

Apodaca, Paul. "Powerful Images: Portrayals of Native America." *American Anthropologist* 101, 4 (2000): 818–825.

Atwood, Margaret. *Strange Things: The Malevolent North in Canadian Literature*. Toronto: Oxford University Press, 1995.

Axworthy, Thomas, and Pierre Trudeau, eds. *Towards a Just Society*. Markham, ON: Viking, 1990.

Backhouse, Constance. *Colour-Coded: A Legal History of Racism in Canada, 1900–1950*. Toronto: University of Toronto Press, 1999.

Bakhtin, M.M. *The Dialogic Imagination: Four Essays*, ed. Michael Holquist and Caryl Emerson. Austin: University of Texas Press, 1981.

Barker, Joanne. "Gender, Sovereignty, and the Discourse of Rights in Native Women's Activism." *Meridians: Feminism, Race, Transnationalism* 7, 1 (2006): 127–161.

Barthes, Roland. *Mythologies*. New York: Hill and Wang, 1972.

Basson, Lauren L. "Savage Half-Breed, French Canadian or White US Citizen? Louis Riel and US Perceptions of Nation and Civilisation." *National Identities* 7, 4 (2005): 369–388.

Baudrillard, Jean. *Simulacra and Simulations*. Translated by P. Foss, P. Patton and P. Beitchman. New York: Semiotexte, 1981.

Baylor, Timothy. "Media Framing of Movement Protest: The Case of American Indian Protest." *The Social Science Journal* 33, 3 (1996): 241–255.

—. "Modern Warriors: Mobilization and Decline of the American Indian Movement (AIM) 1969–1979." PhD diss., University of North Carolina, Chapel Hill, 1994.

Beauregard, Claude. "The Military Intervention in Oka." *Canadian Military History* 2, 1 (1993): 23–47.

Beck, Paul N. "Military Officers' Views of Indian Scouts, 1865-1890." *Military History of the West* 23, 1 (Spring 1993): 1–19.

Belanger, Yale. "Journalistic Opinion as Free Speech or Promoting Racial Unrest? The Case of Ric Dolphin and the *Calgary Herald*'s Editorial Presentation of Native Culture." *American Indian Quarterly* 26, 3 (2002): 393–417.

Beltrame, Julian. "Chrétien Promises to Help Aboriginals." *Maclean's*, 14 October 2002.

Bentley, D.M.R. "Shadows in the Soul: Racial Haunting in the Poetry of Duncan Campbell Scott." *University of Toronto Quarterly* 75, 2 (Spring 2006): 752–770.

Benton-Banai, E. *The Mishomis Book: The Voice of the Ojibway.* Hayward, WI: Indian Country Communications, 1988.

Berkhofer, Robert. *The White Man's Indian, Images of the American Indian from Columbus to the Present.* New York: Vintage, 1979.

Bernstein, Alison. *Toward a New Era in Indian Affairs: American Indians and World War II.* Norman: University of Oklahoma Press, 1991.

Bertman, Stephen. *Cultural Amnesia America's Future and the Crisis of Memory.* Santa Barbara: Greenwood Press, 2000.

Bhabha, Homi. *The Location of Culture.* New York: Routledge, 2004.

Billinghurst, Jane. *The Many Faces of Archie Belaney: Grey Owl.* Vancouver: Greystone Books, 1999.

Bird, S. Elizabeth, ed. *The Audience in Everyday Life: Living in a Media World.* New York: Routledge, 2003.

—. *Dressing in Feathers: The Construction of the Indian in American Popular Culture.* Boulder: Westview, 1996.

—. "Gendered Construction of the American Indian in Popular Media." *Journal of Communication* 49, 4 (1999): 61–83.

Bivins, Thomas H. "The Body Politic: The Changing Face of Uncle Sam: Cartoonists' Use of Proportion and Body Type Conveys its Own Editorial Image." *Journalism Quarterly* 64 (Spring 1987): 13-21.

Bobo, Lawrence D., and Mia Tuan. *Prejudice in Politics, Group Position, Public Opinion, and the Wisconsin Treaty Rights Dispute.* Cambridge: Harvard University Press, 2006.

Bone, John R., Joseph T. Clark, A.H. Colquhoun, and John F. McKay. *A History of Canadian Journalism in the Several Portions of the Dominion, With a Sketch of the Canadian Press Association, 1859-1908.* New York: AMS Press, 1908.

Bonelli, William G. *Billion Dollar Blackjack: The Story of Corruption and the Los Angeles Times.* Washington: Civic Research Press, 1954.

Bonilla-Silva, Eduardo. "'This is a White Country': The Racial Ideology of the Western Nations of the World System." *Sociological Inquiry* 70, 2 (2000): 188–214.

Boyko, John. *Last Steps to Freedom: The Evolution of Canadian Racism.* Winnipeg: Watson and Dwyer, 1995.

Braz, Albert. *The False Traitor: Louis Riel in Canadian Culture.* Toronto: University of Toronto Press, 2003.

—. "The Modern Hiawatha: Grey Owl's Construction of His Aboriginal Self." In *Auto/biography in Canada*, ed. Julie Rak. Waterloo: Wilfrid Laurier University Press, 2005.

Brian, Denis. *Pulitzer: A Life.* New York: Wiley, 2001.

Brown, Dee. *Bury My Heart at Wounded Knee, An Indian History of the American West.* New York: Holt Paperbacks, 2001.

Bucko, Raymond A. *The Lakota Ritual of the Sweat Lodge: History and Contemporary Practice.* Lincoln: Bison Books, 1999.

Burns, E. Bradford. *The Poverty of Progress: Latin America in the Nineteenth Century.* Los Angeles: University of California Press, 1983.

Canadian Dimension 10, 5 (November 1974): 34.

Cardinal, Harold. *The Unjust Society, The Tragedy of Canada's Indians.* Edmonton: Hurtig Publishers, 1969.

Carpenter, Carole Henderson. "In Our Own Image: The Child, Canadian Culture, and Our Future." Ninth Annual Robarts Lecture (29 March 1995). http://www.yorku.ca/robarts/projects/lectures/pdf/rl_carpenter.pdf (accessed 14 September 2008).

Carr, Paul R., and Darren E. Lund. *The Great White North? Exploring Whiteness, Privilege and, Identity in Education*. Rotterdam: Sense Publishers, 2007.

Carter, Sarah. *Aboriginal People and Colonizers of Western Canada to 1900*. Toronto: University of Toronto Press, 1999.

—. *Capturing Women: The Manipulation of Cultural Imagery in Canada's Prairie West*. Montreal: McGill-Queen's University Press, 1997.

—. *The Importance of Being Monogamous: Marriage and Nation Building in Western Canada to 1915*. Edmonton: University of Alberta Press, 2008.

—. *Lost Harvests: Prairie Indian Reserve Farmers and Government Policy*. Montreal: McGill-Queen's University Press, 1993.

Chapin, David. "Gender and Masquerade in the Life of Grey Owl." *American Indian Quarterly* 24, 1 (Winter 2000): 91–109.

Chomsky, Noam, and Edward S. Herman. *Manufacturing Consent: The Political Economy of the Mass Media*. New York: Pantheon Books, 2002.

Christiano, Kevin J. "Federalism as a Canadian National Ideal: The Civic Rationalism of Pierre Elliott Trudeau." *The Dalhousie Review* 69, 2 (Summer 1989): 248–252.

Churchill, Ward. *Kill the Indian, Save the Man: The Genocidal Impact of American Indian Residential Schools*. San Francisco: City Light Publishers, 2004.

Ciaccia, John. *The Oka Crisis: A Mirror of the Soul*. Dorval: Maren Publishers, 2000.

Clerici, Naila. "The Cree of James Bay and the Construction of their Identity for the Media." *Canadian Issues* 21 (1999): 143–159.

Coates, Kenneth. *Canada's Colonies: A History of the Yukon and Northwest Territories*. Toronto: Lorimer, 1985.

Collins, Ross F. and E.M. Palmegiano, eds. *The Rise of Western Journalism, 1815–1914: Essays on the Press in Australia, Canada, France, Germany, Great Britain and the United States*. Jefferson, NC: McFarland and Company, 2007.

Cooper, James Fenimore. *Deerslayer, or The First Warpath*. New York: Barnes and Noble Classics, [1841] 2005.

—. *The Last of the Mohicans*. New York: Signet Classics, [1826] 2005.

Copeland, David A. "'Securing the Affections of Those Peoples at this Critical Juncture': Newspapers, Native Americans, and the French and Indian War, 1754–1763." *American Journalism* 19, 4 (2002): 37–66.

Cortés, Carlos E. *The Children Are Watching: How the Media Teach About Diversity*. New York: Teachers College Press, 2000.

Coward, John M. *The Newspaper Indian, Native American Identity in the Press, 1820–90*. Urbana: University of Illinois Press, 1999.

Crosby, Alfred W. *The Columbian Exchange: Biological and Cultural Consequences of 1492*. New York: Praeger, 2002.

Cross, Coy F. *Go West Young Man! Horace Greeley's Vision for America*. Albuquerque: University of New Mexico Press, 1995.

Cruikshank, Julie. "Images of Society in Klondike Gold Rush Narratives: Skookum Jim and the Discovery of Gold." *Ethnohistory* 39, 1 (Winter 1992): 20–41

—. *The Social Life of Stories: Narrative and Knowledge in the Yukon Territory*. Lincoln: University of Nebraska Press, 2000.

Cuthand, Doug. *Tapwe: Selected Columns of Doug Cuthand*. Penticton, BC: Theytus Books, 2005.

Dallmayr, Fred. "Modes of Cross-Cultural Encounter." In *Cross-Cultural Conversations*, ed. Anindita Balslev. Kennilworth, N.J.: Value Inquiry Books, 1996.

Day, Richard J.F. *Multiculturalism and the History of Canadian Diversity*. Toronto: University of Toronto Press, 2000.

Dearing, James W., and Everett M. Rogers. *Agenda-Setting*. Los Angeles: SAGE, 1996.

Debord, Guy. *Society of the Spectacle*. Translated by Ken Knabb. Oakland: AK Press, 2006.

DeGuzman, Maria. *Spain's Long Shadow: The Black Legend, Off-Whiteness, and Anglo-American Empire*. Minneapolis: University of Minnesota Press, 2005.

Deloria, Philip J. *Indians in Unexpected Places*. Lawrence: University Press of Kansas, 2004.

Deloria Jr., Vine. *Custer Died for Your Sins: An Indian Manifesto*. Norman: University of Oklahoma Press, 1988.

deMause, Lloyd. *The Emotional Life of Nations*. New York: Karnac, 2002. Desbarats, Peter. *Guide to Canadian News Media*. Toronto: Harcourt Brace, 1996.

Dick, Lyle. "Nationalism and Visual Media in Canada: The Case of Thomas Scott's Execution." *Manitoba History* 48 (Autumn/Winter 2004–2005): 2–18.

Dickason, Olive. *Canada's First Nations: A History of Founding Peoples From Earliest Times*. New York: Oxford University Press, 2001.

Dickson, Lovat. *Half-Breed: The Story of Grey Owl*. London: Macmillan, 1939,

Dippie, Brian W. *Custer's Last Stand: The Anatomy of an American Myth*. Lincoln: University of Nebraska Press, 1976.

Diehl, Digby. *Front Page: 100 Years of the Los Angeles Times, 1881–1981*. New York: Harry N. Abrams, 1981.

Downing, John, and Charles Husband. *Representing 'Race'*. London: SAGE, 2005.

Drees, Laurie Meijer. *The Indian Association of Alberta: A History of Political Action*. Vancouver: University of British Columbia Press, 2002.

Dundes, Lauren. "Disney's Modern Heroine Pocahontas: Revealing Age-old Gender Stereotypes and Role Discontinuity Under a Façade of Liberation." *Social Science Journal* 38, 3 (2001): 353–365.

Eagleton, Terry. *Holy Terror*. New York: Oxford University Press, 2005.

Edgerton, G., and K. Jackson. "Redesigning Pocahontas: Disney, the 'Whiteman's Indian,' and the Marketing of Dreams." *Journal of Popular Film and Television* 24, 2 (1996): 90–98.

Edwards, Janis L., and Carol K Winkler. "Representative Form and the Visual Ideograph: The Iwo Jima image in Editorial Cartoons." *Quarterly Journal of Speech* 83, 3 (August 1997): 289–301.

El Refaie, E. "Understanding Visual Metaphor: The Example of Newspaper Cartoons." *Visual Communication* 2 (February 2003): 75–96.

Ellenberg, George B. "An Uncivil War of Words, Indian Removal in the Press, 1830." *Atlanta History* (Spring 1989): 48–59.

Evans, Michael Robert. "Hegemony and Discourse: Negotiating Cultural Relationships Through Media Production." *Journalism* 3, 3 (2002): 309–329.

Fanon, Franz. *The Wretched of the Earth*. New York: Grove Press, 1963.

Faragher, John Mack. *Daniel Boone: The Life and Legend of an American Pioneer*. New York: Holt Paperbacks, 1993.

Fetherling, Douglas. *The Rise of the Canadian Newspaper.* Toronto: Oxford University Press, 1990.

Fiamengo, Janice. *The Woman's Page: Journalism and Rhetoric in Early Canada.* Toronto: University of Toronto Press, 2008.

Flanagan, Thomas. *Louis 'David' Riel, 'Prophet of the New World'.* Toronto: University of Toronto Press, 1996.

—. *Riel and Rebellion: 1885 Reconsidered.* Toronto: University of Toronto Press, 2000.

Fleras, Augie, and Jean Leonard Elliott. *Unequal Relations: An Introduction to Race, Ethnic and Aboriginal Dynamics in Canada.* Toronto: Pearson, 2007.

Fleras, Augie, and Jean Lock Kunz. *Media and Minorities: Representing Diversity in a Multicultural Canada.* Toronto: Thompson Educational Publishers, 2001.

Fletcher, Kim. *The Journalist's Handbook.* London: Macmillan, 2005.

Forgacs, David, and Eric Hobsbawm, eds. *The Antonio Gramsci Reader: Selected Writings 1916–1935.* New York: New York University Press, 2000.

Foster, W. Garland. *The Mohawk Princess: Being Some Account of the Life of Teka-hion-wake (E. Pauline Johnson).* Vancouver: Lion's Gate Publishing, 1931.

Francis, Daniel. *The Imaginary Indian: The Image of the Indian in Canadian Culture.* Vancouver: Arsenal Pulp Press, 1992.

—. *National Dreams: Myth, Memory, and Canadian History.* Vancouver: Arsenal Pulp Press, 2005.

Frideres, James, and Rene, Gadacz. *Aboriginal Peoples in Canada: Contemporary Conflicts.* Scarborough: Prentice Hall, 2000.

Freud, Sigmund. *Jokes and Their Relation to the Unconscious.* Translated by James Strachey. New York: W.W. Norton, 1990.

Furniss, Elizabeth. *The Burden of History: Colonialism and the Frontier Myth in a Rural Community.* Vancouver: University of British Columbia Press, 2000.

Garber, Marjorie. *Vested Interests: Cross-Dressing and Cultural Anxiety.* New York: Routledge, 1992.

Garcia Marquez, Gabriel. *Chronicle of a Death Foretold.* New York: Vintage, 2003.

Geertz, Clifford. *The Interpretation of Cultures.* New York: Basic Books, 2000.

Giroux, Henry. *Education and Cultural Studies: Toward a Performative Practice.* New York: Routledge, 1997.

—. *The Mouse that Roared: Disney and the End of Innocence.* Lanham, MD: Rowman and Littlefield, 1999.

Glassner, Barry. *The Culture of Fear: Why Americans Are Afraid of the Wrong Things.* New York: Basic Books, 2000.

Goldie, Terry. *Fear and Temptation: The Image of the Indigene in Canadian, Australian, and New Zealand Literatures.* Montreal: McGill-Queen's University Press, 1993.

Goodwill, Jean Cuthand, and Norma Sluman. *John Tootoosis: Biography of a Cree Leader.* Winnipeg: Pemmican Publications, 1992.

Gottlieb, Robert. *Thinking Big: The Story of the Los Angeles Times, Its Publishers, and Their Influence on Southern California.* New York: Putnam, 1977

Gramsci, Antonio. *Selections From the Prison Notebooks.* New York: International Publishers, 2008.

Grandin, Greg. *The Blood of Guatemala: A History of Race and Nation.* Durham: Duke University Press, 2000.

Gray, Charlotte. *Flint and Feather: The Life and Times of E. Pauline Johnson*. Toronto: Harper Collins, 2002.

Green, Joyce. "Canaries in the Mines of Citizenship: Indian Women in Canada," *Canadian Journal of Political Science* 34, 4 (2001): 715–738.

—. "Sexual Equality and Indian Government: An Analysis of Bill C-31 Amendments to the Indian Act." *Native Studies Review* 1, 1 (1985): 81–95.

Green, Joyce, ed. *Making Space for Indigenous Feminism*. New York: Zed Books, 2007.

Green, Rayna. "The Pocahontas Perplex: The Image of Indian Women in American Culture," *The Massachusetts Review* 16, 4 (Autumn 1975): 698–714.

Greer, Margaret R., Maureen Quilligan, and Walter D. Mignolo, eds. *Rereading the Black Legend: The Discourses of Religious and Racial Difference in the Renaissance Empires*. Chicago: University of Chicago Press, 2008.

Grenier, Marc, ed. *Critical Studies of Canadian Mass Media*. Toronto: Butterworths, 1991.

—. "Native Indians in the English-Canadian Press: The Case of the 'Oka Crisis.'" *Media, Culture, and Society* 16, 2 (1994): 313–336.

Grey Owl. *The Collected Works of Grey Owl: Three Complete and Unabridged Canadian Classics*. Toronto: Key Porter Books, 2002.

—. *Men of the Last Frontier*. Herzberg Press, 2007

—. *Tales of an Empty Cabin*. Whitefish, MT: Kessinger Publishing, 2007.

Gunn, Simon. *History and Cultural Theory*. London: Pearson, 2006.

Gwyn, Richard. *John A.: The Man Who Made Us, The Life and Times of John A. Macdonald*. Toronto: Random House, 2007.

Haig-Brown, Celia. *Resistance and Renewal: Surviving the Indian Residential School*. Vancouver: Arsenal Pulp Press, 2002.

Hale, William Harlan. *Horace Greeley: Voice Of The People*. New York: Harper and Brothers, 1950.

Hall, Stuart, ed. *Representation: Cultural Representations and Signifying Practices*. Thousand Oaks, CA: SAGE, 1997.

Hanks, Christopher C., Gary Granzberg, and Jack Steinbring. "Social Changes and the Mass Media: The Oxford House Cree, 1909–1983." *Polar Record* 21, 134 (1983): 459–465.

Harding, Robert. "Historical Representations of Aboriginal People in the Canadian News Media." *Discourse and Society* 17, 2 (2006): 205–235.

—. "Media Discourse About Aboriginal Self-Government in 1990s British Columbia." First Nations, First Thoughts Conference, May 2005, University of Edinburgh. http://www.cst.ed.ac.uk/conferences.html (accessed 22 October 2007).

Harmon, Alexandra. *Indians in the Making: Ethnic Relations and Indian Identities around Puget Sound*. Berkeley: University of California Press, 1998.

Harris, Roy. *Pulitzer's Gold: Behind the Prize for Public Service Journalism*. Columbia, MO: University of Missouri Press, 2008.

Hartley, John. *The Indigenous Public Sphere: The Reporting and Reception of Aboriginal Issues in the Australian Media*. New York: Oxford University Press, 2001.

Haycock, Ronald Graham. *The Canadian Indian as a Subject and a Concept in a Sampling of the Popular National Magazines Read in Canada, 1900–1970*.Waterloo: Waterloo Lutheran University Press, 1971.

Hays, Robert. *Editorializing 'The Indian Problem,' The New York Times on Native Americans, 1860–1900*. Carbondale: Southern Illinois University Press, 1997.

Henry, Frances, and Carole Tator. *Discourses of Domination, Racial Bias in the Canadian English-Language Press*. Toronto: University of Toronto Press, 2002.

—. *Racial Profiling in Canada*. Toronto: University of Toronto Press, 2006.

Henry, Wade A. "Imagining the Great White Mother and the Great King: Aboriginal Tradition and Royal Representation at the 'Pow-wow' of 1901. *Journal of the Canadian Historical Association* 11 (2000): 87–108.

Hess, Stephen, and Sandy Northrop. *Drawn and Quartered: The History of American Editorial Cartoons*. Montgomery: Elliott and Clark, 1996.

Holmes, Joan. "Bill C-31, Equality or Disparity? The Effects of the New Indian Act on Native Women." Native Women's Association of Canada Conference on Bill C-31, Ottawa, March 1998.

Holmes, Malcolm D., and Judith A. Antell. "The Social Construction of American Indian Drinking: Perceptions of American Indian and White Officials." *The Sociological Quarterly* 42, 2 (2001): 151–173.

hooks, bell. *Black Looks: Race and Representation*. Toronto: Between the Lines, 1992.

Horsman, Reginald. *Race and Manifest Destiny: The Origins of American Racial Anglo-Saxonism*. Cambridge: Harvard University Press, 1981.

Hudon, Marc. "La crise d'Oka: rumeurs, médias et icône. Réflexion critique sur les dangers l'mage." *Cahiers de Géographie du Quebec* 38, 103 (April 1994): 21–38.

Huhndorf, Shari. *Going Native: Indians in the American Cultural Imagination*. Ithaca: Cornell University Press, 2001.

Hunter, Ernest. "Images of Violence in Aboriginal Australia." *Aboriginal Law Bulletin* 42, 2 (1990): 11–19.

Huntzicker, William E. "The 'Sioux Outbreak' in the Illustrated Press." *South Dakota History* 20, 4 (1990): 299–322.

Hynes, Jim. *Montreal Book of Everything*. Lunenburg, NS: MacIntyre Purcell Publishing, 2007.

Ignatieff, Michael. *True Patriot Love*. Toronto: Viking Canada, 2009.

Innes, Robert. "'I'm on Home Ground Now. I'm Safe.' Saskatchewan Aboriginal Veterans in the Immediate Postwar Years, 1945–1946." *American Indian Quarterly* 28, 3–4 (2004): 645–718.

—. "Socio-political Influence of the Second World War: Saskatchewan Aboriginal Veterans, 1945–1960." MA thesis, University of Saskatchewan, 2002.

Innis, Harold. *Empire and Communications*. Toronto: Dundurn Press, 2007.

Itwaru, Arnold Harrichand, and Natasha Ksonzek. *Closed Entrances, Canadian Culture and Imperialism*. Toronto: TSAR Publications, 1994.

Iyengar, Shanto, and Richard Reeves, eds. *Do the Media Govern?: Politicians, Voters, and Reporters in America*. Los Angeles: SAGE, 1997.

Iyengar, Shanto, and Donald R. Kinders. *News That Matters: Television and American Opinion*. Chicago: University of Chicago Press, 1989.

Jacobs, Ronald N. *Race, Media and the Crisis of Civil Society: From Watts to Rodney King*. New York: Cambridge University Press, 2000.

Jacobson, Eleanor. *Bended Elbow, Kenora Talks Back*. Kenora: Central Publications, 1975.

Jiwani, Yasmin, and Mary Lynn Young. "Missing and Murdered Women: Reproducing Marginality in News Discourse." *Canadian Journal of Communication* 31 (2006): 895–917.

Johnson, E. Pauline. *Flint and Feather*. Toronto: Musson Book Co., 1931.

Johnson, John J. *Latin America in Caricature*. Austin: University of Texas Press, 1993.

Kadish, Lesley V. "Reading Cereal Boxes: Pre-packaging History and Indigenous Identities." *The Journal of American Popular Culture* 3, 2 (Fall 2004). http://www.americanpopularculture.com/journal/articles/fall_2004/kadish.html (accessed 9 September 2009).

Keating, Bridget. "Raping Pocahontas: History, Territory and Ekphrasis in the Representation of an Indigenous Girl." MA thesis, University of Regina, 2008.

Keller, Betty. *Pauline: A Biography of Pauline Johnson*. Toronto: Douglas and McIntyre, 1981.

Kellstedt, Paul M. *The Mass Media and the Dynamics of American Racial Attitudes*. New York: Cambridge University Press, 2003.

Kemnitz, Thomas Milton. "The Cartoon as a Historical Source." *Journal of Interdisciplinary History* 4, 1 (1973): 81–93.

Kessler, Donna Barbie. "Sacagawea: The Making of a Myth." In *Sifters: Native American Women's Lives*, ed. Theda Perdue. New York: Oxford University Press, 2001.

Kesterton, Wilfrid. *A History of Journalism in Canada*. Ottawa: Carleton University Press, 1967.

King, Richard C. "De/scribing the Sq*w: Indigenous Women and Imperial Idioms in the United States." *American Indian Culture and Research Journal* 27, 2 (2003): 1–16.

Knight, Alan. *The Mexican Revolution*. 2 vols. Lincoln: University of Nebraska Press, 1990.

Kovach, Bill, and Tom Rosenstiel. *The Elements of Journalism, What Newspeople Should Know and the Public Should Expect*. New York: Three Rivers Press, 2007.

Krosenbrink-Gelissen, Lilianne E. "Caring Is Indian Women's Business, But Who Takes Care of Them? Canada's Indian Women, The Renewed Indian Act, and Its Implications for Women's Family Responsibilities, Roles, and Rights." *Law and Anthropology* 7 (1994): 107–130.

Kuhn, Thomas S. *The Structure of Scientific Revolutions*. Chicago: University of Chicago Press, 1996.

Kulchyski, Peter. *Like the Sound of a Drum: Aboriginal Cultural Politics in Denendeh and Nunavut*. Winnipeg: University of Manitoba Press, 2005.

Lackenbauer, P. Whitney. "Carrying the Burden of Peace: The Mohawks, the Canadian Forces, and the Oka Crisis." *Journal of Military and Strategic Studies* 10, 2 (2008): 2–71.

Lacroix, Celeste. "Images of Animated Others: The Orientalization of Disney's Cartoon Heroines From The Little Mermaid to The Hunchback of Notre Dame." *Popular Communication* 2, 4 (2004): 213–229.

Lambertus, Sandra. *Wartime Images, Peacetime Wounds: The Media and the Gustafsen Lake Standoff*. Toronto: University of Toronto Press, 2004.

Langston, Donna Hightower. "American Indian Women's Activism in the 1960s and 1970s." *Hypatia* 18, 2 (2003): 114–132.

Lavery, Daniel, and Brad Morse. "The Incident at Oka: Canadian Aboriginal Issues Move to the Front Burner." *Aboriginal Law Bulletin* 2, 48 (February 1991). http://www.austlii.edu.au/au/journals/AboriginalLB/1991/4.html (accessed May 2009).

Law, Ian. *Race in the News*. New York: Palgrave, 2002.

Lawrence, Bonita. "Gender, Race, and the Regulation of Native Identity in Canada and the United States: An Overview." *Hypatia* 18, 2 (2003): 3–31.

—. *"Real" Indians and Others: Mixed-Blood Urban Native Peoples and Indigenous Nationhood*. Vancouver: University of British Columbia Press, 2004.

—. "Rewriting Histories of the Land: Colonization and Indigenous Resistance in Eastern Canada." In *Race, Space, and the Law: Unmapping a White Settler Society*, ed. Sherene H. Razack. Toronto: Between the Lines, 2002.

Limerick, Patricia Nelson. *Legacy of Conquest, The Unbroken Past of the American West.* New York: W.W. Norton, 1987.

—. "Turnerians All: The Dream of a Helpful History in an Intelligible World." *American Historical Review* 100, 3 (June 1995): 697–715.

Lischke, Ute, and David T. McNab, eds. *Walking a Tightrope, Aboriginal Peoples and Their Representations.* Waterloo: Wilfrid Laurier University Press, 2005.

Loew, Patty. "Natives, Newspapers, and 'Fighting Bob,' Wisconsin Chippewa in the 'Unprogressive' Era." *Journalism History* 23, 4 (Winter 1997–1998): 149–157.

MacDougall, Curtis D. *Principles of Editorial Writing.* Dubuque: William C. Brown, 1973.

MacLaine, Craig. *This Land is Our Land: The Mohawk Revolt at Oka.* Maxville, ON: Optimum Publishers, 1990.

MacLennan, Hugh. *Two Solitudes.* Toronto: New Canadian Library, [1945] 2003.

Mageo, Jeannette Marie, ed. *Power and Self.* London: Cambridge University Press, 2002.

Mahtani, Minelle. "Representing Minorities: Canadian Media and Minority Identities," Commissioned by the Department of Canadian Heritage. http://www.metropolis.net (accessed 12 December 2006).

Mann, Charles C. *1491: New Revelations of the Americas Before Columbus.* New York: Vintage, 2006.

Martin, Lee-Ann, and Gerald McMaster. *Indigena: Contemporary Native Perspectives on Contemporary Art.* Vancouver: Craftsman House, 1992.

Martin, Lee-Ann, and Bob Boyer, eds. *The pow wow: An Art History.* Regina: MacKenzie Art Gallery, 2001.

Mattingly, Cheryl. "Pocahontas Goes to the Clinic: Popular Culture as Lingua Franca in a Cultural Borderland." *American Anthropologist* 108, 3 (2006): 494–501.

May, Elizabeth. *Losing Confidence: Power, Politics and the Crisis in Canadian Democracy.* Toronto: McClelland and Stewart, 2009.

McCombs, Maxwell. *Setting the Agenda: The News Media and Public Opinion.* Cambridge: Polity Press, 2004.

McCombs, Maxwell, Donald L. Shaw, and David Weaver, eds. *Communication and Democracy.* Mahwah, NJ: Lawrence Erlbaum Associates, 1997.

McDougal, Dennis. *Privileged Son: Otis Chandler and the Rise and Fall of the L.A. Times Dynasty.* Cambridge: Da Capo Press, 2002.

McFarlane, Peter. *Brotherhood to Nationhood: George Manuel and the Making of the Modern Indian Movement.* Toronto: Between the Lines, 1993.

McGrath, Ann. "Playing Colonial: Cowgirls, Cowboys, and Indians in Australia and North America." *Journal of Colonialism and Colonial History* 2, 1 (2001).

McGuffin, Gary, and Joanie McGuffin. *In the Footsteps of Grey Owl: Journey into the Ancient Forest.* Toronto: McClelland and Stewart, 2002.

McLuhan, Marshall. *Understanding Media.* New York: Routledge, 2005.

McMurtry, Larry. *Oh What a Slaughter: Massacres in the American West: 1846–1890.* New York: Simon and Schuster, 2005.

Meadows, Michael. *Voices in the Wilderness: Images of Aboriginal People in the Australian Media.* Westport: Greenwood Press, 2000.

Meyer, Carter Jones, and Diana Royer, eds. *Selling the Indian, Commercializing and Appropriating American Indian Cultures*. Tucson: University of Arizona Press, 2001.

Meyer, Michael C., William L. Sherman, and Susan M. Deeds. *The Course of Mexican History*. New York: Oxford University Press, 2005.

Mihesuah, Devon. *American Indians: Stereotypes and Realities*. Atlanta: Clarity Press, 2001.

—. *Indigenous American Women: Decolonization, Empowerment, Activism*. Lincoln: University of Nebraska Press, 2003.

Miller, Autumn, and Susan Dente Ross. "They Are Not Us: Framing of American Indians by the *Boston Globe*." *The Howard Journal of Communication* 15 (2004): 245–259.

Miller, David R., Carl Beal, James Dempsey, and R. Wesley Heber. *The First Ones: Readings in Indian/Native Studies*. Regina: Saskatchewan Indian Federated College, 1992.

Miller, J.R. *Shingwauk's Vision: A History of Native Residential Schools*. Toronto: University of Toronto Press, 1996.

—. *Skyscrapers Hide the Heavens*. Toronto: University of Toronto Press, 2000.

Miller, J.R., ed. *Sweet Promises*. Toronto: University of Toronto Press, 1999.

Milloy, John S. *A National Crime: The Canadian Government And the Residential School System*. Winnipeg: University of Manitoba Press, 1999.

Mitcham, Allison. *Grey Owl: Favorite Wilderness*. Manotick, ON: Penumbra Press, 1981.

Monture, Rick. "'Beneath the British Flag': Iroquois and Canadian Nationalism in the Work of E. Pauline Johnson and Duncan Campbell Scott." *Essays on Canadian Writing* 75 (Winter 2002): 118–141.

Monture-Okanee, Patricia. "The Rights of Indian Inclusion: Aboriginal Rights and/or Aboriginal Women." In *Advancing Aboriginal Claims:Visions/Strategies/Directions*, ed. Kerry Wilkins. Edmonton: Purich Publishers, 2004.

Morris, Martin J. "Overcoming the Barricades: The Crisis at Oka as a Case Study in Political Communication." *Journal of Canadian Studies* 30, 2 (1995): 74–92.

Morrison, William R. *True North: The Yukon and Northwest Territories*. New York: Oxford University Press, 1998.

Morrison, Bruce R., and C. Roderick Wilson, eds. *Native Peoples. The Canadian Experience*. Toronto: Oxford University Press, 2004.

Morton, Desmond. "Reflecting on Gomery: Political Scandals and the Canadian Memory." *Policy Options* (June 2005): 14–21.

Murphy, Sharon. "American Indians and the Media: Neglect and Stereotype." *Journalism History* 6, 2 (Summer 1979): 39–43.

Nancoo, Stephen E., and Robert S. Nancoo, eds. *The Mass Media and Canadian Diversity*. Mississauga, ON: Canadian Educators Press, 1996.

Nash-Smith, Henry. *Virgin Land: The American West as Symbol and Myth*. Cambridge: Harvard University Press, 2007.

Nemiroff, Diana, Charlotte Townsend-Gault, and Robert Houle. *Land, Spirit, Power: First Nations at the National Gallery of Canada*. Ottawa: National Gallery of Canada, 1992.

Nesbitt-Larking, Paul. *Politics, Society, and the Media, Canadian Perspectives*. Peterborough, ON: Broadview Press, 2001.

Newhouse, David R., Cora J. Voyageur, and Dan Beavon, eds. *Hidden in Plain Sight: Contributions of Aboriginal Peoples to Canadian Identity and Culture*. Toronto: University of Toronto Press, 2005.

Nichols, Roger L. *Indians in the United States and Canada: A Comparative History*. Lincoln: University of Nebraska Press, 1998.

Parkinson, Robert G. "From Indian Killer to Worthy Citizen: The Revolutionary Transformation of Michael Cresap." *William and Mary Quarterly* 63,1 (January 2006): 97–122.

Paz, Octavio. *The Labyrinth of Solitude: The Other Mexico, Return to the Labyrinth of Solitude, Mexico and the United States, the Philanthropic Ogre.* New York: Grove Press, 1994.

Perrin, Andrew J., and Stephen Vaisey. "Parallel Public Spheres: Distance and Discourse in Letters to the Editor." *American Journal of Sociology* 114, 3 (November 2008): 781–810.

Phillips, Ruth B. "Making Sense out/of the Visual: Aboriginal Presentations and Representations in Nineteenth-Century Canada. *Art History* 27, 4 (September 2004): 593–615.

Pike, Fredrick. *The United States and Latin America: Myths and Stereotypes of Civilization and Nature.* Austin: University of Texas Press, 1991.

Ponting, Rick. "Internationalization: Perspectives on an Emerging Direction in Aboriginal Affairs." *Canadian Ethnic Studies* 22, 3 (1990): 85–109.

Pratt, Richard H. *The Advantages of Mingling Indians with Whites, Americanizing the American Indians: Writings by the Friends of the Indian, 1880-1900.* Cambridge: Harvard University Press, [1892] 1973.

Priest, Lisa. *Conspiracy of Silence.* Toronto: McClelland and Stewart, 1989.

Radforth, Ian. "Performance, Politics, and Representation: Aboriginal People and the 1860 Royal Tour of Canada." *Canadian Historical Review* 84, 1 (March 2003): 1–32.

Rak, Julie, ed. *Auto/biography in Canada.* Waterloo, ON: Wilfrid Laurier University Press, 2005.

—. "Double Wampum, Double Life, Double Click: E. Pauline Johnson by and for the World Wide Web." *Textual Studies in Canada* 13, 14 (1996): 153–170.

Rankin, Charles E. "Savage Journalists and Civilized Indians, A Different View." *Journalism History* 21, 3 (Autumn 1995): 102–111.

Razack, Sherene. *Race, Space, and the Law: Unmapping a White Settler Society.* Toronto: Between the Lines, 2002.

Reader, Bill. "An Ethical 'Blind Spot': Problems of Anonymous Letters to the Editor." *Journal of Mass Media Ethics* 20, 1 (2005): 62–76.

Robertson, Carmen. "Trickster in the Press." *Media History* 14, 1 (2008): 72–93.

Rollins, Peter C., and John E. O'Connor, eds. *Hollywood's Indian: The Portrayal of the Native American in Film.* Lexington: University of Kentucky Press, 2003.

Root, Deborah. *Cannibal Culture: Art, Appropriation, and the Commodification of Difference.* Boulder: Westview Press, 1996.

Rosner, Cecil. *Behind the Headlines: A History of Investigative Journalism in Canada.* Toronto: Oxford University Press, 2008.

Roy, Arundhati. *An Ordinary Person's Guide to Empire.* Cambridge, MA: South End Press, 2004.

Ruffo, Armand G. *Grey Owl: The Mystery of Archie Belaney.* Regina: Coteau Books, 1996.

Rutherford, Paul. *A Victorian Authority: The Daily Press in Late Nineteenth-Century Canada.* Toronto: University of Toronto Press, 1982.

Ryan, Allan J. *The Trickster Shift: Humor and Irony in Contemporary Native Art.* Seattle: University of Washington Press, 1999.

Sadar, Ziauddin. "Walt Disney and the Double Victimization of Pocahontas." *Third Text* 10, 37 (1996): 17–26.

Said, Edward. *Covering Islam: How the Media and the Experts Determine How We See the Rest of the World*. New York: Vintage, 1997

—. *Culture and Imperialism*. New York: Vintage, 1994.

—. *Orientalism*. New York: Vintage, 1979.

Sangster, Joan. "'Queen of the Picket Line': Beauty Contests in the Post-World War II Canadian Labour Movement, 1945–1970." *Labor* 5, 4 (2008): 83–106.

Sarmiento, Domingo F. *Life in the Argentine Republic in the Days of the Tyrants; Or, Civilization and Barbarism*. New York: Hafner, [1868] 1974.

Saul, John Ralston. *A Fair Country, Telling Truth About Canada*. Toronto: Penguin, 2008.

Schoultz, Lars. *Beneath the United States: A History of U.S. Policy Toward Latin America*. Cambridge: Harvard University Press, 1998.

Seed, Patricia. *Ceremonies of Possession in Europe's Conquest of the New World*. Cambridge: Cambridge University Press, 1995.

Sheffield, R. Scott. *The Red Man's on the Warpath: The Image of the 'Indian' and the Second World War*. Vancouver: University of British Columbia Press, 2004.

Shipton, Vicky. *Grey Owl*. London: Penguin, 2008.

Shkilnyk, Anastasia. *A Poison Stronger Than Love: The Destruction of an Ojibwa Community*. New Haven: Yale University Press, 1985.

Siegel, Marc. *False Alarm: The Truth about the Epidemic of Fear*. New York: Wiley, 2006.

Siggins, Maggie. *Bitter Embrace: White Society's Assault on the Woodland Cree*. Toronto: McClelland and Stewart, 2005.

—. *Riel: A Life of Revolution*. Toronto: Harper Collins, 1994.

Skea, Warren H. "The Canadian Newspaper Industry's Portrayal of the Oka Crisis." *Native Studies Review* 9, 1 (1993–1994): 15–31.

Slatta, Richard. *Gauchos and the Vanishing Frontier*. Lincoln: University of Nebraska Press, 1992.

Slotkin, Richard. *The Fatal Environment: The Myth of the Frontier in the Age of Industrialization, 1800–1890*. Norman: University of Oklahoma Press, 1998.

—. *Gunfighter Nation: The Myth of the Frontier in Twentieth-Century America*.Norman: University of Oklahoma Press, 1998.

—. *Regeneration Through Violence: The Mythology of the American Frontier, 1600–1860*. Norman: University of Oklahoma Press, 2000.

Smith, Andrea. "Not an Indian Tradition: The Sexual Colonization of Native Peoples." *Hypatia* 18, 2 (Spring 2003): 71–85.

Smith, Donald B. *From the Land of Shadows: the Making of Grey Owl*. Saskatoon: Western Producer Prairie Books, 1990.

Smith, Paul Chaat, and Robert Allen Warrior. *Like a Hurricane. The Indian Movement from Alcatraz to Wounded Knee*. New York: The New Press, 1996.

Smith, Sherry L. *Reimagining Indians: Native Americans through Anglo Eyes, 1880-1940*. New York: Oxford University Press, 2000.

Smyth, Heather. "The Mohawk Warrior: Reappropriating the Colonial Stereotype." *Topia* 3 (Spring 2000): 58–80.

Soderlund, Walter C., and Kai Hildebrandt, eds. *Canadian Newspaper Ownership in the Era of Convergence, Rediscovering Social Responsibility*. Edmonton: University of Alberta Press, 2005.

Soroka, Stuart N. *Agenda-Setting Dynamics in Canada*. University of British Columbia Press, 2002.

Sossoyan, Matthieu. "Le silence des Mohawks? La press écrite et le déroulement de l'enquête du coroner Guy Gilbert sur la crise d'Oka (1990)." *Recheras Amerindiennes au Quebec* 28, 2 (1998): 85–93.

Sotiron, Minko. *From Politics to Profit*. Montreal: McGill-Queen's University Press, 1997.

Spurr, David. *The Rhetoric of Empire, Colonial Discourse in Journalism, Travel Writing, and Imperial Administration*. Durham: Duke University Press, 1993.

Stahl, William A. *God and the Chip: Religion and the Culture of Technology*. Waterloo: Wilfrid Laurier University Press, 2002.

Stearns, Peter N. *American Fear: The Causes and Consequences of High Anxiety*. New York: Routledge, 2006.

Stonechild, Blair, and Bill Waiser. *Loyal till Death, Indians and the North-West Rebellion*. Markham, ON: Fifth House, 1997.

Strong-Boag, Veronica, and Carole Gerson. *Paddling Her Own Canoe: The Times and Texts of E. Pauline Johnson, Tekahionwake*. Toronto: University of Toronto, 2000.

Stuart, Charles. "The Mohawk Crisis: A Crisis of Hegemony, An Analysis of Media Discourse." MA thesis, University of Ottawa, 1993.

Sulloway, Frank. *Born to Rebel: Birth Order, Family Dynamics, and Creative Lives*. New York: Vintage, 1997.

Szuchewycz, Bhodan. "Re-Pressing Racism: The Denial of Racism in the Canadian Press." *Canadian Journal of Communication* 25, 1 (2000): 497–515.

Taras, David. *Power and Betrayal in the Canadian Media*. Peterborough, ON: Broadview Press, 2001.

Taylor, Drew Hayden. *Me Funny*. Vancouver: Douglas and McIntyre, 2005.

Tilton, Robert S. *Pocahontas: The Evolution of an American Narrative*. London: Cambridge University Press, 1994.

Titley, E. Brian. *The Frontier World of Edgar Dewdney*. Vancouver: University of British Columbia Press, 1999.

Topik, Steven C., and Allen Wells, eds. *The Second Conquest of Latin America: Coffee, Henequen and Oil During the Export Boom, 1850–1930*. Austin: University of Texas Press, 1998.

Trenier-Gordon, Irene. *Grey Owl, Junior Edition*. Toronto: Altitude Publishing, 2007.

Turner, Frederick Jackson. "The Significance of the Frontier in American History." In *Frontier and Section: Selected Essays of Frederick Jackson Turner*, by Frederick Jackson Turner. Englewood Cliffs, NJ: Prentice-Hall, [1893] 1961.

Turpel, Mary Ellen. "Aboriginal Peoples and the Canadian Charter of Rights and Freedoms." *Canadian Women Studies* 10, 2–3 (1989): 149–157.

Valaskakis, Gail Guthrie. *Indian Country: Essays on Contemporary Native Culture*. Waterloo, ON: Wilfrid Laurier University Press, 2005.

Van Dijk, Teun. *Elite Discourse and Racism*. London: Routledge, 1993.

—. *Racism in the Press*. London: Routledge, 1991.

Vickers, Scott B. *Native American Identities: From Stereotype to Archetype in Art and Literature*. Albuquerque: University of New Mexico Press, 1998.

Vipond, Mary. *The Mass Media in Canada*. Toronto: James Lorimer and Company, 2000.

Voyageur, Cora. "They Think They Own the Land: A Media Account of the Government's Acquisition of Treaty Eight Lands." *Prairie Forum* 25, 2 (2000): 271–282.

Wahl-Jorgensen, Karin, and Thomas Hanitzsch, eds. *The Handbook of Journalism Studies*. New York: Routledge, 2009.

Walker, Margath. "Guada-narco-lupe, Maquilarañas and the Discursive Construction of Gender and Difference on the US-Mexico Border in Mexican Media Re-presentations." *Gender, Place, and Culture* 12, 1 (2005): 95–111.

Weaver, Sally. *Making Canadian Indian Policy: The Hidden Agenda, 1968–70*. Toronto: University of Toronto Press, 1981.

Weston, Mary Ann. *Native Americans in the News: Images of Indians in the Twentieth Century Press*. Westport, CT: Greenwood Press, 1996.

White, Richard. *The Middle Ground: Indians, Empires, and Republics in the Great Lakes Region, 1650–1815*. New York: Cambridge University Press, 1991.

Whyte, Kenneth. *The Uncrowned King: The Sensational Rise of William Randolph Hearst*. Berkeley: Counterpoint, 2009.

Widdowson, Frances, and Albert Howard. *Disrobing the Aboriginal Industry: The Deception Behind Indigenous Cultural Preservation*. Montreal: McGill-Queen's University Press, 2008.

Wilkes, Rima and Danielle Ricard. "How Does Newspaper Coverage of Collective Action Vary? Protest by Aboriginal People in Canada." *The Social Science Journal* 44 (2007): 231–251.

Wilkinson, Gerald. "Colonialism Through the Media." *The Indian Historian* (Summer 1974): 29–32.

Williams, Robert C. *Horace Greeley: Champion of American Freedom*. New York: New York University Press, 2006.

Williams, William Appleman. *Empire as a Way of Life*. New York: Ig Publishing, 2006.

Wills, Garry. *John Wayne's America: The Politics of Celebrity*. New York: Simon and Schuster, 1997.

—. "John Wayne's Body," *New Yorker*, 19 August 1996.

Winfield, Betty H., and Yoon, Doyle. "Historical images at a Glance: North Korea in American Editorial Cartoons." *Newspaper Research Journal* 23, 4 (2002): 97–100.

Winter, James. *Common Cents: Media Portrayal of the Gulf War and Other Events*. Montreal: Black Rose Books, 1995.

—. *Lies the Media Tell Us*. Montreal: Black Rose Books, 2007.

Wister, Owen. *The Virginian*. New York: Simon and Schuster, 2002.

Woodward, Ralph Lee. *A Short History of Guatemala*. Antigua, Guatemala: Editorial Laura Lee, 2005.

Wright, Ronald. *Stolen Continents: The "New World" Through Indian Eyes*. Toronto: Mariner Books, 1993.

Wuttunee, William. *Ruffled Feathers: Indians in Canadian Society*. Calgary: Bell Books, 1971.

York, Geoffrey, and Loreen Pindera. *People of the Pines: The Warriors and the Legacy of Oka*. Toronto: McArthur and Company, 1999.

INDEX